# The JEWS OF EAST CENTRAL EUROPE
## BETWEEN THE WORLD WARS

# THE JEWS OF EAST CENTRAL EUROPE BETWEEN THE WORLD WARS

Ezra Mendelsohn

INDIANA UNIVERSITY PRESS

BLOOMINGTON

This book is a publication of

Indiana University Press
601 North Morton Street
Bloomington, IN 47404-3797 USA

http://iupress.indiana.edu

*Telephone orders*   800-842-6796
*Fax orders*   812-855-7931
*Orders by e-mail*   iuporder@indiana.edu

The paper used in this publication meets the minimum requirements of American National Standard for Information Sciences—Permanence of Paper for Printed Library Materials, ANSI Z39.48-1984.

Manufactured in the United States of America

Library of Congress Cataloging-in-Publication Data

Mendelsohn, Ezra.
   The Jews of East Central Europe between the world wars.

   Bibliography: p.
   Includes index.
   1. Jews—Europe, Eastern—History—20th century.
2. Europe, Eastern—Ethnic relations.   I. Title.
DS135.E83M37   1983      947'.0004924      81-48676
cl. ISBN 978-0-253-33160-1      pa. ISBN 978-0-253-20418-9

6   7   8   9   10      13   12   11   10   09   08

*To Judy, with love*

# Contents

*List of Maps*                           ix
*Preface*                                xi

Introduction                              1
**1.** Poland                            11
**2.** Hungary                           85
**3.** Czechoslovakia                   131
**4.** Romania                          171
**5.** Lithuania                        213
**6.** Latvia and Estonia               241
Concluding Remarks                      255

*Notes*                                 259
*Bibliographical Essay*                 287
*Index*                                 293

# Maps

East Central Europe before World War I                                   xv
East Central Europe between the Wars                                    xvi
Poland between the Wars                                                 10
Hungary between the Wars                                                84
Czechoslovakia between the Wars                                        130
Romania between the Wars                                               170
Lithuania between the Wars                                             212
Latvia and Estonia between the Wars                                    240

# *Preface*

I am well aware of the fact that writing this book has required a good deal of *chutzpa*. I can read only a few of the languages spoken in East Central Europe, and cannot claim to be an expert on the history, either general or Jewish, of most of the countries of that region. Only the chapter on Poland is based on a certain amount of original research. For the rest, I have relied on secondary sources in those European languages I do read in addition to the extensive, but not always satisfying, historical literature in Hebrew and Yiddish. My main reason for taking on this task was to provide students and teachers with a single-volume, comparative study of a particularly important, but very much neglected, chapter in modern European Jewish history. If this book stimulates greater interest in the immediate pre-Holocaust period, and if it inspires much needed further research, then it will have achieved its purpose.

My friend and colleague Jonathan Frankel, with whom I have worked for many years and from whom I have learned so much, took the time to read and criticize the manuscript of this book, as did two other friends and colleagues, Peter Medding and Aryeh Goren. I am most grateful to them, as I am to Roman Szporluk and Hillel J. Kieval, who read the chapter on Czechoslovakia, to Michael Silber, who read the chapter on Hungary, and to Gyorgy Ranki and Todd M. Endelmann, who reviewed the completed manuscript. These scholars saved me from making many errors; any errors that remain are my own responsibility.

I am also indebted to Yehudit Friedgut and Jeanette Ranta, who expertly typed the manuscript.

The decision of Indiana University Press to bring out this book in paperback has enabled me to take into account a detailed critique of the hardcover book by Professor Jerzy Tomaszewski of the University of Warsaw. I wish to record here my gratitude to Professor Tomaszewski and to other reviewers who pointed out various errors and suggested ways of improving the book.

THE
JEWS
OF EAST
CENTRAL
EUROPE
BETWEEN THE
WORLD WARS

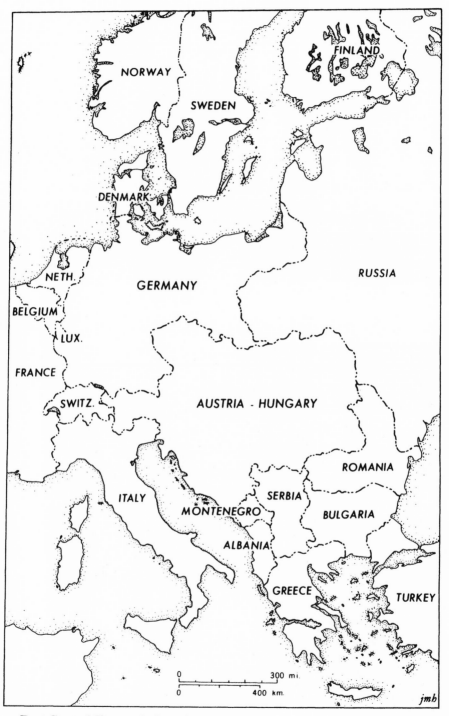

**East Central Europe before World War I**

**East Central Europe between the Wars**

# Introduction

The interwar years in East Central Europe, a short but well-defined period no longer than a single generation, witnessed the dramatic and unexpected triumph of the national principle and the formation of such new states as Poland, Czechoslovakia, Latvia, and Lithuania. During these years previously subjugated nationalities struggled to overcome staggering difficulties and to establish viable states which, so it was hoped, would never again be brought under foreign domination. That their efforts, made possible by the collapse of German, Russian, and Austro-Hungarian power, were doomed by the rise of Nazism and of the Soviet Union should not obscure the considerable achievements of the 1920s and 1930s as the largely peasant peoples of East Central Europe firmly established their national identities and made strong claims for equal acceptance in the family of European nations. Indeed, despite the general failure to cope with seemingly intractable economic, social, and political problems, and despite the rise of local fascist movements in the 1930s, in some ways this period constitutes a golden age wedged between pre–World War I oppression and post–World War II Communist domination.

For the student of modern Jewish history, East Central Europe during the interwar years is of particularly dramatic interest. For one thing, these years may be justly regarded as a period of grim rehearsal for the tragedy of East European Jewry during World War II. In most of the new states, relations between Jews and gentiles were bad from the very beginning (Czechoslovakia and the Baltic States are notable exceptions), and in all of them these relations deteriorated sharply during the 1930s. In Hungary Jewish emancipation was actually revoked, while in Poland and Romania the emancipation won in 1918–1919 proved to be no guarantee of equality. Almost everywhere the "Jewish question" became a matter of paramount concern, and anti-Semitism a major political force. One of the main efforts of this book will be to explain the obsession with the Jewish question and to describe the impact of anti-Semitism both on the various Jewish communities and on East European politics.

A second major consideration is internal developments within the Jewish communities. During the 1920s and 1930s modern Jewish political movements, largely the creation of tsarist Russia, flourished in Eastern Europe as they never had before and as they never would again. In some countries, most notably Poland, secular Jewish nationalism and Jewish socialism were transformed almost overnight into mass movements which were able to wrest control of the Jewish community from its more traditional leaders. The Jewries of Poland, Galicia, Lithuania, Bessarabia, and Bukovina underwent what might be termed a process of politicization and nationalization not unlike that which was affecting their gentile neighbors. Even the Orthodox population, traditionally strong in Eastern Europe, organized itself into modern political parties which adopted many of their secular adversaries' characteristics. Along with the striking politicization of East European Jewry went efforts to implement the tenets of the now triumphant ideologies. In fact, East Central Europe between the wars was the major testing ground for modern Jewish politics: thus the remarkable, though ultimately unsuccessful, efforts to establish extraterritorial national autonomy for the Jews, one of the chief aims of most Jewish nationalist parties; thus Zionist efforts to promote mass emigration (*aliyah* in Hebrew) to Palestine, which for the first time became a practical option for large numbers of Jews fleeing Eastern Europe. And then there was the attempt made by the Jewish left both to promote a proletarian Jewish culture and to forge alliances with the non-Jewish left in order to topple the "bourgeois" states of the region and to replace them with socialist or Communist regimes. Finally, the antinationalist Orthodox Jewish parties sought to perpetuate the old Jewish way of life by establishing new institutions and by instituting working relationships with the various regimes.

Aside from Jewish politics, this book will devote considerable attention to other internal developments within the various Jewish communities. The demographic condition and demographic decline of East European Jewry will be discussed, as will the more important process of economic decline, which resulted by the 1930s in the impoverishment of hundreds of thousands of Jews in Poland, Romania, and the Baltic States. An additional theme emphasized here has to do with the different though related processes of acculturation (by which is meant the Jews' adoption of the external characteristics of the majority culture, above all its language) and assimilation (by which is meant the Jews' efforts to adopt the national identity of the majority, to become Poles, Hungarians, Romanians "of the Mosaic faith," or even to abandon their Jewish identity altogether). Were the Jews in these lands growing closer to their neighbors, or further apart? And did the Jews' willingness or lack of willingness to acculturate and assimilate have any impact on attitudes toward them? These are among the most vital questions the historian of postemancipation Jewry can ask, along with the no less important question as to the efficacy of the various Jewish political proposals for solving the Jewish question.

East Central Europe is a notoriously difficult region to define, and it has been defined differently by different scholars.[1] Of the lands lying between Germany and Soviet Russia, the following are treated here: Poland, Hungary, Czechoslovakia, Romania, Lithuania, Latvia, and Estonia. Here resided the major Ashkenazi (i.e., of German origin) Jewries, almost all of which, except for pre–World War I Romanian Jewry, had previously resided either in tsarist Russia or in Habsburg Austria-Hungary. The relatively small Jewish communities of Bulgaria and Yugoslavia are not included, both because of their size and because they contained a strong Sephardic (i.e., Spanish) component.[2] Even within this rather limited area there was enormous diversity, both in general and among the various Jewish communities. Considering first the general context, we are confronted with a complex picture of different religious, cultural, and political traditions along with different social patterns and widely varying degrees of economic development. The predominant religion was Roman Catholic (in Poland, Czechoslovakia, Hungary, and Lithuania), but Romania was largely Greek Orthodox. The Uniate church was important in certain regions in Czechoslovakia, Poland, and Romania, while there were significant Protestant enclaves as well, represented by some German minorities (as in the Baltic States) or by non-German remnants of the once powerful Reformation in Eastern Europe, as in Hungary and Czechoslovakia. Religious loyalties, in this part of the world, sometimes implied other loyalties as well—to Rome and the West, as in the case of the Catholic Poles, to Moscow and the East, as in the case of some Ukrainians in Subcarpathian Rus and Bessarabia, and of some Belorussians in Poland. The existence of strong Catholic, Uniate, Orthodox, and Protestant churches lent to the area the character of religious pluralism, which did not, however, as the Jewish experience demonstrates, necessarily result in an atmosphere of religious tolerance. The same may be said of the ethnic diversity of the regions; the mix of Slavs, Magyars, Romanians, Balts, and Germans by no means encouraged national tolerance, as we shall have occasion to observe during the course of this study.

Religious and ethnic diversity was paralleled by economic and social diversity. The western regions of Czechoslovakia, namely, Bohemia and Moravia, were among the most advanced in Europe, and such cities as Budapest and Riga were hardly less modern than was Prague. On the other hand, East Central Europe contained some of the most primitive economies in Europe, in such areas as Subcarpathian Rus, eastern Galicia, and Bessarabia. The gentry-peasant societies of the more backward lands of the region stood in sharp contrast to the bourgeois character of the Czech lands. Political divisions were no less apparent, the most striking being between former Russian and former Habsburg territories.

The Baltic States, central and eastern Poland, and Bessarabia had all been part of the tsarist empire and were strongly influenced by its autocratic political traditions. The Czech lands, Slovakia, Galicia, Subcarpathian Rus, Transylvania, Bukovina, and, of course, Hungary had all been part of the Habsburg empire. Here a further division is necessary, namely, between those territories which had been a part of the Hungarian half of the Habsburg empire (Transylvania, Subcarpathian Rus, and Slovakia) and those which had not been. These divisions had important cultural as well as political implications, since they determined in which regions Russian, German, or Hungarian culture was widespread.

Despite this evident diversity, certain shared characteristics imparted to East Central Europe a large measure of unity. Most obvious was the fact that, with the already noted exception of the Czech lands, this was an economically and socially backward region which did not make great economic progress during the interwar years. The majority of the inhabitants were peasants, the percentage of city dwellers was low, and cities were often regarded as foreign enclaves by a hostile peasantry and by the gentry-derived intelligentsia. There was little industrialization, and the commercial class was often "non-native." The old elites—landowners, the clergy—retained considerable power, although they had to share it with the emerging intelligentsia and bourgeoisie, and sometimes even with the rapidly organizing peasantry. To the problems of how to overcome backwardness and poverty was added another shared by most East Central European lands—political inexperience.

The new states faced the extraordinarily difficult task of nation-building after centuries of dependence, a task made all the more difficult by the degree of external hostility to their still fragile independence. The Baltic States had virtually no memories of independence; there had never been a Czechoslovakia, and Poland had been wiped off the map of Europe in the late eighteenth century. Romania had existed as an independent entity before World War I, but after its great postwar territorial acquisitions it was a virtually new state. Hungary had been an equal partner in the prewar Habsburg empire; now, greatly reduced in size, it too was something of a new state. Similar problems, together with similar economic and social structures, helped to produce a fairly homogeneous political situation in the region. All these states were anti-Communist and antirevolutionary, and most perceived the Soviet Union as their most dangerous antagonist. Most began their lives as democracies, at least on paper, and all, with the familiar Czechoslovak exception, moved to the right during the interwar years. This was only to be expected, given their anti-Soviet orientation, the control exerted by the traditional elites, and the weak if not nonexistent traditions of democracy and liberalism. In most of these lands the principal political struggle was not between left and right (the left tended to be quite weak), but rather between right and extreme right. The principal internal threat to the stability of such countries as Poland, Hungary, and Romania in the 1930s emanated from the so-called native fascist movements, such as the Iron Guard in Romania and the Arrow Cross in Hungary. This struggle, in which the Jewish question played a great role, had fateful consequences for the local Jewish communities.

Another major problem which plagued all the lands of East Central Europe was that of the minority nationalities. Despite the triumph of the national principle after World War I, the political boundaries in East Central Europe were not, and indeed could not, be drawn according to strictly ethnic criteria. Most of the countries discussed here regarded themselves as nation-states, but in fact they were not. One-third of the population of Poland, for example, was non-Polish. The minorities were often regarded as threats to the status quo and as disloyal elements interested in redrawing the frontiers in order to accommodate their own national interests. There was something to these accusations. The German minority in Czechoslovakia was transformed into a pro-Nazi force during the 1930s, and the Hungarian minority in Romanian Transylvania wished to live under Hungarian sovereignty. Many Ukrainians of Galicia and other regions in Eastern Europe wanted a state of their own, and some were sympathetic to the Soviet Ukrainian republic. The determined efforts of such countries as Poland and Romania to establish centralized states and to promote the interests of the dominant nationality inevitably clashed with the grievances, real or imagined, of the national minorities. This led to the flourishing of extreme nationalism, which may be regarded as the ruling ideology of East Central Europe between the wars. In this region nation was exalted over class, and unbridled nationalism was rarely tempered by social idealism. Moreover, the existence of the national-minorities problem constituted a standing invitation to intervention on the part of foreign powers interested in upsetting the Versailles settlement. Germany, Italy, and Soviet Russia all promoted various irredentist movements in Eastern Europe, thus greatly contributing to the region's instability.

From the Jewish perspective, the East Central European environment as it has been described here offered little grounds for optimism. Generally Jews have flourished in lands of cultural and religious tolerance, political liberalism, stability, and economic growth. In interwar East Central Europe they were confronted, rather, with chauvinism and intolerance, instability, economic stagnation, and extreme right-wing politics. Moreover, the traditional safety valve of emigration had been blocked by the new restrictions inaugurated by the United States and other Western nations. Many observers were quick to point out, even at the beginning of this period, that the old multinational Habsburg empire was a much more favorable environment from the Jewish point of view than were the successor states, and some went so far as to insist that even the tsarist empire was preferable. It can be argued, too, that the neighboring Soviet Union was a much more friendly place for the Jews than were most of the new East European states. In the Soviet Union the dominant ideology was based on class rather than nation, the old conservative (and anti-Semitic) elites had been destroyed, and economic dynamism was beginning to transform a typically backward East European state into a modern, industrialized colossus. In comparing the fate of the Jews in the Soviet Union with that in East Central Europe during the interwar period, one might conclude that in the latter the environment was bad for the Jews while not necessarily being bad for Judaism—that is, collective Jewish religious, cultural, and even political expression—whereas in the former Jews as individuals were able to prosper while Judaism as a religion, and indeed all forms of specifically Jewish creativity, withered away. We shall see that in certain countries of East Central Europe, most notably Poland, the hostile environment was no impediment to the flourishing of Jewish culture of either the secular or the religious variety.

If East Central Europe was far from being a unified region, despite certain characteristics common to most of its countries, the same was true of the Jewries of East Central Europe. Not only was there no such thing as "East Central European Jewry," but also it made little sense to speak of "Czechoslovak Jewry," "Romanian Jewry," or even "Polish Jewry." There was a world of difference between the basically middle-class, acculturated Jewish communities of Bohemia and Moravia in western Czechoslovakia and the poverty-stricken, Yiddish-speaking, Orthodox Jewry of Subcarpathian Rus in eastern Czechoslovakia. And there was little to unite the Jewish community of Wallachia, in old, pre–World War I Romania, with the Jewish community of Bessarabia, annexed to Romania after the war. The same can be said of the Jews of central (or Congress) Poland and of Polish Galicia, or of the Jews in northern and southern Latvia. In fact, only in Lithuania, Hungary, and Estonia were there fairly homogeneous Jewries. Viewed broadly, two basic "types" of Jewish communities in East Central Europe emerge—a "West European type" and an "East European type." The East European type was characterized by the relative weakness of acculturation and assimilation, the preservation of Yiddish speech and religious Orthodoxy (sometimes of the extremely conservative Hasidic variety), and a lower-middle-class and proletarian socioeconomic structure. A typical East European Jewish community had a high birth rate and a low rate of intermarriage, and, while it was largely urban in nature, many of its members still lived in the old-style *shtetl* (small Jewish town). In such a community a certain degree of acculturation and secularization had occurred, but such acculturation and secularization, which took place gradually in the context of socioeconomic backwardness and general anti-Jewish hostility, most typically led not to assimilation, but to modern Jewish nationalism of one form or another. There existed in this type of community two legitimate forms of Jewish identity—religious (meaning almost always Orthodox, since Reform Judaism was virtually unknown) and national (usually secular national). Finally, East European Jewish communities usually constituted a rather large percentage within the general population, especially within the urban sector, and played a highly conspicuous role in local economic life, particularly in commerce. In lieu of a "native" middle class, these communities were often correctly identified as the local equivalent of a bourgeois class.

The West European type was characterized by a high degree of acculturation, aspirations toward assimilation, and a general tendency to abandon both Yiddish and Orthodoxy, accompanied by a readiness to embrace some form of Reform, or liberal, Judaism. From a socioeconomic point of view, such Jewish communities tended to be middle class; from a demographic point of view, they were highly urbanized, though they rarely constituted a remarkably high percentage within the general urban population. The typical West European Jewry possessed a low birth rate and often a high rate of intermarriage; its sense of Jewish identification was usually religious, not national secular.

The West European type of Jewish community obviously closely corresponds to the Jewries of such Central and West European countries as Germany, France, and England. In East Central Europe it was found in Bohemia and Moravia (the so-called Czech lands), in Hungary, in certain parts of Latvia, and in Romanian Wallachia. The East European type was found in Galicia, central (Congress) Poland, Polish Lithuania, independent Lithuania, Subcarpathian Rus, Bukovina, Bessarabia, and southern Latvia. Other regions, notably Slovakia and Moldavia, possessed Jewish communities of a mixed type, somewhere between the Eastern and Western varieties. There is an obvious correlation between the degree of economic development, and the type of Jewry. Usually, though not invariably, the more developed the region, the more Western the type of Jewry; the less developed, the more Eastern. But if all the Jewries in Central and Western Europe were of the Western type, in East Central Europe, geography notwithstanding, there were besides the predominant East European type some Jewish communities quite similar in most respects to those of Germany and France.

The implications of this typology for the internal development of the various Jewish communities of East Central Europe were very important. In the East European communities, autonomous Jewish culture flourished during the interwar years, as did the new Jewish politics. In these communities Zionism, Jewish socialism, and modern Hebrew and Yiddish schools and literature thrived, along with a new Jewish leadership based on mass support from within the community. Here, too, were voiced demands for Jewish national autonomy. In the West European–type communities, on the other hand, autonomous Jewish politics and culture were much less in evidence. Jews participated much more in the cultural life of the majority nationality and were much less attracted to the various forms of modern Jewish nationalism. Their leaders were quite different, as were the policies they followed. It is extremely doubtful, however, if the type of community had much to do with Jewish-gentile relations.

In modern Jewish history in the Western world, the classical pattern has been progression from nonacculturation and nonassimilation to acculturation and efforts to assimilate, from the physical and spiritual ghetto to integration, of one sort or another, into the broader society. In interwar East Europe this pattern is not in evidence. The East European–type communities, despite a certain, and sometimes even an impressive, degree of acculturation during the 1920s and 1930s, remained basically Yiddish-speaking, lower middle class and proletarian, and strongly influenced both by religious Orthodoxy and by modern separatist Jewish nationalism. Once again we may contrast this situation with that of Soviet Jewry, a typical East European community at the outset of the interwar period, but well on its way to becoming a West European–type community by the end of the 1930s. This dramatic change was a function of the ruling ideology and of the economic dynamism of the Soviet state. In East Central Europe the combination of intolerant, anti-Semitic nationalism, right-wing politics, and economic stagnation made such a change impossible. In the following pages we shall consider the impact of this state of affairs on the Jews of that region.

**Poland between the Wars**

# POLAND / 1

The resurrection of Poland as a free, sovereign state in 1918 was postwar Eastern Europe's most popular and dramatic example of the triumph of the national principle. Unlike the Czechs, Slovaks, Romanians, Lithuanians, and Latvians, the Poles had enjoyed a long and unbroken history of political independence, which came to an end only in the second half of the eighteenth century. The collapse of statehood, however, by no means signaled the collapse of Polish nationalism. In contrast with the situation among most of the peoples of Eastern Europe, the Polish ruling class (*szlachta*) remained intact and succeeded in maintaining the continuity of Polish culture even when the Polish state was no longer in existence. Poland, therefore, was never a peasant nation, although peasants constituted the bulk of the population. During the nineteenth century, moreover, in the wake of industrialization in the Polish lands, a small but significant Polish bourgeoisie and proletariat emerged. Polish national institutions—universities, the Polish Catholic church, even parliaments—also flourished, though certainly not everywhere in the Polish lands and sometimes only for short intervals. The anomaly of a vibrant, powerful people without a state of its own was obvious throughout the nineteenth century, and the Polish cause was enthusiastically adopted by many people and organizations which were far less interested in, or enthusiastic about, the national struggle of the Ukrainians or of the Romanians. Indeed, the "Polish question" became one of the most important and explosive issues in European politics, and its apparent resolution in 1918 was greeted with joy by Poland's many friends and with relief by those who saw in Poland's partition a source of political instability in Europe. If many greeted the creation of Czechoslovakia, Yugoslavia, and the independent Baltic States with skepticism, it was clear to most observers that the creation of an independent Polish state had righted an old and shameful wrong. By the same token, Poland's prospects, thanks to its strong national tradition and cultural and institutional continuity, seemed much brighter than those of the other new East European states. It was therefore hoped that a strong, stable Poland would act as the cornerstone of a stable East Central Europe.

During the nineteenth century the lands which had once constituted the Polish state belonged to the Prussian (later German), Russian, and

Austro-Hungarian states. The condition of the Poles differed widely from one region to the next. Since Prussia, and subsequently Germany, regarded itself as basically a nation-state, whatever autonomy the Poles originally enjoyed in this state was gradually whittled away. By the end of the nineteenth century, the Polish and mixed Polish-German regions of Germany were the scene of a concerted effort aimed at germanization. As a result, Poznań (Posen) and Pomorze (Pomerania), along with Prussian Upper Silesia, witnessed an intense national struggle between Germans and Poles, which in turn produced a particularly strong and xenophobic form of Polish nationalism. (Since the Jews in these regions were identified with German culture, this development had important implications for Polish-Jewish relations.)

In the Habsburg empire the situation was entirely different. Here the prevailing political conception, at least by the second half of the nineteenth century, was that of a multinational empire in which power was shared by certain privileged nationalities. The Poles, along with the Germans and the Hungarians, enjoyed such power and were in effect given home rule in the province of Galicia, a region which they shared with large Jewish and Ukrainian populations. Here they were allowed to establish Polish universities (in Cracow and in Lwów), control the school system, and dominate the local parliament (Sejm). As a result, many Poles in Galicia, particularly the landowning class, developed strong ties of affection and loyalty to the Habsburg dynasty, which they saw not only as a guarantor of continued Polish national existence but also as a bulwark against unwanted social change. There were no major Polish national revolts directed against Vienna during the nineteenth century, although there was a bloody peasant jacquerie in Galicia in 1846 directed against the Polish landlords. Poles were conspicuous in the upper echelons of the Habsburg bureaucracy and rose to the highest positions the state had to offer.

The Russian empire, where the majority of Poles resided in the nineteenth century, was also a multinational state, but if in the early nineteenth century a Habsburg-like policy vis-à-vis the Poles was followed, this policy was abandoned later on. Following the Congress of Vienna in 1815, the autonomous Kingdom of Poland (also known as Congress Poland) was established within the Russian empire, with its own laws, army, parliament, and constitutional monarch (who was also the autocrat of Russia). Former Polish areas outside the borders of the Kingdom, populated mainly by Lithuanians, Belorussians, and Ukrainians, but traditionally dominated by Polish landlords and Polish culture, were also granted a certain degree of autonomy. This policy remained in force until the Polish revolt of 1830, which was followed by the russification of the formerly Polish regions outside the Kingdom and by a cracking down on Polish nationalism in the Kingdom itself. Finally, after the second revolt against Russian rule, in 1863, autonomy was virtually abolished even in Congress Poland, which was now subdivided into ten Russian-style provinces and given a new, politically neutral name—the Vistula lands.

In the Russian empire, in contrast with Galicia and despite the initial Russian efforts to grant special privileges to the Poles, the tradition was one of revolt rather than of accommodation, one of refusal to come to terms with foreign rule. This area was the center of the "romantic" tradition of Polish politics, as opposed to the "pragmatic" tradition which characterized Galician and German Polish politics. Political contrasts were paralleled by sharply different degrees of economic development. Congress Poland underwent something of an industrial revolution during the nineteenth century and became one of the most advanced industrial regions of the tsarist empire. Poznań and Pomorze became major centers of efficient, capitalist agriculture. Galicia and the former Polish regions of the Russian empire not included in Congress Poland, on the other hand, remained economic backwaters, among the poorest regions in all of Eastern Europe, characterized by a wealthy, large landowning class and an impoverished, oppressed peasantry. Such different, and sometimes contrasting, political traditions and economic conditions in the three partitioned regions placed their stamp on interwar Poland, and, if such terms as "Galicia" and "Kingdom of Poland" were no longer in official use during this period, the impact of regional differences remained powerful. We shall see that this was true not only for Poland as a whole, but also for the Jews of the new state, who were vitally affected by the nearly 150 years of partition.[1]

The sudden and unexpected collapse of the three partitioning powers in 1917–1918 made the rebirth of a Polish state inevitable. The borders of the new state, however, were the subject of lengthy diplomatic and military maneuvers, and were not permanently settled until 1923. The new borders did not satisfy those Polish maximalists who hoped for a return to the vast territories of the prepartition Polish state, but they were large enough to satisfy most nationalists. In the east the Poles made good their claims to Vilna (Wilno), and while they failed to annex Kiev, once a Polish city, they did annex the province of Volynia, previously part of the Russian Ukraine. These and other eastern areas were generally known during the interwar period as the "kresy" (borderlands). All of formerly Habsburg Galicia, including its heavily Ukrainian eastern half (whose capital was Lwów), was incorporated into the new state, as was nearly all of Congress Poland. In the west, Poland obtained part of Upper Silesia (after a plebicite in 1921), part of Austrian Silesia (shared with the new state of Czechoslovakia), Poznań, and part of Pomorze. (Danzig, also claimed by Poland, was made a free city.) The national appetite for borders which contained such Polish ethnic islands in non-Polish seas as Vilna and Lwów, as well as extensive territories in mixed Polish-German regions, rendered the new Poland not a nation-state but, rather, a state of nationalities. In this respect, Poland was similar to all the countries surveyed in this book, with the exception of Hungary.

According to the census of 1921, the population of Poland was 27, 176, 717; approximately one-third of this number were non-Poles. The largest non-Polish nationality was the Ukrainian group, followed by Jews, Belorussians, and Germans.[2] The Slavic minorities—Ukrainians and Belorussians—possessed a territorial base in the kresy and in eastern Galicia as well as aspirations for political independence. Indeed, the Galician Ukrainians, whose national consciousness was particularly strong, had proclaimed the independent West Ukrainian Republic in 1918, and, although this state was crushed by Polish arms, the hope of establishing a great Ukrainian state lived on. Ukrainian and Belorussian nationalism was particularly dangerous for the Poles, since both these nationalities might well be tempted to look eastward, to the Ukrainian and Belorussian Soviet republics, for inspiration and assistance. Thus the problem of the Slavic national minorities was inextricably connected with the threat of Soviet irredentism and the spread of Communism within Poland. By the same token, the German population of the western regions was naturally suspected of hoping and working for the return of German rule. It was less logical to accuse the Jews of plotting either to establish their own state within Polish borders or to destroy the Polish state through the intervention of its allies abroad, but such accusations were the stock in trade of numerous Polish anti-Semites. In short, for many Poles the national-minorities problem constituted a serious challenge to the integrity of the state, and the question of how to deal with it became a major issue in interwar Polish politics.

Aside from the nationalities question, the leaders of the new state faced other, no less intractable problems. The difficult legacy of the partitions has already been mentioned. True, Polish nationalism was a powerful force, but would it prove strong enough to overcome the deep-seated political, economic, cultural, and legal differences among the previously Austrian, German, and Russian regions? As the largest of the new states of East Central Europe, Poland might legitimately consider itself to be the "great power" of the region, but would it prove strong enough to overcome Soviet and German revanchism? In addition to its geographic, ethnic, and historical difficulties, Poland suffered from economic deficiencies. It was, despite the indisputable progress of the nineteenth century, a backward nation. Over 60 percent of the population (66.7 percent, if we exclude the Jews) earned a living from agriculture and related professions, while only 16.9 percent of the Christian population derived its income from mining and industry. Polish agriculture was highly inefficient, and the peasant majority suffered from a particularly low standard of living. In the more backward regions of the country, the illiteracy rate exceeded 50 percent. Nonagricultural tasks in Poland had been traditionally performed by non-Poles, and, while a Polish commercial and industrial middle class was very much in evidence by the interwar period, it was still relatively weak. (More impressive, perhaps, was the Polish intelligentsia, to a large extent made up of sons and daughters of the *szlachta*, the Polish nobility.) Would the new state find the resources to raise the living standards of a country ravaged by war and numerically dominated by an impoverished peasant class?

Political stability was obviously essential if these problems were to be solved in a satisfactory manner. In this regard, Poland faced major obstacles which it shared with most other new East European states. The legacy of the partitions ensured the proliferation of political parties, as it did the uneasy coexistence of different economies. It was also responsible for the fact that most Polish politicians traditionally had not over-concerned themselves with social and economic problems, but had concentrated rather on the need to preserve the existence of the Polish nation and to lead it back to political independence. From being leaders of a national minority, these politicians now had to make the difficult adjustment to being leaders of a sovereign state plagued with major internal tensions. All this did not augur well, either for the political health of the new state or for the solution of its socioeconomic problems. Nor did the fact that these politicians were by and large fervent nationalists augur well for their coming to terms with a large non-Polish population with nationalist hopes and ambitions of its own.

The new Poland was constituted as a democratic state in which power was concentrated chiefly in the lower house, or Sejm. Political stability depended on arrangements among the various political parties, since no single party was ever able to achieve an absolute majority. Among the remarkably large number of Polish political parties, three major blocs may be discerned. The left, historically quite strong in Poland (as it was not in Romania and Hungary), was best represented by the Polish Socialist Party (PPS). The PPS, which had a large following among Polish workers, was moderate as European socialist parties went, never dogmatically Marxist, and strongly nationalist. Also part of the left-wing camp was the radical peasant party, Wyzwolenie (Emancipation). Further to the left was the Communist Party, illegal and therefore numerically small during the interwar years, but a potentially powerful force much feared by the Polish establishment. The strongest force on the right was the National Democratic (Endek) movement, which opposed socialist or radical peasant reform in the name of Polish national unity and which led the struggle to "polonize" Poland by, among other things, championing the cause of the "native" (i.e., Christian and Polish) middle class. In the center of the Polish political spectrum stood the strongest peasant party in the state, the Piast, more conservative on social issues than Wyzwolenie and very nationalistic. Also important was the Christian Democratic Party, ideologically close to the National Democrats, though, as its name indicates, closely affiliated with the Catholic church. Another centrist group was the National Labor Party, opposed to the socialist ideology of the PPS and in competition with it for the support of the Polish working class. Finally, there were the numerous parties of the national minorities, which ran the gamut from extreme socialism to extreme nationalism and clericalism. These parties were able to exert, upon occasion, an important influence on Polish political life.

The two leading political personalities in interwar Poland were Roman Dmowski, the ideological leader of the Endek camp, and Józef Piłsudski, whose political roots were in the PPS and who had attained near legendary status as leader of the Polish legions during World War I. Dmowski's nationalistic vision of a united, monocultural and monoreligious Polish state has often been contrasted with Piłsudski's more liberal vision of a multiethnic, multireligious Poland based, if not on socialism, then at least on social justice. But the history of interwar Poland does not demonstrate that these contrasting conceptions, whatever their historical accuracy, had a significant bearing on the policies of the various governments. Up until 1926 Dmowski's party, in alliance with other factions, dominated the political scene. In 1926 Piłsudski engineered a coup d'etat against the Sejm, citing as his justification the never-ending political instability and the inability of the various governments to solve pressing social problems. Thus the former leader of the Polish left, still a hero to many socialists and liberals, instituted a new, authoritarian (but never totalitarian) regime which lasted until his death in 1935. Piłsudski's Poland, far from implementing new social programs or advancing new ways of solving the nationalities problem, proved itself to be no less conservative and nationalistic than the Poland dominated by the Endeks. Successful at keeping the extreme right wing at bay, Piłsudski concentrated on foreign affairs and the army while at the same time condoned severe repression of antigovernment forces. One of his last acts was to replace the old constitution with a new, nondemocratic one which invested power in the president rather than in the Sejm. After his death Poland was ruled by a group of chauvinistic and antidemocratic army officers much influenced by (though still to some extent rejecting) the growing native fascist movement and the growing influence of Nazism. The post-Piłsudski regime participated in the partition of Czechoslovakia in 1938, but was too weak to put up much resistance to the German and Soviet invasions of Poland in 1939. As a result of this "fourth partition," the Polish state once more ceased to exist.[3]

Polish politics in the interwar years followed the typical East European pattern of progression from democracy to authoritarianism, with the major political struggle by the late 1930s taking place between the moderate right, personified by Piłsudski's followers, and the extreme right-wing offshoots of the Endeks. There were, however, certain local peculiarities. The Polish left remained an important political force until the end, in contrast with the situation elsewhere. Moreover, despite the alarming growth of the extreme right in the 1930s, no major native fascist party emerged in Poland, as it did in Hungary and in Romania. Nonetheless, as in Hungary and Romania, the governments of Poland, whether of the pre-1926, 1926–1935, or post–1935 eras, failed to solve the pressing internal problems of the state. The economic situation remained grim, and the lot of the workers and peasants did not improve. The national minorities were no less disaffected from the regime in 1939 than they had been in 1918. The growing political extremism of the late 1930s, among both the Poles and the national minorities, bears witness to this failure. To be sure, there were also successes, particularly in the cultural arena. Much was done in this short period to remold the Poles into a political entity, and the fact is that after World War II there was little thought of denying the Poles a state of their own. But if Poland had been a backward, poor, and internally divided state in 1919, so it remained in 1939.

During the interwar period, as in previous eras, Polish history took a course opposite to that of her Russian neighbor. In Poland traditional elites continued to hold sway; the nobility and the church remained powerful factors. The state was by definition antirevolutionary, fearing above all the subversive dangers emanating from the East. It refrained from radical land reform because it had no desire to alienate the Polish landowners of the kresy and, instead of economic or social programs, preferred slogans calling for national unity. This was one reason for the strikingly poor performance of the Polish economy during the interwar years, and for the failure of the state to solve the problems of the miserably poor peasants and of the urban masses. In this traditional, antirevolutionary, and extremely nationalistic environment resided non-Communist Europe's largest Jewish community, cut off by one of the most hostile borders on the continent from its coreligionists in the Soviet Union, in whose Communist environment Jewish history in the interwar period was to take a very different course.

## 1. The Jewries of Interwar Poland

One cannot speak of a single "Polish Jewry" in the interwar period, just as one cannot speak of a single "Czechoslovak Jewry," "Romanian

Jewry," or "Latvian Jewry." In each of these countries, which either did not exist or (in the Romanian case) existed within very different borders prior to World War I, the Jewish communities were divided by divergent historical, cultural, religious, and political traditions, as were the non-Jewish majority peoples among whom they lived. In Poland the three major Jewish communities were those of Galicia, Congress Poland, and the kresy. There was also the remnant of a once populous Jewry in the former German provinces of Poznań, Pomorze, and Silesia; but most of this Jewry had migrated to other regions of Germany during the nineteenth century, leaving only about 30,000 Jewish inhabitants at the time of the rebirth of the Polish state. This tiny community, which constituted less than one percent of the general population in the formerly German lands, was the only representative in Poland of a Westernized Jewry of the German, Bohemian-Moravian, or Austrian type.

In former Galicia, on the other hand, the Jews made up 9.3 percent of the population (in 1931). Galician Jewry was basically of the East European type, lower middle class and proletarian, extremely conspicuous in local commerce (there was little industry in this very backward land) and in the cities, but still retaining a strong *shtetl* component. Jewish Orthodoxy was traditionally very strong; efforts at religious reform made little headway, and Hasidism possessed in this region one of its greatest strongholds in all Eastern Europe. Indeed, it was from Galicia that the adherents to Hasidism, with their black coats, white stockings, and long side curls (*peyes*), symbols of Jewish foreignness and peculiarity in the eyes of gentiles, spread to such neighboring regions as Bukovina, Moldavia, northern Transylvania, and Subcarpathian Rus. In many of its characteristics, Galician Jewry was similar to the Jewry of the Russian Ukraine. As distinct from Russian Jews, however, Galician Jews lived under favorable political circumstances, at least since their emancipation in 1867; they enjoyed equality of rights, were admitted without difficulty to government schools and universities, and made significant inroads into the professions and even into the government bureaucracy. Although the majority suffered from economic misery, which explains the large migration of Galician Jews to the New World in the late nineteenth and early twentieth centuries, they were not terrorized—there were few Russian-style pogroms in this Austrian province. The coexistence of an Eastern-type Jewry and Western-type political conditions produced important results. Large numbers of Jews took advantage of the situation to attend government schools, and inevitably a process of acculturation took place. If on the eve of World War I most Galician Jews still spoke Yiddish, more and more were speaking Polish, which had by then replaced German as the major cultural orientation of the modernizing Jewish population. We shall see that in the interwar years Galician Jewry was the most polonized of all the great Polish Jewries. The growing Polish cultural orientation was accompanied by a powerful feeling of loyalty toward the Habsburg regime. The Jews in Galicia, as in the Hungarian lands, had good reason to feel grateful to the ruling dynasty which had emancipated them and had refrained from pursuing an anti-Jewish policy on the Russian model.

Like Russia, Galicia was a stronghold not only of Hasidism but also of its great enemy, the Haskalah (Enlightenment) movement. Though the Galician Maskilim (advocates of the Enlightenment) did not go so far as their German colleagues, some of whom advocated radical religious reform, they, too, propagated the cause of modernization, acculturation, and integration. To the Maskilim the Hasidic masses, with their outlandish dress, "fanatic" ways, and unbounded faith in the powers of their rebes (rabbis, in Hasidic parlance), represented all that was negative, and even disgusting, in the Jewish tradition. In Galicia, moreover, as in Russia but not in Germany, the Haskalah produced a revival of Hebrew letters which was later championed by the Zionist movement. The Galician Haskalah gave birth to two sharply divergent views on the Jewish future, one calling for Jewish-Polish assimilation and for the eventual merging of Jews with the Polish nation, the other calling for an affirmation of modern Jewish nationalism. The former option, which appealed to the Jews to become "Poles of the Mosaic faith," was not encouraged by the Polish majority, which unlike the regime in Vienna was strongly anti-Semitic. The rise of modern anti-Semitism in Galicia, along with the peculiar ethnic situation in the eastern half of the province, led many acculturated Jewish youths to Jewish nationalism of one kind or another. By the eve of World War I, Zionism was a powerful movement in Galicia, and Jewish Yiddish-oriented socialism, though much weaker than in Russia, was also in evidence.

Galicia was divided into two parts. In the smaller, western region, whose capital was Cracow, the Jews were the only sizable ethnic and religious minority. In the more populous, eastern region, however, there was a large Ukrainian population, which during the course of the nineteenth century developed a strong nationalist movement of its own. The existence of three nationalities in eastern Galicia lent to this region a special character. Among other things it had the effect of retarding Jewish assimilation and encouraging Jewish nationalism, which was inspired to some extent by the Ukrainian example. The bitter nationalist rivalry between Poles and Ukrainians, however, was also a potential danger for the Jews, who found themselves caught in the middle and whose polonizing tendencies were bound to be resented by the Ukrainians. In this sense the Jewish condition in eastern Galicia resembled that in such other multiethnic regions as Transylvania, Slovakia, and Bohemia.[4]

The largest of all Polish Jewries in the interwar period, comprising over

50 percent of the total number of Polish Jews, resided in the central provinces of the state, which were more or less coterminous with prewar Congress Poland.[5] Here, too, the Jewish community was basically of the Eastern type, in both demographic and economic structure, but since this region was more urbanized and economically more developed, the number of small-town Jews was relatively low. Moreover, in the two great cities of Congress Poland, Warsaw and Lodz, there emerged a wealthy Jewish industrial and commercial class which had no real parallel in Galicia. This class, which played a key role in the economic development of the region, took the lead in the movement calling upon Jews to polonize and financed the important Polish-language Jewish press during the 1860s and 1870s. The ethnic situation in Congress Poland as well as the rapid urbanization of the area encouraged such a movement, since here, as in western Galicia, the Jews were the only important minority group. By the end of the nineteenth century, some Jews in this region were thoroughly polonized and had come to view themselves as Poles of the Mosaic faith, despite the fact that political power was exercized not by the Poles, as in Galicia, but by St. Petersburg. Indeed, Congress Poland provides an unusual example of Jewish willingness to accept the cultural orientation of yet another oppressed minority nationality. (In Transylvania, Slovakia, Bohemia, and Bukovina, the Jews gravitated toward the culture of the politically dominant nationality.) Some Jews even went so far as to take part in the various Polish revolts against Russian rule which broke out in 1794, 1830, and 1863.[6]

Alongside the small but important modernized and polonized Jewish community in Congress Poland stood the much larger Orthodox sector. As in Galicia, Hasidism was extremely powerful; one of the most important of all East European Hasidic leaders, the Rebe of Ger (Góra Kalwaria), maintained his court in a town near Warsaw. As was not the case in Galicia, the Haskalah movement in Congress Poland had never been very strong; the modernizing elite had gone over immediately to Polish, while the Orthodox masses remained in their traditional religious, Yiddish-speaking world. Observers of the Jewish scene in prewar Congress Poland were invariably struck by the domination of two extremist groups—extreme Orthodox and extreme assimilationist. A modern Jewish nationalist politics, which rarely flourished in the absence of a Haskalah tradition, was weaker here than in Galicia, and to a great extent was "imported" from Russia proper by Lithuanian-Belorussian Jews (known as Litvaks). The Litvaks had penetrated Congress Poland in the late nineteenth and early twentieth centuries, attracted by the great economic opportunities there; they had brought with them a Russian cultural orientation and such modern political doctrines as Jewish socialism and Zionism. It was in part thanks to them that Warsaw, with the largest

Jewish community in the Russian empire, had become by the end of the nineteenth century an important capital of modern Jewish politics.[7] Nonetheless, the Zionist leader Chaim Weizmann, who visited the region in 1903, reported that the Polish (as opposed to the Russian) Jews were "a people divided into assimilationists of the worst type and Hasidism, so that there is practically no Zionism."[8]

Relations between Poles and Jews in Congress Poland had their euphoric moments. We have already noted that some Jews collaborated with the Poles in the revolts against Russian rule, and in 1862 the short-lived, semi-independent Polish regime of Aleksander Wielopolski, which one year later raised the flag of revolt, issued a proclamation abolishing many restrictions against Jews.[9] After the collapse of the revolt, however, the situation deteriorated. Conflict between the Jewish and the growing Polish middle class in this industrializing region was particularly sharp, and exclusivist Polish nationalism, directed against efforts at russification, was also very strong. Congress Poland, therefore, was fertile ground for the development of the National Democratic (Endek) movement, which was anti-Semitic from its inception. In 1912 Roman Dmowski organized a boycott against Jewish-owned stores in this region as "punishment" for the Jews' support of a socialist candidate in elections to the Russian Duma (parliament). In pre-1914 Congress Poland, as was not the case in Hungary, the nationalist leaders of the numerically dominant nationality viewed the Jews not as potential allies in its national struggle, but as a disloyal element which constituted a serious obstacle to Polish national goals.

The Jewish historical experience in the kresy was different in many ways from that of the Galician and Congress Poland Jewish communities. Before World War I the kresy, with the exception of the Russian Ukrainian province of Volynia, was part of the "North West" region of the Russian empire. In Jewish parlance this part of the Pale of Settlement (the area within the empire where Jews were allowed to live) was known as Lithuania-Belorussia, or simply as Lithuania, and thus, as we have seen, the Jews themselves were referred to as "Lithuanians" (Litvaks). As a result of the war, the Lithuanian Jewry was partitioned among four states—independent Lithuania, Latvia, Poland, and the Soviet Union. The population of the North West region and Volynia was made up of Lithuanians, Belorussians, Ukrainians, Russians, Poles, and Jews. Historically, the ruling nationality was Polish, but the Polish population was numerically weak (though influential in the cities and among the landowning class) and unable to impose its culture upon the majority. In an area dominated by small and relatively backward nationalities, the modernizing Jewish population adopted Russian culture; virtually no Jews here knew Polish in the prewar period, and the great majority spoke

Yiddish. But if some Jews in this region, as in Congress Poland and in Galicia, were inclined to acculturate, there was less effort to assimilate here than elsewhere. It was obviously more logical to hope to be accepted as a Pole of the Mosaic faith in Warsaw or in Cracow than to be accepted as a Russian of the Mosaic faith in Vilna, where there were few Russians. The multinational character of the region also militated against strong assimilationist tendencies, as did certain internal Jewish developments. Lithuanian Jewry was no less Orthodox than was Congress Polish Jewry; the most celebrated of all East European yeshivahs were located in the region, and Lithuania was also the birthplace of such great Talmudic sages as Elijah of Vilna (1720–1797) and Israel Salanter (1810–1883). But the relative weakness of Hasidism is one reason why the Haskalah movement found in the Lithuanian-Belorussian lands particularly fertile soil. The cities of this region, in particular Vilna, the "Jerusalem of Lithuania," became major centers of the Russian Haskalah, which was characterized by its Hebraic character and, at least in some cases, by its protonationalist spirit. In Lithuania, too, but to an even greater extent than in Galicia, the children of the Haskalah became the founders of modern Jewish politics. The Jewish socialist party known as the Bund was founded in Vilna in 1897. Zionism was strong here, from the very beginning, and the religious Zionist movement known as Mizrachi was established in Lithuania early in the twentieth century. The leaders of the secular political factions were russified, but certainly not assimilated, Jewish intellectuals, whose Jewish nationalism cannot be explained without reference to the peculiarities of the environment in which they lived. If politically ambitious Jewish intellectuals in Warsaw were likely to join Polish movements, in Vilna they were much more likely to join Jewish movements.

In terms of demography and economics, the Jewish communities in Lithuanian-Belorussia and Volynia were not unlike the community in Galicia. The notorious economic backwardness of the region meant that the Jews constituted an important part of the urban population (sometimes even the majority) and were predominant in commerce, but it also preserved the *shtetl* as a viable institution. Relations between Jews and gentiles were probably better here than elsewhere; the pogroms of the tsarist period did not seriously affect the Lithuanian-Belorussian lands, nor did right-wing Polish political movements make serious inroads here in the prewar years. It may well be that here, as in other backward regions such as Subcarpathian Rus, the retarded nature of the national movements of the local nationalities and their failure to develop an important commercial and professional class were responsible for the fact that anti-Semitism of the Congress Poland variety was less in evidence.

If the distinctions among the former Austrian, German, and Russian lands which made up the new state of Poland did not disappear during the interwar period, neither did the distinctions among Galician Jews, Congress Poland Jews, and Lithuanian Jews. They placed their stamp on Jewish cultural and political life in the new republic, and, although by 1939 the Jews of Vilna, Lwów, and Warsaw had much more in common than they had had in 1918, the following pages will demonstrate that throughout the interwar years the differences remained significant.

## 2. The Jews of Poland: Demography, Economic Structure, National Identity

During the interwar period the Polish state conducted two censuses, the first in 1921 and the second ten years later. According to the first census there were 2,855,318 Jews (by religion) in Poland, or 10.5 percent of the population. By 1931 the number had grown to 3,113,933, but the percentage had dropped to 9.8. This was by far the largest Jewish community in non-Communist Europe, and also the community which made up the highest percentage within the general population. Only in British Palestine was there a higher proportion of Jews within the total population.[10] Even more impressive was the extremely high percentage of Jews in Polish cities. In the eight largest Polish cities (outside the former German areas, where there were virtually no Jews) the situation was as shown in table 1.1. In the backward, eastern borderlands the percentage of Jews within the urban population was particularly high (see table 1.2). In 1921 the Jews constituted nearly one-third of the entire urban population of the country, and in the eastern provinces of Volynia and Polesie over one-half. Such numbers were interpreted by Polish anti-Semites as proof that Polish cities were dominated by "foreigners," against whom a holy war must be waged by the native middle class.

TABLE 1.1
**Jewish Population in Major Polish Cities, 1931**

| City | Number | Percentage |
|------|--------|-----------|
| Warsaw | 352,659 | 30.1 |
| Lodz | 202,497 | 33.5 |
| Lwów | 99,595 | 31.9 |
| Cracow | 56,515 | 25.8 |
| Vilna | 55,006 | 28.2 |
| Częstochowa | 25,588 | 21.9 |
| Lublin | 38,537 | 34.7 |
| Sosnowiec | 20,805 | 19.1 |

SOURCE: Refael Mahler, *Yehude polin ben shte milhamot ha-olam* (Tel Aviv, 1968), p. 35.

## TABLE 1.2
### Jewish Urban Population, Eastern Borderlands, 1931

| City | Number | Percentage |
|---|---|---|
| Grodno | 21,259 | 42.6 |
| Brześć | 21,440 | 44.3 |
| Równe | 22,737 | 56.0 |
| Łuck | 17,366 | 48.9 |
| Pińsk | 20,220 | 63.4 |
| Kowel | 12,842 | 46.4 |

SOURCE: Yankev Leshchinski, "Yidn in di gresere shtet fun polyn, 1921–1931," *Yivo bleter* 21 (January–June 1943): 25, 27.

Despite their strong urban bias, the result of rapid urbanization during the nineteenth century, many Polish Jews remained in the countryside. In 1931, 23.6 percent of all Jews resided in villages; in the kresy and in Galicia the percentage was higher than in the more urbanized region of former Congress Poland (see table 1.3). The situation in the kresy, where the Jews constituted the urban class par excellence, but where a very large number of all Jews resided in villages, is typical of the demographic situation in the most backward areas of Eastern Europe. In such regions Jews truly dominated the cities, but the cities were relatively small and relatively few in number, and thus unable to absorb large numbers of Jews who remained in the little towns (*shtetlekh*).

No dramatic changes occurred in the Jewish demographic structure during the interwar period. The tremendous growth which characterized Jewish demography in Eastern Europe during the nineteenth century slowed, although we should emphasize that in Poland the Jewish population continued to grow in absolute terms, whereas it did not in Hungary

## TABLE 1.3
### Jews in Polish Cities and Villages, 1931

| Region | Percentage of All Jews in Cities | Percentage of All Jews in Villages |
|---|---|---|
| Central Region (former Congress Poland) | 80.9 | 19.1 |
| Galicia | 75.8 | 24.2 |
| Eastern Regions (Kresy)* | 61.5 | 38.5 |

SOURCE: Refael Mahler, *Yehude polin ben shte milhamot ha-olam* (Tel Aviv, 1968), p. 25.
*Vilna, Nowogródek, Polesie, and Volynia provinces.

and the Czech lands. Nonetheless, in Poland as everywhere else in East Central Europe, the Jewish percentage within the population declined. In Warsaw, for example, the 310,332 Jews counted in the 1921 census constituted 33.1 percent of the general population, whereas by 1931 the 352,659 Jews constituted 30.1 percent. The Jewish rate of natural increase, though significant, was lower than that of the Poles, the Ukrainians, and the Belorussians (though higher than that of the Germans), and during this period Poles were urbanizing at a faster rate than were Jews.[11] Also, proportionately more Jews than non-Jews emigrated, and, although emigration in general did not have a major impact on Jewish demography, it was fairly substantial during the early 1920s.[12] There was, on the other hand, very little intermarriage or conversion, in contrast with rates of intermarriage and conversion in Hungary and Bohemia-Moravia. In Poland, as elsewhere in East Central Europe, there was no parallel to the demographic revolution which changed the foundations of Jewish life in the Soviet Union—the result of the abolition of the old Pale of Settlement and the dramatic Jewish internal migration to the great cities of the interior.[13]

The economic structure of the Jewish population naturally reflected the urban character of the community. If most Poles were employed in agriculture, the overwhelming majority of Jews were employed in commerce, industry, and the professions. Moreover, if most Poles in the nonagrarian sector tended to be engaged in industry, most Jews, at least in 1921, were employed in commerce. This meant that Jews were relatively more dominant in the latter category than in the former. This was the typical pattern in Eastern Europe, although we shall see that there were several peculiar aspects to the Polish situation.

Table 1.4 shows the economic structure of the Jewish community in 1921, at the time of the first census taken in independent Poland. Between 1921 and 1931 one important change took place. That by the latter date more Jews derived their income from "industry" (42.2 percent) than from "commerce" (36.6 percent) was a most unusual situation so far as the Jews were concerned and unparalleled in any other country in East Central Europe. Some observers called this a process of "proletarization," while others, more realistically, termed it a process of pauperization.

As for the influence of Jews within the general Polish economy, it was most pronounced in commerce and in the professions. The data presented in table 1.5 demonstrate the extent of the Jewish role in Polish commerce in 1921 and also illustrate the general rule that the more backward the region in Eastern Europe, the more predominant the role of Jewish commerce. Thus in Galicia, and most especially in the kresy, the Jews were *the* commercial class, while in the more developed central

### TABLE 1.4
### Economic Profile of Jews in Poland, 1921

| Professional Category | Number (Including Dependents) | Percentage |
|---|---|---|
| Agriculture (including fishing, forestry, gardening) | 159,147 | 5.8 |
| Industry, Mines | 937,073 | 34.0 |
| Commerce, Insurance | 1,136,931 | 41.3 |
| Transportation | 93,057 | 3.5 |
| Services, Liberal Professions | 139,688 | 5.0 |
| Domestic Service | 38,691 | 1.4 |
| Without a Defined Profession, Unemployed, Unknown | 250,467 | 9.0 |

SOURCE: Refael Mahler, *Yehude polin ben shte milhamot ha-olam* (Tel Aviv, 1968), p. 61.

region their role was less conspicuous. The role of Jews in industry was considerably less pronounced; in 1931 a grand total of 2,537,669 people were employed in industry, of whom only 506,690, or 19.97 percent, were Jews. Nearly one-half of all those engaged in the clothing industry were Jews, as were about one-fourth of those employed in food industries, but Jews were underrepresented in heavy industry. Thus of 175,111 people employed in mining, only 1,462 were Jews; and of 331,665 people employed in metallurgy and machinery, only 33,318 were Jews.[14] In Poland, as elsewhere in Eastern Europe, the working class in heavy industry tended to be non-Jewish. In the professions, however, the situation was quite different (see table 1.6).

### TABLE 1.5
### Jews in Polish Commerce, 1921

| Region | Total Number in Commerce (Excluding Dependents) | Number of Jews | Percentage of Jews |
|---|---|---|---|
| All Poland | 518,748 | 324,612 | 62.6 |
| Central Poland | 277,397 | 176,161 | 63.5 |
| Galicia | 137,724 | 101,997 | 74.1 |
| Eastern Regions | 47,672 | 42,078 | 88.3 |
| Western Regions* | 55,955 | 4,376 | 7.8 |

SOURCE: Refael Mahler, *Yehude polin ben shte milhamot ha-olam* (Tel Aviv, 1968), p. 127.
*The former German territories and Cieszyn.

TABLE 1.6
**Jews in the Professions in Poland, 1931**

| Profession | Number | Percentage |
|---|---|---|
| Medicine (doctors in private practice) | 4,488 | 56.0 |
| Lawyers, Notary Publics, Legal Advisors | 6,454 | 33.5 |
| Journalists, Publishers, Librarians | 1,315 | 22.0 |
| Private Teachers, Educators | 13,320 | 43.3 |
| Druggists, Laboratory Workers | 2,256 | 24.1 |

SOURCE: Refael Mahler, *Yehude polin ben shte milhamot ha-olam* (Tel Aviv, 1968), p. 159. See also idem, "Jews in Public Service and the Liberal Professions in Poland, 1918–1939," *Jewish Social Studies* 6, no. 4 (October 1944): 291–350.

In general, the Jewish population in interwar Poland may be termed lower middle class and proletarian, with a numerically small but important intelligentsia and wealthy bourgeoisie. A leading Polish historian and student of the period has estimated that the Jewish bourgeoisie numbered 100,000 (including dependents); the petty bourgeosie, 2,000,000, the working class, 700,000; the professionals and intelligentsia, 300,000.[15] The Jewish proletariat, as we have already seen, was not a proletariat of the great factories and mines, it was, rather, a proletariat consisting almost entirely of craftsmen employed in light industry. The typical Jewish worker was a shoemaker, baker, or tailor who worked in a small shop, possibly with a few other journeymen, but often alone. Table 1.7 illustrates another general rule in Eastern Eu-

TABLE 1.7
**Jews in Polish Industry, 1931**

| Factory or Workshop | Total Number Employed | Number of Jews |
|---|---|---|
| Largest Establishments (graded A-C) | 563,872 | 10,396 |
| Middle-Sized Establishments (graded D-G) | 387,915 | 50,473 |
| Smallest Establishments | 1,585,882 | 445,821 |

SOURCE: Refael Mahler, *Yehude polin ben shte milhamot ha-olam* (Tel Aviv, 1968), p. 79.

rope—the larger the industrial establishment, the smaller the number of Jewish workers. Fully 88 percent of all Jews active in industry were employed in small shops, and 44.4 percent were self-employed craftsmen who did not employ workers.

Various factors were at work in producing this anomalous situation. It was often asserted, with some degree of accuracy, that Jews preferred to be self-employed and resisted being absorbed into the factory proletariat. More important was the fact that Jews were rarely employed in non-Jewish firms, and relatively few Jews owned large factories. The problem of Saturday work was also of importance in this regard, since Jews usually refused to work on the Sabbath, and any factory that employed both Jews and non-Jews would therefore have to close down two days a week. Finally, that non-Jewish workers often regarded factory jobs as their monopoly and resisted Jewish incursions was a natural phenomenon in light of the existence of chronic unemployment.[16] In the 1930s there were some signs in Poland that the situation was changing, as more and more Jews, driven by economic necessity, sought work in factories. But until the very end the Jewish working class, though large and politically as well as socially important, remained a most un-Marxian unit, in the sense that it was far from being a working class of the great industrial establishments.

If the typical Jewish worker was a tailor, the typical Jewish "merchant" was a small shopkeeper, or owner of a stall in the local market, working alone or with the help of his family. Of all Jews active in commerce in 1931, 78.6 percent were self-employed and did not employ workers (among non-Jews the percentage was significantly lower, 42.5).[17] There were, of course, wealthy Jewish merchants, just as there were wealthy Jewish industrialists, and in general the Jewish bourgeoisie played an important role in the Polish urban economy.[18] But great Jewish industrialists, merchants, and bankers were much more prominent in the economic life of nineteenth-century Russian Poland than they were in the interwar period, when the state came to play a dominant role in economic life and did its best to exclude Jews from positions of influence. Such families as Kronenberg and Bloch, which occupied a conspicuous place in the growth of banking and industry during the Russian period, had no real analogues in the 1920s and 1930s. In this regard, as in so many other ways, the situation in Poland was somewhat different from that in Hungary, where the Jewish financial and commercial oligarchy, so vital in the nineteenth century, continued to play a great role in Hungarian economic life in the twentieth century as well.

The Jewish economic condition in Poland at the outset of the interwar period, as in other economically backward regions of Eastern Europe, was undeniably gloomy. On the one hand, it could be asserted, and often was, that Jews "dominated" the economy; on the other, the community itself was poor, existing to a dangerous extent on foreign relief funds and cursed with an unhealthy economic structure. One of the great questions which faced the Jewries of independent Poland was whether the economic performance of the new state, and its economic and social policy, would permit the kind of economic breakthrough into the ranks of the middle class which had been experienced by the Jews of Central and Western Europe and which would be experienced by the Jewish communities of North America and the Soviet Union during the interwar period. The future of Polish Jewry depended to a great extent on the answer to this fateful question.

The two Polish censuses of 1921 and 1931, along with their demographic and economic data, also supply very interesting and revealing material on the national character of the Polish Jewries. The number of Jews in Poland cited above refers to "Jews by religion," but Polish citizens were also asked to state their national affiliation (in 1921) and their mother tongue (in 1931). Obviously the largest number of Jews is yielded by the question "What is your religion?" but a very large number of "Jews by religion" also declared themselves to be "Jews by nationality." In the 1921 census, 2,044,637 Jews declared themselves to be Jews by nationality, or 73.76 percent of the total number of Jews by religion; the territorial breakdown, as shown in table 1.8, is of particular interest. Among those who declared themselves to be Poles by nationality were found the so-called assimilated Jews, of whom the famous mathematician S. M. Ulam was a typical example. Ulam, who grew up in Lwów, barely mentions his Jewish origins in his autobiography, save to note that a university career was difficult in Poland, "especially for people with Jewish backgrounds like myself."[19] Such highly polonized Jews often regarded "the Jew with his long caftan . . . as something very primitive, dirty in the physical sense, and rather undignified."[20] But it is certain that not all those who felt themselves to be "Poles of the Mosaic faith" would have agreed to be termed assimilationists, just as it is certain that not all Jews who declared themselves to be Jews by nationality identified with the various modern doctrines of Jewish nationalism.[21] Representatives of the large Hasidic population, for example, who rejected modern Jewish nationalism but who were certainly not assimilated, were doubtless found both among Jews by nationality and among Poles by nationality. It is not surprising that the most nationalist Jewish community was to be found in the kresy (Volynia), and that the least nationalist area was Galicia, where acculturation had made such deep inroads among the Jews. But not all Galician Jews who registered as Poles by nationality were necessarily

TABLE 1.8
**Jewish Identities in Poland, 1921**

| Province | Jews by Religion | Of Whom Jews by Nationality | | Of Whom Poles by Nationality |
|----------|------------------|--------------|--------|------------------|
| Central Poland | | | | |
| Warsaw (excluding city of Warsaw) | 203,425 | 163,355 | (80.3%) | 39,522 |
| City of Warsaw | 310,334 | 251,241 | (80.1%) | 58,776 |
| Lodz | 326,973 | 269,261 | (82.3%) | 57,304 |
| Lublin | 287,639 | 227,804 | (79.2%) | 59,719 |
| Kielce | 300,489 | 215,007 | (71.55%) | 85,400 |
| Białystok | 193,963 | 162,734 | (83.9%) | 30,769 |
| Kresy | | | | |
| Nowogródek | 74,334 | 56,103 | (75.5%) | 16,550 |
| Polesie | 110,639 | 91,157 | (82.4%) | 17,822 |
| Volynia | 164,740 | 151,691 | (92%) | 11,277 |
| Galicia | | | | |
| Cracow | 152,926 | 76,776 | (50.2%) | 75,632 |
| Stanisławów | 141,524 | 90,276 | (63.8%) | 50,566 |
| Lwów | 313,206 | 190,293 | (60.75%) | 121,768 |
| Tarnopol | 128,965 | 68,891 | (53.4%) | 59,794 |

SOURCE: *Pierwszy powszechny spis Rzeczypospolitej Polskiej z dnia 30 Wrzesnia 1921 roku* (Warsaw, 1927). The figures for the entire country (not including parts of Vilna and Silesia) are in ibid., p. 56.

anti-Zionist, just as we may assume that some Jews who registered (in Warsaw, for example) as Jews by nationality were fierce opponents of Zionism and, indeed, of all modern Jewish national movements.

The data from the 1931 census on language affiliation are no less interesting, and perhaps even more revealing (see table 1.9). All in all, 79.9 percent of Polish Jewry declared Yiddish to be its mother tongue, and 7.8 percent obeyed the command of the Zionist movement and declared (falsely) its mother tongue to be Hebrew. Those who described themselves as Polish-speaking from childhood obviously belonged to the acculturated segment of the Polish Jewish community. They were extremely rare in kresy, whose Jews, as we know, were not much affected by Polish culture before World War I, and particularly in evidence in Galicia and in former Congress Poland. It may be noted that there is no absolute correlation between the choice of national affiliation and mother tongue. In Lodz Province, for example, many Jews whose mother tongue was Yiddish chose to be considered Poles by nationality. The acculturated

## TABLE 1.9
### Languages of Polish Jews, 1931

| Province | Number Indicating Yiddish as Mother Tongue | Number Indicating Hebrew as Mother Tongue | Number Indicating Polish as Mother Tongue |
|---|---|---|---|
| Central Poland | | | |
| Lodz (excluding city of Lodz) | 158,749 (90.2%) | 8,950 | 8,190 |
| City of Lodz | 177,232 (87.5%) | 14,289 | 10,578 |
| Lublin | 245,907 (78.3%) | 13,527 | 54,565 |
| Kielce | 293,122 (92.5%) | 11,715 | 11,915 |
| Białystok | 172,130 (87.2%) | 22,771 | 2,208 |
| City of Warsaw | 298,849 (88.9%) | 19,180 | 18,111 |
| Kresy | | | |
| Nowogródek | 69,781 (84.2%) | 7,243 | 5,695 |
| Polesie | 96,493 (84.65%) | 16,452 | 935 |
| Volynia | 174,131 (83.8%) | 31,388 | 1,975 |
| Vilna (without city of Vilna) | 47,655 (85.5%) | 6,576 | 1,515 |
| City of Vilna | 47,509 (86.4%) | 7,073 | 393 |
| Galicia | | | |
| Cracow (excluding city of Cracow) | 74,464 (63.6%) | 7,743 | 34,414 |
| City of Cracow | 23,316 (41.4%) | 22,487 | 10,517 |
| Lwów (excluding city of Lwów) | 143,466 (59.2%) | 14,139 | 84,518 |
| City of Lwów | 67,495 (67.8%) | 7,793 | 24,007 |

SOURCE: *Drugi powszechny spis ludności z dn. 9.XII 1931 r.* (Warsaw, 1937). Data on Warsaw Province and Tarnopol Province are missing.

Jews, like the Jews who described themselves as Poles by nationality, were by no means all assimilated. Within the ranks of the Zionist movement, there were some Jews who spoke Yiddish with difficulty, or not at all, and in Galicia the language of the Zionist press was Polish. Some Zionist organizations, such as the famous youth movement Ha-shomer ha-tsair (Young Guard), were Polish rather than Yiddish- or Hebrew-speaking. The language a Polish Jew might speak in his home, along with the nationality he might wish to indicate on a census form, certainly tells us something about his degree of acculturation and assimilation. But his answers do not enable us to predict with total accuracy his attitude toward his Jewishness and toward the dilemma of being a Jew in Poland.

The data presented above portray a Jewish community which despite its evident heterogeneity was basically lower middle class and proletarian, and both unassimilated and unacculturated—although, as we shall see, by the 1930s acculturation was making rapid strides forward. It was not only largely Jewish in speech and in national feeling, but also, of course, deeply rooted in traditional religious Judaism, whether of the Hasidic or anti-Hasidic (misnagdic) variety. In all these respects it was quite different from the Jewry of interwar Hungary, for example, which was mostly middle class, acculturated, strongly identified with the Hungarian nation, and for the most part far removed from the traditional Jewish world. The cultural and political activities of the interwar Polish Jewry were determined both by its essentially Eastern-type characteristics, inherited from the past centuries, and by its confrontation with the nationalistic, anti-Semitic, backward, but nonetheless modernizing Polish state.

### 3. The Jewish Question in the New Poland: Jewish Demands, Polish Responses

The political frontiers of postwar East Central Europe were determined first and foremost on the field of battle as the nations of the region rose up against the multinational empires and eventually fought among themselves over the inheritance of these once mighty states. After the hostilities ended came the complex diplomatic negotiations, during which the victorious Western powers sought to extend their influence over the region. The Jewish population was naturally unable to play any independent role in the various military campaigns, but it did attempt, through the medium of various representative (and not so representative) organizations to bring its influence to bear upon the negotiating parties. Indeed, World War I and the immediate postwar period was a high water mark of Jewish diplomatic activity, among other reasons because both sides in the conflict were interested in obtaining Jewish support. Thus the

Germans and Austrians looked to the vast Jewish population of Eastern Europe as a possible partner in the establishment of a new German-dominated order in the former territories of the tsar, while the Western powers, recognizing and perhaps exaggerating Jewish influence and wealth, took steps to neutralize German influence. The Jews therefore possessed a considerable degree of leverage, hitherto unknown and never to be repeated. (During World War II, after all, German policy was to annihilate the Jews, not to court them.) This leverage was translated into at least one great diplomatic victory—the Balfour Declaration of 1917. In Eastern Europe there were no such dramatic triumphs, but this does not mean that there were no achievements. True, the new political divisions took no heed of Jewish interests—Lithuanian Jewry, for example, united under tsarist rule in the prewar period, now found itself divided among four different states. But Jewish pressure, exerted above all at the peace conference at Paris, helped to ensure equal rights, at least on paper, for Jewish communities in those new states where there had been no emancipation before the war. Moreover, this pressure succeeded in bringing about a limited but seemingly meaningful recognition on the part of some of the new states that the Jews constituted a *national* minority, deserving not only of civil equality but also of collective national rights, including the right to establish national Jewish schools funded by the state. The Jewish effort to win recognition as a national minority was above all a struggle to win such recognition in the new Polish state, which both was the largest of the successor states of Eastern Europe and contained by far the largest Jewish population. It was apparent to all that Poland was a test case for this rather new concept, upon which so many Jewish leaders pinned such extravagant hopes.

One of the hallmarks of the new Jewish politics in Eastern Europe, which developed chiefly in the late-nineteenth-century Russian empire (and which is discussed in greater detail below), was the principle that the Jews were a nation like all other nations. The fact that they had no territory of their own was not regarded as an indication that they were no less a legitimate national entity than the Ukrainians or the Poles. Whether or not the Jews ought to aspire to a territory and state of their own was a bone of contention among the competing Jewish political parties, but most Jewish nationalists, whether Zionist or anti-Zionist, believed that so long as Jews lived in the East European diaspora they should enjoy both civil and national rights. The doctrine of extra-territorial national autonomy which the Austrian Social Democratic Party set forth as a possible model for the restructuring of the Habsburg empire was enthusiastically embraced by Jewish nationalists in prewar Russia. And if there was little hope of realizing it in the oppressive Russian "prison of nationalities," the new postwar states of Eastern

Europe appeared to offer a much more favorable environment for such schemes.[22]

Jewish national autonomy meant different things to different people. Its most fundamental meaning was that the Jews, like other minority nationalities, whether territorial or extraterritorial, should be granted the right to develop their national life with the help of public funds. In practical terms this meant above all the right to establish state-supported Jewish schools conducted in Jewish languages (either Yiddish or Hebrew). More far-reaching plans called for state support for a wide range of Jewish cultural, social, and economic institutions and, on the political level, for a state-recognized official Jewish democratic body whose elected leaders would represent the Jews in parliament and in the government. Some Jewish nationalists even demanded that the Jewish national representation in parliament be guaranteed in accordance with the Jewish proportion of the general population. Most advocates of national Jewish autonomy regarded the traditional organ of Jewish self-government, the kehile (*kehila* in Hebrew), as the basic unit in the organization of Jewish national autonomy. They insisted, however, that it undergo a process of democratization and secularization.

It is important to emphasize that not all East European Jews were interested in the various schemes for Jewish national autonomy. This was obviously true of the assimilationist sector, and it was true of many acculturating Jews as well. It was also true of most Orthodox Jews. The last were naturally hostile to all secular ideologies, and the fact is that almost all the adherents to Jewish national autonomy had in mind secular national autonomy—secular Jewish national schools, for example, and also secular kehiles. That the religious leadership of the Polish Jewish communities could no more support the secular ideology of national autonomy than they could support the Marxist ideology of the Jewish socialist Bund was a fact known, and exploited, by the Polish government.

Jewish demands for national autonomy in Poland were set forth by Jewish leaders at the Paris peace conference of 1919, at which time these leaders attempted to persuade both the great powers and the Polish politicians that the granting of such demands would serve both the Jewish and the Polish interests. The most prominent Jewish representatives at Paris were from America, but the Polish Jewries were also well represented by a delegation dominated by Zionists. The Polish Zionists entered into negotiations with prominent Polish politicians, to whom they presented their plan for Jewish autonomy. The plan called for proportional Jewish representation in the Polish parliament, a democratic kehile as the basic Jewish autonomous institution, and a national Jewish council elected by the Jewish population. This last body would propose candidates to deal with Jewish affairs within the Polish government. No one on the Polish side was willing to satisfy these demands; the Polish left, which as we shall see adopted the line that the Jews should merge with the Polish population, rejected them out of hand as reactionary, while the anti-Semitic Polish right, though somewhat more willing to consider some limited form of Jewish autonomy, also turned against the Zionist schemes. Negotiations held at the same time in Poland between Jewish leaders and Polish politicians also got nowhere and were eventually broken off by the Poles.[23] The Jewish representatives at Paris were more successful in persuading the great powers that Poland should be bound by some sort of international agreement regulating the treatment of its national and religious minorities. The Poles resisted this, too, but while they could refuse to listen to the Jews they could not afford to alienate the Allies. In the end, Poland signed (in June, 1919) a Minorities' Treaty with the victorious powers, of which two articles specifically mentioned the Jews. The first called upon the Polish government to allow for the existence of Jewish schools, controlled by Jewish authorities and funded by the state. The second forbade the government to compel the Jews to violate their Sabbath. No mention was made of the status of the Jewish kehile, of a representative Jewish organization, of proportional Jewish representation in the Polish parliament, or of a Jewish official whose task it would be to look after Jewish interests in the Polish government.[24]

The Poles bitterly resented having been coerced into signing the Minorities' Treaty. They regarded it as an intolerable act of interference on the part of the great powers and blamed the Jews for having engineered its acceptance. The treaty was ratified by the Sejm only after all shades of opinion had denounced it, and its text was first published by the Polish government in its official organ as late as December, 1920. The secular national Jewish leadership, on the other hand, regarded its passage as a great victory. It was, so thought the optimistic Zionists, a "magna carta" in that it specifically referred to the Jews as a minority with national, not only religious, rights. It signified, so they thought, the beginning of a new era in Polish-Jewish relations and a foundation upon which the glorious edifice of Jewish national autonomy in Poland would be erected.[25] From our vantage point, however, such optimism is difficult to understand. Whatever the attitude of the great powers (and they were clearly unfavorable to the more extensive national-autonomy schemes), the Poles showed by their behavior in Paris and Warsaw that they did not believe that Jewish support was necessary to ensure the victory of their cause. In this they differed from the Lithuanians and Latvians, for example, and even from the Czechs, all of whom made special efforts to gain the support of world Jewry. Polish nationalism was so strong, and the Polish cause so universally supported, that Jewish help was seen as superfluous. Moreover, for most Polish leaders it was also undesirable. As we shall see, the traditional anti-Semitism of the Polish political elite was reinforced by the experience of World War I and by the events in Poland, particularly in the ethnically mixed border regions, during the immediate postwar period. Far from being regarded as potential allies, as they were in Lithuania and in Bohemia, the Jews were generally regarded as enemies of the Polish cause. Their effort to force Jewish national autonomy down the Poles' throats with the aid of foreign powers was seen as yet another example of their basically hostile attitude toward the Polish state.

Apart from the Minorities' Treaty, the Jewish legal status in Poland was governed, at least on paper, by the Polish constitution of 1921. This document guaranteed equality of rights to all citizens of the state, irrespective of religion or nationality, thereby emancipating those Jews resident in the former Russian-controlled regions. It also promised to each religious and ethnic group the right to develop its own cultural life according to its own desires, thus affirming that the state would not promote coercive polonization. The Jews were not specifically mentioned in the constitution, and therefore the question of whether they were a religious or a national minority was left undecided, but they hailed this document both as a model of West European liberalism and as a commitment to a multinational and pluralistic Polish state.[26]

Before we consider what the real, as opposed to the theoretical, condition of Polish Jewry was in the early years of the new state, a brief survey of Polish attitudes toward the Jewish question is in order. The first thing that needs to be said in this connection is that attitudes toward the Jews were part and parcel of attitudes toward the nationalities question as a whole. If the Jews represented, as always, a special and particularly troublesome case, they could not be isolated from the more general difficulty posed by one-third of the Polish population's being ethnically non-Polish. The basic issue which confronted Polish politicians was whether Poland was a multinational state by definition or a Polish nation-state despite the undeniable existence of numerous non-Poles. Adoption of the first position implied granting extensive national rights to the "territorial minorities" in the east, the Ukrainians and the Belorussians, as well as giving special status to the German minority in the west. It also implied a greater willingness, at least, to consider the Jews' demands for national autonomy. If, on the other hand, Poland was to be regarded as a nation-state, the implications were quite different. In this case the nationalities would not receive special rights, efforts would be made to polonize the country, and the interests of the Polish element within the population would be promoted at the expense of the non-Poles. It was this latter position which was adopted by the great majority of Polish political parties and was, in fact, implemented. The Ukrainians and the Belorussians were often regarded as an "ethnic mass" which, with the right treatment, eventually could be merged with the Polish nation. Ukrainian demands for autonomy in eastern Galicia were turned down, as were their requests to establish a Ukrainian university in Lwów. Ukrainian- and Belorussian-language elementary schools were permitted to exist but were under strong pressure to polonize; their numbers declined over the years. Members of these Slavic nationalities did not have an easy time in pursuing careers in the Polish civil service, and they encountered discrimination in all walks of life. The Germans, too, faced similar discrimination and received little satisfaction so far as their nationalist demands were concerned. True, negotiations were occasionally held between the Poles and the various nationalities (including the Jews), but the "agreements," if reached, failed to endure. The fact is that most Polish leaders adhered to the slogan "Poland for the Poles." The non-Poles would have to conform, suffer in silence, and in the end either emigrate or undergo polonization.[27] The Polish nation, it was felt, had not shed its blood and sacrificed its sons in order to establish a state in which vast territories and important financial resources would be controlled by non-Poles.

The Jewish question, of course, was quite different from the Ukrainian, Belorussian, or German question. On the surface it appeared to be a less dangerous and difficult one. The Jews, after all, possessed no territorial ambitions in Poland and had no armed allies on Poland's borders. They were traditionally a politically loyal, if culturally and religiously nonconformist, population, and there was no reason why they should not prove to be loyal citizens of the Polish state. It cannot be denied, however, that they constituted a problem for the rulers of the state. The vast majority of Jews were clearly very different from the Polish majority—in religion, speech, culture, customs, and economic behavior. Should the state attempt to polonize them or not? Should they be allowed to continue to predominate in Polish cities and in Polish commerce? Polish politicians brought to the Jewish question a set of attitudes much more complex than those they brought to the Ukrainian or even the German question. The Jews, after all, were not Christians, and the Catholic church, one of the most influential of all Polish institutions, had long waged a campaign against them. Anti-Semitism was not at all the same as anti-Ukrainian feeling—it had much deeper and more emotional roots. Moreover, the Jews were to be found everywhere in Poland and were highly visible. If the Ukrainians and the Belorussians were concentrated in the far-off villages of Galicia and the kresy, the Jews were to be found in great numbers in the very centers of Polish political and cultural life—in Warsaw, Cracow, Lwów, and Vilna. What was to be done with them?

As might be expected, there was no unanimity of views on this subject. The Polish left, as represented by the PPS, was not anti-Semitic and maintained relations, though not particularly friendly ones, with the Jewish socialist movement. While at times championing the cause of the Slavic minorities in the East, it maintained a Jewish policy that was strongly assimilationist. In the West, argued its leaders (among whom there were several prominent Jews), economic development had led to a merging of the Jews with the general population. In Poland this would also occur once the Polish state had overcome its medieval, "feudal" character. Assimilation, therefore, was inevitable. It was also desirable, since the Jews were not really a nation in the proper sense of the word and had no real reason for continuing to exist as a group apart. Of course, no one in the party advocated the abolition of synagogues and rabbinical seminaries, but Jewish secular national autonomy was regarded as a step backward to the medieval ghetto. The Jews should therefore secularize and polonize. They should not demand separate schools. In all this the party's leaders were echoing Western Marxism's well-known assimilationist attitude toward the Jews, voiced by Marx himself and by such illustrious Marxists as Kautsky and Lenin. It goes without saying that the PPS rejected both the Bund's national program and the Zionist position.[28]

Quite different was the attitude of the Polish right, as exemplified by the leaders of the National Democratic movement. There were two main components in their attitude: first, hostility to the Jews as enemies of the Polish cause; second, the belief that most Jews were unassimilable and therefore could never become Poles. The chief ideologue of the National Democratic movement, Roman Dmowski, declared (in a collection of articles written during the war and published in book form in 1926) that the Jews had long served German interests and were formidable enemies of Poland. Moreover, he also believed that the Jews possessed tremendous power, that they had succeeded in taking over the Paris peace conference, and that their Zionist program was nothing less than an effort to rule the world from Palestine.[29] Most of his colleagues felt the same way about the "Jewish danger," if not about Zionism, and even representatives of the centrist parties, such as the Piast leader Wincenty Witos, shared his views.[30] The antiassimilationist views of the right were summed up by Dmowski when he wrote (before the war):

> . . . in the character of this race [the Jews] so many different values, strange to our moral constitution and harmful to our life, have accumulated that assimilation with a larger number of Jews would destroy us, replacing with decadent elements those young creative foundations upon which we are building the future.[31]

One should not imagine, however, that such views prejudiced Dmowski and his allies in favor of granting Jews national autonomy. If they rejected the doctrine of Polish-Jewish integration favored by the left, they also opposed transforming Poland into a flourishing center of state-supported Jewish national culture. Poland, they felt, had arisen in order to further Polish interests, not to sponsor Yiddish or Hebrew schools. Thus they, too, like the PPS, were hostile to all aspects of the Jewish national-autonomy program.

The National Democrats' attitude toward the Jewish question, if carried to its logical conclusion, could mean only one thing—ridding Poland, in one way or another, of its Jewish population. In fact, by the 1930s emigration had become this party's solution to the Jewish problem. In the short run, however, it meant something rather different, namely, an effort to strike at the Jewish population in order to weaken it as much as possible. Since the National Democrats, together with allied forces, constituted the preponderant influence in the Polish state up to 1926, and since their ideology, at least so far as the Jewish question was concerned, was more or less adopted by Piłsudski in the post-1926 era, this position became the guiding principle of the Polish state. To be sure, it is difficult to speak of a single, coherent "Jewish policy" in the interwar years. There was no lack of zigzags and reversals, of periods of oppression followed by efforts to reach a negotiated agreement with the Jewish population. But behind the strategic maneuvers was a basic purpose—to lessen the Jews' influence, real or imagined, in Poland, and eventually to reduce significantly the number of Jews in the country.

Since virtually all Polish political leaders agreed in denouncing the idea of modern Jewish national autonomy, it is hardly surprising that no such autonomy came into existence. Jews were allowed to establish Yiddish- and Hebrew-language schools, but only at their own expense. The state, despite the Minorities' Treaty, refused to subsidize these institutions. Indeed, it hampered the existence of such schools in a multitude of ways and saw to it that graduates of Yiddish- or Hebrew-language high schools would not receive the right to enter Polish universities.[32] For this reason, and for others mentioned below, the modern Jewish national school failed to attract enough Jewish children to make it a cornerstone of Jewish national cultural autonomy. The kehile, which in the autonomists' scheme of things was to serve as the administrative framework of national autonomy, was defined by Polish law as a basically religious institution and was dominated, in part thanks to government intervention, by representatives of Orthodox, antinationalist Jewry.[33] A democratically elected all-Polish Jewish institution never came into existence. Nor did the various Polish governments consider appointing an official, chosen by the Jewish community, to deal with Jewish affairs. While most Jewish parties continued to promote the idea of national autonomy till the bitter end, little came of their demands. The Poles would have nothing of it.

If this was a blow to Jewish hopes, far worse was the fact that the promises of equality before the law were not fulfilled. During the first decade of the new Poland, both the state and its people displayed a hostility toward the Jewish population which found expression in systematic discrimination and in widespread anti-Semitic violence. The latter's impression upon Poland's Jews was all the more terrible since pogroms accompanied the very founding of the new, free Poland. The first major pogrom occurred in Lwów in November, 1918, when this city was captured by the Poles from the Ukrainians (who had established here the capital of their short-lived West Ukrainian Republic). Although early reports of the casualties were exaggerated, the fact that Polish troops had been permitted to kill and loot in Jewish neighborhoods without the intervention of the state was justly interpreted by Polish Jews as a sign of how precarious their situation was. The leading Hebrew newspaper in Warsaw commented that "in this hour, the hour of the rebirth and reunification of Poland, the hour of Poland's victory over her enemies, who arose to tear away from her the city of Lwów—in this hour we Jews sit and mourn for our victims, the victims of the terrible pogroms, the slaughtered and murdered."[34]

Not only Lwów but also many other Galician cities were the scene of anti-Jewish disorders, perpetrated both by soldiers and by peasants. From this point on, Galician Jewry began to long for the "good old days" of the Emperor Francis Joseph, when, as we know, Galicia was relatively free of anti-Jewish violence. In 1919 the wave of pogroms spread to Polish-controlled Lithuania, another region which had not known many pogroms before the war. In April Jews were shot by Polish soldiers in Pińsk, a pogrom took place in Lida, and, most shocking of all, anti-Jewish riots broke out in the Jerusalem of Lithuania, Vilna. In Congress Poland, too, Jews were terriorized, particularly in railroad trains, where their beards were cut off by Polish patriots. The anti-Semitic tide reached new heights during the Soviet invasion of Poland in 1920, especially in the summer when Warsaw was threatened by the Bolsheviks. During the Polish-Soviet war the Polish government went so far as to intern in a concentration camp Jewish officers serving as volunteers in the Polish army, thus demonstrating to the public at large that it regarded all Jews as potential traitors.[35]

After the satisfactory conclusion of the Polish-Russian war and the final demarkation of the Polish frontiers, anti-Semitic violence died down, though it did not disappear altogether. So far as the Jews were concerned, the wave of pogroms demonstrated that the new state was the personification of anti-Semitism. "Poland," we read in a Zionist newspaper of 1919, "we who are about to die salute you." "Poland" wrote another, "has been reborn with bloodstains on its forehead."[36] How are we to explain this sudden outburst? It was, of course, part of a much larger anti-Semitic wave which enveloped most of the countries of Eastern Europe in the immediate postwar period. The "white terror" in Hungary and the terrible pogroms which cost thousands of Jewish lives in the Russian Ukraine were the most dramatic examples outside Poland of this anti-Jewish offensive. Anti-Semitism in the Polish lands was not a new phenomenon, and we have already noted that it was on the rise before the war. Dmowski's effective call to boycott Jewish shops was made, after all, in 1912. But there is no doubt that the war, the national conflicts within Poland among Poles, Ukrainians, Germans, and Lithuanians, and the Soviet invasion greatly exacerbated the situation. The German and Austrian occupation of the Polish lands in 1915 placed the Jews in a difficult situation, and they were inevitably accused, both during the occupation and after it, of having collaborated with Poland's enemies. It was pointed out by Dmowski and others that the Jews of the former German regions had germanized and sided with the Reich's nefarious efforts to depolonize the area. In Congress Poland, too, it was asserted that the Jews had welcomed the arrival of German troops and had cooperated with German plans to transform Poland into a German colony. There is no doubt that relations between Jews and Poles deteriorated sharply during the occupation, not only because of political tension but also because of economic hardship.[37] The postwar struggle over the borders of the new country also cost the Jews dearly, and it is no accident that two of the worst pogroms took place in ethnically mixed regions where Polish aspirations were opposed by other nationalities. In Lwów, where the Jewish leadership had declared neutrality in the Polish-Ukrainian conflict, the Jews were "punished" for having allegedly sided with the Ukrainians. In Vilna, a city claimed by Poles, Lithuanians, and Belorussians, the Jews were similarly accused of having supported Lithuanian aspirations. (We shall see that this accusation had some basis in fact.) Finally, the Soviet invasion of 1920 greatly increased Jewish vulnerability to the old charge that Jews were left-wing radicals bent upon destroying the old order. The undeniable fact that some Jews were prominent in the Soviet Bolshevik regime and in the Polish left lent substance to this charge. In short, we may assume that the general violence and turbulence of the years 1914–1920, along with the terrible economic hardships of those years, created a climate of opinion and a mass mood most conducive to translating long-harbored anti-Semitic feelings into anti-Semitic acts. There is no doubt, too, that the triumph of unbridled Polish nationalism was bound to be accompanied by anti-Semitism, given the legacy of Polish-Jewish relations and the supreme Polish nationalist doctrine, "Poland for the Poles." The fact is that the triumph of nationalism nearly everywhere in Eastern Europe lent impetus to such feelings, and in Poland, where relations before the war were particularly bad and where the turmoil of the immediate postwar period was particularly great, such feelings were especially strong. Poland is an excellent example of how the fall of the old order and the triumph of nationalism was no blessing for the Jews, just as it was no blessing for the other peoples of the region who found themselves without a state of their own.

The decline in the number of anti-Semitic excesses from 1921 on brought relief to the Jewish community, but it did not lead to a new era of peace and understanding between Poles and Jews. It soon became clear that the Polish state, though committed by its constitution to treat all of its citizens as equals, was no less committed to the National Democratic mission to weaken the Jewish population. One way in which this was done was to see to it that virtually no Jews were hired in those sections of the economy controlled by the state. For example, the Polish bureaucracy was to all intents and purposes *Judenrein*. In Galicia, where Jews had been employed in the civil service before the war, they were pensioned off. Outside Galicia the situation (in 1931) was as shown in table 1.10. In municipal bureaucracies the same situation prevailed.[38] Of 72,721 elementary school teachers in Poland in 1931, only 2.2 percent were Jews; and of 4,429 high school teachers, only 2.8 percent.[39] Jewish doctors were not hired in state hospitals, and Jewish lawyers were not employed by state institutions. Jewish professors in Polish universities were virtually unknown; even the great historian Szymon Askenazy, one of Poland's most distinguished scholars, could not obtain a chair in Warsaw. There were hardly any Jewish officers (aside from doctors) in the Polish army. The number of Jewish students in Polish universities, which were here as elsewhere in Eastern Europe hotbeds of anti-Semitism, declined dramatically during the interwar years—from 24.6 percent in 1921–1922 to 8.2 percent in 1938–1939.[40] True, an effort in 1923 to institute a legal *numerus clausus* (Jewish quota) in the universities was thwarted by Jewish protests in Poland and by opposition abroad, but the universities as autonomous institutions were able to see to it that fewer and fewer Jews were admitted.

TABLE 1.10
**Jews in Government Posts in Poland (Excluding Galicia), 1931**

|  | Total Number of Clerks | Number of Jews |
|---|---|---|
| Post, Telegraph, Telephone | 16,840 | 21 |
| Railroads | 28,895 | 44 |
| Government Offices and Courts | 41,905 | 534 |

SOURCE: Refael Mahler, *Yehude polin ben shte milhamot ha-olam* (Tel Aviv, 1968), p. 161.

Aside from not hiring Jews in the civil service, other ways were found to strike at the Jewish economic interest. Jewish businessmen found it difficult to get state loans, and Jewish artisans found it no less difficult to obtain work licenses. The government passed a law forbidding work on Sunday, which was hailed by some as a progressive piece of legislation, and which had in fact been a long-standing demand of the Polish labor movement, but which was interpreted by the Jews quite differently, since it meant that many Jews were unable to open their businesses two days out of the week.[41] The effect of this law on the Jewish economy, and the impact of the other measures described, led one Jewish leader to accuse the Poles of carrying out a policy of economic "extermination" against the Jewish population and of creating an environment even more hostile to the Jews than that of tsarist Russia.[42] This assessment was influenced by other anti-Jewish acts inspired by the government, such as the effort to expel from Poland Jews accused of not having Polish citizenship and the electoral law which made it especially difficult for Jews and other scattered minorities to elect representatives to the Sejm.

"Extermination" was certainly far too strong a word to use, at least in the 1920s, but even in this first decade of Polish independence, which later appeared to many Jews as a kind of golden age of Polish democracy and tolerance, it was clear that the Jewish condition was tragic. The triumph of Polish nationalism meant the unleashing of latent anti-Semitism which struck at all Jews, assimilated and unassimilated, Orthodox and secular. This triumph, along with the generally bad economic situation, made much worse by the Depression of the 1930s, meant the end to any reasonable hopes that the Jews might improve their already desperate economic situation and make a breakthrough into the middle class. On the contrary, the poverty of the land and the policy of its government led toward the ever-increasing impoverishment of large sections of the Jewish community, whose miserable plight was one aspect of the general impoverishment of the Polish population in the 1930s. (Whether the Jewish tailors were worse off than the Polish peasants is a moot point.) Jewish politics in Poland, to which we now turn, were as much a reaction to this impoverishment as they were to the official anti-Semitism of the state.

### 4. The Jewish Response: Jewish Politics in Poland in the 1920s

The political map of the interwar Polish Jewish community was drawn in the prewar tsarist empire. There were, it is true, several new political organizations which were born only after the war—the very important Zionist youth movements, for example, and the powerful anti-Zionist

Orthodox political party Agudes yisroel. But the creation of modern Jewish politics was basically the work of prewar Russian (and to some extent also Galician) Jewry, and it was an important part of the legacy inherited by the Jewish communities of the successor states.

While we cannot deal here in detail with the emergence of modern Jewish political parties in the late nineteenth and early twentieth centuries, the basic issues which divided these parties and which shaped their ideologies must be briefly surveyed.[43] Perhaps the most divisive issue in Jewish politics in the Russian empire was that concerning where the Jewish question should be solved—"here," in Russia and in the other lands of the Jewish diaspora, or "there," in Palestine or in some other territory where the Jews would enjoy political sovereignty and become the masters of their own fate. Zionism, which had become a force in Russian Jewish life after the pogroms in the Ukraine in 1881–1882, stood for a territorial solution to the Jewish question in the Jews' ancestral home; other Jewish organizations, rejecting the Palestino-centric view, sought a Jewish homeland somewhere else (such groups being known as "territorialist" as distinct from "Zionist"). Opposing the idea that the Jews must look outside the Russian empire for their salvation was a formidable array of Jewish political forces—socialists, diaspora autonomists, and Orthodox Jews. The last were certainly not opposed to the return to Zion, but believed that such a return would be made possible only through divine intervention. The secularist opponents of Zionism and territorialism held up the banner of *doikeyt* (literally "hereness"), a Yiddish term indicating their belief that the struggle for Jewish equality and national rights must be fought and won in the Russian empire and in the other centers of East European Jewish life.

Another, no less basic division in Jewish political life was between secular and religious forces. As already mentioned, in the late-nineteenth-century Russian empire a new type of Jewish identity had emerged, based not on traditional religious concepts but rather on the notion that the Jews were a nation like all other nations, possessing as they did a language (or languages) of their own, a common culture, and a unique historical legacy. Religion, of course, was a part of this legacy, but not the only part, and it was postulated that the abandonment of religious Judaism by no means implied the end of the Jewish people. On the contrary, the "modern" Jew did not go to synagogue, but he was proud of his Jewishness, spoke a Jewish language, and fought for the creation of a new, secular Jewish nation freed from the religious constraints of the past but emphasizing at the same time its distinctiveness among the nations. Such views were denounced by Orthodox Russian Jewry, which clung to the traditional notion that Jews without religious Judaism could not maintain their existence. For Orthodox Jews a secular Jewish identity was (and remains today) a contradiction in terms. This was one reason why so many Orthodox Jews rejected Zionism, which they regarded as a substitute for authentic Judaism and as a movement which might eventually lead the entire Jewish people to spiritual destruction. There were, however, religious Zionists who tried to create a synthesis between modern Jewish secular politics and religious Judaism. Their task was not easy, as they were condemned by the secular Zionists for their religious conservatism and by the extreme Orthodox camp for collaborating with the secular enemy. Orthodox Jewish organizations also denounced the doctrine of Jewish national autonomy in the diaspora, since it, too, was a basically secular concept. What they wanted was religious autonomy, which most governments in Eastern Europe were willing to grant. Thus in many East European countries governments unwilling (as in Poland) to consider the grandiose programs of Jewish national autonomy often received the tacit (and sometimes not so tacit) support of organized Jewish Orthodoxy, which feared even more than the governments themselves the consequences of such secular schemes.

Another basic division within the Jewish political community, more typical of the general political scene in Europe than were the previously mentioned ones, had to do with social ideologies. For some Jewish political leaders the solution of the Jewish question was inextricably connected to the establishment of a new and just society, whether in the East European diaspora or in some other territory. Those among them who favored *doikeyt* naturally emphasized the need to forge a coalition between the Jewish oppressed and the oppressed classes of other nationalities in order to transform Russia into a socialist, federal republic, while the Zionists and territorialists championed the establishment of a sovereign but socialist Jewish society either in Palestine or in some other land. Among the Jewish socialists were Marxists and non-Marxists, determinists and voluntarists, Social Democrats and Populists. All sought support among the Jewish "working masses," who were perceived as being both nationally and socially oppressed, by the regime as well as by the Jewish and non-Jewish bourgeoisie. This double oppression dictated the formulation of both national and social demands, and the various Jewish socialist parties invariably put forth Jewish national demands as well, either for national autonomy or for a Jewish territory. The tension between the nationalist and social platforms of these parties was to lead, in the immediate postwar period, to a series of splits within the Jewish left which mirrored to a certain extent the splits within European socialism at that time. These splits were viewed with satisfaction by the antisocialist Jewish parties, whether nationalist or not, which placed emphasis upon the unity of the Jewish people and rejected its division into classes. If the Jewish socialists emphasized the internal struggle between the Jewish rich and the Jewish poor, the antisocialists played down such internal strife and claimed to speak for the entire Jewish people, whose oppressors did not distinguish between one Jewish social class and another. And if some Jewish socialists insisted that the Jewish people's social structure was "abnormal" and that an internal revolution "on the Jewish street" was necessary in order to transform the Jews into a healthy, productive people, the antisocialists rejected such demands and championed the cause of the Jewish shopkeeper and artisan, believing that the central problem was not the Jews' social structure but their oppression and lack of rights. For the Orthodox community, of course, atheistic, materialistic socialism was anathema, and its political parties, whether nationalist or antinationalist, stood in the forefront of the antisocialist struggle.

Yet another source of political divisiveness among the Jews of the old Russian empire was the language question. Those political parties which believed that the Jews would remain in the diaspora either indefinitely or until the coming of the Messiah were advocates of Yiddish. For the diaspora socialists Yiddish was the language of the Jewish proletariat. For the Orthodox, Yiddish was revered as the traditional spoken language of the East European diaspora, while Hebrew, the "holy tongue," was reserved for prayer and religious writings. The Zionists, on the other hand, stood for the revival of Hebrew as the language of the new Jewish community and of the "new Jewish man" to be created in Palestine and as the chief language of Jewish national autonomy in the diaspora. The struggle of "Hebraists" versus "Yiddishists" was particularly sharp, since it involved the confrontation between two very different visions of the Jewish future. One should add that some Jews rejected both the Hebrew and the Yiddish orientations and preached cultural assimilation, whether of the Polish or of the Russian variety. Small groups of so-called assimilationists were organized in the late nineteenth century, and among their main demands was that Jews learn and speak the language of the land. The Jewish-language question in Russia was therefore three dimensional, and it continued to be so during the period of Polish independence.

The basic divisions described above produced a large number of political parties. By 1918 the most important parties of the left were the Jewish Workers' Union in Poland (the Bund) and Poale Zion (Workers of Zion). The first was diaspora-oriented and Yiddishist, while the second was Zionist. Both were Marxist, and both claimed to represent the Jewish proletariat. More moderate and still in the early stages of organization was the Zionist movement known as Zeire Zion (Youth of Zion), radical but not yet clearly socialist, let alone Marxist. The most important centrist Zionist parties were the so-called General Zionists, Hebraist and secular, and the Mizrachi, Hebraist but religious. Another centrist party was the Folkspartey (People's Party), whose adherents were known as

Folkists. This group was Yiddishist, diaspora-oriented, strongly anti-Zionist and antisocialist. The chief organization of the anti-Zionist and antimodern nationalist sector was the religous party Agudes yisroel (League of Israel, usually referred to as the Agude). Agudes yisroel was brought to Poland during the war years from Germany, where it had been founded in 1912. During the interwar period factionalism, particularly on the left, resulted in the appearance of new parties and new movements. The most dramatic developments took place within the Zionist movement, which in the 1920s witnessed the emergence of various "pioneering" youth movements whose members trained themselves to go to Palestine and build there, through their own physical labor, a new Jewish society. Graduates of these youth movements normally joined the Pioneer (*He-haluts* in Hebrew), a movement based in Poland whose members, after a certain amount of training in the diaspora, were expected to "go on *aliyah*" (i.e., emigrate to Palestine). In the mid-1920s a new Zionist faction, known as Revisionism, began to take shape within the General Zionist movement. It was to play a very prominent role in the Polish Zionist movement of the 1930s.

When viewed as a whole, Jewish politics in Poland possessed certain special characteristics. For one thing, the degree of divisiveness and factionalism was surprisingly great, all the more so in view of the relatively homogeneous nature of the Jewish social structure. The Jews, unlike the other national groups of the region, possessed neither a peasantry nor a landed aristocracy and thus were spared political parties based on these two groups. Nonetheless, the number of Jewish political organizations in independent Poland was remarkable. To be sure, political divisiveness in Eastern Europe was not a Jewish monopoly, but there were certain specific reasons for its prevalence among the Jews. The question of where the Jewish problem was to be solved, "here" or "there," did not confront any other national group in the region, and neither, except in a few marginal cases, did the question of linguistic orientations. Moreover, the question of which identity to assume, secular national or religious, was more acute among the Jews than among the other nationalities. Finally, since the Jews enjoyed no political power, there was little incentive to prevent political factionalism. The absence of real rewards for sticking together meant that ideological differences led almost inevitably to organizational splits. On the other hand, traditional notions of Jewish unity and the fact that the anti-Semites often made no distinctions among Jews usually failed to lead to Jewish political unity.

Along with divisiveness went a remarkably high degree of political mobilization within the Jewish community. Not all Jewish parties were mass organizations; some, in fact, were the creations of one man and a typewriter. But on the whole the historian of interwar Polish Jewry cannot fail to be struck by the fact that Polish Jewry, especially Polish Jewish youth, was highly politicized. An important collection of hundreds of autobiographies of Jewish teenagers, available in the archives of the Jewish Scientific Institute (Yivo) in New York, demonstrates that for young Polish Jews, particularly in the 1930s, joining a political youth movement or party was the norm, the expected thing to do. Why was this the case? One obvious reason was the very acuteness of the Jewish question itself, which obliged many Jews, young people particularly, to seek solutions in the political arena. If political activism is a function of extreme situations, we should not be surprised that so many Jews turned to politics. The Jewish dilemma in Poland, in both its economic and its political aspects, also had the effect of lessening the traditional authority of the parents and of religion in the Jewish household. Economic collapse and violent anti-Semitism, along with the secular, democratic, and modernizing character of the new Polish state, meant that Jewish children were less likely to look to their parents or to their rabbis for guidance and more likely to place their hopes in one or another of the new political organizations, both Jewish and non-Jewish. They were, in other words, more likely to "run away" to the Pioneer, to the Bund, or to the Polish Communist Party. Parental opposition, once formidable, weakened during this period and was usually not strong enough to dissuade them. The generational war between parents and children often took the form of a war over the political orientation of the youth, whose rejection of parental attitudes and whose growing indifference to religious authority resulted in the swelling of the ranks of the Jewish parties.

Another characteristic of Jewish politics in Eastern Europe was that the party or the youth movement took on the attributes of a state within a state, dispensing a wide range of services not always connected with its ideological position. Such services, from running elementary and high schools to administering summer camps, helped give party members the feeling that they resided in a "new world," as opposed to the "old world" of the home and the synagogue. It is clear that the party served as a kind of substitute both for the family and for the secular state, which notably failed to treat its Jewish citizens equally and was not interested in granting them the kind of services they needed. To be a Bundist or a member of Poale Zion was to belong to a separate world with its own cultural, social, and economic institutions. The parties, therefore, were important in aiding Polish Jews in compensating for their alienation from the anti-Semitic, Catholic, Polish nationalist state.

All the major Jewish parties in Poland, with the important exception of Agudes yisroel, were committed to what they termed the "new Jewish politics." This signified that they had broken once and for all with the old Jewish political traditions of seeking a modus vivendi, at all costs, with the authorities. They denounced such traditional behavior as demeaning, as *shtadlones* (a Yiddish-Hebrew word meaning, literally, "intercession" and designating traditional Jewish efforts to intercede with the authorities). The "new Jew," they reasoned, possessed national pride and would proudly demand his rights as a Jew and as a free man. Adherents to the new Jewish politics would therefore not be afraid to anger the gentiles. It was this point of view which lay behind Jewish political activity at the Paris peace conference, where Jewish national rights were demanded even though such demands obviously angered the Poles. And the fact that Agudes yisroel rejected this stance in favor of time-honored Jewish political practices made this religious party the object of disgust and scorn in Zionist, Folkist, and Bundist circles. The new Jewish politics flourished in interwar Poland as nowhere else in the diaspora. How effective it was is a question which will be posed later on in this chapter.

During the tsarist period the modern Jewish political parties were either illegal (as was the Bund) or semilegal (as were the Zionists). With the German and Austrian occupation in 1915 this situation changed radically, and a new era of relatively unhampered political activity began. The years 1915–1918 witnessed the rapid rise in influence of the Jewish nationalist parties, both because of the politically liberal German occupation and because of the powerful tide of nationalism which swept over all the peoples of Eastern Europe. Polish Zionism was the greatest beneficiary of the new situation, and it also benefited greatly from the publication, in 1917, of the Balfour Declaration. England's presumed readiness to establish a Jewish homeland in Palestine made a great impact in Poland, where the Jewish population suffered terribly from the economic hardships of the war. But not only the Zionists found their influence on the increase. The anti-Zionist Orthodox forces began to organize, the Folkists emerged as a significant force, and so did the Jewish Marxists, of both the Zionist and the anti-Zionist varieties.[44] These modern Jewish parties were destined to take over the political leadership of Polish Jewry. And since the new Poland was a secular, democratic, and highly nationalistic state, the secular, democratic, and nationalist forces within the Jewish community dominated the Jewish political scene, relegating to the sidelines the old-style *shtadlonim* and assimilationists and, to a lesser extent, the traditional religious leadership now represented in the political arena by Agudes yisroel.[45]

The triumph of the new Jewish politics was demonstrated during the fateful year 1918, which saw both the dramatic resurrection of a Polish state and the beginning of anti-Jewish disturbances unprecedented in modern Polish history. In response to these events Jewish national councils were established in the major cities of Poland and Galicia. In the latter region the councils were set up without much internal feuding and were almost totally dominated by Zionists. In Congress Poland, however, the situation was quite different. Here, in contrast with Galicia, anti-Zionist forces were strong; the Agude, for example, was much stronger here than anywhere else in the new Polish state, and the same could be said of the Folkists. The Bund, too, was more influential in the industrialized cities of formerly Russian Congress Poland than in Galicia, where it had been virtually nonexistent in the prewar period. The result was that efforts to establish a unified Jewish political leadership in the region inhabited by over fifty percent of Polish Jewry failed. The Bund, emphasizing class solidarity over the traditional Jewish belief in *klal yisroel* (a Yiddish-Hebrew term denoting the unity of all Jews), refused to take part, as did, for the same reasons, Poale Zion. The Orthodox, for their part, rejected an alliance with secular forces hostile to religious Judaism. The Folkists, bitter enemies of the Zionists, withdrew from the negotiations when it became apparent that the Jewish national council in Warsaw, if established, would be dominated by Jews who wanted to abandon Poland and settle in the Middle East. In the end, the middle-of-the-road General Zionists, as well as the Mizrachi (religious Zionists), were left alone, and they, along with certain nonparty elements, established the Temporary Jewish National Council, which was to become permanent only after elections could be held to establish a more representative organization. Such elections, however, never took place.[46]

The events in Congress Poland had important repercussions for Polish Jewry and are extremely instructive to the historian. They illustrated the extreme divisiveness of Polish Jewish politics, all the more remarkable if we recall that the negotiations to create a Jewish national council in the capital took place in an atmosphere of rising anti-Jewish violence. Such divisiveness was particularly striking in Congress Poland and remained a decisive aspect of Jewish political life in that region during the entire interwar period. But it was not limited to Congress Poland alone. The failure of 1918 was a preview of a series of failures to establish an all-Polish unified Jewish leadership during the interwar period, the result not only of ideological differences but also of deep-seated regional distinctions among the various Jewries of the Polish state. These failures, in turn, made it easier for the Polish state to wage its anti-Jewish campaign and made it more difficult for the Jews to defend themselves. Even in the late 1930s, when anti-Semitism reached new heights and when the physical threat to Polish Jewry was apparent to all, no unified Jewish leadership emerged to speak for the endangered community.[47]

The Galician and Polish Jewish national councils formed in 1918 sent delegations to the peace conference in Paris; the reception their national-autonomy schemes received in that exalted forum has already been described. The next major political test for the Jewish parties was in 1919,

when elections were held for the constituent Sejm. These elections revealed the great strength of Zionism in western Galicia, where the General Zionists won an overwhelming majority of the votes given to Jewish
lists. In Congress Poland the Zionist-dominated Temporary Jewish
National Council received about twice as many votes as the Orthodox
anti-Zionists did, and the Folkists, though not the Bund, made a respectable showing.[48] On the basis of the returns "on the Jewish street," at least
four generalizations may be made concerning the political leanings of
Polish Jewry. First, the great majority of Polish Jews gave their votes to
Jewish, rather than to Polish, parties. Second, the "new Jewish politics"
in the form of Zionism and Folkism established itself as the major force in
Jewish political life. The old-style "Poles of the Mosaic faith," who
played a major role in Jewish affairs before World War I, were routed by
the combination of democracy and nationalism which ruled political life
in the new Poland. Third, the antinational Orthodox party proved to be a
formidable force, in Congress Poland if not in Galicia. Fourth, the Jewish
left, whether of the Bundist or of the Poale Zion variety, was revealed as
extremely weak, thus demonstrating that the radicalization of the Jewish
population evident to some extent in socialist Russia, was not present in
nationalist Poland.[49] Indeed, the election results of 1919 clearly belied
Polish accusations that the Jews were pro-Bolshevik. On the contrary,
they demonstrated the moderate social views of a basically conservative
population much more interested in protecting its civil and national rights
than in promoting social change.

The newly elected representatives of Jewish factions in the Sejm, of
whom there were eleven, became automatically the political leaders of
Polish Jewry. The question now arose as to the strategy to be worked out
in order to protect Jewish interests in the new and hostile environment of
independent Poland. To a certain extent this question had already arisen
before 1919, during the struggle for the borders of the new state, when
Jewish politicians and parties had been obliged to chose sides among
various possible national orientations. In Congress Poland, once the
withdrawal of the German and Austrian occupying forces had begun, the
Jews had no choice but to proclaim their support for the establishment of
a Polish state. The same was true in western Galicia, where the Poles were
also the dominant ethnic group. In eastern Galicia and in the Lithuanian-
Belorussian borderlands, the situation was far more complex and dangerous, for there the Jews found themselves caught between competing
national claims, as they did in other ethnically mixed regions of Eastern
Europe such as Transylvania, Bohemia and Moravia, and Slovakia. In
eastern Galicia the Jewish population was strongly identified with Polish
culture and had certainly acquiesced in the granting of political supremacy in the prewar period to the Poles. Most Jews were ignorant, and

perhaps also contemptuous, of the Ukrainian language and indifferent to Ukrainian national aspirations. On the other hand, the short-lived West Ukrainian Republic, proclaimed in Lwów in the fall of 1918, promised the Jews civil equality and national autonomy, while the Poles in the region made no effort to hide their anti-Semitic tendencies. Uncertain as to who the ultimate victor would be, and unwilling to alienate either the Poles or the Ukrainians, the local Jewish National Council proclaimed neutrality. As we already know, some Poles regarded this as a sign of pro-Ukrainian feeling and took revenge on the Jews of Lwów after their capture of the city in November 1918. The Ukrainians also denounced Jewish neutrality, interpreting it as a continuation of the Jews' traditional pro-Polish attitude. Nonetheless, the decision of the Jewish National Council is difficult to fault, for the out-and-out support of one side against the other might well have resulted in even more disastrous consequences. Whatever the case, the experience of the Polish-Ukrainian war of 1918–1919 persuaded many Jews that only independent, nationalist Jewish politics could save the Jews from the wrath either of the politically dominant nation in the area or of the numerically dominant one.[50]

In the Lithuanian-Belorussian borderlands, the situation was even more complicated than in eastern Galicia and led to a different Jewish political strategy. Here there were a number of "weak nationalities"—Lithuanians, Belorussians, and Jews—and little Russian or Polish presence on the ground (with the exception of the important Polish element in the urban centers, especially in Vilna). The Jews were not culturally or politically identified with the Poles, in contrast with the situation in Galicia, and had no reason to favor Polish rule. Instead, most of their political leaders opted for a pro-Lithuanian orientation, based on the assumption that the Lithuanians, desperately in need of international support, would make far-reaching concessions to the large and influential Jewish minority. In their pro-Lithuanian orientation the Jewish leaders held up the banner of a "large Lithuania," with its capital in the great Jewish center of Vilna, both because such a large state would include a great many Jews and because it would be by definition a nationalities state rather than a Lithuanian nation-state. This environment, they felt, would be ideal for the development of Jewish national autonomy, since the Jews were not tempted to adopt Lithuanian culture, and the relatively good track record of the Lithuanians so far as their relations with the Jews were concerned was also regarded as a great advantage.

As things turned out, the large Lithuania championed by the Jews did not come to pass; the Poles captured Vilna and rewarded the Jews for their pro-Lithuanian orientation with the pogrom mentioned above. The Jews' political strategy won them some favor in the eyes of the masters of the new, small Lithuanian state, but was naturally bitterly resented by the

Polish nationalists, who regarded Vilna as no less Polish than was War-saw, Cracow, or Lwów.[51]

By the early 1920s territorial issues had ceased to play a role in Jewish politics. The Polish state had established its frontiers, and the old neutral and pro-Lithuanian orientations ceased to exist. The problem now be-came one of promoting the Jewish interest in Poland. On this issue there was a conspicuous lack of unanimity among the Jewish factions, which perceived the Jewish interest in different ways. Viewed broadly, four separate approaches to this problem may be discerned.[52] When con-fronted with the question of how the small and relatively powerless Jewish minority could combat anti-Semitism and oblige a hostile govern-ment to respond to its national demands, the Bund answered by seeking an alliance with the Polish left. True to its opposition to the concept of *klal yisroel* and to its nature as a class party, the Bund struggled to build bridges to the proletarian, class-oriented parties of the Christian popula-tion, which, so the Bund believed, were free of anti-Semitism and would be prepared, once in power, to grant the Jewish proletariat its economic, social, and national demands. In the last analysis the Bund's strategy, also adhered to by certain sections within the Poale Zion party and by Jews active in the underground Communist Party, was to work for revolution-ary change within Polish society. Only a Marxist revolution could lead to a satisfactory solution to the Jewish question.[53]

For the nonsocialist Jewish parties, a close alliance with the Polish socialist movement was neither realistic nor desirable. Instead, some of these sought alliances among the "bourgeois" representatives of the other national minorities. This was particularly true of the General Zion-ists of Congress Poland, whose leader, Yitshak Grünbaum (1879–1970), labored long and hard in order to establish a national minorities' bloc among the Jews, Ukrainians, Germans, and other national minorities of the state. The ideological basis for this approach was the assumption that all the national minorities, whatever their special peculiarities might be, shared a common interest in forcing the Polish state to cease behaving as a Polish nation-state, which it was not, and begin behaving as a nationalities state in which the Poles were only one, albeit the most important, na-tional community. Only coercion, Grünbaum argued, could bring about such a revolution in the state's nationalities policy, and the minorities, by banding together in a mighty bloc, possessed the political clout to achieve their just aims. After the adoption by the state of an electoral law which clearly discriminated against the national minorities, such a bloc did come into existence and contested the Sejm elections of 1922, with considerable success.[54]

Alliance with other oppressed minorities, a strategy not entirely new to Jewish politics, was obviously dangerous. Grünbaum himself, the main

Jewish architect of the 1922 bloc, was not blind to these dangers, but claimed that the Poles, by their provocative behavior, had forced the Jews into a desperate act of self-defense. Nonetheless, support for Grünbaum's strategy was not forthcoming from the important Zionist strongholds in Galicia, where most leaders objected to the bloc as a potentially tragic mistake. Ignacy (Yitshak) Schwarzbart (1888–1961), a western Galician Zionist leader, summed up in his memoirs the Galician objections to linking up with Germans, Ukrainians, and Belorussians:

> The minorities' bloc will be able to do nothing in the Sejm, its [Galician] enemies claimed, because of the differences in principle which exist among the territorial minorities and the Jewish minority . . . the bloc will fall apart in the next elections, since the nationalities are not homogeneous and have different party attitudes, based on social and on national demands. [Moreover] the nationalities' bloc will call forth the frontal opposition of the entire Polish people and will alienate from us even the relatively friendly groups within the Polish people, especially the Polish Socialist Party.[55]

Rather than siding openly with an "anti-Polish" force which included Ukrainian, Belorussian, and German revisionists, whose interest in altering the borders of the state was certainly not shared by the Jews, the Jewish minority should carry on its own, self-reliant political line, as it had attempted to do during the Polish-Ukrainian war in eastern Galicia. Leon Reich (1879–1929), leader of the eastern Galician General Zionists, noted in 1927 that "we are caught between two peoples, Poles and Ukrainians, and thus we must conduct only an independent Jewish policy."[56] In 1922, therefore, the Zionist organizations of both parts of Galicia ran their own lists to the Sejm elections, leaving the Zionists of Warsaw and the kresy to take the plunge and adhere to the national minorities' bloc.

If the Galicians rejected the politics of coercion, what did they suggest? Basically, they favored efforts to seek an accommodation with the regime, whatever its views on the minorities and on the Jews might be. Rather than dogmatically oppose the government and rally support among the socialists or among the minorities, the Galician Zionists stood for negotiations. The Poles, they reasoned, would eventually realize that there was no sense in alienating the large and economically powerful Jewish population. The Jews, for their part, should not make the fatal error of alienating the Poles through ill-conceived electoral alliances. In the end, the enlightened Jews and the enlightened Poles would reach an agreement in which Jewish demands for an end to anti-Semitism and for national rights would be recognized. This political position led logically to the so-called Ugoda ("agreement") signed in 1925 between the Galician

Zionist leaders of the Jewish faction in the Sejm (the koło) and the Polish government.[57]

The different policies of the Galician and Congress Poland Zionists in the 1920s suggest the existence of two distinct schools of Jewish politics within the General Zionist movement—the "Austrian" school, favoring flexibility, compromise, and accommodation, and the "Russian" school, which refused to do business with anti-Semites and which sought other ways of bending the regime to its will. In the vocabulary of the times, the Galicians were depicted as cowardly *shtadlonim*, and the Russians as fanatics, nurtured on the Russian revolutionary tradition and "capable of fighting to the end over trivialities."[58] All this hyperbole aside, an important distinction between the two political schools clearly reflected the very different political environments in which the leading Jewish politicians had grown up. This distinction, maintained to the very end of the interwar period, was one of the reasons for the failure of Polish Jewry to establish a unified political leadership.

The leaders of the anti-Zionist Orthodox party Agudes yisroel advanced yet another political strategy. The Agude, the most traditional of all major Jewish political factions, went beyond the Galician model of accommodation and held up the banner of active cooperation with and support for the government. To be sure, such a strategy was not always possible. In the early years of the new state, the attitude of the government was such as to force even the Agude to join the opposition, and it went so far as to support, for tactical rather than for ideological reasons, Grünbaum's minorities' bloc of 1922. With the decline of violent anti-Semitism, however, and especially after Piłsudski's coup d'etat in 1926, the Agude found it possible to make a firm alliance with the government. Such an alliance was useful to both sides. The regime preferred to do business with the Orthodox, whose social conservatism and lack of interest in secular national rights was to its liking and whose voting power was an important factor in many large towns of Congress Poland. In return for its political support, the Agude received several important concessions: the government recognized its religious schools as satisfying the requirements of the compulsory-education act and did its best, through legislation and through administrative acts, to ensure the Agude's control over the kehiles. Throughout the Piłsudski era no efforts were made to curtail Jewish religious freedom, which the Agude was naturally most concerned to preserve. It was only after Piłsudski's death, when violent anti-Semitism once again rose to the fore and when the Polish government did attempt to strike at the religious interests by legislating against the *shkhite* (ritual slaughter, without which Jewish dietary laws cannot be maintained), that the alliance between the Agude and the Polish government broke down.[59]

It cannot be claimed that any of the political strategies devised by Polish Jewish parties in the 1920s was particularly effective. The Bund's efforts to forge an alliance with the Polish left, though occasionally crowned with success, did not reverse the anti-Semitic trend in Poland. The inability of the Polish Socialist Party to challenge the right for political supremacy and its unwillingness to be too closely associated with a Jewish organization were responsible for this failure. The minorities' bloc, though an electoral success in 1922, did not lead to a close working arrangement among the various nationalities and did not gain the necessary political clout in the Sejm to alter the direction of Polish policy. Indeed, as the Galicians predicted, it had the effect of uniting Polish public opinion against the minorities in general and the Jews in particular. But the Galicians' strategy, brought to fruition in the Ugoda of 1925, was also a failure. The government refused, despite solemn promises and a protocol signed by Reich and Władysław Grabski, the prime minister, to make meaningful concessions to the Jewish minority, thus making a mockery of the predictions of the Galician Zionists in 1925 that a new era would dawn in Polish-Jewish relations. The Agude could claim certain real achievements deriving from its strategy, but in the long run even its modest demands were rejected.

The ultimate failure of the four political strategies outlined above reveals the essential powerlessness of the three-million-strong Jewish minority in Poland, which had no really strong allies within Polish society and no powerful allies abroad. (World Jewry, which occasionally intervened on behalf of Polish Jewry, proved to be of little political assistance.) We may assume that Jewish political activity in the Sejm had some impact and that things would have been even worse without it. But the hopes that the new Jewish politics, in contrast with the discredited tradition of *shtadlones*, would enable the Jews to deal with the majority nationality on terms of equality and would win for the Jews both civil and national rights were dashed on the rocks of Polish reality.

Jewish politics, however, were concerned not only with protecting Jewish rights and improving relations with Poles. The various Jewish parties were concerned also with shaping the Jewish community in their own image—whether Zionist or anti-Zionist, Orthodox or secular, socialist or antisocialist. What was the balance of political power on the Jewish street during the 1920s? How successful were the various parties in mobilizing support? And what impact did they have? It is not surprising that the Polish Zionist movement was the single strongest Jewish political force during these years, since Poland provided the ideal environment for this brand of modern Jewish nationalism to flourish. Political freedom, extreme nationalism, and anti-Semitism, combined with a huge unacculturated Jewish community rooted in traditional Judaism but undergoing a process of secularization, produced a mass Zionist movement without precedent in modern Jewish history. The typical Zionist of the interwar period was the product of traditional Jewish education, but also, almost invariably, of modern Jewish or non-Jewish secular schools. The pattern is well illustrated by the following autobiographical notes written by an applicant to the Zionist-run Tarbut teachers' seminary in Vilna:

> I was born in Oszmiana in 1908. At the age of six I was sent to kheyder, but was forced to stop studying because of the war. Two years later I returned to the kheyder and remained there till my twelfth year. Then I went to a yeshiva where I studied for two years, and during that time I learned a good deal of Talmud and also general subjects.
>
> At that time the spirit of enlightenment began to influence many of my fellow yeshiva students, who left the yeshiva and went to high school. I too fell under the spell of the enlightenment, and searched for ways to free myself from the yeshiva. To my joy a Hebrew high school was opened in Oszmiana and I was immediately accepted to the sixth grade. I finished the school, and now that I possess the requisite knowledge I wish to be accepted to the first course of the Tarbut seminary.[60]

Zionism was aided also by the various immigration laws which ended mass Jewish migration to the New World. In the first three Sejm elections, the Zionists did much better than any other Jewish faction, and in 1921 they claimed to have sold the remarkable number of 400,000 *shkalim* ("coins," the purchase of which indicated membership in the World Zionist Organization).[61] Zionist strength was particularly strong in Galicia, as we have seen, and in the eastern borderlands, or kresy, whose multinational character and nonpolonized Jewish population made it an ideal arena for Jewish nationalism.

Zionism was the only Jewish political movement which could hope to attract a following among all types of Jews—religious as well as secular, socialist as well as antisocialist. But its appeal to all sections of Polish Jewry was paralleled by its extraordinary divisiveness. Along with the classical issues which divided Jews into different political camps, certain special problems confronted Zionism. Among these was the question as to whether the Zionist movement should concentrate solely on the Zionist concern of creating a viable Jewish society in Palestine or whether it should play an active role in local Polish Jewish politics. This issue divided Zionism into two camps, one composed of Palestino-centric forces, which were strongest in the Pioneer movement and in the various Zionist youth movements (to be discussed below), the other composed of socialist and General Zionists who wanted not only to build Palestine but also to play a dominant role in Polish Jewish life. The most prominent exponent of what Zionists called *Gegenwartsarbeit* (work in the diaspora) was Yitshak

Grünbaum, who placed great emphasis on political work in the Sejm and who adhered to the slogan that nothing Jewish could possibly be alien to the Zionist movement. His critics complained that such "Sejm Zionism" neglected proper Zionist activities in favor of useless parliamentary maneuvers; the main thing was to get Jews to Palestine, not to spend valuable time and money on election campaigns. On the whole, at least during the 1920s, the advocates of *Gegenwartsarbeit* were able to impose their will upon the Zionist movement. Theirs was a typically East European Zionism, rooted in the life of the Yiddish-speaking, national-minded Jewish masses and committed to the struggle for Jewish national rights both "here" in Poland and "there" in Palestine. It was, too, a brand of Zionism which spoke to the masses in Yiddish and which rejected the traditional anti-Yiddish bias of the Palestino-centric, strongly Hebraic classical Zionist tradition.[62] The Zionist left, which identified with the Jewish working class in Poland, was often extremely Yiddishist, despite its ideological commitment to Hebrew as the language of Jewish Palestine.

Another peculiarly Zionist issue which divided the movement concerned the ultimate goal of Zionism. Was it merely the transfer of Jews to Palestine or was it to bring to pass an internal Jewish revolution, meaning the creation of a new Jew totally different from the Jew of the East European exile? The latter viewpoint was enthusiastically espoused by the so-called pioneering movement, which included the Pioneer and the various Zionist youth movements. For the Pioneer the aim of Zionism was to transform the downtrodden, East European *luftmentsh* (literally "man of the air") into a productive worker, who by his labor would build up a new and just Jewish society in Palestine "without exploiters and without the exploited." Indeed, the Jewish right to Palestine, in the Pioneer's view, was based not on the ancient covenant between God and Abraham and on "historical rights," but on the Jews' determination to undergo a revolutionary process of proletarianization leading to the establishment of a Jewish workers' society in the ancient Jewish homeland. This radical conception, linking Zionism with a profound internal revolution, was shared by some General Zionists and, to a certain degree, by the Zionist socialist parties, who also believed that the emerging Jewish society in Palestine must be based on social justice and (in the case of the doctrinaire Marxists) on the class rule of the Jewish proletariat. It was rejected, however, by most General Zionists, who denounced the "social experiments" of the Zionist left and who thought in terms of building up Palestine as quickly as possible through mass emigration. This ideological conflict was quickly transformed into a serious dispute as to who should go to Palestine—"plain Jews" who wished to escape from anti-Semitic Poland and to reclaim the Jews' ancestral homeland or young pioneers who often viewed Palestine as an instrument through which Jewish life would be both revolutionized and normalized. The dispute was especially heated during the period of the so-called fourth *aliyah* (1924–1926), when the Zionist left denounced the unexpected desire on the part of "plain Jews" to go to Palestine and to convert it (so the left feared) into a Middle Eastern version of Nalewki, the main Jewish thoroughfare and business district in Warsaw.[63]

Finally, regional differences divided the Zionist camp into warring factions. We have already noted the different approaches of the "Austrians" (i.e., Galicians) and the "Russians" (from Congress Poland and the kresy) in matters of local Jewish politics. To this must be added the insistence of Zionists from the four main centers—Warsaw, Lwów, Cracow, and Vilna—on maintaining their autonomous status. As a result, there were at first four quite separate General Zionist organizations in Poland, and all efforts to establish a unified, single Zionist federation for the entire country failed. Indeed, it was sometimes noted that the Galician Zionists had closer ties with Western Europe than with the Zionist center in Warsaw.[64]

Jewish political divisiveness is well illustrated by the diversity of groups which constituted organized Polish Zionism in the first decade of Polish independence. There were no less than six Zionist socialist or Zionist labor parties, ranging in fine ideological gradations from Poale Zion-left, which was pro-Communist, Yiddishist, and opposed to cooperation with the bourgeois Zionists, to the reformist, nonsocialist, Hebraic party Hitahdut (Union). In between were Poale Zion-right, the Zionist socialists, Poale Zion in eastern Galicia, and Dror (Freedom). There were also no fewer than five General Zionist organizations, the result of regional separatism and of an ideological split in the Zionist Organization of Congress Poland. There were also a number of Zionist youth movements, whose impact on the Zionist movement and on Polish Jewry in general was considerable. The first to organize was called Ha-shomer ha-tsair (The Young Guard), which eventually assumed a radical, left-wing, Marxist character. It was followed by such organizations as Gordonia (named after A. D. Gordon, one of the leaders of the Palestinian labor movement), The Young Pioneer, Frayheyt, and Betar. Most of the youth movements were associated with political parties, while some, such as Ha-shomer ha-tsair, zealously maintained their independence from any parent organization.

We have already seen that the appearance of Jewish youth movements in Poland, whether Zionist or anti-Zionist, was symptomatic of the general crisis in which Polish Jewry found itself during the interwar years, a crisis which particularly affected the youth. In the 1930s it was common to refer to the new Jewish generation as "a youth without a future," but even

in the 1920s it was clear that Polish anti-Semitism and the general economic crisis in the country was endangering the economic future of young
Jews. In such circumstances the appeal of Zionism was obvious. The urge
to join movements specifically geared to the problems of youths up to the
age of eighteen was also linked to the failure of the Jewish home to offer
adequate guidance to the new generation, which therefore sought guidance elsewhere. It is no accident that youngsters joining these movements
referred to them as their "new home," a home which offered hope for the
future as well as a new and exciting social environment. If the traditional
Jewish family could propose no economic solutions to the problems of
Jewish youth, the fact that it often clung to traditional Jewish religious
and social customs also made it unbearable for many secularizing youths.
Into this vacuum stepped the youth movements, with growing success. By
the 1930s they played a great role in Jewish life, and in certain regions
(particularly in the kresy) whole classes of Jewish school children joined
one movement or another.[65]

The strengths of Polish Zionism were apparent, but so were its weaknesses. Of these the most glaring was its dependence on forces outside its
control. What Zionism was all about, of course, was building a new
Jewish homeland in Palestine, but the almost Messianic expectations in
the wake of the Balfour Declaration were soon replaced by bitter disillusionment. It quickly became clear that the World Zionist Organization was incapable of funding mass aliyah and that the English government was not prepared to allow unlimited emigration to its new territory.
Thus during most of the 1920s aliyah meant a mere trickle of Jews, mostly
young pioneers, to Palestine, with little impact upon the huge Polish
Jewish population. The only exception was the period 1924–1926, when
(according to Polish Zionist statistics) a grand total of 32,536 Jews went to
Palestine. For the first time more Polish Jews went to Palestine than to
America. But the "fourth aliyah" ended in 1926, when Palestine entered
a period of economic crisis which had the effect not only of stopping
aliyah but also of forcing many Polish immigrants to return to Eastern
Europe.[66] The Polish aliyah certainly strengthened the still tiny Jewish
community in Palestine, but its failure to solve the Jewish question in
Poland also supported the claims of the anti-Zionist Jewish parties that
Zionism was unrealistic, if not utopian.

There were other difficulties as well. We already know that the Zionists' national-autonomy program was given short shrift by the Poles, and
we shall see that the Zionist-sponsored schools, intended to produce a
new Zionist-minded Jewish generation, were not a great success.
Moreover, the Zionists were unsuccessful in their efforts to penetrate
both the trade unions of the organized Jewish working class and the
Hasidic world. They were therefore unable to make good their efforts to

"conquer" Polish Jewry. Dominant in the Sejm, they were much less strong in the kehiles and in the city councils. The weakness of Zionism, to become especially evident in the late 1930s, was a result of events both in Palestine and in Poland itself.

The Bund, in contrast with Zionism, could appeal only to the secular, antireligious elements in Jewish life and to those who sympathized with its class approach to the Jewish question. Its strength resided in its influence within the Jewish trade-union movement, in its emphasis on the day-to-day economic struggle of the Jewish masses, and in its occasionally successful efforts to link up with a strong Polish political force. This party, well organized despite its internal factionalism (mostly caused by general socialist issues), was rooted in Jewish working-class life, and its emphasis on the need to develop Yiddish secular culture in Poland won it a following among the Yiddishist Jewish intelligentsia. It never succeeded in electing a deputy to the Sejm, but it polled over 80,000 votes in 1922 and tended to do well in city council elections in the large cities of Congress Poland, its electoral base. Yet, like the Zionists, the Bund was unable to realize its platform. It certainly did not succeed, during the 1920s, in ameliorating the conditions of the Jewish working class, and its various campaigns for "the right to work" ended in failure. It did not succeed in establishing a solid proletarian front with the socialist parties of the other nationalities, and its vision of secular Jewish national autonomy based on Yiddish won no converts among the Poles and relatively few among the Jews. The heroic period in the history of the Polish Bund was to come later, in the immediate pre–World War II years, when for reasons not entirely related to its political ideology it emerged as the strongest single Jewish party in Poland.

Agudes yisroel, the third great force in Polish Jewish politics, derived its strength from the Orthodox population and particularly from the Hasidic element in Congress Poland. The most influential of all Polish Hasidic rebes, the Gerer Rebe, was the religious leader of the movement. Outside Congress Poland the Agude was much weaker; in Galicia, for example, the famous Hasidic Rebe of Bełz refused to support it, and in the kresy Hasidism was in general much weaker than in other areas of the state.

The Agude possessed a loyal, mass following, and, while its representatives were overshadowed in the Sejm by the better educated and more acculturated Zionist politicians, it was the most important single political faction in the kehiles and controlled the largest of all private Jewish school systems. Demanding less of the government than the secular Jewish parties did, it was less affected by the regime's attitude. Upholding the banner of traditional Jewish life and castigating the religious Zionists for their willingness to cooperate with secular forces within the godless

Zionist camp, the Agude clearly did succeed in protecting the Orthodox interest. In this sense it may be considered the most successful of all Jewish parties. But it just as clearly did not halt the trends toward secularization within Polish Jewry, neither was it able to protect the economic interests of the generally impoverished Hasidic masses. It is an interesting question whether it won the great debate with the Mizrachi, the Orthodox Zionist party, as to how to preserve Jewish Orthodoxy in a secular, democratic age. The Mizrachi argued that Judaism must move with the times, and, while it strongly condemned the reforming trends in Western and Central European Judaism, it stressed the need for more modern Jewish education, for a degree of acculturation, and for a synthesis of general and Jewish culture. The Agude, on the other hand, hoped to preserve as much as possible the closed Jewish Orthodox world of Eastern Europe and argued that the Mizrachi's path led, ultimately, to assimilation. This argument was not resolved in Poland, and still goes on today in the world of Jewish Orthodoxy. Just as the Mizrachi succeeded in drawing many Orthodox Jews into the Zionist orbit, so the Agude's fierce opposition to secular Jewish nationalism cost the Zionist movement the support of tens of thousands of other Orthodox Jews.

Of the smaller Jewish parties, only the Folkists were able to gain some influence in the early 1920s, but this secular, anti-Zionist, strongly Yiddishist faction declined rapidly thereafter.[67] As for Jewish participation in non-Jewish political organizations, it was naturally evident only on the left. Among the leaders of the Polish Socialist Party were several Jews, but, since the PPS was a mass party based on the organized Polish working class, the percentage of Jews within the membership was not very great. Such was not the case within the illegal and very small Polish Communist Party, where Jewish involvement was extremely conspicuous. As everywhere in East Central Europe, in Poland, too, Communism found many of its supporters among national minorities alienated from the established political system; it is hardly surprising that a relatively large number of Jews found their way into the ranks of this urban-based movement which had a great need for intellectuals and which was not successful in building up much support among the anti-Soviet, nationalistic, and Catholic Polish masses.[68] The Jewish Communists, some of whom carried on propaganda in Yiddish, pointed to the Soviet Union as a society in which (so they thought) anti-Semitism no longer existed and compared it to "fascist" Poland with its official anti-Semitic policies. Their advocacy of the pro-Soviet orientation and of "returning" the Eastern borderlands to the Soviet Union earned them the detestation of the national Polish majority, which in turn equated Bolshevism with Judaism. The fact that the great majority of the Jewish population was anti-Communist and gave its votes to anti-Communist

Jewish parties did not mitigate one of the most effective anti-Semitic canards of the interwar period.

## 5. Aspects of Jewish Cultural Life

Just as interwar Poland became the center of autonomous Jewish politics in the Jewish diaspora, so it also became the center of autonomous Jewish culture, whether secular or religious, whether in Hebrew or in Yiddish. The yeshivas for which Poland had been so famous in the Jewish world continued to flourish, and new institutions of traditional Jewish learning were founded by the two new religious parties, Agudes yisroel and the Mizrachi.[69] Along with the preservation of traditional Jewish culture went the remarkable experiment to create in Poland a secular Jewish national culture based on Yiddish which was designed to serve as one of the cornerstones of Jewish national autonomy. Never before in modern Jewish history, and for that matter never again, would this version of autonomous Jewish culture make such deep inroads into Jewish life. If in the Soviet Union the regime clamped down on Yiddish culture in the 1930s, and if in America acculturation and assimilation sentenced Yiddish to a gradual but inevitable decline, Poland remained the ideal setting in which the "folk language" and the "folk culture," in its new, modern form, could thrive. Moreover, the unification of Congress Poland with Galicia and the eastern borderlands, while causing serious problems for Jewish politics, was a blessing for Jewish culture. Indeed, the role of Litvaks in Yiddish cultural life in the capital was so great as to cause some grumbling in Polish Jewish circles with regard to the "foreign invasion" from the Lithuanian-Belorussian lands.[70]

One dramatic example of the success of Yiddish culture in Poland was the Yiddish press, with its two mass-circulation dailies in Warsaw (*Haynt* and *Moment*) and hundreds of other daily and weekly newspapers in the provinces. Jewish newspapers also appeared in Hebrew and in Polish, but neither of these languages, especially not the former, could compete with Yiddish.[71] Another example was the flourishing of the Yiddish theater.[72] Interwar Poland also became a great center of Yiddish literature. True, the most celebrated Polish Yiddish writer, Y. L. Perets, died in Warsaw in 1915, another famous author, I. M. Weissenberg (1881–1938), wrote little in the interwar years, and Sholem Asch (1880–1957), of Polish birth, wrote his most famous works in America. But interwar Poland produced such talented authors as Y. Y. Trunk (1887–1961), Oizer Varshavsky (1898–1944) and I. J. Singer (1893–1944). It was also the milieu in which the most famous of modern Yiddish writers, Isaac Bashevis Singer (b. 1904, known simply as Bashevis in Yiddish) made his literary debut.[73] Along with literature went the development of Yiddish literary criticism and new efforts to promote an understanding of Jewish history and culture. In 1925 the Jewish Scientific Institute (Yivo) was founded in Vilna, mostly by secular Yiddishist intellectuals sympathetic to the Folkists or to Jewish socialism. The Yivo quickly became the main scholarly institution of the secular Yiddish cultural movement, and its various publications helped lay the foundation for modern academic work on Yiddish language and literature. It also encouraged work on East European Jewish history, and during the interwar period a distinguished group of Jewish historians, mostly from Galicia, such as Majer Bałaban (1877–1942) and Ignacy Schipper (1884–1943), made lasting contributions to this field.[74]

For those Jewish intellectuals committed to the cause of secular Yiddish culture, education was surely the single most important issue, and it is not surprising that tremendous efforts were made to educate the young generation in this spirit. In 1921 a conference in Warsaw created the Central Jewish School Organization (known as Tsisho after its Yiddish initials), which aimed at establishing elementary and high schools that would use Yiddish as the language of instruction and promote a national, diaspora-centered, secular Jewish culture. From the very beginning the Tsisho school system was highly politicized, and it was riddled by political conflicts among Bundists, Zionist socialists, Folkists, and even Communists. Its leaders endlessly debated such questions as whether or not its goal was to produce "class-conscious socialists" and whether or not to allow the teaching of Hebrew. Its greatest dilemma, however, was the nature of the new secular Yiddish culture it sought to promote in the classroom, for such a concept was obliged to reject not only the Jewish religion, but Hebrew culture as well, and to replace it with the still very young Yiddish secular culture of Eastern Europe. There were no models in the Jewish historical experience for the kind of schools that Tsisho wanted to establish, and its revolutionary character—revolutionary both in the sense of its socialist ideology and in the sense of its radical departure from traditional Jewish education—doubtless alienated many parents. The success of Tsisho was also hampered by other problems which it shared with most other Jewish school systems—government harrassment and the state's refusal to share the financial burden. Tsisho schools did best in the kresy, where they were less politicized than in Congress Poland and where the general cultural situation was most favorable to national Jewish schools. They did not penetrate beyond the old Austrian border into Galicia.[75]

In late 1923 Tsisho could claim 120 elementary schools (with 12,400 pupils), 26 kindergartens, three high schools, and two teachers' seminaries. By 1934–1935 the grand total of pupils attending Tsisho institutions was 15,486.[76] This was, of course, a very small minority of all

Jewish pupils in Poland and a far cry from the hopes of the ideologues of the new Yiddish secular culture. The extremely high pedagogical level of the Tsisho school system, which was generally acknowledged, could not conceal its failure to attract the young generation. This failure, partly financial and partly ideological, certainly calls into question the viability of what may be called the Yiddishist program for Polish Jewry.

Granted the existence in interwar Poland of a Yiddish literary "renaissance," how deep were its roots?[77] It would appear that, despite the unparalleled flourishing of the Yiddish press, theater, and literature, the secular Yiddish movement encountered grave difficulties both because of its militant secularism and because, in the final analysis, many Jews must have asked themselves just what their children would gain by acquiring a Yiddish education. It was all very well to study the works of Sholem Aleichem and Perets, and to learn how to write a proper Yiddish sentence, but what good would this be to someone growing up in Poland? The question of *takhles* (the Yiddish-Hebrew word denoting practical purpose) loomed large, and if the Zionists could claim that their Hebrew schools were preparing young Jews for life in the Palestinian, Hebrew-speaking homeland, the Tsisho schools could make no such claims. In this sense, at least, the Jewish demands for cultural national autonomy did not find mass support among the Jewish population—at least not in Poland. In other areas of East Central Europe, for reasons to be explained in subsequent chapters, the program of cultural national autonomy received considerably more support.

If modern Yiddish culture in the interwar period found a center in Poland, modern Hebrew culture fared less well. The Hebrew press, supported by the Zionist movement, was not nearly so successful as its Yiddish rival, and the new Hebrew theater and literature were now concentrated in Tel Aviv and Jerusalem rather than in Warsaw and Vilna. Hebrew, of course, was not a spoken language of Polish Jewry, and in an age of mass-circulation newspapers and novels, the small, cultural elite which had traditionally supported Hebrew culture could not compete with popular tastes and habits. Nonetheless, the idea of promoting a modern Hebrew culture in Poland did lead to the establishment of the remarkable Tarbut school system. The Tarbut (the word means culture in Hebrew) school system, which was backed by the General Zionist and other, moderate left-wing Zionist parties, took upon itself the awesome task of making Hebrew a living language for Jewish elementary and high school pupils. In the Tarbut schools the language of instruction for all subjects save Polish language and history was Hebrew; with the establishment of Tarbut kindergartens and high schools it became possible for Polish Jews to spend their entire educational career in a Hebrew-speaking environment. The Tarbut schools became islands of Hebrew speech and modern Hebrew culture, drawing inspiration from the rapidly developing modern Hebrew school system in Palestine.[78]

From a linguistic point of view, the Tarbut schools were more alien to Polish Jewry than were the Tsisho institutions, but the Zionist schools were less radical politically and more closely related to traditional Jewish education. This, along with their Palestinian orientation, made them rather more popular among the Jews. According to a census of the Tarbut schools taken in 1921, the total enrollment was 25,829. By mid-1923 there were 30,672 pupils and as many as twelve high schools; by 1934–1935 the number of pupils had risen to 37,000.[79] Like Tsisho, Tarbut was mainly a phenomenon of the kresy, and in the various towns of the eastern border-lands the Tarbut school system became a focal point of local Zionist activity, especially for the various youth movements. It was much less successful in Congress Poland and in Galicia, where the more accultur-ated and the more Hasidic elements within the Jewish population were both unfriendly to its brand of Jewish education.

There were other Zionist-sponsored schools in Poland, some of which favored bilingual programs—Polish and Hebrew, as was the case with the so-called Braude high schools, and Yiddish and Hebrew, as was the case with the Shul-kult schools sponsored by Poale Zion-right.[80] The religious Zionist schools of the Mizrachi, known as Yavne, were particularly important. But a glance at the statistics of Jewish schools and the division of Jewish youngsters among the various systems reveals two important facts. First, the most attractive Jewish school system in interwar Poland was that of Agudes yisroel (the Khoyrev schools for boys, and the Beys yankev schools for girls), despite the great popularity of the new Jewish politics and the undoubted process of secularization within the Jewish community. According to one set of statistics, the number of students in the Khoyrev and Beys yankev schools reached nearly 110,000 in 1934–1935, as compared with slightly over 50,000 pupils in the Tsisho and Tarbut networks. Particularly impressive was the development of the Beys yankev school system, whose establishment was the work of one of the most remarkable Jewish women of interwar Poland, Sarah Shenirer. The Beys yankev schools offered a somewhat modernized education to the Orthodox girls of Poland, whose Jewish cultural needs were tradi-tionally ignored by the community and who, as a result, often ended up entirely ignorant of Judaism. These schools had a considerable impact, and they provide clear evidence that even Agudes yisroel was prepared, however grudgingly, to move with the times.[81] In their choice of a Jewish school, therefore, Polish Jewish parents revealed a markedly con-servative character, preferring the traditional religious schools to the Bundist or Zionist alternatives. Second, the majority of all Jews of school age attended Polish state schools rather than Jewish private ones.

According to Kazdan, about sixty percent of all Jewish pupils studied in state schools, although it should be emphasized that this figure includes Jewish pupils in those state schools which catered exclusively to Jews (the so-called Szabasówki, which exempted Jews from writing on Saturday) and that many Jewish pupils studied both in Jewish and in state schools.[82] On the high school level the majority of Jewish pupils attended Jewish schools, since Polish high schools, unlike Polish elementary schools, discriminated against Jews.

The reasons for the preference of state over Jewish education among Polish Jews are obvious. Polish state schools, after all, were free. And even if they were sometimes anti-Semitic, they dispensed a Polish education. Moreover, in Galicia, if not in the former Russian areas, Jews had long since been accustomed to attending state schools, and they maintained this tradition during the interwar period. What this meant, of course, is that even within this population acculturation, it not assimilation, was making rapid strides forward. The new Jewish generation was at least to some extent becoming culturally polonized, whatever the findings of the 1931 census, and in this sense the old Polish Jewish assimilationist dream of a Polish-speaking Jewry was realized during the interwar period. During 1931–1932 the Zionist historian A. Druyanov paid a visit to Poland; his comments on the process of polonization are worth quoting:

> Linguistic assimilation is increasing among the Jews of Poland to the degree that it appears as though, in front of our very eyes, the language which they spoke for hundreds of years is being forgotten. The elderly know Yiddish and speak Yiddish, but when they want to act important they speak Polish. As for the youth, some know Yiddish and some don't, and most speak Polish. The children virtually don't know Yiddish at all and speak Polish. This is the situation in the big cities, and usually in the middle-sized cities, and sometimes even in the little towns of Congress Poland, and of course in Galicia too. For many hours I walked around the Kazimierz quarter in Cracow, which was full of Jews, and I heard a bit of Yiddish and a lot of Polish. On the Sabbath and on holidays I attended the synagogues in this city, and I heard Jewish children speaking among themselves only in Polish. I heard this language, too, among the children who went with their fathers to the Hasidic synagogues of Ger. I was invited to speak at conferences of Ha-shomer ha-tsair and Gordonia in Lodz, and I found there several boys and girls who didn't know Yiddish, but all knew Polish.[83]

The ever-growing encroachment of Polish on Jewish life did not mean that the Jews were assimilating into Polish society. It did, however, indicate the severe obstacles confronted by the adherents to Jewish national cultural autonomy everywhere in Poland, with the exception of the still not polonized kresy. Moreover, the continued cultural conservatism of the Jewish population, demonstrated by the strength of the Orthodox school networks, showed that the efforts of Tsisho and Tarbut activists to formulate a new, secular Jewish culture based either on Yiddish or on Hebrew were also unsuccessful. Such efforts were more successful in the Baltic States, but it is legitimate to wonder whether, in the long run, the very concept of secular national Jewish culture was viable in the Jewish diaspora. It is safe to assume that, had independent Poland survived for another twenty years, modern Yiddish and Hebrew culture and schools would have inevitably declined, to be replaced by Jewish cultural creativity in the Polish language.

Before the war some Jews had played a major role in Polish cultural life, and this trend continued into the interwar period. Indeed, only in Hungary, and of course in interwar Soviet Russia, did Jews penetrate so deeply into the cultural life of the majority nationality in Eastern Europe. Among the leading poets of interwar Poland were two of Jewish origin, Julian Tuwim (1894–1953) and Antoni Słonimski (b. 1895; the baptized grandson of a famous Haskalah figure), and among the leading historians of the period was the Jew Szymon Askenazy (1867–1937). The presence of a small but important Polish Jewish cultural elite demonstrates the heterogeneous character of Polish Jewry and belies any meaningful comparison with other oppressed groups such as the American Blacks, whose contribution to the high culture of the majority was much less striking.[84] So far as the anti-Semites were concerned, the prominence of Tuwim and Askenazi was yet another sign of the impending takeover of Poland by the Jews, and the biographies of these and other famous Polish cultural figures of Jewish origin are eloquent testimony to one of the most tragic aspects of Polish Jewish history.

### 6. The 1930s: The Reemergence of Violent Anti-Semitism and the Jewish Reaction

During the 1930s, and particularly in the last four years of Poland's existence as an independent state, violent anti-Semitism made a dramatic reappearance. It was accompanied by redoubled efforts to strike at the Jews' economic interests and to remove the Jews, as many as possible, from Polish economic and intellectual life. A complex combination of factors, having to do with the transition from democracy to right-wing authoritarianism, economic depression, and events outside Poland's borders, was responsible for these ominous developments. In Poland, as in most other states of East Central Europe, the last decade of the interwar period witnessed a struggle for power between moderate and extreme right-wing nationalists in the context of an economic crisis and the rising influence of Nazi Germany. The Jewish question, in Poland as elsewhere, proved to be an integral part of a political struggle the outcome of which was to determine who would rule the country.

The first great blow to Poland's democratic form of government—Piłsudski's coup d'etat of 1926—was regarded by most Polish Jews as a positive event. This was not because they opposed democracy, but rather because they regarded Piłsudski as a moderate nationalist, a federalist and therefore possibly sympathetic to the concept of national autonomy, a bitter enemy of the National Democrats, and a former socialist opposed to anti-Semitism as a political or economic weapon.[85] He was also seen as a strong man who would put a stop to the endless political and social strife which some Jews believed was the main cause of Polish anti-Semitism. To a certain degree Piłsudski's ten years in office as the supreme arbiter of Poland's fate justified these expectations. He was successful in holding the extreme anti-Semites in check and welcomed the participation of Jews in his government lists during elections to the Sejm. His prime minister in the years immediately following the coup, Kazimierz Bartel, was generally regarded as friendly to the Jews and made a few statements opposing economic anti-Semitism. However, Piłsudski and his camp, popularly known as the Sanacja (cleansing), took no steps to alter the state's basic attitude toward the Jews, just as they did little to win the affection of the Ukrainians and Belorussians.[86] The Jews continued to receive virtually no state funds for their cultural institutions, and they remained the victims of wide-ranging economic discrimination. The Great Depression, which struck Poland with a vengeance in 1929, rendered the impact of this economic anti-Semitism all the greater. In short, despite Piłsudski's refusal to embrace anti-Semitic slogans, the Jewish crisis intensified. If the Jews sincerely mourned Piłsudski after his death in May, 1935, they mourned him as the lesser evil, as a man much to be preferred to his National Democratic and fascist-leaning opponents. From the Jewish point of view, he was surely a more desirable leader than such other "moderate" nationalists as Horthy of Hungary and King Carol of Romania, but he has not been regarded, as has Masaryk of Czechoslovakia, as a friend of the Jewish people.

The roots of the unprecedented wave of anti-Semitism which characterized the post-Piłsudski period are certainly to be found in pre–1935 Poland. One is the already mentioned economic crisis, which heightened social tensions and inevitably worsened Polish-Jewish relations. Another important factor was the rise of Nazism in Germany. Polish nationalists had much to fear from a resurgent Germany, but they were greatly impressed by Hitler and by the prominent role of anti-Semitism in the Nazi ideology. Of particular significance was the influence of Nazism on the younger National Democrats. In 1934 some right-wing radical youths split off from Dmowski's party and formed the National Radical Camp (ONR), clearly based on the Nazi model; its members were described by Moshe Kleinbaum (Sneh), a leading Zionist, as "Polish Hitlerites."[87] And the National Democratic movement itself, called since 1928 the National Party, veered ever more sharply to the right, its anti-Semitism "greatly encouraged by the impunity with which Hitler was able to deprive of political rights the wealthiest and most powerful Jewish community in Europe."[88] As was the case elsewhere in East Central Europe, particularly in Romania, the universities became centers of anti-Jewish agitation and riots, much of it in emulation of the Nazis. Dmowski himself, despite his longstanding anti-German views and his devotion to Catholicism, did nothing to stem the growing tide of pro-Nazi feeling within his party.[89]

While the right-wing opposition took comfort from Hitler's triumph, the Polish government took steps to come to terms with the new regime on its western border. In 1934 Poland and Germany signed a nonaggression pact, thus signaling the Polish government's apparent belief that it had nothing to fear from Hitler. This in turn naturally increased Nazi influence within Poland. In July of the same year, Goebbels visited Poland and lectured at the University of Warsaw. Many Polish dignitaries, including the prime minister, attended his lecture, which dealt, among other things, with the National Socialist attitude toward the Jewish question.[90]

In Poland a broad-based, right-wing radical movement on the Romanian Iron Guard or on the Hungarian Arrow Cross model failed to develop. In contrast with its counterparts in other East Central European states, the Polish left retained a considerable following.[91] Neither of these facts, however, was to have a crucial impact upon the fortunes of the Jewish community. After the death of Piłsudski, Poland was ruled by a small circle of Piłsudski loyalists who lacked their revered leader's charisma and who enjoyed little popular support. The new regime's legitimacy was based on an antidemocratic constitution, initiated by Piłsudski himself, which supplanted the liberal constitution of 1921.

In 1936 a new ruling political organization called the Camp of National Unity (OZON) was established, the electoral success of which was guaranteed by the new constitution. It should be stressed, however, that even now Poland did not become a totalitarian state. The most serious threat to the rule of the "colonels," as Piłsudski's followers were called, came from the right—from the National Party and its fascist offshoot, the ONR. In the struggle which took place in the context of growing social unrest and an increasingly dangerous international situation, the Jewish question became a major issue, as each side, seeking popular support among the impoverished Polish masses, attempted to outdo the other in its devotion to the anti-Jewish campaign.[92]

During the post-Piłsudski years the government's attitude toward the Jewish question was fairly clear. In the short run, the Jews' role in the Polish economy and in all other walks of life was to be drastically reduced. In the long run, emigration was the only solution. In a declaration of 1937 the government, which refused to allow Jews to join the ruling party, defined its Jewish policy as follows:

> We have too high an idea of our civilization and we respect too strongly the order and peace which every state needs to approve brutal anti-Semitic acts which harm the dignity and prestige of a great country. At the same time, it is understandable that the country should possess the instinct compelling it to defend its culture, and it is natural that Polish society should seek economic self-sufficiency.[93]

This last reference to "self-sufficiency" meant that the government lent its official sanction to unbridled economic anti-Semitism. This policy was given its most famous formulation by Prime Minister Sławoj-Składkowski, who said in 1936, "Economic struggle [against the Jews] by all means [owszem]—but without force."[94] But the main thrust of official policy towards the Jews was to promote the cause of Jewish emigration. The problem was, of course, that it was not clear where the Jews could go. The Polish government did its best to soften British opposition to emigration to Palestine, and, if Zionism meant Jewish emigration to that country, no one was more Zionist than Poland's leaders in the late 1930s. Poland also linked the issue of Jewish emigration to its demands for colonies overseas. Thus in 1936 Madagascar was put forward as a suitable Polish colony and as a promising region for Polish Jewish settlement.[95] Jabotinsky's famous "evacuation" plan of 1936, according to which large numbers of Jews would leave Poland and other East European countries for Palestine, where they would establish a Jewish state on both banks of the Jordan, was received with great enthusiasm both by the government and by the right-wing opposition—with much more enthusiasm, as we shall see, than it was received by the Jewish community.[96]

Both economic anti-Semitism and "pro-Zionist" leanings were very much present in pre-1935 Poland, and neither can be regarded as a new departure. What was new was the government's open and vocal espousal of these principles, the immediate causes of which were its weakness, its fear of the extreme right, and its antidemocratic tendencies. In its Jewish policy it received the full support of the Polish Catholic church, long a bastion of anti-Semitism and, of course, an institution of great influence and authority. The church was a veteran supporter of the National Democrats, and some priests were among the most active propagators of anti-Semitism in the country. In 1936 Cardinal August Hlond, head of the

Polish hierarchy, published a special pastoral letter on the Jewish question in which he opposed Nazi racist doctrines but condemned the Jews as atheists and revolutionaries. He also lent the authority of the church to economic anti-Semitism.[97]

The main difference between the attitude of the extreme right-wing opposition and that of the government and the church to the Jewish question had to do with means, not ends. While the political and religious establishments deplored violence, the right embraced it. And if the church, at least, resisted Nazi racism, thereby seeking to protect Jewish converts to Catholicism, the right had no such scruples. Both establishment and opposition, the Endeks and the Sanacja, agreed that "Jewish influence" in Poland must be done away with. What this meant was clear, although how it was to be achieved was not. The centrist Peasant Party, an amalgam of the various peasant factions of the 1920s, also lent its voice to the anti-Jewish chorus. In 1935 this party declared that

> all citizens in Poland irrespective of creed and nationality must enjoy equal rights. The Jews, however, as has been proved, cannot be assimilated and are a consciously alien nation within Poland. As a middle class they occupy a far more important position in Poland than in other countries, so that the Poles have no middle class of their own. It is, therefore, most vital for the Polish state that these middle-class functions shall more and more pass into the hands of the Poles. We must realize this objective not through fruitless acts of violence, which only brutalize the nation, but above all through the development of the cooperative movement in the country. While we profess the principle of equal rights for the Jews in Poland, we shall nevertheless aim to solve the Jewish problem through the emigration of Jews to Palestine and other places.[98]

This left the Polish Socialist Party as the only important political organization clearly opposed to anti-Semitism, and even within its ranks there was no unanimity on the Jewish question. Thus in 1936 one of its spokesmen published a pamphlet advocating Jewish emigration, a position denounced by the Jewish ally of the PPS, the Bund.[99] Nonetheless, in Poland, as was not the case in Hungary, a political organization of considerable and even growing strength set its face clearly against the government-inspired anti-Semitic campaign. Gentile opposition to anti-Semitism, therefore, was not restricted, as it was in other countries, to a courageous but lonely and isolated group of intellectuals and priests who viewed with alarm the emergence of virulent racism on the Nazi model. From the Jewish point of view, and particularly from the point of view of the Jewish left, this was a fact of some importance. But it is also true that the PPS was too weak to blunt the anti-Semitic campaign. Its stand, therefore, was of greater moral than practical significance.

The war against the Jews during 1935–1939 took many forms, ranging from legislative efforts to brutal attacks. In 1936, for example, legislative action was initiated in the Sejm to outlaw *shkhite* (ritual slaughter). This attack on one of the most fundamental aspects of Jewish religious practice caused a tremendous storm in the Jewish world, where it was interpreted as a first step toward revoking Jewish emancipation. A law forbidding *shkhite*, closely modeled on Nazi German legal precedents, was actually passed by the Sejm in 1936, but was eventually amended by the government to allow a certain amount of ritually slaughtered meat for Jews in areas where they made up more than three percent of the population.[100]

Another dominant theme in the anti-Semitic movement was the effort to establish "ghetto benches" in Polish universities. In some of these institutions the Jewish students, whose number was rapidly dwindling, were required to attend lectures in segregated areas of the classroom; this system was inaugurated at the Lwów Polytechnicum in 1935, and later at the University of Vilna. From 1937 on, physical attacks against Jewish students became ever more common, and several Jewish students were actually murdered. The ghettoizing of Jewish students was the first skirmish in the campaign to segregate (and eventually oust altogether) Jews in the white-collar professions. In 1937 various associations of doctors and journalists adopted the "Aryan paragraph," thereby making Jewish membership impossible.[101]

Most serious, however, was the economic boycott of Jewish businesses, an age-old tactic which now resurfaced with explicit government support. Bands of anti-Semitic enthusiasts invaded the marketplaces of Polish towns and villages and warned Christian Poles not to do business with Jewish merchants. Behind them stood a well-organized movement, spearheaded by National Democrats but supported by the various Polish economic organizations of merchants and artisans. Christian businessmen were supplied with special signs attesting to their "Aryan" nature, which were displayed for all to see. Pressure (not all of it gentle) was brought to bear on Christian Poles not to do business with Jewish firms, not to deal with Jewish agents, and not to rent apartments to Jews. The right-wing press often published the names of Christians who failed to obey the boycott. Thus in 1937 the *Warszawski Dziennik Narodowy* informed its readers that a certain Von Richwald had purchased a radio from a Jewish store in Poznań Province and that a civil servant from Radom had taken a ride in a Jewish cab.[102]

The enforcers of the boycott had frequent recourse to violence. Jewish stalls in marketplaces and at fairs were destroyed; Jewish storekeepers and artisans in little towns were terrorized and forced to abandon their shops. In such an atmosphere it did not require much for attacks on Jewish shopkeepers to degenerate into pogroms directed against the entire local Jewish population. From 1936 on, such pogroms were a common occurrence, once again reviving a phenomenon familiar in Poland during the prewar period. The most notable pogroms occurred in Grodno (1935), Przytyk (1936), Mińsk-Mazowiecki (1936), and Brześć (1937). According to a list prepared by Yankev Leshchinski, during 1935–1936 1,289 Jews were wounded in anti-Semitic attacks in over 150 towns and villages in Poland, a number based on reports in the Polish press and probably much too low. "Hundreds of Jews were killed."[103]

The impact of all this on the Jewish population, both from the economic and psychological point of view, was enormous. During the 1930s, the period of the Great Depression when the entire population of Poland underwent a process of pauperization, it began to appear as though not only the Polish Jewish youth had "no future" in the country, but that the entire Jewish community was in dire peril. The most telling aspect of the economic crisis was the decline in the number of Jewish-owned stores. During the years 1932–1937 the Jewish economist Menakhem Linder carried out a study of the Jewish-owned shops in eleven towns in the Białystok region. The results are given in table 1.11. In 1932 there were 663 Jewish-owned shops in these towns, which constituted 92.0 percent of the total number of shops; by 1937 there were 563 Jewish-owned shops, which constituted 64.5 percent of the total number. The figures show that the crucial year in this decline was 1936–1937, the reason being the renewed boycott. The decline was nationwide, although it was particularly evident in the eastern borderlands, where Jewish domination of commerce was so pronounced. By 1938, according to one authority, the share of Jewish-owned enterprises in Polish commerce had sunk below 50 percent, and no end to the precipitous decline was in sight.[104]

That the economic boycott was less effective in the industrial sector (which, as we know, meant chiefly craft production) is one reason for the Jewish tendency toward "proletarianization" in the 1930s. But more important than proletarianization was pauperization. The Great Depression, the anti-Semitic campaign, and the competition of a "native" bourgeoisie and of peasant cooperatives combined to push more and more Jews below the poverty line. As early as 1934 the percentage of Jews who appealed for some form of relief during the Passover holiday was alarmingly high—in Galicia nearly one-third of the Jewish population, in fifty-eight selected urban localities needed such aid.[105] And the worst was yet to come. The vigorous, even heroic efforts of foreign Jewish relief organizations to halt the economic decline saved many Jews from starvation, but were unable to reverse the trend.[106] By the eve of World War II, Polish Jewry was an impoverished community with no hope of reversing its rapid economic decline. There was, of course, no lack of poverty among the Christian population, but in the Jewish case the "artificial"

TABLE 1.11
Jewish-Owned Shops in Białystok Region, 1932–1937

| Town | 1932 | | 1936 | | 1937 | |
|---|---|---|---|---|---|---|
| | Total Number of Shops | Jewish Shops | Total Number of Shops | Jewish Shops | Total Number of Shops | Jewish Shops |
| Śniadowo | 22 | 18 | 21 | 12 | 28 | 8 |
| Rutki-Kossaki | 30 | 27 | 27 | 24 | 34 | 13 |
| Jedwabno | 29 | 25 | 31 | 23 | 50 | 22 |
| Ciechanowiec-Maz. | 29 | 28 | 31 | 29 | 38 | 24 |
| Ciechanowiec-Bielski | 69 | 68 | 67 | 64 | 81 | 55 |
| Sokoły | 59 | 54 | 64 | 51 | 73 | 48 |
| Sokołów Podl. | 188 | 174 | 220 | 174 | 223 | 153 |
| Czyżew | 73 | 70 | 78 | 72 | 83 | 60 |
| Wysokie Maz. | 68 | 62 | 74 | 63 | 81 | 56 |
| Tykocin | 38 | 38 | 37 | 35 | 46 | 35 |
| Zambrów | 116 | 99 | 121 | 95 | 136 | 89 |

SOURCE: Menakhem Linder, "Der khurbm funem yidishn handel in bialistoker rayon," *Yidishe ekonomik* 1 (1937):17.

causes of the crisis, when added to the repercussions of the general economic crisis, made the situation particularly intolerable.

The psychological impact of the crisis of the 1930s is more difficult to measure, but it was obviously great, perhaps greater, because of the anti-Semitic component, than it was among non-Jews. One indication of its scope was the rise in the number of suicides among Polish Jews.[107] Another was signs of apathy and despair which the celebrated Jewish scholar Maks Vaynraykh found in his study of autobiographies of Jewish Polish youth. For many members of the new Jewish generation, on the whole better educated and more ambitious than the prewar generation, the situation in the 1930s was one of absolute gloom. One youth wrote, "If one were to ask me to give a single definition of the period in which I live, I would answer: a hopeless generation."[108]

The despair of the 1930s, however, was manifested not only in suicides and apathy. We must now ask how the crisis of the 1930s affected the organized Jewish community, and how the community reacted to the new and perilous situation. So far as Jewish politics is concerned, the 1930s gave rise to a definite trend toward extremism, expressed in an increase in the strength of both the right and the left at the expense of the center. Within Zionism occurred the remarkable rise of the Revisionist movement, which challenged the Zionist establishment from the right. Revisionism, led by Vladimir (Zev) Jabotinsky (1880–1940), emerged from the General Zionist movement in the mid-1920s. Its main principles were the emphasis on the establishment in Palestine of a Jewish state on both banks of the Jordan, its sharp opposition to what Jabotinsky regarded as Chaim Weizmann's policy of appeasement vis-à-vis the British and the Arabs, its hostility to socialism as a "foreign creed" within the Jewish national movement, and its belief in the efficacy of military means to win Palestine for the Jewish nation. Jabotinsky and most of his early followers were Russians, but between the two wars the movement, inevitably, was based in Poland. Although it had been a relatively small faction in the 1920s, its call for the immediate creation of a Jewish state, its rejection of left-wing "experiments," and its denunciations of the British and the Arabs won it ever-greater strength in the 1930s. Indeed, Revisionism, with its great stress on integral Jewish nationalism, untrammeled by a socialist dimension, was well suited to gain adherents in a period of growing Polish nationalism and at a time when the various strategies of the General Zionists to improve the lot of Polish Jewry— whether of the Galician or of the Polish variety—revealed themselves to be bankrupt. And its frequent calls for mass Jewish emigration to Palestine also caught the imagination of a Jewish community many of whose members were coming to regard an exodus from Poland as its only hope. In 1931 the Polish Revisionists received 29,985 votes in the elections to the biennial Zionist Congress; in 1933 they received 64,370. Two years later Jabotinsky abandoned the World Zionist Movement and founded his own New Zionist Organization, which held its first world convention in that year. According to party figures (which may not be wholly accurate), some 450,000 Polish Jews participated in the elections to this convention, a number which enabled Jabotinsky to say (in 1936) that "no other Jewish party in Poland was ever backed by such a plurality."[109]

The Revisionist movement also included a powerful youth movement, Betar. Betar, one of whose leaders in the 1930s was Menachem Begin, differed from the other Zionist youth movements in its rejection of socialist pioneering and the ideology of renewal through labor. Instead, it emphasized military discipline. But it too called upon its members to cast aside the old *goles* (exile) way of life and devote themselves single-mindedly to building up the new motherland. By 1930, at the time of its first all-Polish census, the movement numbered some 16,000, and it was to grow during the last decade of Polish independence.[110]

The emergence of a powerful right-wing Zionist movement was paralleled by growth on the left. The worsening conditions in Poland and the relatively positive economic situation in Palestine gave birth, in the early 1930s, to a new *aliyah* movement (sometimes called the "fifth *aliyah*"). New opportunities for *aliyah* brought about a remarkable rise in the number of Polish pioneers and in the number of youths involved in agricultural and craft training (*hakhshara*) in preparation for *aliyah*. In 1933 there were about 41,000 pioneer members in Poland (Congress Poland and the kresy) and an additional 17,800 in Galicia.[111] The number of those in training for *aliyah* reached 18,958 in the summer of 1935.[112] And in the elections to the Zionist congresses in 1933 and 1935, the Zionist left won crushing victories in Poland, largely at the expense of the General Zionists.

Outside the Zionist camp the most dramatic political development was the growing strength of the Bund. During the 1920s this party had maintained its influence amoung the organized Jewish working class, but had not played a great role in Jewish politics. It had not succeeded, for example, in electing a single representative to the Sejm. In the late 1930s the situation changed greatly. In elections to the Lodz city council in 1936, the Bund emerged as the single largest Jewish party. Even more surprising was its victory in elections to the Warsaw kehile in the same year, when it won fifteen mandates whereas the traditional leader of the kehile, Agudes yisroel, won ten. It repeated these victories in 1938, most notably in elections to the Warsaw city council, when it won 61.7 percent of the votes given to Jewish lists. Such results enabled the Bundists to proclaim, with some justification, that their party was now the single most powerful of all Jewish organizations.[113]

The reasons for the Bund's startling successes are connected with its leading role in the Jewish struggle against anti-Semitism (to be discussed presently) and with its partial success in finding allies within the Polish community at a time when no other Jewish party could do so. They derived also from the Jewish public's growing disgust with the failure of the General Zionists' political strategies and, above all, from the collapse of the Zionist movement's program for Palestine after 1936. Great Britain's decision to close the gates of Palestine to substantial Jewish immigration, just at a time when anti-Semitic pressure was increasing in Poland, led to disillusionment with Zionism in general and a readiness to support a party whose *doikeyt* was accompanied by excellent organization, ties with the Polish left, and the courage to demonstrate against Polish fascism. Under these conditions the Bund's secularism and Marxism ceased to impede its growth within the generally conservative and religious Polish Jewish community.

In the 1930s, then, the slogans of Jabotinsky, the Pioneer, the Bund, and the Communist Party (which also attracted a growing number of Jewish youths) were rapidly gaining ground, while the more moderate Agudes yisroel and General Zionists were on the decline. This was also the period when political mobilization on the Jewish street reached its greatest heights. Graduates of elementary and high schools streamed in unprecedented numbers into the youth movements and parties. A young man from a *shtetl* in Volynia Province, writing in 1934, gave the following explanation for his decision to join the Pioneer:

> [I joined the organization] because I saw that Jewish youth here in Poland had no hope of improving its situation in the future. I saw how Jewish youths went about in our little town with nothing to do. If someone wants to learn to be a blacksmith he is asked, "Have you finished seven classes of a general [state] school? If not go home, there is nothing to be done for you." Thus the Jewish youth is driven away from various good professions in which work is available.[114]

Another Jewish youth, writing in the late 1930s, remarked that

> at home there were no prospects for the future. Business was bad. I did not see any prospects for a future after I finished school. And at home I was being threatened with an interruption of school. And even in this tragic situation, despite no prospects for the future, I wanted to finish school. . . . If anyone asked me then what I would do after finishing school, I would not have known how to answer. In this terrible situation I took to Zionism like a drowning person to a board.[115]

A youngster from a town near Łuck (also in Volynia), after describing the great poverty of his *shtetl*, wrote that "the one aim, which is shared by almost the entire youth, is to go to Palestine." This sentiment brought almost everyone to the Pioneer.[116] A young man from Beresteczka joined Ha-shomer ha-tsair and decided to go to Palestine because "here, among the gentiles [goyim], one can see the abyss in which people lie about without a future, without prospects for a bearable human existence."[117] Not everyone, of course, joined the Pioneer. A young tailor from a Polish town, after beginning his political career as a Zionist, abandoned Zionism for "Leninism" after becoming convinced that only socialism could solve the Jewish question.[118] But there was a general feeling that, in the absence of parental or religious guidance, the "organization" was the only hope left. Thus a young man from Horodenko, born in 1919, wrote that at the tender age of eleven "all my friends were entering organizations and taking a great interest in politics." He himself became a Revisionist because he liked the idea of marching like a soldier, but eventually decided that Zionism was immoral because of its anti-Arab character and became a Bundist.[119] Such moving about from one party to another was typical of the times, as was the often very bitter division of families into opposing ideological camps. In fact, it is quite impossible to predict, on the basis of sociological data, the political preferences of Polish Jewish youth in the 1930s. But the remarkable politicization of this youth is beyond doubt.

How efficacious this political activity was is another question. The Zionist program of emigration to Palestine, which seemed quite promising in the middle 1930s, was thoroughly discredited by British policy from 1936 to 1939. (Table 1.12 illustrates the decline of the aliyah movement.) All in all, during the period 1919–1942, 139,756 Polish Jews went to Palestine. This number was very significant so far as the Jewish community in Palestine was concerned, even though many did not remain in the Holy Land, but it represented less than five percent of Polish Jewry as of 1931. If aliyah as a solution to the Polish Jewish question was a failure, more glaring was the failure of Zionist politics within the state. Even in

### TABLE 1.12
#### Polish Emigrants to Palestine, 1930–1939

| Year | Number | Year | Number |
|------|--------|------|--------|
| 1930 | 2,470 | 1935 | 30,593 |
| 1931 | 1,726 | 1936 | 13,256 |
| 1932 | 3,299 | 1937 | 3,708 |
| 1933 | 13,251 | 1938 | 3,642 |
| 1934 | 17,723 | 1939 | 4,532 |

SOURCE: David Gurevich and Aharon Gerts, Ha-aliya, ha-yishuv ve-ha-tnua ha-tivit shel ha-ukhlusiya be-erets yisrael (Jerusalem, 1944), p. 61.

the late 1930s the old hostility between Galician and Congress Polish Zionism continued to plague Jewish politics. Thus in the 1935 Sejm elections the Galician Zionists participated while many Congress Polish Zionists (along with the Jewish and Polish left) boycotted them. On the other hand, efforts to convene an all-Polish Jewish congress in 1938, while championed by the Zionists of Congress Poland and the kresy, were regarded with suspicion by the Galicians. The congress never took place.[120] The great storm which erupted over Jabotinsky's "evacuation" scheme, though chiefly pitting Zionists against anti-Zionists, also contributed to internal Zionist tensions. In 1936 the Revisionist leader published in the Polish conservative newspaper *Czas* a plan which called for the "evacuation" to Palestine of 1.5 million Jews from Eastern Europe over the course of ten years, of whom 750,000 would come from Poland. According to the plan the various governments of Eastern Europe, in cooperation with the Zionist movement, would bring pressure to bear upon the British government to open the gates of Palestine to mass Jewish immigration.

The evacuation plan was greeted with enthusiasm by the Polish government, but was bitterly denounced by the Bund, which accused Jabotinsky of openly allying himself with the Polish anti-Semites in order to compel the Jews to quit the country. Agudes yisroel also opposed the idea, and even many Zionists were unhappy with its apparently coercive character.[121] The uneasiness which many Zionist leaders felt over this plan did not, however, deter them from cooperating closely with the Polish government. In general, during the late 1930s many acts of collaboration took place between the anti-Semitic colonels and the Polish Zionist leadership. These included an agreement on the purchase of Polish goods by Polish Jews going to Palestine and on the military training of young Polish Jews before their departure for the Middle East. Unfortunately for the Zionist cause, the Poles were unable to persuade the British to alter their immigration policy.

If the Zionist slogans of evacuation and pioneering *aliyah* appeared by the late 1930s to be utterly bankrupt, and if the Zionists were so divided that they could not even cooperate in the convening of a Jewish congress, other Jewish parties were not notably more successful. The Agude, its alliance with the government shattered by the campaign against the *shkhite*, had little to offer the Jewish masses. The Bund was much more active, and its activism, as we know, helped to bring it the great electoral successes of the late 1930s. This party organized several impressive general Jewish strikes against anti-Semitism, most notably in March, 1936, following the pogrom in Przytyk. It was also extremely conspicuous in organizing Jewish self-defense (*zelbshuts*) against anti-Semitic hooligans.[122] In short, the Bund became the main force in the organized Jewish opposition to anti-Semitism, a rather surprising though not wholly new development for this class-oriented party which had always denounced the concept of *klal yisroel*. On the other hand, the Bund's traditional hostility toward the Jewish bourgeoisie helped doom any effort to achieve Jewish political unity in the face of the anti-Semitic offensive.

Indeed, the most striking aspect of the Jewish political reaction to growing Polish anti-Semitism was precisely that of disunity. It is perhaps utopian to imagine that a community so deeply split as that of Polish Jewry could ever have created a unified political leadership, and it is questionable how effective even the most unified leadership would have been in stemming the anti-Semitic tide. It is a fact, however, that increased pressure from outside did nothing to bring together the advocates of *doikeyt* and the advocates of emigration, the Orthodox and the secularists, the socialists and the "bourgeoisie." It is also probable that the continued divisiveness facilitated the Poles' anti-Jewish onslaught. Thus on the eve of World War II Polish Jewry was no less divided than it had been immediately after World War I. It was certainly much more demoralized. Divided, demoralized, and impoverished, it now entered a new and unimaginably terrible period which ended with the virtual destruction of Polish Jewry.

## 7. Concluding Remarks

It is clear, in retrospect, that interwar Poland served as the laboratory for the crucial testing of the various modern Jewish approaches to the Jewish question. Never before had conditions been so favorable for the flourishing of national Jewish politics and culture in the diaspora, and it is safe to say that they never will be again. What conclusions, then, can be drawn from the Polish experience? Clearly, modern Jewish national politics won a mass following, in both its Zionist and its anti-Zionist forms. No less clear, however, were the failures of modern Jewish nationalism. The great expectations of Zionism, unleashed after the Balfour Declaration, were never fulfilled, partly because the fortunes of the movement depended on forces outside its control. The Bund had only mixed success in its efforts to forge an alliance with the Polish left and virtually none in its struggle to improve the condition of the Jewish working class. The effort to gain national extraterritorial autonomy, championed by all the modern Jewish parties, was a failure. Efforts to create a secular Jewish national life in Poland based on Yiddish schools and Yiddish culture, whereas they certainly resulted in certain impressive achievements, cannot be said to have had more than a limited success. The various strategies of the "new Jewish politics" to combat anti-Semitism were not notably more efficacious than the traditional *stadlones* of the pre-World War I period. No party and no strategy were able to stem the disastrous economic decline of Poland's Jews.

As for the vision of Agudes yisroel, which hoped to preserve Polish Jewry in a basically premodern, Orthodox form, there can be little doubt that the direction taken by Polish Jewry during the interwar period was the opposite of what it hoped for. True, Poland remained a bastion of Judaism in the traditional sense, but the processes of modernization, secularization, and acculturation, begun in the old Austrian and Russian empires, accelerated. More and more Jewish children and young adults attended state schools, learned Polish, read newspapers, joined youth movements and political parties, and entered the secular world. In this regard the Jewish experience in interwar Poland bore at least some resemblance to the Jewish experience in America and in the Soviet Union, although the processes were slower in Poland and also led in different directions—toward Jewish nationalism rather than toward efforts at integration. From a cultural viewpoint, there is little doubt that Polish Jews had much more in common with non-Jewish Poles by the end of the interwar period than they had had at its beginning.

If the Jewish experience in Poland demonstrates the weaknesses of modern Jewish politics and of autonomous modern Jewish culture in the diaspora, it also demonstrates how dangerous, from the Jewish point of view, was the emergence of the new nation-state in East Central Europe of which Poland was the prime example. In this new state, beset with seemingly intractable internal and external problems, only nationalism and the Catholic church served as unifying factors. Both Polish nationalism and Polish Catholicism were by their very nature exclusive, anti-pluralistic, and anti-Semitic. And, since there was little in the way of a tolerant, pluralistic, liberal political tradition in modern, as opposed perhaps to medieval, Poland, nothing stood in the way of the triumph of extreme national-religious intolerance from which all the minorities in the state suffered and which, because of the special nature of the anti-Jewish tradition and the economic vulnerability of the Jews, was particularly threatening to the Jewish minority.

It is true that the Polish state, unlike Hungary and Romania, refrained from enacting anti-Jewish legislation in the late 1930s. It is also true that in Poland, unlike in most other East European countries, there was considerable opposition to the extreme anti-Semitism of the late 1930s. But, in the development of Jewish-gentile relations, there was little essential difference between Poland and the other major states of the region, with the important exception of Czechoslovakia. The combination of traditional hatred of Jews, the triumph of nationalism, internal weakness, and the role of the Jewish question in the struggle for power between the moderate right and the extreme right typified the situation not only in Poland, but in other East European states as well. In this respect, as with regard to internal Jewish developments—acculturation, economic decline, political divisiveness, the failure of national autonomy and Zionism to solve the Jewish question—Poland may serve as a paradigm of the Jewish experience in interwar East Central Europe. It remains only to add that, when Hitler's soldiers, aided by Soviet troops, stamped out Polish independence in 1939, Nazi anti-Semitism, though far more extreme and thorough than the Polish variety, struck a highly responsive chord among large sections of the Polish population. In this respect, too, Poland was typical of East Central Europe.

**Hungary between the Wars**

# HUNGARY /2

In some crucial ways the situation of interwar Hungary was the very opposite of that which prevailed in the other lands of East Central Europe. Far from being an oppressed, "nonhistorical" people which had unexpectedly achieved statehood as a result of World War I, the Magyars had been one of the great ruling nations of prewar Europe. Indeed, they had ruled an empire of their own. Ever since 1867 Hungary had been an autonomous part of the Habsburg state, with its own government. A minority in their part of Austria-Hungary, just as the German-speaking Austrians were a minority in theirs, the Magyars dominated Slovakia, Croatia, Transylvania, Subcarpathian Rus, the Burgenland, and the Banat. Unlike most of the nations of East Central Europe, they had a strong stake in preserving the status quo.

The war, a great opportunity for so many East European nations, was an unmitigated disaster for Hungary. It lost all of the above-mentioned territories, which constituted more than seventy percent of its former territory and about sixty percent of its population. How different was Hungary's fate from that of Poland, Romania, Czechoslovakia, and the Baltic states, all of whom emerged from the war with previously undreamed of successes. Trianon Hungary (so called after the treaty, signed with the victorious powers in 1920, which defined its frontiers) was a small, landlocked country of little importance in European affairs. Not only had the Hungarians lost their multinational empire, but some three million Magyars were now living under foreign rule in Czechoslovakia, Yugoslavia, and Romania. True, Hungary was now rid of the nationalities problem—interwar Hungary was, in contrast to Poland, Romania, and Czechoslovakia, a true nation-state, with only a small German minority of about one-half million to contend with. But national homogeneity was not regarded as a blessing, while the loss of territory was regarded as a terrible national humiliation. And this was not the only severe shock, for Hungary had also endured during 1918–19 a two-stage social revolution, beginning with the moderate left-wing rule of the Károlyi government, which overthrew the old regime, and culminating in a Bolshevik regime led by Béla Kun. Kun was finally overthrown in the summer of 1919 and "order" was restored, but not before the country had experienced first a "red terror," then foreign intervention by the despised

85

Romanians, and finally a "white terror." Thus Hungary suffered not only from the tremendous losses of the war but also from a national humiliation and a social upheaval unparalleled elsewhere in East Central Europe.

Nineteenth-century Hungary was a classic gentry-peasant society. True, toward the end of the century it had undergone something of an industrial and financial boom, which particularly affected the Budapest region. As a result, the country was somewhat more industrialized than were its neighbors. But much of the work of modernization was carried out by non-Magyars—in particular by Jews and Germans—and the Magyars, while developing an intelligentsia and a bureaucracy, did not develop a strong bourgeoisie. In this they were similar to the Poles and the Romanians, and unlike the Czechs. As in Poland, in Hungary the gentry, and above all the great landowning magnate group, was synonymous with the political nation. In prewar times the Hungarian gentry had an absolute monopoly on politics, and after the post-Béla Kun restoration it continued to rule the now much reduced country. Only in the 1930s was its position seriously threatened by the growing power of the radical right.

Interwar Hungary was obsessed with one great issue—revision of the Trianon treaty. The old regime, having been returned to power, had as its overriding aim the reestablishment of the Hungarian empire. For this reason, and for other, more traditional ones, it also set its face firmly against any social or political change. The left, demoralized after its abortive seizure of power, was unable to offer a serious challenge to the political establishment. Hungary during the interwar years was among the least democratic of all East Central European countries, and among the socially most conservative. Its peasantry, by far the largest class, remained impoverished and powerless. Revision meant, of course, the overturning of the East European status quo and hostility toward those countries which had annexed parts of old Hungary, above all toward Czechoslovakia and Romania. It also meant an invitation to foreign states to intervene, since obviously the Hungarians alone lacked the power to revise the Versailles settlement. Above all it was a green light for German intervention in East European politics and for a German-Hungarian alliance, based on mutual hatred for the postwar settlement. This alliance, welcomed by so many Hungarians because it promised a return of the lost provinces, linked Hungary's fate with that of Hitler's Germany and was in the long run a disaster for the country. It was even more of a disaster for the country's Jews.

If nearly all Hungarians, of all parties and factions, agreed on the need for revision, there was no agreement on how and when such a revision was to be implemented. During the 1920s Hungary was ruled by "moderate revisionists," whose commitment to the restoration of the old empire was tempered by caution, by the old "liberal" Hungarian political style (what this meant shall be discussed shortly), and by pro-Western, particularly pro-English, views. But already in the early 1920s there existed in the country a radical right-wing political force, which rejected the moderation of the traditional leaders and pressed for more drastic action. The great political struggle in interwar Hungary, given the absence of a strong socialist movement, was fought out between these two forces, with the radical right growing ever stronger until it finally took over the state in the late 1930s. The triumph of the radical right, which owed much to the revisionist obsession but which also fed on social and economic unrest, had important implications for the Jews, since the ferocious revisionists were also pro-Nazi and extremely anti-Semitic. It was they who violated traditional Hungarian practice and made the Jewish question a national obsession, which came almost to rival the national obsession with blotting out the infamous Trianon treaty.[1]

## 1. The Historical Context

If Hungarian history was unique in the context of East Central European history, even more unique was the history of the Jews in this country in the context of East European Jewish history. For one thing, by the eve of World War I most Hungarian Jews had adopted Hungarian culture and had become as acculturated as were the Jewries of Bohemia and Moravia. Moreover, the process of magyarization, which had been preceded by a process of germanization, was accompanied by a considerable degree of what is often termed "assimilation," which was definitely not the case in the Czech lands or in the other regions where acculturation had made considerable inroads before the war, such as Wallachia or Courland. That is to say, in Hungary many Jews not only spoke Hungarian but also regarded themselves and were regarded by others as "Magyars of the Mosaic persuasion." In this respect they resembled not so much the Jewries of Bohemia and Moravia but, rather, German Jewry.

What were the reasons for this unusual situation? One has to do with political power. Ever since 1867 the Hungarians were masters of their own home, and the Jewish minority, which to the extent that it is attracted to a secular culture is usually attracted to the secular culture in power, was naturally inclined to gravitate toward the cultural orientation of Budapest. The same factor prompted Prague Jews to adopt a Viennese cultural orientation, and at least some Vilna Jews to adopt the Russian orientation emanating from St. Petersburg. Moreover, the Hungarian political elite, that is the landowning class, actively encouraged the Jews not only to acculturate but also to regard themselves as members of the Magyar nation. This was partly the result of a longstanding Hungarian policy to encourage non-Magyars—in particular Slavs, Germans, and Romanians living in the lands of St. Stephen—to become Hungarians, a policy resulting from the awareness that there were not enough ethnic Magyars to impose their will on the vast, multinational region known as Hungary. Hungarian nationalists, at least during the prewar period, were always prepared to welcome into their ranks sons and daughters of other nations so long as the latter were willing to renounce their former ethnic allegiance and become full-fledged Magyars. And, since joining the ranks of the politically dominant nation obviously paid off, socially and professionally, it is scarcely surprising that during the nineteenth century numerous Germans, Slovaks, Romanians, and Croats magyarized. Some, as is so often the case, became fanatic Hungarian chauvinists.

But the traditional openness of the Hungarians was accompanied by extreme intolerance toward those who did not wish to become Magyars, and this intolerance in turn helped kindle the flames of nationalism among the subject peoples of the Hungarian empire. This fact rendered it all the more necessary for the Hungarians to enlist assistance, and the Jews proved themselves to be ideal allies. For unlike some Slovaks, Croats, Germans, and Romanians, the Jews did not develop their own nationalist, anti-Magyar movement in the Hungarian lands. Rather, they opted almost exclusively for the Hungarian cultural and political orientation, accepting with enthusiasm the offer of alliance held out to them by the Hungarian ruling elite. The Jews, after all, have almost always been prepared to support the established regime, all the more so if that regime treats them well, and in Hungary the various governments, from 1867 on, did their best to combat popular anti-Semitism and recognized the Jews as first-class citizens.

Even before 1867 some Jews, inspired by the liberal views of the Hungarian revolutionaries, had demonstrated their Hungarian patriotism. Many of them had rallied around Lajos Kossuth in 1848, at a time when they were still second-class citizens and had much to gain from a revolutionary triumph, and that legendary hero became one of the first in a long line of pro-Jewish Hungarian statesmen. Indeed, one of the last acts of his revolutionary government was to emancipate the Jews.[2] Kossuth and his successors clearly grasped the great value of the Jews as Magyars and as magyarizers, particularly in the borderlands where the Hungarians were in a minority—in Slovakia, in Transylvania, and in Subcarpathian Rus. And the Jews willingly—all too willingly in the view of the minority nationalities and their supporters—played the role of magyarizers in these regions. They therefore linked their fate to the fortunes of the regime in Budapest, which seemed perfectly logical in prewar Europe.[3]

We have noted that the prewar leaders of Hungary, among them such famous statesmen as Baron József Eötvös and Ferenc Deák, were strong advocates of Jewish emancipation and assimilation (the only major exception being the famous reformer István Széchenyi). Such a stance was adopted not only because of the unique national problem within the Hungarian empire but also because these leaders, despite their gentry origins, were interested in economic modernization. They therefore recognized the usefulness of the Jews both as cultural magyarizers and as economic modernizers, as people who could perform economic tasks which the magnates approved of but could not or did not wish to perform themselves.[4] These magnates also subscribed to a peculiar brand of liberalism, which certainly did not mean either democracy or social justice but which was far removed from modern racism and did allow for a certain degree of political pluralism and tolerance of minority groups, so long as these groups toed the Magyar line. As a result of all these factors, the Hungarian ruling class of the prewar period was uniquely open to the ideology of Jewish assimilation—more so, certainly, than was the German ruling class, not to mention the Romanian, Polish, or Czech elites.[5]

It was not only the government's friendly attitude which encouraged the Jews of Hungary to acculturate and to attempt to assimilate. The rapid economic development of the last half of the nineteenth century was no less important. As in the Czech lands, Hungarian Jews began moving from towns to cities, above all to Budapest, and rapidly improved their economic status. By the end of the century many of them, in ethnic Hungary, at least, if not in the borderlands, had become solidly middle class, as they had in Bohemia, Moravia, and Germany. Thus Hungarian Jewry was on its way to becoming a Jewry of the West European-type despite its location in East Central Europe. Economic upward mobility, as always, hastened acculturation and assimilation. And both these processes developed with remarkable speed, engulfing a relatively young Jewry many of whose members had arrived in Hungary from the East during the nineteenth century. One of the most dramatic demonstrations of their impact was the Jews' readiness to magyarize their names. They were not the only ones to participate in this highly symbolic act, which was much encouraged by the government, but they did so en masse. This was noted with disgust by the enemies of magyarization. As the famous historian Robert Seton-Watson, the friend of the Slovaks and Romanians, put it, "Weiss, Kohn, Löwy, Weinberger, Klein, Rosenfeld, Ehrenfeld, Gansl, Grünfeld conceal their identity under the pseudonyms of Vészi, Kardos, Lukács, Biró, Kis, Radó, Erdélyi, Gonda, Mezei."[6] The celebrated traveler and orientalist, Arminius Vámbéry, was born Hermann Vamberger, and Ferenc Molnár, the famous playwright, had as his original name Neumann. Nowhere else in nineteenth-century East

Europe, even in the interwar years, did a similar phenomenon occur; in the nineteenth-century Polish lands, after all, Jews were usually forced to adopt non-Jewish family names. Its occurrence in Hungary reveals the depth of Jewish pro-Magyar sentiments.

Another important indication of the acculturation and assimilation process was the emergence of Reform Judaism as a force in Hungarian Jewish life. The Reform movement, which stood for the modernization of Jewish religious life, made only a limited impression in Russia, Poland, or Romania, but spread rapidly from its German homeland to Bohemia and Moravia and to Hungary. By the 1840s it was already a factor in the Hungarian lands, led by such notable figures in the history of Reform Judaism as Leopold Löw (1811–1875) and Aron Chorin (1766–1844), who served as rabbis in Szeged and Arad.

Reform Judaism in Hungary was certainly less extreme than in Germany or in the United States. Hebrew was retained as the language of prayer, and the liturgy was barely altered. But services were held in a quiet, dignified atmosphere, sermons were given in German or in Hungarian, and a choir and organ were often employed. While this sort of "conservative" reform was generally accepted in the Czech lands of Bohemia and Moravia, there was furious opposition in Hungary to its modernizing message. This was particularly the case in the poorer borderlands of Transylvania, Slovakia, and Subcarpathian Rus, whose Jews were much less prosperous and much less inclined toward acculturation and assimilation. In 1868 a great religious schism occurred within Hungarian Jewry, which eventually split into three groups: Reform (known as Neolog), Orthodox, and "Status Quo" (a small group closer to the Orthodox side than to the Reformers). Reform predominated in the more prosperous regions of inner Hungary, and above all in the great middle-class community of Budapest, while Orthodoxy prevailed in the small towns and in the ethnically mixed borderlands. Slovakia, particularly its major city, Pressburg (Pozsony, Bratislava), remained a great center of Orthodoxy close to the German variety, while Northern Transylvania and Subcarpathian Rus remained great Orthodox centers of the Hasidic type.[7] But the Western-type Jewry of inner Hungary now proceeded to build its Reform synagogues, in which Hungarian sermons were more and more frequently heard and whose minutes were taken in the Hungarian language.[8] The cause of Reform came to be associated with loyalty to Budapest and with Hungarian patriotism (although the Orthodox, if less acculturated, were no less loyal and patriotic). The schism of 1868 was of momentous importance in Hungarian Jewish history. It ruled out any effective united action by Hungarian Jews and lent institutional confirmation to the internal division between small-town Orthodox Jews and Budapest Neologs, between Jews from inner Hungary and those from the periphery, between richer Jews and poorer Jews. But we should point out that both Orthodox and Neologs agreed that the Jewish people was primarily a religious group, no matter how much they differed on the way to observe that religion. The Jews were definitely not to be regarded as a nation in the modern, secular sense of the word. This made it possible for both to be "Magyars of the Jewish persuasion" and made impossible the kind of schism between religious Jews and national-secular Jews which characterized the East European Jewish communities of Russia and Poland. As might be expected, Zionism made little headway in Hungary, although two of its most famous leaders, Theodore Herzl and Max Nordau, were born in Budapest.

It has been claimed by many observers that by the eve of World War I Hungarian Jewry was one of the most acculturated and most assimilated Jewries in the world, a Jewry whose commitment to serve the national interests of the dominant nationality in the state was absolute. As a leading Hungarian publicist of Jewish origin, Paul Ignotus, has written, the Jews became ". . . more fervently Magyar than the Magyars themselves."[9] Oszkár Jászi, also of Jewish origin and a prominent Hungarian politician and intellectual during the early postwar years, made much of the "intolerant [Magyar] nationalism and chauvinism of the Jews" which, in his view, had done a great deal to poison relations between the Hungarians and the other nationalities of the prewar era; and Seton-Watson declared in 1908 that "the Catholic Church and the Jews form today the two chief bulwarks of Magyar chauvinism."[10] But, while the Jews were mostly Hungarian by speech (although many retained the knowledge and use of German) and while they had concluded a mutually beneficial alliance with the Hungarian ruling class according to which they were to be regarded as Hungarians of the Jewish faith, just as there were Catholic and Protestant Hungarians, this did not mean that they were able to integrate fully into Hungarian society and thus fulfill their assimilationist expectations. The problem was that, from a socioeconomic as opposed to a national point of view, the Jews could not be absorbed. Hungary, after all, was a gentry-peasant society, and neither the gentry (which tended to despise the Jews socially, even if they welcomed them as accomplices in magyarization and economic development) nor the peasants afforded the Jews the possibility of social integration. Thus while in advanced Western nations the Jews did integrate to some extent, though never completely, into the middle class, in Hungary they remained essentially outside the "native" social structure, despite their evident acculturation and fervent magyarism.[11] The process of assimilation, if we define it as identification with and acceptance by the dominant nationality, cut much deeper here than in the Czech lands, where (as we shall see) the acculturated Jews found it difficult to identify themselves as either Czechs or Germans, but it did not go as deep as it did in France and, eventually, in the United States. The Jews in Hungary remained a group very much apart, although their self-definition as "Hungarians of the Mosaic faith" enjoyed the recognition of the ruling elite.

The Jews were, however, a group which played a tremendous, probably unparalleled role in their country's economic and cultural life. C. A. Macartney, a leading historian of modern Hungary, has written that "the capitalist development of modern Hungary, insofar as it has been carried out by 'domestic' forces at all, has been almost entirely of their [the Jews'] making, and the results were concentrated chiefly in their hands."[12] Largely excluded from the army (which was a Hungarian and German preserve) and from the bureaucracy, the Jews constituted the industrial and commercial bourgeoisie. By the late nineteenth century a small but potent Jewish oligarchy, mostly ennobled and partly converted to Christianity, "held overriding economic power" and represented "the vanguard of Hungary's capitalist class in Hungary's age of modernization."[13] Closely allied with the ruling political elite (for this reason one scholar has called them a "feudalized bourgeoisie"), the great Jewish financial and industrial families were a power to reckon with. Some Jewish families even became great landowners themselves.[14] The Jewish commercial and industrial bourgeoisie was concentrated, of course, in Budapest, itself a great metropolitan island in a peasant sea, sometimes called, not entirely in jest, "Judapest." Probably nowhere else in Eastern Europe was there a greater gap between city and village than in Hungary, and it was symbolized by the tremendous contrast between rich, industrialized, westernized Budapest and the impoverished, typically East European countryside. The Jews, for better or for worse, were totally identified with capitalist, bourgeois, Westernized, urban Hungary. And they did not win the admiration of the many enemies of capitalism and of the city.

The Jewish impact on Hungarian life in the prewar era was not limited to economic activity. The children of Jewish bankers, industrialists, and businessmen, here as elsewhere in Europe, flocked to the universities and became doctors, lawyers, editors, journalists, scholars, musicians, and perhaps most notably, scientists.[15] Thus in the immediate prewar period Jews constituted some fifty percent of the students in the University of Budapest's medical faculty. They also were attracted to politics, above all to the radical left. Young Jewish intellectuals, disgusted with the conservative views both of the ruling class and of their own bourgeois and petty bourgeois parents, became prominent in the Social Democratic and Radical parties.[16] So it was, here as in Germany, that Jews became identified not only with capitalism but also with socialism, a double curse so far as the radical right was concerned. Far more Jews were capitalists than socialists, of course, but the conspicuous Jewish role in the small and historically weak Hungarian left was to become a major issue in post–World War I, and post–Béla Kun, Hungary.

How are we to explain the unprecedented Jewish penetration of Hungarian economic and cultural life in the prewar period? The fact is that the general environment was unusually favorable to the Jews. The regime, as we have seen, was basically pro-Jewish. There was, of course, no lack of anti-Semitism in prewar Hungary, as elsewhere in Europe. Ignaz Goldziher (1850–1921), Hungary's greatest orientalist and one of Europe's most famous scholars, was one of its most notable victims. While still a young man he had been granted a scholarship to study in Germany by Baron Eötvös, the minister of culture. Upon his return from Germany, however, and despite his ever-growing international reputation, Goldziher was unable to support himself by university teaching and was obliged, much against his will, to take a position as secretary of the Neolog Jewish community in Budapest.[17] Social anti-Semitism, of the type so common in the West, was extremely strong, as the following description by an acute observer of the Hungarian scene indicates:

> You could be the richest, the best educated, even officially the highest ranking man in the kingdom, but if you had Jewish blood you could not hope to play *chemin de fer* on the premises reserved for the upper-middle-class gentry in Budapest. I knew a converted Jew, gentleman farmer, and ex-member of Parliament, titled and dandified, who could out-duel his circle; and he married a dowerless, most attractive girl of the ancient lesser nobility, the "belle of the county hall" and of gentry parties in Budapest. After their wedding, she was still invited to the country balls, but they received a tactful warning that *he* had better plead public duties on that occasion. And he—and she—agreed; after all, she must not lose her old friends, and there was no way of getting round such limitations.[18]

This sort of anti-Semitism, however, did not prevent the majority of Hungarian Jewry from rising rapidly on the social ladder and from attaining middle-class status. Popular anti-Semitism was limited in the prewar period. The peasants were traditionally not much interested in the Jews, and there was as yet no powerful Christian bourgeoisie to resent Jewish commercial success. Nor were the two Christian churches (Catholic and Calvinist) involved in the anti-Semitic movement. True, a celebrated blood libel case involving the accusation that Jews used the blood of Christians for ritual purposes occurred in 1882 in the town of Tisza-Eszlár. Moreover, a significant political anti-Semitic movement emerged in the 1880s, as it did in Germany and in Austria, but in Hungary it was quickly put down by the "liberal" government, whose attitude in this regard was crucial.[19] The regime's opposition to political and popular anti-Semitism, its commitment to economic (as opposed to political) modernization, and the absence of a competing "native" bourgeoisie in gentry-peasant Hungary facilitated the remarkable Jewish breakthrough into positions of dominance in industry, commerce, and the professions. The situation here was quite different from that in Russian Poland, where, as we know, a growing Polish middle class both despised the Jews and organized against them, where the regime did not act to stamp out political anti-Semitism, where the Jews were often regarded as russifiers and therefore as enemies of Polish nationalism, and where the general economic situation remained one of great backwardness. It was also quite different from the situation in the Czech lands, where anti-Semitism inevitably accompanied the Czech struggle against German political and cultural hegemony.

Thus Hungary appeared to be a "paradise for the Jews," but potential dangers were certainly not absent. One obvious danger was the identification of the Jews with oppressive magyarization in the ethnically mixed regions. Another was the nexus between the Jews and the ruling elite, an elite which was antidemocratic and reactionary despite its pro-Jewish policy. Finally, there was the Jews' conspicuous role in Hungarian life, particularly in the economy. How long would this be tolerated? Prewar Hungary was, clearly, a good place for the Jews, but, as we now know, it would remain thus only so long as the country remained a multinational empire ruled by old-regime gentry liberals. Even before the end of the old regime, Theodore Herzl, a native son, had the prescience to write, in 1903, "The hand of fate shall also seize Hungarian Jewry. And the later this occurs, and the stronger this Jewry becomes, the more cruel and hard shall be the blow, which shall be delivered with greater savagery. There is no escape."[20] Herzl, of course, was speaking as a Zionist, not as an impartial observer of the scene. But the interwar period was to prove him a prophet.

## 2. Hungarian Jewry and the End of the Old Order

We have remarked that World War I and the ensuing peace settlement had a devastating impact on Hungary. The same can be said for Hungarian Jewry.[21] Just as Hungary lost vast territories and millions of people, so Hungarian Jewry was deprived of thousands of Jews in Transylvania (now attached to Romania), Slovakia, and Subcarpathian Rus (both now part of Czechoslovakia). This meant the loss of the most religious and least assimilated of Hungarian Jews, the strongholds of Orthodoxy and Yiddish speech in Pressburg (now called Bratislava), Szatmár (Satu-Mare), and Munkács (Mukačevo). Those who remained in Trianon Hungary tended to be more Neolog than Orthodox and more magyarized. Moreover, the collapse of Habsburg Hungary meant the end of the golden age of Hungarian-Jewish relations, an age which was never to return. One of the reasons for this was the demise of the multinational state. If the Jews were regarded in the prewar period as agents of magyarization, so useful to Hungarian rule in the peripheral regions, in the postwar period they were no longer needed to fulfill this function. Trianon Hungary, after all, was a nation-state, not a state of nationalities; as for the magyarized Jews of Slovakia, Transylvania, and Subcarpathian Rus, it was hoped that they would remain loyal to Magyardom, but it was also realized that they were in no position to bring about a revision of the postwar settlement. Thus one of the main reasons for traditional pro-Jewish feeling among the Hungarian elite, from Kossuth on, no longer applied.

Along with the collapse of multinational Hungary went a series of political upheavals which, although ultimately unsuccessful, were also to strike at the Hungarian-Jewish alliance. In October, 1918, the first (and only) Western-type liberal regime in Hungarian history, headed by Mihály Károlyi, took power. Károlyi's left-leaning coalition, supported by radicals and social democrats and including within its ranks several prominent Jews, was unable to halt the disintegration of the state. In March, 1919, it was replaced by a Communist government headed by Béla Kun (1886–1939), a Transylvanian Hungarian of Jewish origin who had spent most of the war as a Russian prisoner. If many right-wing opponents of Károlyi (who was of impeccable aristocratic origins) accused him of being a "Jewish stooge," there was no doubt in the minds of millions of anti-Communist Hungarians that Béla Kun's regime was Jewish through and through.[22] In fact, the number of Jews who occupied prominent positions in Kun's ill-fated one hundred-day regime was truly remarkable. According to one student of this period, of twenty-six ministers and vice-ministers of the Kun regime, twenty were of Jewish origin.[23] Of course, they were Jews only in the technical sense—Kun himself is quoted as having proclaimed in 1919, "My father was a Jew but I am no longer one, for I became a socialist and a Communist."[24] But this made no difference to anyone. The fact was that the Hungarian Soviet government, despised by large numbers of Hungarians as the antithesis of traditional Hungarian politics and as a Russian effort to gain a beachhead in Central Europe, was from the beginning identified with Hungarian Jewry. The extraordinarily high rate of Jewish representation deserves some comment, for, although Jews were prominent in socialist movements everywhere in Eastern Europe, nowhere, and certainly not in Soviet Russia, did they play so great a role. Not only did Jews dominate the Béla Kun government, but they were also very prominent in the prewar "Galileo Circle," the center of Budapest student radicalism, and in the prewar socialist movement. The traditional explanation for the prominence of Jews in the left, namely, that they were reacting to anti-Semitism, certainly has something to do with this phenomenon. True, prewar Hungary, as we have noted, was not extremely anti-Semitic, but the atmosphere changed radically after the war and even in the prewar period those Jews who were politically ambitious were likely to look to the left rather than to the gentry-dominated establishment political order. We should also recall that Hungarian Marxism was not a mass movement but chiefly an organization of intellectuals (as it was elsewhere in Eastern Europe), and the Hungarian intelligentsia, as we have already remarked, probably had more Jewish members than that of any other East European country. It was, in fact, characterized by the conspicuous presence of precocious and brilliant children of the Jewish bourgeoisie, who found on the left a more attractive environment than that offered by their banker and merchant parents. (More will be said on this subject later on.)

Jászi and other observers of the Hungarian scene have theorized that the Jews' overrepresentation in Hungarian radicalism was the result of the rootlessness, "half-assimilation," and lack of firm national tradition which characterized Hungarian Jewry. Confronting the problem of why so many Jews were involved in Béla Kun's "un-Hungarian" experiment, Jászi wrote in 1923 that

> we must not forget that the contrast between Jewry and the Christian world is much greater in Eastern Europe than in the West. The Hungarian people is much more rural, conservative, and slow thinking than the Western peasant peoples. On the other hand, Hungarian Jewry is much less assimilated than Western Jewries, it is much more an independent body within society, which does not have any real contact with the native soul of the country.

This lack of contact with the Hungarian nation rendered the Jews much more prepared to devote themselves to the Bolshevik ideal than were the "rooted," conservative Hungarian masses.[25] Indeed, for Jászi the peculiar situation of the Jews in Hungary made them prone to ideological excesses of all kinds, including not only Bolshevik internationalism but also Hungarian superchauvinism. The connection between Jewish rootlessness and Jewish Bolshevism, which fitted in well with racial theories about the Jews' inability to assimilate properly, was made ad nauseam by Hungarian anti-Semites during the interwar years. And if there is some truth in this analysis, the fact is that most Jews were patriotic Hungarians who were extremely hostile to Bolshevism and who wanted nothing less than the restoration of the prewar order. Nonetheless, they paid a heavy price for the high proportion of Jews in Kun's government, just as Russian Jewry during the civil war paid a high price for the conspicuous role played by Trotsky and other Jews in the Soviet regime.

Kun's regime, accompanied by considerable chaos and a modest red terror, called into life a voluminous and incredibly venomous anti-Semitic literature, the theme of which was the accusation that Kun was attempting to subjugate Hungary to Jewish domination. "St. Stephen's Hungary," read one typical entry, "has fallen under the rule of Trotsky's agent, Béla Kun, the embezzler."[26] Under Kun, we are informed, "a new Jerusalem was growing up on the banks of the Danube. It emanated from Karl Marx's Jewish brain, and was built by Jews. . . ."[27] Just as ominous, from the Jewish point of view, was that Kun's regime brought forth a powerful counterrevolutionary reaction. A loose coalition of fanatic right-wing anti-Bolsheviks and old-style Hungarian liberals rose up to fight Kun and socialism in the name of ancient Hungarian virtues. The latter group, led by István Bethlen and Pál Teleki, typical aristocrats of the old regime, was concentrated in Vienna, while the former, led by the future profascist prime minister of Hungary, Gyula Gömbös, rallied around the flag in Szeged. (Gömbös and his followers were known as the "men of Szeged.") In the summer of 1919 Kun was overthrown, not so much by internal opposition as by French-backed Romanian military intervention. The counterrevolution took over the country, symbolized by the appointment as regent of Admiral Miklós Horthy, a venerable naval hero and representative of the old ruling class who favored the restoration, as much as possible, of the prewar regime.

The overthrow of Kun and the triumph of counterrevolution was accompanied by a white terror which was, among other things, a series of bloody pogroms directed against leftists and Jews, usually regarded as identical. This was the Hungarian version of the wave of anti-Jewish disturbances which swept over the Ukraine, Poland, Lithuania, and even Czechoslovakia during 1918–1919. But if pogroms were fairly common in the lands of the old Tsarist empire, they were something new in the lands of St. Stephen. The white terror reached its height during August-September, 1919, but continued until the spring of 1920. Jews were murdered in some fifty towns, usually by military detachments. Hungarian public opinion regarded these events as just revenge for the sins of the Kun regime, and Horthy himself, upon his triumphant entrance into Budapest, promised to "punish" that sinful city which, as we recall, was identified in the Hungarian mind with Hungarian Jewry.[28] The Jewish world, and in particular Hungarian Jewry, reacted with horror and amazement to these events, so unexpected in this "philo-Semitic" country. But the Hungarian ruling class, which before the war would never have tolerated such behavior, did not condemn the excesses. Terror, it was felt, had to be fought by terror, and the Jews were clearly guilty of great crimes.[29] They deserved what they got.

The Hungarian experience provides the researcher with a unique example of how a country previously "good for the Jews" is transformed, almost overnight, into a country wracked with pogroms and permeated with anti-Semitic hysteria. How did this happen? We have already seen how the community of interests which bound the Magyar ruling class to the Jews had been shaken by loss of empire and how the prominence of Jews in the short-lived Communist regime infuriated the great majority who were anti-Bolshevik. More generally, it might be said that the Hungarian nation underwent a profound national trauma during 1918–1919, when the humiliation of loss of empire was combined with the humiliation of a political takeover by a group of socially unacceptable intellectuals acting, so it was believed, under the guidance of foreign, anti-Magyar powers. These humiliations, greater than those experienced by any other East Central European nation during this period, created the overriding need for scapegoats. The Jews and the leftists were obvious targets, and if the old regime had once shielded the Jews from anti-Semitism, which was at any rate relatively submerged in prewar Hungary, it was no longer in a position to do so when anti-Semitism burst forth with unprecedented vigor during the white terror. In other words, Jewish well-being during the prewar period was a function of the old regime's ability to retain the empire and maintain social and political tranquility. The collapse of the Habsburg regime signaled the beginning of the collapse of the Jewish-gentry alliance.

To be sure, the restoration of the old regime in 1919 also restored, to a degree, the old situation so far as Hungarian-Jewish relations were concerned. But the restoration was more apparent than real. The Jewish condition in Trianon Hungary was quite different from that in prewar Habsburg Hungary, and even the victory of Horthy and Bethlen could not conceal this fact. The Jews remained great Magyar patriots, but the Hungarian ruling class was no longer pro-Jewish; meanwhile, a new political force, organizing on the extreme right, threatened the Jewish minority as no political force ever had before. But it was not only the attitude of the ruling elite and the emergence of a radical right which were new. If before the war the Hungarian nation was prepared to welcome reinforcements from other national and religious groups, it was now much less so. The traditional open nationalism of the prewar period was replaced by a closed, exclusivist nationalism which found its intellectual justification in the writings of such people as the outstanding historian of the interwar years, Gyula Szekfü.[30] And if the Jews were able to play such a dominant role in economic and intellectual life before the war, when Hungary was a large, multinational empire undergoing rapid economic development, in the interwar period new economic conditions rendered their dominance much less tolerable. Hungary was now a much smaller country, where opportunities were suddenly reduced and where competition for employment was greater. A rapidly growing number of "native" university graduates were now searching for suitable work, and things were made worse by the influx after the war of large numbers of Hungarians from what was now Czechoslovakia, Romania, and Yugoslavia. The old world was gone forever, and Hungary became a most dramatic example, along with Bukovina, Transylvania, and Galicia, of how Jewish fortunes declined with the decline of the Austro-Hungarian empire.

### 3. Interwar Hungarian Jewry: Demography, Socioeconomic Status, Cultural Characteristics

According to the census of 1920, there were in Trianon Hungary 473,355 Jews (by religion, of course—the existence of a Jewish nationality, in contrast with the situation in Poland, was recognized neither by the state nor by the Jews themselves). The Jews constituted 5.9 percent of the total population, a much lower percentage than in Poland but a much higher percentage than in Czechoslovakia. By 1930 the Jewish population had declined to 444,567, or 5.1 percent of the total; this was mostly the result of a very low Jewish birth rate, typical of Western-type Jewish communities and similar to the situation in Bohemia and Moravia, where the Jewish community also suffered a decrease in absolute numbers during the interwar years.[31] Some decrease was also a result of conversion, intermarriage, and emigration.

The most outstanding characteristic of Jewish demography in Hungary was the concentration of Jews in the capital. In 1920, 215,512 Jews resided in Budapest, constituting 23.2 percent of the city's total population and over 45 percent of Hungarian Jewry. The tendency of Jews to concentrate in capital cities is also a Western phenomenon. It was true in Bohemia, for example, where nearly 50 percent of all Jews lived in Prague, but it was not true of Poland, where only about 10 percent of the Jewish population resided in Warsaw. But outside Budapest, Hungarian Jews tended to live in the medium and small towns which characterized Hungary. The only other sizable Jewish communities, and they were none too large, were located in Miskolc (11,300), Debrecen (10,170), and Szeged (6,958). In 1920, 44.1 percent of all Jews resided in areas which were officially designated as rural ("comitats"), where they constituted 3.2 percent of the total population; 55.9 percent resided in "municipal districts," where they made up 17.2 percent of the total population.[32] We must, therefore, modify to some extent our portrait of Hungarian Jewry as a Western group. In most respects it was, but since approximately one-half of its members resided in little towns, mostly in the northeast of the state, it shared some of the characteristics of an Eastern Jewry. Just as Hungary itself was characterized by the sharp division between Budapest and the "country," so Hungarian Jewry was sharply divided between the Jews of the capital and the small-town Jews of the provinces. This was, in fact, the most fundamental division in Hungarian Jewish life.

While there was no such thing as a single Polish, Romanian, or Czechoslovakian Jewry, there was a Hungarian Jewry, bound together by a common political history under the Hungarian crown, by its adoption of Hungarian culture, and by its identification with the Magyar nation. Virtually all Hungarian Jews in Trianon Hungary spoke Hungarian and regarded themselves as Hungarian by nationality. Yiddish could no longer be heard in the country, now that Transylvania, Slovakia, and Subcarpathian Rus were annexed to other states. The major cultural division within the community was not linguistic, as in Romania or in Latvia, but rather religious. In Trianon Hungary the Neologs were stronger than the Orthodox, claiming the allegiance of about 65 percent, but the latter held on, particularly in the small towns and among the poorer Jews of the northeast. The capital of Neolog Hungary was, of course, Budapest, and its symbol was the famous modern rabbinical seminary established there before the war. The seminary, which in American terms would probably be considered more "conservative" than reform, was the home of such celebrated Jewish scholars as the aforementioned Goldziher. Its students, who also studied at the University of Budapest, were expected to be learned both in secular and in Jewish subjects.[33] It was, of course, anathema in the eyes of the Orthodox, whose great religious institutions had been lost to Hungarian Jewry as a result of the Trianon treaty. Some 80 percent of the old Hungarian yeshivas were no longer in Hungary, but a fairly large number continued to function and to turn out Orthodox rabbis in the traditional fashion.[34] Hasidism was confined to the northeast region; the famous rebes of Munkács and Szatmár, along with most of their followers, were now Czechoslovakian and Romanian subjects.

Hungarian Jewry was basically distributed among the various strata of the middle class, ranging from the haute to the lower bourgeoisie. At its apex were the giants of finance and industry, the great Jewish families of Budapest. At the bottom were the artisans and small merchants of the little towns. There was no Jewish factory proletariat, but there was no lack of Jewish poverty, though it was certainly much less pervasive than in the Eastern-type communities.[35] Table 2.1 compares the economic pursuits of all gainfully employed Jews and Christians in 1920. The figures are comparable to those relating to Bohemia and Moravia, except for the fact that a larger number of Jews in Hungary were engaged in "industry and

TABLE 2.1
**Economic Profile of Jews and Christians
in Hungary, 1920 (By Percentage)**

|            | Agriculture | Industry and Crafts | Trade | Civil Service and Professions |
|------------|-------------|---------------------|-------|-------------------------------|
| Jews       | 4.2         | 31.2                | 43.6  | 8.6                           |
| Christians | 59.7        | 17.5                | 3.7   | 4.2                           |

SOURCE: B. D., "Di yidn in ungarn," *Yidishe ekonomik* 1 (1937):191. Slightly different figures are given in "The Occupations of the Jews of Hungary: Census of 1920," *American Jewish Year Book* 32 (1930–1931):259.

crafts;" presumably these were mostly the artisans of the small towns, who were less numerous among the urbanized Jews of the economically more advanced Czech lands. As was almost always the case in East Central Europe, those Christians not employed in the agricultural sector were more likely to be employed in industry than in commerce, whereas among the Jews the opposite was the case. During the interwar period Jews played an insignificant and declining role in the bureaucracy, from which they were now basically excluded, but their role in commerce, industry, and the professions was remarkable. Despite the fact that they constituted only 5.9 percent of the population, the number of Jews active in trade was almost the same as the number of gentiles. In 1920, 50.6 percent of all lawyers, 59.9 percent of all doctors, and 34.3 percent of all editors and journalists were Jews, as were 39.2 percent of all privately employed engineers and chemists, and 28.6 percent of all musicians.[36] In 1930, 61.7 percent of all large commercial firms (employing twenty or more people) were in Jewish hands, as were 47.4 percent of all large industrial establishments (similarly defined).[37] Not appearing in the statistics, but of great importance, were the famous banking and industrial families of Jewish or partly Jewish origin—the Chorins, the Weiszes, the Goldbergers and others. It was their activities, and those of their less wealthy but solidly middle-class coreligionists, which led Macartney to write that the Jews occupied a "commanding position" in the Hungarian economy.[38] And while this was a familiar claim of the anti-Semites, in Hungary as elsewhere, and while the existence of large numbers of poor Jews should not be forgotten, the statistics appear to bear him out.

We have remarked that Hungarian Jewry was basically of the Western type, although this designation applies more to the Neologs of Budapest than to the Orthodox communities of the small towns. There was, as we might expect, a significantly high rate of intermarriage, though the Orthodox community's weight within Hungarian Jewry kept the figures well below the Bohemian-Moravian level. During the years 1931–1935, 19.3 percent of all Jewish grooms in Budapest married outside the faith, while the figure for Jewish brides was 16.5 percent. In the little communities, intermarriage was infrequent.[39] There were also more conversions in Hungary than anywhere else in East Central Europe, and they occurred in bunches, during the white terror of 1919–1920 and again in the late 1930s, when the extreme anti-Semites won the upper hand. In 1919, 7,146 Jews converted, an insignificant number compared with that at the very end of the interwar period.[40] Such statistics reflect the reaction of a part of the acculturated community to outbursts of anti-Semitism previously unknown in Hungarian history.

Intermarriage, low birth rates, Reform Judaism, the lack of an autonomous modern Jewish culture in either Hebrew or Yiddish—these are the characteristics of Hungarian Jewry. If we compare it to the Jewries of Bohemia and Moravia, also distinctly of the Western type, there appear to be at least three significant differences. Hungarian Jewry, which in Trianon Hungary lived in a monocultural setting, failed to develop that kind of Jewish nationalism which in the Czech lands resulted largely from the Jews' delicate position between Czechs and Germans. On the other hand, Orthodox Judaism survived in Hungary, as it did not in the Czech lands, and even the Neologs created an important rabbinical school. Thus both traditional Judaism and modern Jewish scholarship (centered in the Budapest Seminary) were able to exist and even thrive in Hungary. In this respect Hungarian Jewry of the interwar years is more similar to German Jewry than to the Jewish communities of the Czech lands. Finally, as we have seen, the small-town Jewish community survived in Hungary to a much greater extent than either in the more developed Czech lands or in Germany. While it is doubtless true that the Budapest Jewish community dominated Hungarian Jewry, much as New York Jewry dominates Jewish life in the Eastern United States, the presence of the more conservative, more religious, less intellectual, and less wealthy Jewish communities of the Hungarian northeast should not be forgotten.

### 4. The New Hungary and the Jewish Question: Part One

Historians of interwar Hungary usually divide the period into two parts—the period of the "liberal" restoration, when Hungary was ruled by the old aristocratic elite, and the period when the country fell under the control of radical right forces. The first period extends until 1932 and comes to an end with the appointment of Gömbös as prime minister. This scheme is far from foolproof (there was, for example, an old-style "liberal" Hungarian prime minister during the years 1942–1944), but it is useful, and its usefulness extends to our discussion of the position of the Jews in the state. Roughly speaking, so long as the old elite held on to power, albeit in the new environment of Trianon Hungary, Jewish well-being was not seriously impaired. This was not the case under premiers of Gömbös' type, although we shall see that the bark of this first avowed Hungarian fascist to rule the country was considerably worse than his bite.

Two men put their stamp on Hungary of the 1920s: the regent, Admiral Miklós Horthy, and the prime minister for much of this period, István Bethlen. Both were old-style landowners, both were avowed enemies of the Versailles settlement and of Communism, and both wished to pre-serve the social and political system of prewar Hungary. This meant the ascendancy of the old gentry elite along with the preservation of a certain degree of political pluralism. Opposition groups were allowed to exist, but since democracy was foreign to the Hungarian system, and remained anathema to her new leaders, party life on the Czechoslovak or Polish model never developed. So far as its attitude toward the Jews was con-cerned, the political elite was far less friendly than the prewar rulers of Hungary, but in substance its policy during the 1920s differed little from that of its predecessors. Even at the height of the struggle against Kun and his "Jewish government," Horthy was careful not to blame all Hungarian Jews for Kun's crimes. His attitude is reflected in his memoirs, written after World War II, when he noted, "The Jews who had long been settled among us were the first to reprobate the crimes of their co-religionists, in whose hands the new regime almost exclusively rested."[41] This distinction between "real Hungarian Jews" and the others, presumably recent im-migrants, became a common theme in the writings of the leaders of the restoration. It was not wholly reassuring to Hungarian Jewry, but it was at least not a purely racist position, and it allowed for the existence of good, patriotic Hungarian Jews who could be counted on to support the regime. It was made in the clearest possible way by the future prime minister, Count Pál Teleki, a great magnate and establishment politician who, when in the United States in 1921, insisted that Hungarians disliked only the "Galician Jews," by whom he meant recent arrivals from Poland who were clearly not assimilated Hungarians. ". . . it is a mistake," he added, "to think that the anti-Jewish movement, which really existed and which still exists in Hungary, is one against the Jewish religion or Jews in general."[42] In a lecture given in 1926 Teleki elaborated on this theme:

> For centuries we have had a nationally thinking and valuable working Jewry in the process of assimilation. Over the past decades, however, the ratio of immigrants from Russia, Romania, and Galicia has multiplied. The unassimilated, unnational or even antinational Jewry became pre-

dominant, first numerically, then in certain professional lines, such as the press and literature. Its flexible, combatant cosmopolitanism has undermined the way of thinking of individuals, and started destroying the pillars of the state. And in the years subsequent to the World War, the cohesive force of the Jewish thought proved to have been stronger than the national thought.[43]

It makes no difference that the theory of the "Galician invasion" had little basis in fact. So long as Hungarian leaders took out their wrath on the "Galicians," and not on the "nationally thinking and valuable working Jewry," state-inspired anti-Semitism remained limited. And some of the traditional reasons for limiting anti-Semitism still prevailed. Jews might not be able to serve as magyarizers in Transylvania now that that province was attached to Romania, but they could still provide great financial assistance to the government. They did, in fact, support the new-old regime with an enthusiasm born of certain knowledge that this regime's opponents on the right were fanatic anti-Semites whose victory would prove fatal to Hungarian Jewry. For their part, Bethlen and Horthy also had much to fear from the radical right, whose attitude toward social and economic questions posed a threat to the status quo. Thus the old Jewish-Hungarian establishment alliance was reconstructed; it was built on much less firm soil than in the prewar period, but it held so long as the old-regime politicians continued to rule new Hungary. As Macartney has put it, "the big Jewish interests became one of the most powerful pillars of his [Bethlen's] whole system."[44] The Jewish oligarchy continued to co-opt Hungarian aristocrats into its firms and sometimes even intermarried with the sons and daughters of the aristocracy. Jews continued to serve as lessees of large estates. And while the Jewish rich (and, as we shall see, the Jewish political leadership) lent its strong support to the regime, the regime resisted popular pressure from the extreme right to curtail Jewish rights and to strike at the Jewish economic interest. This meant, of course, that Jewish well-being continued to be firmly linked to the preservation of the conservative (or even reactionary) order just as it had been before the war. This was not a happy position for Hungarian Jewry to find itself in, but it is difficult to see what other choice it had. And surely the situation of Hungarian Jewry during the 1920s was happier than that of the Jews of Poland, where the basically racist attitude of the Endek movement prevailed and where the Jews' lower-middle-class and proletarian character made them especially vulnerable to anti-Semitism. Teleki and his colleagues did not love the Jews, and we shall see that they came to love them less and less, but their attitude was preferable to that of Dmowski and other leaders of the Polish right, who could not concede the possibility that Polish Jewry might be of benefit to the state.

There was one attempt during the 1920s to curtail Jewish rights, and that involved the effort to establish a *numerus clausus* at Hungarian institutions of higher learning. In 1920, the year of the signing of the humiliating Trianon Treaty, at a time when the devastated country was being invaded by Magyars from the annexed territories and when Béla Kun was still a fresh memory, the government passed a law limiting attendance at universities to the percentages which various "races and nationalities" constituted within the general population. The word "Jew" was not mentioned, although there were no other possible targets for the law.[45] It was defended in the League of Nations (to which, as we shall see, complaints were brought by international Jewish organizations) as a measure to reduce the too large number of intellectuals in the state. Said the Hungarian representative, "There is no international obligation in existence by which a state could be compelled to give education to a mass of persons of the intellectual class which it would be unable to support."[46] He added, perhaps not entirely facetiously, that the government regarded this measure as something of a favor to the Jews, since universities were unwilling to accept "unpatriotic" candidates and, were it not for the *numerus clausus*, would not accept any Jews at all.

What was alarming about this law was not so much that it limited the number of Jews in universities, but that it defined the Jews as a special "race" or "nationality" and therefore appeared to exclude them from Magyardom. Such a definition, devoutly desired by many Polish Jews, and by Zionists everywhere, went against the grain of Hungarian Jewish history, for it implied that the prewar formula "Hungarians of the Mosaic faith" no longer applied. Vilmos Vázsonyi (1868–1926), minister of justice during World War I and one of the few prominent Hungarian politicians of Jewish origin not identified with the left, pointed this out in an appeal to Bethlen issued in 1923:

> The *numerus clausus* does not speak of religious groups [confessions] but of race. . . . This law therefore considers the Jews to be a race or a distinct nationality. And this at a time when, in Paris, Count Teleki and Count Bethlen have declared that the Romanians and Czechs are wrong to consider the Jews as a separate race, since the Jews [in Slovakia and Transylvania] are Hungarians.[47]

How, Vázsonyi wondered, could the Hungarian government expel Hungary's Jews from Magyardom while claiming, for irredentist purposes, the allegiance of Hungarian Jews in the lost provinces? He could not have been reassured when, in 1925, the Hungarian representative at the League of Nations announced that the Jews were partly a race, partly a religious group, and partly a nationality, and that "a Jewish minority cannot be defined in the same way as other minorities, in view of the unique position occupied by Jews throughout the world."[48] But in the 1920s, at least, the conclusions implied in such statements, which appeared to threaten the legal equality of Hungarian Jewry, were not explicitly drawn. The *numerus clausus* law remained on the books but was not strictly enforced. The number of Jewish students at institutions of higher learning declined sharply in 1920–1921, but in 1921–1922 it rose to 13.4 percent of the total—far higher than the Jewish percentage within the population, although lower than in the prewar years.[49] This was again different from the Jews' experience in Poland, where an attempt in 1923 to institute *numerus clausus* had failed but where the percentage of Jewish students declined steadily during the 1920s. Moreover, the government insisted that it regarded the law as a temporary measure, and it was eventually allowed to lapse.[50] Nonetheless, this episode was a revealing one. It would not have been possible in the Habsburg years, and it demonstrated how tenuous the reconstructed Hungarian-Jewish alliance was. It is an illustration of how acute the problem of competition between Jewish and Christian intellectuals and potential members of the professions had become after the collapse of the Hungarian empire, and it also showed how the Magyar ruling class, while maintaining its close ties with the Jewish oligarchy, was prepared to punish those Jews it considered most responsible for the revolution—namely, the intelligentsia— while making it easier for the "native" middle class and intelligentsia to find employment.[51] Jews were punished in other ways as well during the 1920s. Not only did their members in the universities fall short of prewar figures, but also they were, as has been mentioned, effectively kept out of the bureaucracy as well as out of the army officers corps (the former was a preserve for Magyars of the Christian faith, the latter an important avenue of advancement for the German minority). Such exclusion was not a calamity for Hungarian Jewry, which was much richer and therefore much less vulnerable economically than were the Jewries of the East European type. But it was another sign that things were not as they had been. We have noted that in chauvinist, revisionist Hungary of the interwar years opportunities for Jews were not so great as they were in Habsburg times, and this was particularly true for those young people— and there were many such—who did not wish to follow in the footsteps of their "bourgeois" parents. It was during this period, after all, that such celebrated Jewish scientists as Szilard, von Neumann, and Teller left their native land. We do not find in Hungary the Polish phenomenon of a "youth without a future," certainly not in the 1920s and not during most of the 1930s. But neither was there the feeling, as there was in the Czech lands, that virtually all careers were open to the talented. In retrospect the 1920s seem to have been a good period for Hungarian Jewry. But anti-Jewish statements by Hungarian leaders, the *numerus clausus* law, and discrimination in those areas dominated by the state, along with the rise of the extreme right and the growth of anti-Semitic propaganda, were a taste of what was to come, with much more devastating impact, in the 1930s.

## 5. Jewish Politics and Jewish Leadership in Hungary

Of all the lands of East Central Europe, Hungary was the most unfavorable environment for the emergence of modern Jewish politics. In this sense it was the exact opposite of Poland. In Hungary, as we know, Jews defined themselves as a religious group, not as a nationality, and so long as virtually all Hungarian Jews regarded themselves as Hungarians of the Mosaic faith a Jewish political platform based on the notion that the Jews were a modern nation was impossible. The basic split in Hungary was between Neolog and Orthodox Jews, while in the Jewries of the East European type it was between secular-national Jews and religious Jews. To be sure, in the peripheral regions of old Hungary the multinational situation did make more likely the establishment of a secular Jewish national tradition, but even in such regions as Slovakia and Transylvania modern Jewish politics was very weak in the prewar period. It was even weaker, of course, in the monoethnic Hungarian heartland. True, Herzl and Nordau were Hungarian-born, but they became Zionists after they had left their childhood home. Most Hungarian Jews in the interwar years would surely have agreed with the Neolog rabbi of Buda, Samuel Kohn, who had declared in 1897 (the year of the first Zionist Congress), "I consider political Zionism, which wants to establish a new Jewish state in Palestine, a reckless . . . and dangerous folly."[52] Hungary was the only country in East Central Europe where the dramatic events of 1918–1919 did not lead to a much greater national consciousness on the part of the Jewish community. Even the pogroms of the white terror did not have this effect. The Jews of Trianon Hungary, unlike their coreligionists in Czechoslovakia, Transylvania, Slovakia, and Lithuania, did not suddenly find themselves in a new cultural and political setting. There was no cultural and political vacuum here, as there was in so many other regions. They continued to be Hungarian Jews living under Hungarian sovereignty, as they had since 1867. This, along with the fact that in most respects they were a Western-type Jewry, precluded the process of nationalism which affected most East Central European Jewries, from the Jews of Bohemia to the Jews of Galicia. We should not be surprised, therefore, if in 1937, when extreme anti-Semitism was rampant in Hungary, a mere 6,044 shekels were sold in the state, or that in some years the

Jews of the Vilna region in Poland purchased nearly as many shekels as did all of Hungarian Jewry.[53] There is no better proof that anti-Semitism alone does not inevitably lead to Jewish nationalism. It was only after 1938, when Hungary regained some of her lost territories, and along with them many Jews who had participated in the national movement in Romania and Czechoslovakia, that Zionism was able to make something of an impact in Hungary.

If there was no Zionism, and of course no Bund or Folkist tradition either (we may recall that Yiddish was unknown in interwar Hungary and that the left in general was not very strong), what was the nature of Jewish politics and leadership? Instead of the autonomous "new" Jewish politics of the Polish variety which dominated Jewish communities of the Eastern type and which made great inroads even in the Czech lands, we have the preservation of the old, nondemocratic Jewish leadership, largely drawn from the wealthy Neolog community in Budapest. (The Neologs and the Orthodox maintained separate organizations throughout the interwar years.) The policy of this leadership was to emphasize time and again the loyalty and patriotism of Hungarian Jewry and to denounce any suggestion that the Jews were anything but good Hungarians. This policy made them ferocious enemies of such Jewish separatist doctrines as Zionism, as well as of Hungarian right wingers who believed the Jews to be anti-Hungarian. It also led them to take positions identical to those of the ruling elite. During the white terror the leaders of the major Jewish communities issued statements condemning Béla Kun and his colleagues as violators of the holy precepts of Judaism and emphasizing the readiness of Hungarian Jewry to sacrifice itself for the fatherland.[54] In 1920 an important Hungarian Jewish organization declared itself in favor of revising the Trianon treaty and returning to Hungary her lost provinces, thus proving itself to be no less patriotic than Horthy and Bethlen.[55] (We should recall that such patriotic statements were made during the pogroms of 1919-1920, which were not denounced by the new rulers of Hungary.) Vilmos Vázsonyi, who was not an official Jewish leader but who often spoke out on the Jewish question and was regarded as a Jewish spokesman, was a Hungarian superpatriot, a great opponent of Bolshevism, a revisionist, and a fierce enemy of Zionism. His views on general issues mirrored those of the ruling class, and he was highly valued by the moderate counterrevolutionaries. In 1919 he was recommended to Horthy by Prince Lajos Windischgraetz as "the most pronounced antagonist in Hungary of the revolutionary Jewish journalism, which during recent years has had such a great role, and he bides his time only until he can break those who, also in his opinion, have ruined the country."[56] Thus Vászonyi, the "good Hungarian Jew," was contrasted to the wicked Jewish journalists who paved the way for the victory of Béla Kun. And it is a fact that the official leaders of Hungarian Jewry saw themselves in this light, carrying on the glorious tradition of Jewish Hungarian patriotism which went back to Kossuth and which was responsible, so they believed, for the great achievements and happy condition of Hungarian Jewry. In all this they closely resembled the official leaders of German Jewry, who also lost no opportunity to emphasize the patriotism of German Jewry and its loyalty to the state.

The Magyar patriotism of the Hungarian Jewish leadership had as one of its consequences the tendency not to call undue attention to the anti-Semitism of the new regime. In a discussion between an English Jewish leader and a Hungarian Jewish journalist attached to the Hungarian embassy in London—a certain Dr. Rácz—the latter remarked that "we patriotic Hungarian Jews do not like to discuss the question of anti-Semitism because we feel a little ashamed of ourselves and our people when we think that, after all we owe to Hungary, nearly all the leaders of the Bolshevist revolution should have been Jews."[57] Of course, representatives of the Neolog and the Orthodox communities spoke out against the white terror, but they also were quick to point out that there were some Jewish victims (twenty-seven were discovered) of the red terror as well.[58] Particularly interesting and revealing was their attitude toward the *numerus clausus* law of 1920. One might have expected them to denounce this effort to limit the number of Jewish students at Hungarian universities, as did the Hungarian social democrats and liberal opponents of the regime, but in fact there were no official protests. (Vázsonyi's remarks, quoted above, represented his own views, not those of the official Jewish leadership.) It was left to foreign Jewish organizations—the Foreign Committee of the British Jewish Board of Deputies, and the French Alliance Israélite—to protest to the League of Nations, and their actions were opposed, not supported, by the Hungarian Jewish leadership. Such opposition was based on the belief that outside interference could not help the cause of Hungarian Jewry and would only reinforce anti-Semitic views of the Jewish people as an international body allied with anti-Hungarian powers. Moreover, the intervention was based upon certain clauses in the Trianon treaty that promised equality to all groups within Hungarian society, a treaty which Jewish leaders rejected since it called for the dismemberment of the old Hungarian state. We therefore have the curious spectacle of British and French Jews pleading the cause of Hungarian Jewry at Geneva while Hungarian Jews insisted that they needed and wanted no such help. This situation was naturally exploited by the Hungarian representative to the League, who pointed out with evident delight that opposition to the 1920 law derived from "organizations entirely foreign to the Hungarian Jews—who have, in fact, not only disapproved the action of these organizations but solemnly protested their intrusion. . . ."[59] The Jewish leadership, closely wedded to the Horthy-Bethlen regime, evidently believed that it was best not to make a commotion over the law, which, so it believed, resulted from intense pressures from below and did not signify a real change in policy on the part of the ruling class. How different their behavior was from that of the Polish Jewish nationalists, who actively courted international intervention, Jewish and non-Jewish, on behalf of Polish Jewry and who fought tooth and nail against a Polish effort to institute the *numerus clausus* in 1923. No greater contrast can be imagined in the world of Jewish politics than that between a Grünbaum, for example, and the Neolog leadership of Budapest.

The behavior of the official Hungarian Jewish leadership was regarded with scorn by the Jewish nationalists of Eastern Europe. It has been characterized by modern historians as cowardly, and its practitioners have been accused of ignoring the interests of the Jewish masses.[60] It certainly did appear to deserve the derisive appellation *shtadlones*.[61] But we must be careful not to accept such accusations blindly. The leaders of Hungarian Jewry, whether Neolog or Orthodox, were certainly sincere Magyar patriots. They were also convinced that their only hope in the struggle against radical, racist anti-Semitism was to preserve at all costs their alliance with the regime. It was far better, they thought, to acquiesce in a *numerus clausus* in which (in their view) the leadership did not really believe and which at any rate would be only temporary than to endanger their good working relations with Horthy and his friends. By so doing they were obviously playing an extremely dangerous game, for it was by no means clear where the line should be drawn. How anti-Semitic would the government have to be in order to rouse the leadership into action? On the other hand, what was the alternative? Hungarian Jewish leaders did not believe in the efficacy of foreign intervention at the League of Nations, and they cannot be faulted for this. All minorities need allies, and in Hungary, which lacked a strong left and which possessed no strategically important national minorities, the only possible allies of the Jews who possessed some influence were precisely the moderate anti-Semites. True, they were responsible for the *numerus clausus* law, but they also played bridge with the Jewish oligarchy, despised the radical right, and believed that there were some "positive" elements within Hungarian Jewry. Thus the reaction of the Jewish leadership to the *numerus clausus* affair, which established an important pattern of behavior, to be repeated many times during the 1930s and 1940s, is perfectly understandable. It also highlighted the dilemma of the Jewish leadership in Hungary, to which there were obviously no easy answers.

Whether or not Jewish leaders in interwar Hungary were "cowards," their policies were not seriously challenged during the interwar years. If the masses were inadequately represented, they did not offer any alternative leadership. No nationalist opposition arose to oust the *shtadlonim*, as it did in Poland, Romania, and the Baltic States. No national Jewish party emerged, as it did in Czechoslovakia and Romania. Those Hungarian Jews who did not agree with the established leaders of the two communities, and there were plenty of them, did not vent their displeasure by joining the Zionist movement or by embracing any other form of Jewish nationalism. Rather, in the time-honored prewar tradition, they turned against the bourgeoisie and the reactionary ruling class, both gentile and Jewish, and went into Hungarian left-wing politics. Thus the war between fathers and sons in Hungary did not take the form, as it did in Poland, for example, of joining a pioneering youth movement or the Bund. Those who were disgusted by the official Jewish leadership did not offer an alternative Jewish leadership, but turned their backs entirely on Jewish affairs and plotted revolution. As we have noted, this was nothing new. Ever since the end of the nineteenth century, Jewish intellectuals, sons and daughters of the commercial and industrial bourgeoisie, had been castigating the reactionary behavior of Hungarian Jewry. Thus George Lukács (1885–1971), the famous Communist intellectual, has the following to say about his childhood:

> As is well known I came from a capitalist, *Lipótváros* family. [The Lipótváros is a district in Pest which was then fashionable among the town's richer merchants.] . . . From my childhood I was profoundly discontent with the *Lipótváros* way of life. Since my father, in the course of his business, was regularly in contact with the representatives of the city patriciate and of the bureaucratic gentry, my rejection tended to extend to them too. Thus at a very early age violently oppositional feelings ruled in me against the whole of official Hungary. . . .[62]

The loathing many young, sensitive Jews felt toward the Hungarian Jewish bourgeoisie was truly remarkable and led many to what can only be called a severe case of Jewish self-hatred. An excellent example of this was the radical sociologist Oszkár Jászi, a minister in the Károlyi government, who in his well-known writings denounced the Jews for aiding and abetting the oppression of the minority nationalities and for propping up the reactionary old regime. They were, in his view, "an unscrupulous instrument of feudal and financial class-domination" as well as "the loudest and most intolerant representatives of Magyar nationalism."[63] Many Jewish intellectuals held identical views throughout the interwar years. Even the great Jewish scholar Goldziher, who could scarcely be accused of self-hatred, was driven to despair by his dealings with the Jewish leadership of the Neolog community and by the Jewish "rabble" (*Pöbel*) who ran the yellow press and sat in the Budapest cafes.[64] But, again, this Jewish version of what was considered anti-Semitism when uttered by gentiles did not bring about a new Jewish leadership. In this area, as in so many others, Hungarian Jewry did not undergo anything like the revolutionary change experienced by other Jewries in East Central Europe during the war and in the immediate postwar period. Its cultural orientation and political policy remained, for better or for worse, what they had been.

If there were no autonomous Jewish politics, neither was there much autonomous secular Jewish culture, certainly not on the Polish model. Jewish education in Jewish languages was nonexistent, although there were a number of private Jewish schools.[65] There were many Jewish newspapermen, but no newspapers in Jewish languages. Jewish writers, scholars, and journalists, such as the celebrated playwright Ferenc Molnár, were extremely conspicuous in Hungarian cultural life, but regarded themselves first and foremost as Hungarians working in and contributing to the Hungarian cultural tradition. There can be no doubt that there was a special Jewish subculture in interwar Hungary, but its contribution to modern Jewish culture was certainly not striking. This acculturated community offered little scope for specifically Jewish activity to those among its children who no longer took any interest in religion or in preserving the status quo. The alternative Jewish identity afforded by secular Jewish nationalism was not available in Hungary. Someone like Jászi, a disaffected son of middle-class parents, might have become in Poland a Jewish socialist or a member of Ha-shomer ha-tsair; here, his most natural course was to become active in the Hungarian left. If one was not willing to take the position of Vázsonyi, that was the most obvious choice available.

### 6. The Beginning of the End: Hungarian-Jewish Relations in the 1930s

During the 1930s the radical Hungarian right, kept out of government by Bethlen and his allies in the 1920s, finally rose to power. That this happened was to some extent the fault of Bethlen and his allies, since during the 1920s the established regime, while persecuting the left and effectively banning it from political life (we should note here the contrast with the situation in Poland), was ambivalent toward the extreme right and even agreed with it in some ways, as in its demand for total revision of the postwar settlement. And its search for allies in its revisionist policy led the moderate right to establish friendly relations with fascist Italy, a country much admired by Hungary's extreme right wing. In the late 1920s and early 1930s, new factors combined to strengthen the extreme right. One of the signal achievements of Bethlen was the restoration of economic prosperity, but this broke down under the devastating impact of the Great Depression. Economic misery in the countryside grew worse, as did the lot of the too numerous university graduates with little hope of suitable employment. Meanwhile, the Nazis were growing ever stronger in Germany, and the extreme right in Hungary, losing interest in the Italian alliance, was ideologically inspired by Hitler and began to see in him the key to the revision of the Trianon settlement. In this connection we should note the dramatic and foreboding turnabout in the politics of Hungary's one-half-million-strong German (Swabian) minority. During the nineteenth century this community had undergone a process of magyarization not unlike that of the Jews, although as Christians they certainly found it easier to integrate into Hungarian society. During the 1920s their leaders maintained their traditional loyalty to Hungary and behaved much like the Jewish leaders. Their position changed in the 1930s, when, like the other *Volksdeutsch* communities of East Central Europe, the German Hungarians fell more and more under Nazi influence. They now began to "demagyarize" and reassert their "germanism," providing an interesting example of how a long process of denationalization may be arrested and even reversed. (Once again, there are suggestive Jewish parallels.) The Hungarian Germans, always more anti-Semitic than the Magyars were, played a particularly important role in military life, and the result was that the Hungarian army became a center of the radical right, of Nazi influence, and of fierce anti-Semitism.[66] We shall see that this army had a good deal to do with the tragic fate of Hungarian Jewry.

Thus more and more people fell under the sway of various organizations which preached extreme Hungarian chauvinisim, hatred both of capitalism (and Budapest, the center of modern Hungary) and Bolshevism, and admiration for European fascism. The undisputed leader of this camp during the 1920s was Gyula Gömbös, a military officer of partly German origin who had led the "men of Szeged" during the counterrevolution of 1919–1920 and who had, even in the 1920s, expressed his admiration for German National Socialism. In 1932 the regent of Hungary, Admiral Horthy, yielded to pressure from the right and appointed Gömbös to lead a new Hungarian government, thus putting an end to the rule of the moderates.

The advent of Gömbös appeared to be extremely dangerous for Hungarian Jewry. Here, for the first time in modern Hungarian history, was a prime minister who was an open racist, who stood for a "Christian Hungary," free of Jewish influence, and who in 1925 had helped organize an international anti-Semitic conference in Budapest. No sharper break could be imagined with that pro-Jewish tradition of Hungarian statesmen which extended from Kossuth to the last premier of Habsburg Hungary and which, at least to a certain degree, was carried on by Bethlen in the 1920s. The platform of the new government, published in 1932, spoke in traditional terms of the need to revise the Trianon settlement and to increase the "national strength" of Hungary, but it also included a more ominous clause which stated, "We desire to secure our own national civilization based on our own special racial peculiarities and upon Christian moral principles."[67] In 1933 Gömbös became the first prime minister of a foreign country to visit the recently elected Chancellor Adolf Hitler in Berlin, and close ties were established between the two leaders.[68] And during his term in office, which lasted until his death in 1936, Gömbös was a great proponent of a German alliance, which he supported both for ideological reasons and because he believed that only Germany had the strength and will to revise the postwar settlement. Moreover, he made clear his contempt for the political pluralism and personal liberty which had been part of the old Hungarian liberal system and which had been maintained by Bethlen. His government persecuted the insignificant left with new vigor, and, while it did not in fact succeed in transforming Hungary into a fascist, one-party state à la Italy and Germany, it did not conceal the fact that those were its political models.

All this augured badly for Hungarian Jewry. And yet, to everyone's surprise, Gömbös' reign did not appear to signal a radical departure with the past so far as the Jewish question was concerned. While this five-year period did contribute greatly to the eventual conversion of Hungary into an extreme right-wing state wedded to a Nazi alliance, it did not witness any concentrated effort to strike at the half-million Hungarian Jews. Indeed, upon taking power, Gömbös, the convinced anti-Semite, performed something of an ideological somersault. The new prime minister quickly came to an agreement with the leaders of the Neolog community in Budapest, and in return for Jewish support (presumably financial) he announced that he had "revised his ideas on the Jewish question."[69] Sounding precisely like Bethlen and Horthy, he now declared that "that part of Jewry which recognizes that it has a common fate with our nation, I wish to consider my brothers as much as my Hungarian brethren. I saw in the war Jewish heroes. I know Jews who have the golden medal and I know that they fought courageously."[70] Once again appeared that famous distinction between "good Hungarian Jews" and "bad Jews," although Gömbös indicated that even the "good Jews" were not quite "Hungarian." Nonetheless, Hungarian Jewry was able to take solace in these remarks. And Gömbös made no move to emulate the Nuremburg laws or even to revive the *numerus clausus*.

How is this remarkable turnabout to be explained? In the opinion of Gömbös' right-wing allies, he had sold out to the Jewish interests and had treacherously moved toward a Bethlen-like position. For others, his shift to the center was a statesmanlike reaction to his sudden and unexpected ascendancy to power.[71] Whatever the case, it is clear that Gömbös discovered that it was to his advantage to secure Jewish support. And just as Bethlen, during the 1920s, fought off his enemies on the right, now Gömbös, called by one historian a "conservative fascist," had to wage war not so much against the weak and demoralized left as against even more extreme rightist forces who now regarded him as a traitor to the movement.[72] By 1935 these ever-growing forces were chiefly organized in the Arrow Cross Party, led by Ferenc Szálasi, Hungary's most prominent "radical" fascist leader during the second decade of the interwar period. So far as the Jewish leadership was concerned, the devil they knew was far better than the devil they did not know, all the more so since Gömbös turned out to be not nearly so bad as they had feared. They now clung to him, as they had once clung to Bethlen.

But for those with eyes to see, by the mid-1930s it was clear that the tide was turning against the Jewish interest. The extreme right was there to stay, and, if Gömbös refrained from striking at the Jews, those who came after him did not. Personalities may have had something to do with this, but more important were the growing ties with Germany and the linkages established among the Nazi alliance, the hopes for revision, the strengthening of Hungarian fascism, and government anti-Semitism. It is true that these trends were offset to a certain extent by old Hungarian liberal traditions, which refused to die out altogether, along with an aversion in some circles to the alliance with Nazi Germany, considered by many to be, along with Austria, the hereditary enemy. Nonetheless, Hungarian-Jewish relations during the second half of the 1930s were shaped by the triumph of the extreme right and of the Nazi alliance. The alliance won back for Hungary much of its lost empire, at least temporarily, but it also led it into World War II and eventually into the Soviet orbit. As far as the Jews were concerned, it signaled the end of their legal emancipation and the beginning of their physical destruction.[73]

If 1932 is regarded by most Hungarian historians as the great turning point in interwar Hungarian politics, for Hungarian Jewry the crucial year was 1938. This, of course, was the year of the German takeover of Austria and of the first partition of Czechoslovakia. The latter event was of great significance for Hungary, since it returned to Hungary parts of Slovakia and Subcarpathian Rus. Here was proof that the Nazi alliance was strong enough to begin the righting of the terrible wrong of 1920. In this atmosphere of growing affection for the Nazi ally and of a surge of nationalism fed by the prospects of revising the Trianon settlement, along with rising fears within the government due to the rapid growth of the Arrow Cross Party, pressure mounted to "solve" the Jewish question. The pressure came not only from within Hungary but from Germany as well, since the

Nazis strongly urged their Hungarian friends to emulate their Jewish policy. In May, 1938, even before the return of parts of Slovakia, the pro-German prime minister, Kálmán Darányi, enacted the so-called first Jewish law, the first such law to be passed in East Central Europe. The major provisions of the law were summed up by an official Hungarian publication as follows:

> Industrial and commercial undertakings and banking houses employing more than ten persons are given five, or in certain cases ten, years in which to adjust the proportion of employees and of salaries, bonuses, and so on, to conform with the general rule that does not allow the Jewish share under any of these headings to exceed twenty percent of the total. In chambers of industry and commerce and in the legal, medical, and engineering professions, new Jewish members will be admitted at the rate of only five percent, until the Jewish proportion is reduced to the limit of twenty percent. New chambers in journalism and in the entertainment industry will be set up by the end of the year, and the twenty percent *numerus clausus* will come into force at once.[74]

Jews who had converted to Christianity prior to August, 1919 were exempt from these draconian measures (but those who had participated in the rather large wave of conversions following the fall of Béla Kun and during the white terror were not). Exempt too were Jews who had fought at the front during World War I, as well as the widows and children of Jews killed in the war.

Government spokesmen justified this law on three grounds. First, the high percentage of Jews in commercial, industrial, and professional life was obviously "abnormal" and could not be allowed to continue forever, certainly not when thousands of Christian Hungarians were starving. Second, the growing strength of Nazi Germany had caused great panic among the Jews, who were under the impression that they would be subjected to the same kind of anti-Jewish terror prevalent in the Reich; therefore, "it was necessary to reassure the Jews by laying down the limit of the restrictions which the Government was prepared to approve as just and equitable."[75] In other words, the state had done the Jews a favor. Finally, it was claimed that the great majority of Jews had not really become proper Magyars, that they had not really assimilated, despite a superficial process of acculturation. Thus they were not worthy of equal treatment before the law. All these claims were rejected by the Jewish leadership, which, now, in contrast with its reactions during the 1920s, registered a strong public protest. The Union of Hungarian Jews pointed out that the law "creates a distinction between Hungarian citizens of the Jewish and of other faiths [and] is a gross offense against the principle of equality of rights." It was, in fact, a violation of the noble tradition of

Hungarian tolerance, embraced by the great Hungarian statesmen and revolutionaries of the nineteenth century—by Kossuth, Deák, and Eötvös. The Jewish leadership declared, logically enough but rather naively, that

> since no field of occupation was closed to Hungarian Jews, no one has the right to accuse them of having taken up too great a number of positions in economic life—particularly in fields from which, according to the motivation of the Bill, citizens professing other religions have kept away. No one can deny that without the activity of Hungarian Jews, the most important areas of industry, commerce, and credit in Hungary would not have been cultivated to their needed extent. Neither has anyone the right to reproach the Jews of Hungary for having participated in every field of intellectual endeavor to the best of their ability, and for faithfully serving the country's interest, the people's welfare and national culture in this as in other spheres of endeavor.[76]

Having established the obvious unfairness and un-Hungarian character of the law, the Jewish organization went on, in time-honored fashion, to denounce the view that the Jewish population was not fully assimilated and did not identify itself wholeheartedly with the Hungarian cause:

> We protest against making our Jewish faith appear as if adherence to it is opposed to the faithful observance of the nation's historical traditions and as if these traditions do not represent the same values for Hungarians of Jewish faith as they do for other Hungarians. We protest against the pretense that the adherence to the Jewish faith could in any way influence assimilation to the Hungarian spirit. And we particularly protest against terming the abandonment of the Jewish faith as assimilation to the Hungarian spirit, and thus terming loyalty to religion as incompatible with loyalty to the nation. This declaration of reasons for the Bill is a condemnation of the Jewish religion before the forum of the nation. It is an insult to the most sacred patriotic feelings of more than four hundred thousand Hungarian citizens of the Jewish faith.
>
> We maintain and declare that we are and will remain faithful Jews by religion, faithful Hungarians by sentiment. We suffer from the doom of Trianon equally with all our compatriots. Our efforts are directed towards the realization of the great aims of the nation. We will share in the newly initiated work of saving the nation with the same utmost effort and faculty for sacrifice that we have demonstrated in the past, fighting against every attempt at disturbance from whatever quarter it may come. The spirit of Rákóczi, Kossuth, Vörösmarty, Petöfi, Jókai, and Arany stand before us as our national ideals.[77]

Such ringing declarations show that even the cautious and conservative Jewish leadership would not remain silent in the face of such an obvious attempt to make the Jews into second-class citizens, although they also demonstrate that its Hungarian superpatriotism remained firm. Moreover, now as in 1920, the Jewish leaders rejected the idea of foreign intervention on behalf of Hungarian Jewry and were even prepared, at least in private, "to accept a tolerable level of anti-Jewish measures."[78] In return for not attempting to rally world and Jewish opinion against the law, they hoped that the government would do its best to subdue the extreme right.

The first Jewish law was debated in parliament, where members opposed to the government, few and ineffectual as they were, were allowed to voice their opposition. One common theme in this opposition, one which was likely to strike a responsive chord among many Hungarians, was that the new law was "made in Germany," that is, drafted with an eye toward appeasing the Nazis.[79] Another theme was the unequal treatment meted out to Jews and to the Swabian Germans, Hungary's only national minority. Why, asked the socialist deputy Peyer, were the Jews told that their failure to assimilate had cost them their equal status while the German Hungarians (whose cause was dear to the hearts of the Nazi government and who were disliked by many Hungarian nationalists) were allowed to remain loyal to their ethnic heritage?[80] Finally, there was opposition on moral grounds. The law, some deputies thought, was obviously contrary to that Hungarian tradition which had consistently opposed racism and whose only criterion for legal equality was loyalty to the Hungarian state. These arguments had no effect on the government, of course, and it is interesting that the law was defended by such representatives of the old ruling class as Pál Teleki, whose views on the Jewish question are quoted above. Writing in early 1939 to an English acquaintance, Teleki had the following to say:

> It was in 1919 or 1920 when I told some Jewish leaders of our public life: "You are Jews and you are Magyars. There is a conflict between the Christian Magyars and between the Oriental [i.e., East European] Jews who came in great masses to our country in the last half-century, and the continual infiltration of which did not stop and does not stop. You have to choose your place in this conflict because it is an earnest conflict, it is a problem of life and death for the Hungarian people. You must choose between your Magyar compatriots and between your Oriental co-religionists." Unhappily the greatest part of Hungarian Jews chose the latter. They help the Oriental Jew with money, by way of adoption and by giving them work, to come into the land, to get here a footing, to stay and fight his life [sic] in competition with the autochthonus Christian people.[81]

Such were the views also of Horthy and other pillars of the establishment. The Catholic church, less active in the anti-Semitic campaign here than in

Poland, and fearful lest the anti-Jewish hysteria strike at Christians of Jewish origin, nonetheless also supported the 1938 law.[82]

The first Jewish law was not one-hundred-percent racist in character. It did, after all, exempt some Jews and also recognized pre-1919 converts as Hungarians. Teleki, Horthy, and their allies maintained the old tradition of allowing for the existence of "Magyar Jews." Moreover, these "moderates" insisted that the first Jewish law, even if it was not justified on moral grounds and even if it violated the spirit of Hungarian history and the Hungarian constitution, was a reasonable way out of a situation in which external and internal pressures combined to make some sort of action necessary. Thus Teleki informed his disapproving English correspondent that "I have probably more connections with most different circles of people than many parliamentary politicians. And I know quite well how public opinion wishes a very radical solution of the Jewish problem." Failure to act might provide "the opportunity to any neighbor and especially the big one [Germany] to interfere."[83] And besides, it was argued that the law was not very harmful to the Jews, since it was to be implemented over a long period of time and since Hungarians were at any rate not nearly so efficient as Germans.

Such arguments, first trotted out during the *numerus clausus* affair of the 1920s, continued the old pattern of behavior according to which "moderate" Hungarian politicians argued for the acceptance of "moderate" anti-Semitic measures as an alternative to the great danger of a revolt from below (that is, a takeover by the Arrow Cross Party) which would finish off the Jews (and the old elite) altogether.[84] It is by no means clear to what extent the views of Horthy and Teleki were shaped by expediency—the need to buy off the extreme right and the Nazis—and to what extent they reflected a growing acceptance of Nazi racism. Whatever the truth of the matter, one thing was clear: the Hungarian ruling class did not hesitate to strike cruelly at its erstwhile Jewish allies, much preferring such action to social reform and knowing full well that the Jews, lacking any other allies, would continue to support it in preference to the still worse alternative. From the Jewish point of view, as we have already noted, this was a very dangerous game, since the stakes were constantly rising. One might live with a *numerus clausus* not strictly enforced, but could one live with the law of 1938? And would this be the last Jewish law?

It turned out that this was not the end, but rather the beginning. During 1938–1939 the links with the Nazis grew stronger (and bore fruit in the return, in 1939, of the rest of Subcarpathian Rus to Hungary) and so did the Arrow Cross Party. The need to steal the thunder of the extreme right in order to maintain the power of the "moderates" was now even greater. In late 1938 the government of Béla Imrédy initiated a "second Jewish law," and after Imrédy's fall (in ironic circumstances, described below) the measure was passed by the new prime minister, Pál Teleki, whose strong anti-Nazi and anti–Arrow Cross views did not prevent him from steering it through parliament. The new law, which took effect in May, 1939, was far more severe than its predecessor. Its definition of a Jew was still not entirely racial; children of Jewish parents both of whom had converted were not regarded as Jews, although children one of whose parents was a nonconverted Jew were, and exemptions were still granted to Jewish war veterans who had won medals and to invalids. Champions of Olympic games" of Jewish origin were also exempted. But the *numerus clausus* was made more restrictive, and a host of other limitations were introduced. The following is a contemporary summary of the regulations:

> The Law limits the Jews to 6 percent of the membership of the Chambers of the liberal and academic professions; restricts the participation of the Jews in public contracts to 20 percent, and from 1943 to 6 percent; forbids them to occupy any controlling, managerial, or influential position in newspaper offices, theatres, cinemas, or film studios; utterly excludes them from the Civil and Municipal services, and from the staff of social insurance organizations and all public institutions, as well as from the vocations of notary and sworn interpreter. It requires that all Jewish professors and teachers in colleges and higher grade schools, and all Jewish district notaries shall be retired by January 1st, 1943, and all Jewish public prosecutors by January 1st, 1940, with compensation. Jewish students at Universities and higher grade schools are to be limited to 6 percent. All licenses held by Jews for the sale of State monopoly articles must be withdrawn within five years and not renewed, and trade licenses issued to Jews must be limited to 6 percent of the total held in the local community. Jews have no right to buy or sell land, except by permission, and they can be compelled at any time to sell or lease their agricultural property on terms fixed by the authorities—a provision that amounts to forcible expropriation. In industrial concerns, mines, banks, money exchanges, and insurance companies Jews must be limited to 12 percent; they can be dismissed at any time on short notice, and their compensation or pension depends upon the generosity of the employer.[85]

As was the case with the first Jewish law, there was opposition to this law—and this time not only from the handful of left-wing and Jewish deputies in the parliament. In January, 1939, the former premier Bethlen and other distinguished Hungarians voiced their opposition in a letter to the regent, Horthy. To be sure, Bethlen did not take a pro-Jewish position. He too believed that the Jewish question (along with the question of land reform) had to be solved immediately:

If these two problems remain unsolved before elections are called, any internal or external revolutionizing tendency will attempt by way of these problems to deflect our nation—a nation small, and therefore hardly able to accept great risks and loads—from the lawful path of historical development, and divert it to the path of unforeseeable revolutionary risks. If these two problems are not settled, the agitation of the Arrow Cross men will roll over the four thousand communities of our country, in an unprecedented manner, and it is beyond doubt that they will dispose of abundant financial means from foreign sources.[86]

"The essence of the Jewish problem," Bethlen continued, "is that there are too many of them and their influence is too great." But the proposals of the Imrédy government would not provide the cure, according to Bethlen, since they created panic among the Jewish population and threatened to destroy the Hungarian economy. The former ruler of Hungary therefore attacked the second Jewish law, not on moral grounds and not even on the grounds that it was "made in Germany," but on the same pragmatic grounds which were responsible for Gömbös' moderate position during his tenure as prime minister:

Within the country the Government are about to turn close to one million [sic] intelligent Jews over to an internal element hostile to the Hungarian nation [apparently Communism] and capable of doing anything. The growth of strength which the reannexation of the Highlands [Slovakia] means might be completely offset by a faulty settlement of the Swabian and Jewish problems, moreover such a settlement might call into jeopardy our position as a nation in every respect. For the future development of our foreign trade and our finances the settlement of the Jewish problem might be of decisive importance, and it may perhaps suffice to mention that on the day of the march into Kassa [a Slovakian city, in November, 1938] the pengö was quoted at about 70 centimes in Zurich, while during the past week it was already around 35 centimes. The revolutionizing policy of the Government, and the Jewish Bill drafted for purposes of propaganda have reaped their first fruit: throughout the country enterprise has come to a standstill, and normal business life is on the decline. The expanded employment of the armament industry may for a short time cover up the decay, yet the catastrophe will come to pass as soon as the extraordinary requirements of the army will be covered. The level of government revenue is sinking, the budgetary equilibrium has been upset, and panic among the Jews and the liquidation of Jewish business turns tens and hundreds of thousands of Christians into unemployed. The present Jewish Bill does not serve Hungarian interests, but aims at satisfying base passions with the intent to prop up the position of a weak government in the eyes of irresponsible elements, irrespective of how much this success costs the country.[87]

Here is the authentic voice of the old Hungarian seigneur, fearful of the masses, afraid of German expansionism, and conscious of the vital (and even beneficial) role played by the Jews in the economy. Horthy also was unhappy with Imrédy's policy and complained that the latter had tabled the law "without my previous consent."[88] But while the existence of these and other critical voices demonstrates that Hungary in 1939 was not Nazi Germany, the fact that Teleki agreed to see the second Jewish law through parliament demonstrates to what extent the old ruling class had become the captive, whether willingly or not, and for whatever reason, of the radical anti-Semitism of the extreme right. The passage of the two laws also demonstrates the extent to which Hungarian politics had become obsessed with the Jewish question by the late 1930s, an obsession resulting from economic distress, the triumph of Hungarian chauvinism, the great prestige and influence of Nazi Germany, and the government's fears of the ever-growing fascist movement. One of the victims of this obsession was the highly anti-Semitic prime minister Béla Imrédy, author of the second Jewish law, who was forced to resign from office when his enemies (among them Horthy) published documents showing that he possessed a Jewish great-grandfather.[89] The victims of the anti-Jewish hysteria were therefore not confined to the Jewish population alone. But this was small comfort to a Jewish community now augmented by the annexation of thousands of coreligionists from Slovakia and Subcarpathian Rus.

What was the impact of the first two Jewish laws on Hungarian Jewry? In the view of some it was very limited. The new regulations were enforced in the "Hungarian way," that is, inefficiently, and not as in Nazi Germany. Macartney remarks that "the business went on as before, all the real work being done by the Jews, while the requisite changes in the proportions of Jewish and non-Jewish employees, etc., were effected by simply taking on extra non-Jewish employees, many of whom did little more than draw their salaries."[90] The efficient Germans looked on with contempt, believing that the anti-Jewish legislation was merely for show and not really intended to harm the Jewish interest.[91] And, of course, the local Hungarian fascists agreed with their Nazi allies. The truth seems to be that the first two laws left the Jewish financial and industrial elite untouched, but did strike fairly hard at the middle and lower middle class and at the professionals. Thousands were discharged and reduced to poverty. In some small towns (where one-half of all Hungarian Jews resided) Jewish landowners' property was confiscated, the few Jewish civil servants were dismissed, and Jewish artisans lost their licenses, but in others the laws were simply not enforced.[92] Much depended upon the attitude of the local authorities. But it is clear that the laws signaled a new and dangerous deterioration of relations between Jews and gentiles, since they legitimized anti-Semitic attitudes in a way in which even the white terror had not and made the Jews fair game for job hunters. The "aryanization" of the Hungarian economy might have been bad for the status of the currency, as Bethlen pointed out, but it gave thousands of Hungarians a stake in the new anti-Semitic "system," as well as official sanction to the baser instincts of the Hungarian population.

In one sector of Hungarian life, the military, the situation became particularly ominous in 1939. According to the second Jewish law, Jews were no longer allowed to serve as officers, but the question as to whether they were worthy of serving at all alongside Christian Hungarians remained open. In May, 1939, some progress was made toward solving this issue by founding several special "labor battalions." These battalions were at first not earmarked for Jews alone, but in subsequent years Jews were deprived of the right to bear arms and were drafted exclusively into such formations. The results, as we shall see, were disastrous.[93]

The impact upon the Jews of the laws of 1938–1939 was not limited to economics. The leadership, as we have noted, was no longer content to remain silent, but on the other hand it did not offer new guidelines to the Jewish community. It held fast to its traditional line—the reiteration of Jewish-Magyar patriotism, denunciation of any effort to separate Hungarians of the Mosaic faith from other Hungarians, and a willingness (now born out of desperation) to go along with any regime so long as it was not a regime of the Arrow Cross.[94] Samu Stern, President of the Jewish community of Pest, spoke for assimilationist Hungarian Jewry when he wrote, in 1938:

> It is easy to love the homeland when . . . the homeland offers glory and happiness to those who love it; but the homeland must be loved even when it does not bestow upon us the totality of its love. God must be worshipped even when he reduces us to dust . . . we worship him whether he rewards or punishes us. We worship him even when he appears to turn his love away from us and we worship our earthly God, our homeland, whatever our fate may be in this homeland.[95]

But for many Jews this position was no longer satisfactory. Ever since the mid-1930s the idea of emigration had been growing more popular, and, although emigration could never become a mass movement (since there was nowhere for the masses to go), some left, including Jewry's most famous writer, Ferenc Molnár.[96] Another response to the Jewish laws was a new wave of conversions, more significant than that of 1919–1920. During 1938–39 over 14,000 Jews converted, a number unparalleled anywhere else in Eastern Europe—even though conversion, as we know, did not exempt Jews from the various disabilities imposed upon them.[97] Finally, during the years 1939–1944 Jewish nationalism finally came to play a role in Hungarian Jewish life. That it did so was the result not so much of an emerging Jewish nationalism among the Jews of Trianon Hungary, but rather of the return to Hungary of Slovakian, Subcarpathian, and (in 1940) large numbers of Transylvanian Jews. The Jewries of these three regained or partially regained provinces were much more nationalist- and Zionist-inclined than Trianon Jewry, and their national leaders, some of whom moved to Budapest, established a new Jewish leadership which, if it did not supplant the traditional one, at least offered an alternative. Zionist youth movements sprang up as well. Another indication of the new mood among some Hungarian Jews was the rather dramatic rise in the number of students attending the rabbinical seminary in Budapest.[98] None of this indicates any change in the basically acculturated and anti-nationalist nature of Hungarian Jewry, but the virulent anti-Semitism of the late 1930s and early 1940s did induce some Jews to convert to Zionism, just as it induced others to convert to Christianity. Neither phenomenon, however, was to save Hungarian Jewry.

## 7. The War Years

In strict adherence to the scope of this book, our survey of Jewish history in interwar Hungary should end with the second Jewish law of 1939. However, because Hungary retained its national sovereignty until 1944, a brief description of the fate of Hungarian Jewry during the first six years of World War II is in order. This period was a truly remarkable one, since, despite the outbreak of war and Hungary's entry into it as a loyal ally of Nazi Germany, the traditional tug-of-war over the Jewish question continued with no real resolution. As in the late 1930s, the German Nazis pressured Hungary to solve the Jewish question along German lines, as did the local fascists, while the Hungarian regime, now much more in German thrall than before the war, continued to pass anti-Semitic laws while to some extent resisting Nazi pressure. The great symbol of the preservation of traditional Hungarian policy even in the new wartime environment was Horthy, the old Habsburg admiral, still regent of Hungary and still a force in political life. In the course of his efforts to preserve Hungarian sovereignty, he continued to differentiate between "good" Hungarian Jews and "bad," while at the same time acquiescing in the ever-harsher treatment meted out to all the Jews. This approach meant, among other things, solving the Jewish question in the "Hungarian way"; as late as July, 1944, Horthy wrote to Hitler that he preferred to solve the Jewish question without having recourse to "brutal and inhumane methods."[99] New anti-Jewish legislation was enacted in 1941, this time prohibiting intermarriage between Jews (defined in this context as a person with one Jewish grandparent) and gentiles. In 1942 the status of the Jewish region was reduced from that of an "established cult" to that of a "recognized" one.[100] Hungarian officials continued to argue, however, as had Bethlen in 1939, that it was simply impossible on practical grounds to do what the Germans had done. In 1943 the Hungarian Foreign Office prepared a memorandum for use during discussions between Germany and Hungary. While pointing out that Jews were by now virtually excluded from the professions and intellectual life, the memorandum noted that the Jews were proportionately far more numerous in Hungary than in Germany and played a much greater role in economic life. It followed that they could not be excluded from the Hungarian economy without dreadful consequences which would serve neither Hungarian nor German interests.[101] In 1942 Horthy managed to assure the appointment of Miklós Kállay as prime minister, a man whose views were similar to those of Bethlen in that he disliked both the Nazis and the Hungarian fascists. Under this last "liberal" Hungarian premier yet another act in the already familiar Hungarian-Jewish drama was played out, according to the by now well-established rules. Like his predecessors, and under much greater foreign pressure than either Darányi (the premier at the time of the first Jewish law), Imrédy, or Teleki, Kállay announced in parliament that "the restriction of the Jew in the economic field is a basic condition for the economic progress of the Hungarian people, at which none can take offense." He then proceeded to initiate more anti-Jewish legislation (this time confiscating Jewish-owned estates) while at the same time making no secret of his anti-Nazi views and urging Jews to "understand" his actions in light of the terrible situation of wartime Hungary. As he put it, in what was fast becoming a truly classical style,

> . . . my introduction and commendation of the Expropriation bill was— for all the injustice of it, like any discriminatory action or any interference with individual liberty perpetrated—a successful move on my part. I had to gain time, I had to provide a safety valve for the overstrained anti-Semitic feeling in the country and to divert it from the racialist line and from the threatening possibility of individual action. I therefore chose a solution which—as will be seen later—was never finally followed up and could have been partly or wholly undone after the war or at least equalized with similar measures applied to non-Jewish land.[102]

How similar this sounds to official apologies for the *numerus clausus* law of 1920. And now, as then, the wealthy pillars of the Jewish community continued to look to "moderates" like Kállay and Horthy for aid and comfort, pleading yet again the cause of Hungarian-Jewish partnership in the face of the Nazi–Arrow Cross onslaught. As always, they had nowhere else to turn.

We may be skeptical about how moderate Horthy and his allies were during the war years, and we have observed how such "moderation" had led to severe anti-Jewish legislation. Nonetheless, it is a fact that so long as Hungary remained sovereign and under the control of such men, Hungarian Jewry was far better off than were the Jewries of Nazi-occupied East Central and Eastern (Soviet) Europe. True, Hungarian Jews were humiliated and impoverished. With Hungary's entry into the war, Jews were drafted into labor battalions and sent, unarmed, mostly to the eastern front, where they were brutally treated and died in great numbers.[103] Others were employed in slave labor in Yugoslavia, where their fate was no happier. In 1941 thousands of Jewish refugees were forcibly "repatriated" to Poland, where most were murdered by the Nazis, and in 1942 thousands of Jews and Serbs were butchered by Hungarian forces in the region of Újvidék (Nori Sad), formerly part of Yugoslavia. But up until 1944 the "final solution" had not yet been attempted, despite intense Nazi pressure. However, after the occupation of Hungary by German troops in March, 1944, the Nazis, aided by Hungarian collaborators, began the process of ghettoization and deportation organized by Adolph Eichmann. Between May 5 and June 7 of that year close to 300,000 Hungarian Jews were sent to death camps. Horthy, who still retained some power despite the German occupation, was able to prevent the deportation of Budapest Jewry. (This was his last service to the Jews of the capital, the "real" Hungarian Jews whom he and his friends consistently distinguished from the "Galician" Jews of the hinterland.) In October, 1944, the Nazis engineered a coup which placed Szálasi and his Arrow Cross Party in control of the country, and, in the few months which remained before the liberation of Hungary by the Soviet Union, pogroms and death marches took their toll of the Jews of Budapest as well.[104] Horthy, arrested by the Germans and then taken into custody by the Allies, eventually made his way to the West, where he received financial support from some of his millionaire friends of Jewish origin—the final act of the ancient alliance between the Jewish elite and the Hungarian ruling class. At the time of the Soviet conquest of Budapest, over half of the capital's Jewish community remained alive. The Jewish communities of the provinces had been almost entirely wiped out.[105]

## 8. Some Final Thoughts

The peculiar relationship between Jews and Magyars in Trianon Hungary was based to a large extent upon illusions. The spokesmen of the Jewish community believed that their community's long history of loyal service to the Hungarian cause and to the ruling class would ensure its continued prosperity. How pathetic were the words of the son of Vilmos

Vázsonyi, a deputy in parliament, who stated during the debate on the first Jewish law, "When the fatherland calls again, then Hungarian Jewry will find itself at the front."[106] Its Jewish sons did, in fact, find themselves at the front during World War II, but in humiliating labor battalions, without the right to bear arms, persecuted by anti-Semitic officers and contributing to the Nazi cause in Russia. Jews were sent to these battalions and removed from the Hungarian economy with the express consent of that same ruling class which was supposed to be opposed to anti-Semitism. In the end it became apparent to all that the Telekis, Horthys, and Kállays, moderates though they might be in comparison with the men of the Arrow Cross, and opposed as they might be to brutal Nazi measures, were willing to sacrifice Hungarian Jewry—not only the so-called Galicians but all Hungarian Jews—to the exigencies of the German alliance and to the need to buy off the radical right by passing anti-Jewish laws.

For their part, at least some of the moderate Hungarian leaders cherished the illusion that they could play the Jewish game according to their rules—that they could pass anti-Jewish laws while making clear their aversion to racism and, at a given point, put a halt to the deterioration in the Jews' status and in Hungarian-Jewish relations. This was part of a larger illusion that Hungary could regain its empire, accept the Nazis' embrace, and yet retain its freedom of action. The high price for this belief was paid not only by Hungarian Jewry but by all Hungarians.

There were, of course, good reasons for the behavior both of Hungarian Jews and of the Hungarian leadership. The former were wedded to a ruling class which was obviously not adhering to its liberal traditions. Horthy, moreover, was no Masaryk, and the fact that he and his allies were capable of condoning the Jewish laws demonstrates the essential difference between Czech and Hungarian liberalism. In the Czech case liberalism meant a commitment to political democracy and a firm rejection of religious discrimination. In the Hungarian case, in the new interwar environment, it did not. But the Jews could not turn, as they could in Poland, to possible allies on the moderate left or among the nation's minorities, and we have seen how the history and nature of Hungarian Jewry precluded the possibility of the rise of Jewish nationalism as a rallying point. The marriage between Jewry and the traditional Hungarian ruling class may have been based on an illusion, but there were no other possible partners. And there was therefore no likelihood that the Jews would seek a divorce.

As for the Hungarian leaders, they too could claim that, given the obsession with revision, there was no choice but to act as they did. And they could also claim that, while they bent in response to Nazi and Arrow Cross pressure, they preserved the physical safety of Hungarian Jewry until the German occupation and even, to a degree, until October, 1944. If Horthy was no Masaryk, neither was he a Hitler. He and his circle may have betrayed the traditional pro-Jewish views of the Magyar ruling class, but they preserved at least some elements of that tradition until the very end.

In the final analysis it was a truly disastrous and unexpected set of circumstances which combined to doom Hungarian Jewry. There were, as we know, observers who had predicted before World War I that the Hungarian-Jewish honeymoon would not endure, but few would have predicted so rapid a disappearance of all those factors which had made Hungary a promised land for its Jewish population. For this particular type of Jewish community, the interwar period was an especially cruel tragedy. Having so enthusiastically magyarized and having embraced the ideology of "Hungarians of the Mosaic faith," although never really succeeding in integrating into Hungarian society, these Jews were less prepared for the blows which fell upon them and less capable of defending themselves than were the nationalist-minded Jewries of the Eastern type. Their fate is proof of the fact that what the Jews did and how they behaved had little impact on what happened to them. The bulk of Hungarian Jewry remained, during the years 1918–1944, as it had been during the last half of the nineteenth century. With the exception of a vocal but small radical left faction, attracted to Hungarian socialism or Communism, its ideology did not change. It was not more prominent in the economy of 1935 than it had been in 1910, and no less patriotic. The utterly different treatment it received was a function of the collapse of the old Hungarian empire destroyed by the first World War.

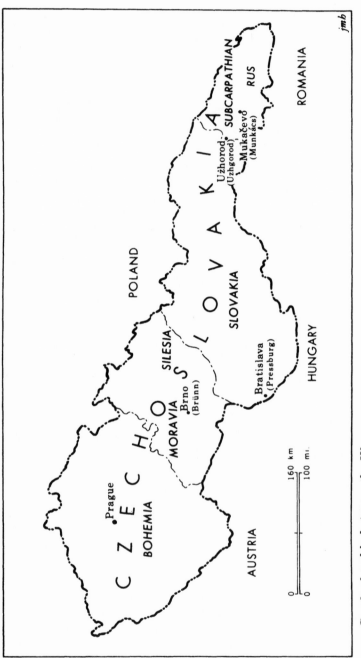

**Czechoslovakia between the Wars**

# CZECHOSLOVAKIA / 3

Czechoslovakia is justly regarded as the great exception in interwar East Central Europe. Within its frontiers lay the highly industrialized and wealthy regions of Bohemia, Moravia, and part of Silesia (together called the "Czech lands"). The Czechs, alone among the Slavic peoples, had by World War I developed a solid bourgeoisie. Their politics, the product of the Habsburg empire, were marked by a considerable degree of moderation, liberalism, and democracy. Unlike the Poles, they lacked a native aristocracy. Moreover, many of their leaders tended to be anticlerical, regarding the Catholic church, along with the German landowners, as symbols of Austrian-German oppression. Here again the contrast with neighboring Poland is striking. The Czech national movement was able to develop freely during the last decades of the Habsburg empire, and, while the struggle against Austrian-German control was fierce enough, Czech nationalism was more pragmatic and moderate than was its Polish counterpart. Its most renowned leader, Thomas Masaryk, was the very model of the Western-oriented, liberal, and moderate nationalist, quite unusual in the East European context. Unlike Poland, Hungary, and Romania, the state over which he presided remained a liberal democracy until the very end of the 1930s.

But this is not the whole story. Czechoslovakia consisted not only of highly developed Bohemia and Moravia, but also of much less developed Slovakia and of Subcarpathian Rus, one of the most backward regions in all Europe, which became part of interwar Czechoslovakia because, among other reasons, no one else was interested in its acquisition. Czechoslovakia may have been something of a democratic outpost in an area of authoritarian regimes, but it faced a nationalities problem of great difficulty. It was also a brand new state whose borders were under constant pressure from irredentist attacks emanating chiefly from Germany and Hungary. In these ways Czechoslovakia was a typical East European state.

All of the regions which constituted the Republic of Czechoslovakia were part of the prewar Habsburg empire, but while the Czech lands had been in the Austrian half, Slovakia and Subcarpathian Rus had been Hungarian provinces. The distinction is crucial in all respects. The former Hungarian lands were economically more backward and were characterized by a dominant Magyar or magyarized aristocracy, an impoverished peasantry, and the absence of a strong native middle class. The political system had been more autocratic than that of the former Austrian lands, and the non-Magyar nationalities—Slovaks and Rusyns[1] —had been subjected to relentless pressure to adopt Hungarian culture. Some Slovaks and Rusyns had, in fact, magyarized but others had resisted, mounting their own national movements which were by definition anti-Hungarian. In both Slovakia and Subcarpathian Rus the church played a great role in local life—Roman Catholic in the former region, Uniate and Orthodox in the latter. The Slovaks, and even more so the Rusyns, were peasant peoples whose sense of national identity was weaker than that of the Czechs. In the case of the Rusyns, there was no consensus as to whether they represented a separate people, a part of the Ukrainian nation, or a part of the Russian nation. The Slovaks possessed a stronger sense of nationhood, which developed as a reaction to Magyar onslaughts, but they too were not certain whether a similar language and culture bound them to the Czechs or whether their unique history justified the establishment of a separate Slovak state. Culturally, economically, and politically less developed than the Czechs, the Slovaks and Rusyns during the interwar period were spared one major problem which had such fatal consequences in Bohemia and Moravia, namely, the presence of a large (some three million strong) German minority in what came to be called the Sudetenland. By comparison, the Magyar minorities remaining in Slovakia and Subcarpathian Rus after the dismemberment of prewar Hungary were small and much less troublesome.[2]

The enemies of interwar Czechoslovakia, and they were numerous, referred to it as an "artificial" entity, with no historical justification for existence. It is true that there had never been such a state, and it is equally true that internal national divisions—above all between Germans and Czechs and between Slovaks and Czechs—hastened its collapse in 1938–1939. But it is no less the case that the achievements of this stable, prosperous, and democratic state in the 1920s and 1930s were remarkable, and they included improving the quality of life in the eastern, non-Czech regions of the country. One thing is certain: from a Jewish point of view Czechoslovakia provided by far the most favorable environment in Eastern Europe.

## 1. The Historical Context

There were three separate and very different Jewries in interwar Czechoslovakia—the Jewry of the Czech lands (Moravia, Bohemia, and Silesia), the Jewry of Subcarpathian Rus, and Slovakian Jewry. The first was the best example in East Central Europe of a West European-type Jewish community, the second was a typical East European-type Jewry, and the third was something of an intermediary case. The historical development of Bohemian and Moravian Jewry was quite similar to that of the Jewries of the various states which eventually became part of unified Germany. Final emancipation was achieved in 1867, at which time all Jewish subjects of the Habsburg empire became equal citizens. By then the Jews of the Czech lands, like the Jews of the German and Austrian lands, had already undergone a rapid process of acculturation, urbanization, and embourgeoisement, somewhat more pronounced in Bohemia than in more rural Moravia. They had mostly stopped speaking Yiddish and had abandoned Orthodoxy in favor of Reform Judaism, or no Judaism at all. These were the fruits of the Haskalah (Jewish Enlightenment) movement, strong here as it was in Germany and lacking, in contrast with the Russian and the Galician Haskalah, a Hebraic national component. As for their new cultural orientation, we must note an important difference between the situation in Bohemia and Moravia and that in Germany, Austria, and what was to become Trianon Hungary. In contrast to the monocultural character of the latter regions, the former were bicultural, and the Jews were obliged to choose between German and Czech. To be caught between two competing cultures is always a dangerous situation for a minority, and we have already had opportunity to observe how much the Jews suffered as a result of being identified by one nationality as allied with the other. In this case, their choice (if we can call it that) often was German. German, after all, was the high culture of the region during most of the nineteenth century, as well as being the official language of the dynasty which promoted the German orientation and to which the Jews owed loyalty. Czech was regarded by many as the language of a peasant, lower-class culture, the language of the village rather than of the city. And as more and more Jews left the village for the city, they became more and more a part of German urban culture. This is not to say that many did not know Czech. But, even if they spoke Czech with their neighbors, they tended to send their children to German schools and often proved willing instruments of the germanizing campaign of the central government.[3]

The bicultural aspect of the Czech lands, and the increasingly fierce struggle between Germans and Czechs for supremacy, had at least two important implications for the Jews. The Jewish predilection for German, naturally resented by the Czechs, was used by nationalist Czech politicians as justification for anti-Semitism. On the other hand, the fact that there were competing secular cultures here—as in East Galicia, Transylvania, and Lithuania—had a retarding effect upon Jewish efforts at assimilation, if not acculturation, and encouraged the development of Jewish nationalism. We shall see how the unwillingness of some Jews to take sides in the national conflict persuaded them to take a Jewish national position despite their evident acculturation. In this sense Jewish history in Bohemia and Moravia was quite different from that in Germany or in the Hungarian heartland.

Modern Jewish history in the Czech lands presents a dramatic example of the rapid process of secularization and acculturation which took place in many European countries during the nineteenth century. This region could boast of several ancient and celebrated Jewish centers of learning— Prague, of course, in Bohemia, and Nikolsburg (Mikulov) in Moravia. Prague had been, during the sixteenth and seventeenth centuries, one of the most vital and influential Jewish communities in Europe, and as late as the early nineteenth century its rabbi was the great Galician scholar Shlomo Yehuda Rappaport (known as Shir, 1790–1867). The nineteenth-century founder of modern Orthodoxy, Samson Rafael Hirsch (1808–1888), served for a time as rabbi in Nikolsburg. But by the mid-nineteenth century little if anything of this glorious religious and cultural tradition remained. True, new and lavish synagogues, in which services were conducted according to Reform practice—complete with choir, organ, and German sermon—were built. But the region was not producing its own rabbis (they came from Germany or Hungary), and the synagogues were filled only on the High Holidays. Unlike the situation in Germany and Hungary, where Judaism split into Reform and Orthodox factions, formal unity prevailed in Bohemia and Moravia. But there were virtually no yeshivas and little in the way of Jewish schools. Here, as in Germany, the antinational and acculturating ideals of the Haskalah movement, which urged the Jews to integrate into the larger society, had triumphed. Unlike the situation in Germany, however, there was no parallel to the vigorous religious revival led by Hirsch and others.[4]

In short, by the turn of the century Bohemian and Moravian Jewry had become one of the most de-Judaized communities in Europe. As one of the leading Jewish intellectuals of Prague, Max Brod (1884–1968), wrote in his memoirs, "In the Prague of my youth there were only a few families who were completely faithful to the Jewish tradition."[5] And one of the leading Czech playwrights of the interwar period, František Langer (1888–1965), recalled that "the way of life in which religion played an important role had ended with our grandfathers."[6] The most famous of all Prague Jews, Franz Kafka (1883–1924), wrote of this religious void in a well-known letter to his father, in which he reproaches him for the "insignificant fragments of Judaism you preserved." Kafka's impressions of his father's brand of Judaism are worth quoting, since they epitomize the Jewish crisis of his generation:

You really had brought some traces of Judaism with you from the ghetto-like village community; it was not much and it dwindled a little more in the city and during your military service; but still, the impressions and memories of your youth did just about suffice for some sort of Jewish life, especially since you did not need much help of that kind, but came of robust stock and could personally scarcely be shaken by religious scruples unless they were strongly mixed with social scruples. At bottom the faith that ruled your life consisted in your believing in the unconditional right-ness of the opinions of a certain class of Jewish society, and hence actually, since these opinions were part and parcel of your own nature, in believing in yourself. Even in this there was still Judaism enough, but it was too little to be handed on to the child; it all dribbled away while you were passing it on. . . . The whole thing is, of course, no isolated phenom-enon. It was much the same with a large section of this transitional generation of Jews, which had migrated from the still comparatively devout countryside to the cities.[7]

Kafka is right, of course, to link the urbanization (and the embourgeoisement which accompanied it) of his father's generation with the dilution of Judaism. (In less urban Moravia Jewish religious life was somewhat more alive.) Langer also notes that his father had moved to the big city, where "the new environment, the new way of life, the daily bustle, and all the secular cares and ideas which pressed in upon them [his father's generation] provided no stimulus to their religious feeling and made it difficult for them to keep up some of the old customs."[8] We may find the same sociological pattern in the family histories of Sigmund Freud, Gustav Mahler, and Franz Werfel, all of whom came from the Czech lands. And since their fathers' vague sense of Judaism could not be passed on to the sons, the latter naturally tended to regard it as not very important. Langer wrote, "So long as anti-Semitism did not rear its head too close to us or too noisily, our generation looked upon the register of births as its only link with Judaism."[9] Many did not even maintain their fathers' tradition of being "four-day Jews," that is, Jews who attended synagogue four days a year, three days during the High Holidays and once upon the occasion of the emperor's birthday.

And yet, despite this departure from Judaism, greater here than in either Germany or Hungary, the members of Kafka's generation were certainly not assimilated Jews. After all, with whom were the Jews of Moravia and Bohemia to assimilate? In Germany they could hope to become Germans of the Mosaic faith, and in Hungary, where the absence of a native middle class made integration difficult, they could also hope to be recognized as true and loyal Magyars. But the situation in the Czech lands was more complex. The Germans of this region were distinguished by their extreme German nationalism and extreme anti-Semitic tradition.

Unlike the Magyars, who courted the Jews as allies in their efforts to control multinational Hungary, they did not welcome Jewish support. Even in Prague, where there was a strong German liberal tradition warmly supported by the Jewish population, relations between Jews and Germans were far from being close—the relationship is described by Brod as being one of *Distanzliebe*.[10] As for the possibility of integration into the Czech community, which was growing ever stronger during the course of the nineteenth century and which was rapidly turning German towns into Czech towns, this was even less likely than the German alternative. We have already observed that Jews often preferred German to Czech culture and that their political loyalties lay with the Habsburgs in Vienna rather than with the Czech nationalists in Prague. Moreover, the Czechs, like the Germans, did not appear to want the Jews even to make the attempt to become part of their nation. In 1846 a Bohemian Jew, Siegfried Kapper (1821–1879), wrote several poems in Czech and called upon his fellow Jews to identify with Czech culture. For his pains he was denounced by the Czech publicist and national leader Karel Havlíček-Borovský, who proclaimed in the same year that Jews could not possibly become Czechs:

> With regard to the Jews one should bear in mind not only their creed and religious confession, so that there could be Czechs equally of Catholic, Protestant, Mosaic or, perhaps, Mohammedan faith, but primary consideration should be given to their origin and nationality. If so, how can the Israelites belong to the Czech nation since they are obviously of Semitic origin? We could more easily regard Germans, French, Spaniards, Englishmen, etc. as belonging to our nation than the Jews, for all these nations have a greater affinity with us than have the Jews. Therefore it cannot be asserted that the Jews living in Bohemia or Moravia are Czechs of the Mosaic persuasion, but we must regard them as a separate—Semitic—nation which lives only incidentally in our midst and sometimes understands or speaks our language. . . . Therefore, anyone who wants to be a Czech must cease to be a Jew.[11]

This cold reception, along with various manifestations of Czech anti-Semitism, doubtless helped to destroy any hope of a pro-Czech movement among the Jewish intelligentsia in the mid-nineteenth century. True, such a movement did start up later on. In 1876 a pro-Czech Jewish academic society was established in Prague, and in 1884 a special organization was established to promote the use of Czech in the synagogue. In the 1880s and 1890s the first Jewish journals in the Czech language appeared, advocating the Czech orientation and opposing the prevailing pro-German attitude within the community, and in 1904 the journal *Rozvoj*, the organ of a growing Czech-Jewish assimilationist movement led by Viktor Vohryzek (1864–1918), made its appearance. The Czech orientation was clearly gaining strength. Its impact on Jewish life in Bohemia and Moravia was certainly greater than traditional Czech-Jewish historiography allows. Indeed, by the eve of World War I, if Austrian statistics are to be believed, the majority of Bohemian Jewry declared Czech to be its *Umgangssprache* (language of common usage).[12] But the high culture of urban Bohemian and Moravian Jewry, which continued to prefer German- over Czech-language educational institutions for its children, remained German. And the Czech nationalists remained unfriendly. If the Germans rejected the Jews as possible partners in maintaining their domination in the Czech lands, the Czechs often regarded them as germanizers who could not possibly be useful allies in the struggle against German rule.

In short, the Jews of the Czech lands found themselves disliked both by the old ruling nation of the region and by the nation which was challenging the status quo. In this regard their situation differed from that in certain other multinational regions in prewar Eastern Europe—in Transylvania, for example, they enjoyed a close and mutually beneficial alliance with the Hungarians, and the same might be said of Slovakia. To some extent the Czech lands were reminiscent of eastern Galicia, also a bicultural (Polish-Ukrainian) region, where a Jewish-Polish assimilationist movement active in the 1880s received little encouragement from the Polish community (but where a Jewish-Ukrainian movement never developed). The Jews' reaction naturally varied. Most simply shrugged their shoulders and carried on with their traditional political and cultural loyalty to the German dynasty in Vienna. But for the more sensitive Jewish youth, growing up during the immediate prewar years, the complex ethnic situation in the Czech lands produced something of a Jewish national reaction. The celebrated historian Hans Kohn (1891–1971) recalls in his memoirs how he had become a nationalist in Prague because of "its persuasive mood of nationalist stirrings," but he did not become a German or Czech nationalist—rather, he turned to Zionism. The same was true of Brod, and to some degree it was true of Kafka.[13] A number of Jews who enrolled at the University of Prague (which in 1882 was divided into two—one German, the other Czech) discovered, or rediscovered, their own Jewish identity after being rejected by both opposing groups. It has even been argued that Albert Einstein's journey from assimilation to Jewish consciousness was at least in part the result of the short time he spent as a professor at this university in 1910. There is an interesting Czech parallel: Thomas Masaryk made his final decision to become a Czech rather than a German only after he had gone to Prague and had become a professor at the Czech university.[14] It is clear, therefore, that the intense nationalistic atmosphere in Bohemia and Moravia imposed upon many the need to choose between competing nationalisms—and, in the Jewish case, to opt for Jewish nationalism.

It is not surprising, therefore, that in 1893 a group of Jewish students in Prague banded together into an organization with the romantic name Makabäa and proclaimed that "the Jews are neither Germans nor Slavs, they are a people in their own right."[15] They therefore acknowledged as accurate Havlíček's analysis of 1846. In 1899 the famous Prague Zionist group Bar Kochba was founded, and it attracted such notable intellectual figures as Hans Kohn and the philosopher Hugo Bergmann (1883–1979). Many of its members were from acculturated, German-speaking families, while others came from Czech-speaking backgrounds and had identified previously with Czech nationalism. Their new feelings of Jewish nationalism were accompanied by a search for their Jewish roots. Some regarded old Jewish Prague, with its picturesque synagogues and cemeteries, still very much in evidence, as sufficient, while others, notably Bergmann, made field trips to neighboring Galicia to encounter what they believed to be authentic Judaism.[16] Of course, such idealistic young Jewish nationalists were very much of a minority within Bohemian-Moravian Jewry, but the mark they made on Jewish history in these provinces was considerable, especially in view of the indisputable fact that this was very much a Western-type Jewish community. There was nothing comparable within Hungarian Jewry, the other major example of a Western-type Jewry in the region. The members and sympathizers of Bar Kochba were among those who established, in independent Czechoslovakia, a national Jewish party which exerted a great deal of influence during the interwar period.

During the entire nineteenth century Czech-Jewish relations were clouded by the Jews' cultural and political pro-German position, just as Romanian-Jewish relations in Transylvania were so adversely affected by the Jews' Magyar alliance. And the image of the Jew in the popular imagination was probably no better in the Czech lands than elsewhere in Eastern and Central Europe. Masaryk himself, growing up in rural Catholic Moravia, had believed the infamous blood libel accusation to be true and had stared at the fingers of his Jewish acquaintances to see if any traces of blood remained.[17] And yet, while there was no lack of popular anti-Semitic manifestations during the nineteenth century, Czech politics on the whole remained relatively free of anti-Semitism. To be sure, the powerful Young Czech Party was not above using anti-Semitism in its political campaigns, but it did not become obsessed with the Jewish question—as did the Polish National Democrats, for example; and the strong Czech left, like its Polish counterpart, rejected Jew-hatred as a political program.[18] If in prewar Hungary a specifically anti-Semitic political party emerged, no such organization came into existence in the Czech lands. Even Havlíček, who did not think Jews could become

Czechs, favored Jewish emancipation. Moreover, Masaryk, who was to become during World War I the undisputed Czech nationalist leader, took a courageous public position against anti-Semitism when, in 1900, he denounced the belief in the blood libel which had led to the arrest and conviction on a murder charge of the Jew Leopold Hilsner in the little town of Polna in Bohemia. By taking this stand Masaryk exposed himself to a ferocious campaign of slander emanating from Czech national circles, which accused him of favoring the "pro-German" Jew over his just Czech accusers. Much of this campaign was centered at the Czech university in Prague, where Masaryk was castigated by his nationalist colleagues—in Bohemia, as everywhere in East Central Europe, universities were focal points of anti-Jewish feeling. But Masaryk stood his ground and weathered the storm, becoming in the process a hero of Bohemian and even world Jewry (which status did not hurt him when he toured America during the war seeking support for a Czechoslovak state). The Hilsner affair blew over. It did not have anything like the impact of the Dreyfus affair in France, and the anti-Semitic storm it occasioned also dissipated.[19] Although Masaryk was obviously not hurt by his advocacy of the unpopular Jew, it is difficult to imagine a Polish or Romanian politician of the period taking such a stand and surviving to become a national hero. Indeed, in interwar East Central Europe Masaryk was the only dominant politician firmly identified with the campaign against anti-Semitism. This was a fact of considerable significance for Jewish history in the interwar Republic of Czechoslovakia.

Just why anti-Semitism played a fairly small role in Czech politics is an interesting question. It may have had something to do with the small size and "European character" of the Jewish community, although such things are usually not determining factors in the extent of anti-Jewish feeling. It was more likely related to certain unique aspects of Czech history and society—the anticlerical attitude of the intelligentsia, which owed something to the Hussite tradition and the dislike of the Catholic church as a Habsburg institution; the "advanced" state of Czech society, with its solid middle class and well-organized proletariat, which meant among other things the existence of a powerful but moderate left wing which was lacking in both Romania and Hungary; the economic prosperity of the region, which rendered unlikely right-wing political extremism; and the fact that the Czech national struggle had been shaped in Austria rather than in Russia or Hungary, implying a more flexible and liberal political tradition. Whatever the case, the Jewish question in the Czech lands never received anything like the obsessive attention paid to it in Poland, Romania, or Hungary.

It must be emphasized, however, that such conditions prevailed only in the Czech lands. Things were quite different in Slovakia. Indeed, in this former Hungarian possession Jewish history in the prewar years had taken quite a different course in every respect. Slovakian Jewry was part of greater Hungarian Jewry, though a more backward, less modernized part than the Jewry of "ethnic" Hungary. This meant, first of all, that it was formally split into three religious factions—Neolog (Reform), Status Quo, and Orthodox. In this peripheral Hungarian area, poorer than central Hungary, Orthodoxy remained very strong. In western Slovakia it was basically of the German variety, meaning a combination of extremely strict adherence to Mosaic law and a readiness to acculturate to some extent in matters of language and dress. In eastern Slovakia Jewish Orthodoxy was more of the East European type, including a certain Hasidic influence which emanated from Galicia. The largest city in Slovakia, Bratislava (Pozsony in Hungarian, Pressburg in German) was a celebrated center of Orthodox Judaism, home of a great yeshiva and seat of one of the most renowned sages of early nineteenth-century European Judaism, Moses Sofer (known as the Hatam Sofer, 1762–1839). As everywhere in Hungary, the wealthier, more urban, and more bourgeois elements within the Jewish community gravitated toward Reform Judaism, but in backward Slovakia such elements were in the minority. The region, therefore, in sharp contrast to Bohemia and Moravia, was a bastion of orthodox Jewish religious life.[20]

Jewish acculturation in Slovakia was less pronounced than in the Czech lands and followed a rather different course. Historically, the first non-Jewish language learned was German, and German remained important until the end of the prewar period. This was particularly true in Pressburg, only a short journey from Vienna and the home of a sizable German national minority. But by the century's end Hungarian was rapidly gaining among the Jewish population. Slovakia was subjected to a fierce magyarization campaign after 1867, and many Jews, along with many Slovaks and Germans, were glad to adopt the culture of the ruling nation, all the more so since it consciously adopted a pro-Jewish policy. If in the Czech lands neither the Germans nor the Czechs welcomed Jewish support, in Slovakia (where the German minority was much smaller than in Bohemia and Moravia) the Hungarians courted it. As for Slovak culture, it lagged behind that of the Czechs, and thus held virtually no attraction for the Jews. There was, therefore, no parallel here to the Czech-Jewish movement to the west. Instead, by the century's end Hungarian began to be heard in the Reform synagogues, and in many Jewish families the parents conversed in German while the children, who attended Hungarian schools, spoke to each other in Magyar.[21] Again in contrast to the situation in the Czech lands, Yiddish also survived into the twentieth century, particularly in the small towns of eastern Slovakia, where Jewish life in many ways resembled that of neighboring Galicia.

The Jews in Slovakia were closely identified with Magyar domination, which was social, cultural, and political. The Magyars ruled with an iron hand, suppressing any sign of autonomous Slovak political or cultural activity. The situation was again quite different here than in Bohemia and Moravia, where by the late nineteenth century the Czechs were making even greater gains at the expense of the Germans, and it was to be expected that the Jews, allies of oppressive Budapest rather than of more benign Vienna, would be far more disliked by Slovak than by Czech nationalists. Here is one reason why, while many Czech national leaders were not anti-Semites, most Slovak leaders were. No less a factor in Slovak anti-Semitism was the close connection between Slovak nationalism and the Catholic church, more influential among leading Slovaks than among leading Czechs. In addition, the economic conflict between the Slovaks, whose bourgeoisie was very weak, and the middle- and lower-middle-class Jewish community, which played a great role in local commerce, was sharper than in the advanced Czech lands, where the Jews' economic role was much less conspicuous. Finally, the Jews were proportionately much more numerous in Slovakia than in Bohemia and Moravia. In short, this backward, oppressively ruled land, where the Jews were identified with the social and national enemy, was a much more likely arena for extreme anti-Semitism and extreme politics in general than were the Czech lands. In fact, in interwar Slovakia, finally liberated from Hungarian rule but now resentful of Czech domination, the Jewish question assumed a prominence reminiscent more of Poland than of Bohemia and Moravia.

Being less acculturated than Bohemian and Moravian Jewry, Slovakian Jewry was potentially more likely to nurture strong Jewish national movements. But the absence of a Russian- or a Galician-type national Haskalah tradition, the prevalence of the "Hungarian pattern" of Jewish identification by religion, and the strong Orthodox hold militated against such a possibility, at least in the prewar period. An important conference of the Orthodox Zionist movement was held in Pressburg in 1912, but nothing remotely like Bar Kochba arose in Slovakia. It was only after World War I that the situation changed.[22]

The Jewish community of Subcarpathian Rus, also a part of prewar Hungarian Jewry, possessed its own very special character. This was the most backward region in all Hungary, inhabited by the peasant Rusyns (often called Ruthenians, sometimes Ukrainians), Hungarian landowners and bureaucrats, and a Jewish community of the classic East European type. There were only two cities of any importance, and most Jews, like most Rusyns, lived in small towns and villages. A small magyarized Jewish elite could be found, but the overwhelming majority spoke Yiddish and remained faithful to Orthodox Judaism. Hasidism, unknown in the Czech lands and not very strong in Slovakia, was extremely influential. The Jewry of Subcarpathian Rus was something of an offshoot of Galician Jewry, whence its Hasidic Judaism derived, but it lacked Galicia's highly cultured urban centers and modernizing Haskalah tradition—Munkács (in Czech, Mukačevo) and Uzhgorod (in Czech, Užhorod; in Hungarian, Ungvár) could not be compared with Lwów and Cracow. No greater contrast with the Jewry of the Czech lands could be imagined. Here, as in Slovakia, the Jews were loyal subjects of Budapest, but being much less magyarized they were less likely to incur the wrath of the Hungarian-dominated Rusyn majority. And the latter, much less politically and nationally conscious than the Slovaks, did not articulate strong anti-Jewish feelings during the prewar period. In this regard, extremely backward Subcarpathian Rus appeared less dangerous an environment than less backward Slovakia, though certainly not nearly so promising a one as advanced Bohemia and Moravia.[23]

## 2. The Jews of Interwar Czechoslovakia:
### A Profile

According to the census of 1921, there were 354,342 Jews (by religion) in Czechoslovakia. In 1930 the figure was virtually the same, 356,830, representing 2.42 percent of the total population, a considerably lower percentage than in most other states of East Central Europe.[24] The Jews were unevenly distributed among the three major historical units which constituted the country, and, as was so often the case, the farther east one went the higher the Jewish percentage in the general population. (The regional distribution in 1930 is shown in table 3.1.) The low percentage of Jews in the Czech lands was typical of the West European Jewish demographic pattern. In Subcarpathian Rus, on the other hand, the Jews constituted an extremely high proportion of the population.

The situation in the major cities also demonstrates the dramatic contrast between East and West (see table 3.2). Here too the Slovak case lies

TABLE 3.1
**Jewish Population of Czechoslovakia, 1930**

| Region | Number | Percentage |
|---|---|---|
| Bohemia | 76,301 | 1.07 |
| Moravia-Silesia | 41,250 | 1.16 |
| Slovakia | 136,737 | 4.10 |
| Subcarpathian Rus | 102,542 | 14.12 |

Source: Franz Friedmann, *Einige Zahlen über die tschechoslovakischen Juden* (Prague, 1933); Bruno Blau, "Yidn in der tshekhoslovakay," *Yidishe ekonomik* 3 (1939):27–54.

TABLE 3.2
**Jewish Population in Major Czechoslovak Cities, 1930**

| City | Percentage |
|---|---|
| Prague | 4.17 |
| Brno (Brünn) | 4.15 |
| Bratislava (Pressburg) | 12.02 |
| Mukacěvo (Munkács) | 43.34 |
| Užhorod (Uzhgorod) | 27.58 |

SOURCE: Franz Friedmann, *Einige Zahlen über die tschechoslovakischen Juden* (Prague, 1933); Bruno Blau, "Yidn in der tshekhoslovakay," *Yidishe ekonomik* 3 (1939):27–54.

somewhere between the Western pattern in Prague and Brno, the capitals of Bohemia and Moravia, and the classically Eastern pattern in the two largest (though none too large) cities of Subcarpathian Rus. As for the internal Jewish demographic situation, the Jews of the Czech lands were highly urbanized and highly concentrated in the capital cities. In Bohemia nearly 50 percent of all Jews (35,463) lived in Prague, while in less urban Moravia more than 25 percent (11,003) resided in the capital city of Brno. In Subcarpathian Rus, on the other hand, less than 20 percent of the Jewish community resided in the two major cities, the rest living in small towns (*shtetlekh*) and villages. In Slovakia slightly more than 10 percent of the Jews lived in Bratislava, the rest being scattered among the smaller cities and towns of the region. To summarize the two Jewish demographic patterns in Czechoslovakia, the typical East European Jewry of Subcarpathian Rus constituted a very high percentage in the cities, but at the same time numerous Jews resided in small towns and villages, while the typically West European Jewish community of the Czech lands was almost entirely urbanized, although the Jews there made up an insignificant percentage within the large cities. These patterns reflect the general socioeconomic situation in the region. In the more advanced areas the Jews were drawn into city life, but so were the much more numerous non-Jews. In the more rural areas, where the vast majority of the population engaged in agriculture, the few existing cities bore a marked Jewish character, but they were not large and prosperous enough to absorb the entire small-town and village Jewish population. These patterns obviously had important implications for all aspects of Jewish life, since small-town Jews were likely to be more religious and less acculturated than their big-city brethren. This is certainly borne out by the situations in the Czech lands, Slovakia, and Subcarpathian Rus.

In other respects, too, there were important demographic distinctions among the three Jewries of the state. In the Czech lands the Jewish percentage within the general population had been on the decline since the turn of the century, and in fact during the interwar years there was a significant decrease in the absolute number of Jews in Bohemia and Moravia (see table 3.3). The principal reason for this decline, at least during the interwar period when emigration to Vienna or America did not play a major role, was the very low birthrate which characterized Central and West European Jewish communities, most notably that of Germany, the usual consequence of urbanization and embourgeoisement. It was so striking that some experts predicted the eventual "natural" demise of German and Bohemian Jewry, just as today they predict a similar fate for the highly urbanized and middle-class Jewish community in the United States. Intermarriage also was a factor. In the eastern provinces, however, this was definitely not the case. In Slovakia, while the proportion of Jews also decreased during the interwar period, their absolute number increased, though not by very much. In Subcarpathian Rus there was a more sizable increase in the absolute number of Jews, though here too the increase did not keep up with that of the non-Jewish population. The Jewish natural increase in the most backward of Czechoslovakia's provinces was similar to that of Polish Jewry, whereas the situation in the Czech lands was similar to that in Germany. As usual, the Slovak case lies somewhere in between.[25]

The economic activities of the Jewries of the Czech lands closely conformed to the typical West European pattern. About 60 percent of the economically active Jews of Bohemia and Moravia were engaged in business, finance, and communications. In Bohemia 22.6 percent were engaged in industry and crafts, while in Moravia the figure was 28.5 percent. Virtually no Jews were active in agriculture, still the single most important economic sector for the non-Jewish population, but a significant number were employed in public service and the professions—14.8 percent in Bohemia, and 14.6 percent in Moravia.[26]

In Subcarpathian Rus the situation was quite different. According to statistics compiled by the Joint Distribution Committee in 1921, of 11,760

TABLE 3.3
**Decline of Bohemian and Moravian Jewry**

| Year | Region | Number of Jews | Region | Number of Jews |
|------|--------|---------------|--------|---------------|
| 1890 | Bohemia | 94,479 | Moravia | 55,367 |
| 1921 | " | 79,777 | " | 45,306 |
| 1930 | " | 76,301 | " | 41,250 |

SOURCE: Jan Herman, "The Development of Bohemian and Moravian Jewry," in *Papers in Jewish Demography*, ed. O. Schmelz, P. Glikson, and S. Della Pergola (Jerusalem, 1969), p. 200.

Jewish families surveyed 2,500 were engaged in agricultural pursuits, and an additional 2,000 were day laborers in the towns and villages. There was a small Jewish professional class, but most others were artisans, store-keepers, and innkeepers. In addition there was a very large number of *luftmentshn*, (people who "lived off the air"), beggars, and so forth.[27] This was the region with the largest Jewish peasantry, if such a term may be used, in all of Europe, and on the whole the poorest and most involved in physical labor of all European Jewries.

The Slovakian Jewish economic profile resembles more the Bohemian-Moravian than the Subcarpathian Rus model, but there is at least one important difference which should be pointed out. In Slovakia, as in Subcarpathian Rus, the Jewish middle and lower middle class played a much more conspicuous role in the nonagricultural economy, both in the towns and in the villages, than did the more solid Jewish bourgeoisie of the Czech lands. Thus, even if the backward eastern regions possessed a much larger Jewish working class than did the more prosperous west, the Jewish storekeeper, merchant, and industrialist in these regions was more likely to be regarded as "dominating" the local economy. And Jewish professionals, especially doctors and lawyers, constituted an inordinately high proportion; even in the late 1930s 40 percent of all doctors in Slovakia were Jews.[28] This is simply the result of the fact that the Czechs had developed a sizable bourgeoisie and professional class of their own, whereas the Slovaks and Rusyns had not. In Slovakia and Subcarpathian Rus, as in Polish Lithuania, independent Lithuania, Bessarabia, and elsewhere in East Central Europe, the middle class was often perceived as being synonymous with the local Jewry, despite the fact that Jewish population was largely lower middle class and proletarian in character. It was this paradoxical and "abnormal" situation which local political leaders set out to correct, often with disastrous results so far as the Jews were concerned.

A profile of the Jews of Czechoslovakia would not be complete without consideration of certain data regarding the state of their Jewish consciousness and identity. It will come as no surprise that the rate of intermarriage, always a good test of how "Jewish" a given community is, was quite high in the Czech lands. Thus in Bohemia, in 1931, 32 of every 100 Jewish grooms married gentile women; for Jewish brides the figure is a bit lower.[29] In Slovakia the figures are much lower, and in Subcarpathian Rus scarcely any intermarriage occurred. Few conversions took place anywhere in Czechoslovakia, as in East Central Europe in general, with the single exception of Hungary.[30] As for the way the Jews perceived themselves, there are some very interesting, though probably somewhat misleading, data on their national identification. When asked to what religion they belonged, all Jews presumably answered "Jewish." When asked their national affiliation, in 1921, they responded as indicated in table 3.4. These figures, however, should be regarded with some caution. As we already know, the choice of Jewish nationality by no means indicates, in every case, acceptance of the modern Zionist notion of a secular Jewish nation; it may simply indicate that, as in the case of Subcarpathian Rus, the Jews did not identify with any other nation. Moreover, the Jews may have been responding the way they imagined the census taker, or the state, wished them to, not according to their own beliefs. We shall see that in interwar Czechoslovakia the government preferred the Jews to be Jewish by nationality rather than German or Hungarian, and this may have prompted some Jews to answer as they did. Finally, there is no clear explanation for the glaring discrepancy in regard to Jewish national consciousness between Bohemia and Moravia, whose Jewries were so similar in other respects. Nonetheless, these figures are a further indication of the extremely Jewish character of the Jewish community in the most backward of Czechoslovakia's regions, and of the acculturated nature of the Jewry of its most developed region. All in all, in 1921, 53.86 percent of all of Czechoslovakia's Jews declared themselves to be not only of the Jewish religion, but of Jewish nationality. This was considerably lower than the Polish and Romanian percentages, but incomparably higher than that of Hungary, where hardly any Jews regarded themselves as belonging to a separate Jewish nation.

### 3. The State and Its Jewish Citizens

Whatever the Czechoslovak Jews' sense of national identification, and however loyal they had been to their prewar masters in Vienna and Budapest, they had good reason to be enthusiastic about their new state. Their feelings may be contrasted with those of the Galician, Bukovinian,

TABLE 3.4
**National Identities of Czechoslovak Jews, 1921 (By Percentage)**

| Region | Nationality | | | | |
|---|---|---|---|---|---|
| | Jewish | Czecho-slovak | German | Hungarian | Rusyn |
| Bohemia | 14.6 | 49.49 | 34.63 | | |
| Moravia-Silesia | 47.84 | 15.71 | 34.85 | | |
| Slovakia | 54.28 | 22.27 | 6.68 | 16.49 | |
| Subcarpathian Rus | 86.81 | 0.78 | 0.29 | 7.49 | 3.85 |

SOURCE: Franz Friedmann, *Einige Zahlen über die tschechoslovakischen Juden* (Prague, 1933), p. 23; Bruno Blau, "Nationality among Czechoslovak Jewry," *Historica Judaica* 10 (1948):147–54.

and Transylvanian Jews, who had no cause to be happy about the transition from Habsburg to Polish and Romanian rule. For if the new states of Poland and Romania were clearly anti-Semitic from the very beginning, the rulers of Czechoslovakia appeared to be not only opposed to anti-Semitism, but in a way even pro-Jewish. Like the Lithuanians, but very much unlike the Poles, Romanians, and interwar Hungarians, the Czech nationalists actively courted Jewish support during World War I and the immediate postwar period. Masaryk noted how the Balfour Declaration had won Great Britain the support of world Jewry, and set out to win similar Jewish support for his cause. In America during the war he found that "the Jews stood by me" because of his position during the Hilsner affair and because of his support for Zionism and Jewish national rights. "In America," he writes in his memoirs, "as in Europe, Jewish influence is strong in the press, and it was good that it was not against us."[31] This remark indicates just how much importance Masaryk, the leader of a small and little-known nation which had lost its independence in the premodern period, placed on world public opinion. Czechoslovakia, after all, had never existed before as an independent state, and therefore its need for international support of all kinds was greater than that of Poland, Hungary, or Romania. In this sense its position was similar to that of the Baltic States, and it is no accident that the Lithuanians and the Latvians, along with the Czechs, made great efforts to gain Jewish backing for their national causes. It appears, then, that in some cases a new state's feelings of insecurity and vulnerability may work to the advantage of its Jewish minority.

This is not to suggest that Masaryk's views on the Jewish question were formed solely by expediency. That they were not is indicated not only by his position in the Hilsner affair, but also by the fact that he was a consistent advocate of the Jewish right to national self-determination in Palestine and national autonomy in the diaspora. Masaryk was certainly not the only East European leader to take a pro-Zionist stance; insofar as Zionism meant the mass departure of Jews from Europe, it was a very popular doctrine in Polish and Romanian anti-Semitic circles. But Masaryk did not think that Zionism meant simply or even principally the removal of the Jews to Palestine. Nor is there any evidence that he wanted the Jews of Czechoslovakia to go elsewhere. Rather, he believed that just as Czech nationalism imparted dignity and pride to the Czech people, so Jewish nationalism would grant the oppressed Jewish people the same vital ingredients. As he said in 1918, "I am completely sympathetic toward Zionism and National Judaism because I see in them a problem of moral regeneration."[32] In his grasp of this dimension of Jewish nationalism, as opposed to its more easily understood aspect of fleeing from persecution, Masaryk was unique among the great nationalists of East Europe.

Masaryk was unusual, too, in his championing of Jewish national rights in the diaspora. Here too, of course, the possibility of expediency cannot be dismissed. In multinational Czechoslovakia, with hostile German and Hungarian minorities, the authorities naturally preferred Jews to identify themselves as "Jews by nationality" rather than as Germans (in the Czech lands) or as Hungarians (in Slovakia). The same kind of reasoning led Romanian authorities to encourage, at least for a while, Jewish national identity in Bessarabia, which was preferred to identification with the Russian nationality. But if it was convenient for the Czech leaders that the Jews register as "Jews by nationality," given the likelihood that most would not be prepared to register as Czechs or Slovaks, it was nonetheless the case that they accepted the legitimacy of Jewish nationalism, went to some lengths to satisfy the demands of Jewish nationalists in the country, and did not engage in the kind of coercive assimilation which was occasionally attempted in other East European states.

The tolerant attitude toward Jewish nationalism, of course, must be understood in the broader context of Czechoslovak nationality policy. Czechoslovakia, unlike Poland and Romania, was a multinational state not only in fact but also by definition. Whatever the grievances of the minorities, above all of the Germans and the Slovaks, national minority rights were upheld, and there was no concerted effort to treat the Germans, Hungarians, Slovaks, and Rusyns as "ethnic material" (the term is borrowed from the vocabulary of the Polish National Democrats) to be transformed into Czechs. Those Jews who wished to promote Jewish national culture in Czechoslovakia naturally benefited from this general policy. They may also have benefited from the traditional Czech view, expressed so clearly by Havlíček in the mid-nineteenth century, that Jews could not really become Czechs at all. But even if Masaryk and his allies shared that view (and despite Masaryk's appreciation of the Jewish-Czech movement, in contrast to Havlíček's dislike of Kapper, it seems that he did), there is no evidence that the Jews who did not favor a Jewish national identity suffered as a result.[33] In this regard Czechoslovakia was in sharp contrast with Poland, where the prevailing view that the Jews could not possibly become Poles was accompanied both by an established, state-sponsored campaign of anti-Semitism and by opposition to Jewish national rights on Polish soil. "Chauvinism," Masaryk wrote, "that is to say, political, religious, racial, or class intolerance, has, as history proves, wrought the downfall of all states."[34] Some observers have noted that the Czech leader's insistence on incorporating the Sudetenland and Subcarpthian Rus into the new state contradicted such views, and many Germans and Slovaks certainly felt themselves to be second-class citizens. But so far as the Jews were concerned, the Republic under Masaryk lived up to these lofty sentiments.

The Czech-Jewish alliance, if we may call it that, was therefore the result on the Czech side of a mixture of self-interest and the peculiar brand of Czech liberal nationalism. It was a unique alliance, for according to its unwritten terms the Jews were not necessarily expected to become "Czechs of the Jewish persuasion," as they were expected to become Hungarians, Frenchmen, and Germans of the Jewish persuasion. In other words, the two major Jewish modes of identification of modern times— religious and national—were both granted legitimacy. For their part, the Jews were expected to be loyal to Czechoslovakia, and, while some Jews remained "German" or "Hungarian" by culture and nationality during the interwar years, it was certainly easier and more logical for them to display such loyalty than it was for the Christian Germans and Christian Hungarians, so easily won over by the nationalism of a Hitler or a Horthy. After all, Jewish-German acculturation had not been accompanied by the Jews' transformation into German political nationalists in the Czech lands, and, while some Slovak Jews clung to Magyar patriotism, even they could not but respond positively to a Czechoslovakia which compared so favorably with anti-Semitic Hungary. The alliance, based on the real interests of both sides, worked, though of course Jewish loyalty could not possibly offset the disaffection of the larger minorities in the state. As the old saying went, there were Czechs and Slovaks (and, it should have been added, Germans, Hungarians, and Rusyns), but the only real Czechoslovaks were the Jews. And while the other minorities tended to become less and less loyal to Czechoslovakia as time went on, subjected as they were to relentless propaganda from their "protectors" abroad, in the Jewish case the opposite was true. Here is an example of how a tolerant policy can ensure Jewish loyalty and support—a policy which might have been followed, but which was not, in Poland and in Romania.

This is not to say that everything went smoothly in Czech-Jewish relations in the early years of the Republic, for there were problems both in negotiations between the leaders of the two peoples and on a popular level. Despite the fact that Masaryk and his chief partner, Eduard Beneš, were willing to acknowledge the Jews as a nationality with clearly defined national rights, they were unwilling to adhere to the "Jewish clauses" in the Versailles Minorities' Treaty. When, in 1919, the Zionist leader Nahum Sokolow met with Beneš and requested him to sign the Minorities' Treaty, the latter replied that "the two articles represented a sort of 'yellow badge' of which only Poland and Romania were deserving. Unlike these countries, Czechoslovakia was at the head of the Slavic nations and was a Western state. Moreover, she was not anti-Semitic and suspicion must not be allowed to rise in the world that she was."[35] This attitude caused a temporary crisis, with Sokolow threatening the Czechs with the loss of world Jewish support. Such threats did not deter Beneš, and the

Jews had to make do with two kinds of assurances: first, the general provisions in the treaty between Czechoslovakia and the allies in 1919 and in the Czechoslovak constitution promising equality for all nationalities and the right of all nationalities to use their languages in their primary schools (which would receive government subsidies) and before the courts; and, second, the recognition of the Jews as a nationality. The usual criterion for national status, namely, the use of a particular national language, was waived in the Jewish case, thus allowing Czech-, Slovak-, German-, and Hungarian-speaking Jews to register as Jews by nationality.[36] This was good enough for most Jewish nationalists and Jewish organizations, whose advanced state of acculturation was responsible for the fact that their national demands were minimal by East European standards. Thus the Minorities' Treaty issue did not prove to have any lasting effect.

More serious were the many instances of popular anti-Semitism in the early years of the interwar period. The fact is that the wave of anti-Jewish feeling which swept over East Central Europe immediately after World War I did not spare the lands of Czechoslovakia, though it was certainly much less devastating than in Poland or in Hungary. In Czechoslovakia, too, wartime dislocation, the collapse of the old order, social revolution, and the national conflicts which accompanied the process of drawing the new frontiers in Eastern Europe, resulted in what the Jewish National Council termed "pogrom-like incidents which have occurred within the territory of the Czechoslovak state. . . ."[37] Although such incidents occurred all over the state, they were most serious in Slovakia, where Béla Kun's short-lived Communist regime in 1919 created political and social dislocation not experienced in the Czech lands, and in regions where there were important German communities. Pressburg (Bratislava), the capital of Slovakia but a German-Hungarian-Jewish city where there had been serious anti-Jewish disturbances during the nineteenth century, was probably the single most important center of popular anti-Semitism during 1918–1919.[38] Indeed, it is worth remembering that the Czech-Jewish alliance, while claiming the loyalty of Jews everywhere in the state, was emphatically not adhered to by the other nationalities in Czechoslovakia—not by the Germans and, particularly, not by the Slovaks. In July, 1919, Chaim Weizmann, speaking in the name of the World Zionist Organization, complained about the anti-Semitic campaign in Slovakia. He was answered by the Slovak leader Vavro Šrobár, who noted that the Jewish question in Slovakia "has an aspect and character completely divergent from that in Western countries." Along with Magyar nobles and officials, "Jewish estate owners and innkeepers . . . for whole decades did the most serious harm to the Slovak people." The Magyar government, he went on, was astute enough to make a tool of the Jews in Slovakia to carry out their violent policy of Magyarization, and only too often they found them devoted helpers, informers, agents-provocateurs, spies and agitators against the Entente. It is unfortunately necessary to assert, and this assertion can be substantiated by thousands of proofs, that the Jews in Slovakia became the exponents of the most active intrigues. For this, it is to the interest of all right-minded Jews in the world that this system, which corrupted the race, was destroyed in Austria-Hungary. During the war this hostile activity towards the Slovak people became more violent. As the result of information lodged by the Jews, persons were imprisoned and executed. In return for all this they were rewarded by the Government with various concessions and privileges, to the detriment of the Slovak people. When the revolution occurred, and the Czechoslovak nation threw off the tyrants' yoke, it was the Jews who worked as Magyar agitators against our Republic. During the Bolshevist invasion of June, 1919, it was again the Slovak Jews who proved themselves an element hostile to the people and Republic, who led Bolshevist troops, showed them the way, and denounced the loyal Slovaks, so that these were shot or tortured by the Bolshevists.[39]

We should note that Šrobár was an ally of Masaryk and an opponent of Slovak separatism. More nationalistic Slovaks, who in the 1930s were to set the tone for Slovak politics, disliked the Jews not only for their economic behavior, their Bolshevism, and their pro-Hungarian attitudes, but also for their evident loyalty to the Czechoslovak state. As one Slovak historian has written, "After helping the Magyars to realize their aims at domination in Slovakia, they did not hesitate to render the same service to the Czechs."[40]

The Jews were thus despised, both as "Magyars" and as "Czechoslovaks," however illogical that might appear. By the same token the other national minorities in the state, to the extent that they felt discriminated against by the dominant Czechs, resented the Jews as enthusiastic supporters of the state. This was the inevitable price the Jews paid for upholding their part of the alliance with the leading nationality in Czechoslovakia. And as national tensions between the Czechs and the minorities heated up in the 1930s, the Jews could not fail to bear some of the burden. It was precisely this unhealthy situation of being identified with the dominant nationality and thus being despised by the other national groups which persuaded many Jewish leaders in Eastern Europe to call for a commitment to Jewish national politics and an avoidance of unwritten alliances with one or another nationality. But this policy did not work; the fact is that in eastern Galicia, for example, many Ukrainians continued to regard the Jews as "polonizers" despite the strength of Zionism in that region and despite the Jews' declaration of neutrality in the Polish-Ukrainian dispute. Likewise in Czechoslovakia the undoubted triumphs of the Jewish national party, which we shall turn to shortly, did not convince the Germans, Slovaks, Hungarians, and Rusyns that the Jews were not working hand in glove with the Czechs to suppress the others' just national aspirations.

Despite the manifestations of popular anti-Semitism during 1918–1919, and the obvious anti-Jewish feeling of some Slovak, German, and Rusyn politicians, it cannot be said that anti-Semitism constituted a serious obstacle to Czechoslovak Jews, at least not during the 1920s and early 1930s. Economic prosperity obviously had something to do with the low profile of anti-Semitism. Popular anti-Semitism existed, but the various governments which ruled the country, maintaining the liberal tradition of Czech politics, would have nothing to do with it, and it is usually the attitude of the government rather than the attitude of some of its subjects which determines the impact of anti-Semitism upon the Jewish population. Jews did not, on the whole, suffer discrimination in the state bureaucracy or in the universities, unlike the case almost everywhere else in East Central Europe. A few rose to prominence in Czech politics.[41] Even in Slovakia, where there was a clearcut policy of hiring Slovaks first, the situation was tolerable. Thus in 1933 the German representative in Prague reported with regret to his superiors in Berlin that "in Czechoslovakia there is no discrimination of any sort against Jews, neither in their administrative careers, nor in social, economic, or other respects, or in the field of sport. Any such measures would be contrary to President Masaryk's principles. . . ."[42] So long as those principles endured, in the face of both internal and external pressures, the well-being of the Jews in all three regions of the state was guaranteed.

### 4. Internal Jewish Developments: Politics and Culture

The story of Jewish politics in Czechoslovakia is both complex—as might be expected, given the diversity of the Jewish communities there—and surprising, since the most acculturated Jewish communities were the pioneers of national Jewish politics. We have already noted the peculiar conditions in the prewar years which propelled some young Jews in the Czech lands toward Jewish nationalism. The war years, here as elsewhere in Eastern Europe, raised the national consciousness of many more, who were inspired by the triumph of Czech nationalism but who did not necessarily seek to become Czechs. In this connection the collapse of the old German-Habsburg political-cultural orientation is important, since it brought to an end the long process of Jewish-German acculturation which had characterized the nineteenth century. This is not to say that all Jews suddenly stopped speaking German, but it did mean the emergence of a new cultural situation, in which German was no longer the language of the government and in which the new leading language, Czech, was not yet well known to many Jews. In such circumstances a Jewish national stance was a logical reaction, just as it was in Transylvania after the end of Hungarian rule and in Polish Lithuania after the fall of the tsar. Moreover, in the Czech case the government actually encouraged Jewish nationalism. This is the background to the establishment, in October, 1918, of the Jewish National Council in Prague, which claimed to speak for "the nationally oriented Jews of the Czechoslovak state."[43] How many such Jews there were is not clear, since the Council was not elected by anyone but rather appointed by the Zionist Federation of Bohemia, the most active Jewish political force during this period. Among its prominent leaders was Max Brod. Naturally in favor of establishing a Jewish national home in Palestine, the Council nonetheless was chiefly concerned with the Jewish situation in Czechoslovakia. Like many other Zionist-dominated organizations elsewhere in Eastern Europe, it immersed itself in *Gegenwartsarbeit* (work related to the diaspora, as different from work for Palestine).

The Jewish National Council in Prague was founded at about the same time as other Jewish national councils emerged in such cities as Lwów, Cracow, Warsaw, Vilna, Kaunas, and Cernăuţi (Czernowitz). Representing as it did a largely acculturated Jewry, its national program was rather moderate if compared with that of similar Jewish organizations to the east whose constituencies were much more nationalist-minded. It stood for recognition of the Jews as a nation, of course, subsidies for Jewish schools and other cultural institutions, and the democratization of the Jewish communal bodies (the *Kultusgemeinde*). The Council specifically disavowed any intent to ask for "separate status in matters of national defense, national politics, law, civil service, or industrial or vocational life," since this would be regarded as "an attempt to restore the old ghetto."[44] Turning to the Jews of the new state, the Council made a plea for a national Jewish orientation rather than one based on assimilation:

> We national Jews grant that there are some Jews who have so completely identified with the Czech or German people that they are capable of participating fully in the inner life of the nationality in whose midst they live. We have no intention of opposing these Jews who have become assimilated, for we respect all individual convictions which are sincerely held. What we have fought against, and are still fighting against, is that vacillating, insincere sort of assimilation which is to be blamed not on the unfortunate Jewish people, but on the conditions of their dispersal, and on the fact that the Austrian government (particularly under Magyar influence) consistently opposed the recognition of the Jews as a national-

ity group. The governments of Austria and Hungary continually sought to use the Jews as tools for opposing the small nationalities, an exploitation which we Zionists have always emphatically deplored.[45]

In order to promote these views the Council convened a conference of "National Jewry" in 1919 at which time the Jewish Party of Czechoslovakia was established.[46] The Jewish Party, despite its obvious Zionist origins, was conceived as a middle-of-the-road organization, above political parties, which would unite Jews of all factions and from all the regions of the state. It viewed as its task not only the propagation of the ideals of Jewish nationalism but also the defense of Jewish interests, which were broadly defined so as to attract the greatest number of Jewish supporters. Here was another Zionist effort, not unlike that made in Warsaw in 1918, to establish a broadly based Jewish organization which while remaining under Zionist leadership would unite religious and secular Jews, Zionists and non-Zionists, socialists and nonsocialists. And if in Poland such an effort foundered, the victim of deep and longstanding divisiveness among the various Jewish political parties, it was much more successful (though certainly not entirely successful) in Czechoslovakia, where modern Jewish politics was younger and more amorphous. Its success was reflected in national election returns during the 1920s, when the Jewish Party received 79,714 votes in 1920, 98,845 votes in 1925, and 104,539 votes in 1929.[47]

The election figures represent a remarkable achievement for the Jewish Party. We must recall not only that we are dealing with a much less nationalized Jewry in Czechoslovakia than in Poland, for example, but also that the moderate and non–anti-Semitic nature of Czech politics, in contrast to that of Poland, meant that Jews had the option of voting for the major Czech parties. Nonetheless, about one-half the Jewish vote went to the Jewish Party in 1920. The Jewish Party's high watermark in 1929, however, was reached only with the help of an alliance with two Polish parties representing the small Polish minority in Czechoslovakia. This coalition was the Czech version, albeit on a much less grandiose scale, of the minorities' bloc established in Poland in 1922, and it is ironic that the Poles, who so vigorously denounced this tactic in Poland as an anti-Polish act, were willing to cooperate with the Jews in Czechoslovakia. The reason for the formation of the minorities' alliance was the same in both countries, namely, the desire to overcome electoral laws which made it difficult for minorities to return candidates to parliament. In both cases the maneuver succeeded, and in 1929, for the first time in Czechoslovakia, the Jewish Party sent two representatives to the parliament in Prague. This success was repeated in 1935.

The Jewish Party by no means encountered smooth sailing within the Jewish community, despite its considerable electoral triumphs. On the left the small Poale Zion party refused to follow its lead, but this was not nearly so important as ideological opposition from the right, which emanated from the dominant Orthodox circles in Slovakia and Subcarpathian Rus. The strength of Hungarian-style Orthodoxy in Slovakia and of Hasidism in Subcarpathian Rus meant that efforts to propagate the view that the Jews were a modern, secular nation with national rights both in Czechoslovakia and in Palestine would be met with determined opposition. Thus, paradoxically, the modern Jewish national views of acculturated Jews in Bohemia and Moravia were resisted by many much less acculturated Jews of the eastern provinces. There was more opposition to national Judaism in these regions than in Poland, where the basic division within the Jewish community was between Orthodox and national Jews rather than between adherents to Orthodoxy and adherents to Reform. In Slovakia the anti-Zionist Orthodox party Agudes yisroel (League of Israel), a German import at first viewed with some suspicion by the rabbis of this ultra-Orthodox region, did well during the interwar years. The religious leaders here, who in the 1920s faced for the first time a serious Zionist national challenge, responded by flocking to the Agude's banner and urged the faithful not to support the atheistic Jewish Party. In 1925 the Slovakian Agudes yisroel formed an electoral list of its own, called the Jewish Economic Party, which polled some 17,000 votes and ruined the Jewish Party's chances of returning representatives to parliament.[48]

Opposition to the Jewish Party in Slovakia was subdued compared to that in Subcarpathian Rus, where even Agudes yisroel was regarded as a radical organization. The Hasidic rebes in this region, and particularly the famous Mukačevo Rebe, Haim Eliezer Shapira (1872–1937), were known for their extreme hostility to any secularizing tendency within Judaism and in particular to Zionism—a hostility which in this former Hungarian backwater was much more pronounced than in Poland. In 1935 the Mukačevo Rebe issued a characteristic proclamation in which he forbade all aid and comfort "to the representatives of the Zionists, the heretics [minim] and atheists" and villified the Zionist-run, modern Hebrew High School in his city, "from which issue heresy and atheism." All those who vote for the Zionists, the Rebe continued, "are aiding transgressors and criminals [poshim]."[49] In their determination to thwart the ambitions of the Jewish Party in Subcarpathian Rus, the Mukačevo Rebe and his allies favored electoral arrangements with Czech parties. Just as the powerful Polish Agude allied itself with Piłsudski after 1926, so the leader of Hasidism and his allies in eastern Czechoslovakia cooperated with the highly nationalistic Czech Agrarian Party, which they much preferred over any secular Jewish force.[50] What mattered to them, after all, was not the precise nature of the Czech party they were supporting (so long as it was not too anti-Semitic), but the preservation of traditional Jewish life, which they believed to be threatened, not by Czech, but by Jewish nationalists. Not all Jews in Subcarpathian Rus followed their lead in this matter; in 1925, for example, the Jewish Party received 19,098 votes there.[51] But the rebes were strong enough to keep this most Jewish of all Czechoslovak regions from lending all-out support to the secular nationalists, though we shall see that they were not strong enough to isolate the region from modern Jewish political doctrines emanating both from the Czech lands and from Poland.

The Jewish Party's most vocal opposition derived from Slovak and Subcarpathian Rus Orthodoxy, but of course many acculturated Jews also opposed it on ideological grounds. Some in the Czech lands remained loyal to German liberalism, some continued to support the Hungarian cause in Slovakia, and some supported either centrist Czech parties or the Czech left. As elsewhere in East Central Europe, Jews were fairly prominent in the Communist movement, though it enjoyed nothing like the support given it by Jews in Poland.[52] On the whole, it should be noted that the electoral successes of the Jewish Party did not imply the victory of Zionism as a mass movement in Czechoslovakia. Nor, as we shall see in our discussion of Jewish educational trends, did it represent Jewish support for a national Jewish school system in a Jewish language, one of the principal demands of the National Council and the Jewish Party. What it did imply was that many acculturated and Orthodox Jews, probably none too friendly to secular Jewish nationalism, voted for the Jewish Party because they believed in the need for a strong Jewish political organization devoted to protecting general Jewish interests in the new state, and because they believed that the delicate situation of Czechoslovakian Jewry dictated following an independent political line rather than siding with one nationality against another, or with one non-Jewish party against another. The multinational aspect of Czechoslovakia helped make the Jewish Party a success, just as its absence helped doom to failure any similar organization in Hungary or the Romanian Regat. But one should emphasize that in Czechoslovakia, as in Poland and Romania, it was the secular Zionists who proved themselves not only the most active political force within Jewry but also the most capable of defending the interests of all Jews, not simply those of Zionists. And the reason for this, here as elsewhere, resided in the fact that the secular Zionist leaders, usually talented and energetic professionals, possessed the tools for dealing with representatives of the new states of the region, were in tune with the democratic nature of the political system, and were therefore able to persuade the Jewish electorate that they would be more effective spokesmen for Czechoslovak Jewry on the national level than would the Orthodox leaders whose religious convictions carried so much weight within the various Jewish communities. In Czechoslovakia, as in other East European countries, the Jews supported something of a dual leadership—a secular-national leadership to represent them in parliament along with the traditional religious leadership in the *Kultusgemeinde*.

During the 1930s the Jewish Party continued to wage energetic and effective war against all manifestations of anti-Semitism, despite a split in 1935 which occurred over the issue of the party's choice of allies. As everywhere else in Eastern Europe, the issue was a most divisive one for Jewish politicians. In 1929 the Polish alliance had been generally accepted, but in 1935 a decision to make a formal electoral alliance with the Czech Social Democrats provoked a revolt and caused the resignation of many, including the former Jewish Party chairman and prominent Zionist leader Emil Margulies (1877–1943).[53] Despite the split the Jewish Party retained its two representatives in the parliament and remained the chief Jewish voice protesting the rising tide of anti-Semitism in the late 1930s.

Of all the major modern secular Jewish political tendencies, only Zionism developed roots in Czechoslovakia. The socialist-nationalist tradition represented by the Bund was lacking, since there was no Jewish working class to speak of in the Czech lands and since the impoverished, preindustrialized, and mostly Orthodox community of Subcarpathian Rus could not sustain a Marxist party. Moreover, in neither Slovakia nor Subcarpathian Rus was there much of a general Marxist socialist movement from which a Jewish movement might derive, as in Russia. As for the kind of secular Yiddish tradition represented by the Folkist party, it too was lacking in a country where Yiddish was spoken mostly by Orthodox Jews and not at all by the secularized Jews of the western region. But Zionism was another matter. Its advocacy of Palestine received a tremendous shot in the arm after the Balfour Declaration and the establishment of the British mandate, and both the triumph of nationalism everywhere in East Europe in 1918 and the rise of anti-Semitism made its appeal even stronger. Moreover, a Zionist tradition had existed in prewar Bohemia and Moravia, if not in the eastern provinces. But we must not exaggerate. Czechoslovakia, though a much more favorable environment for Zionism than mononational and monocultural Hungary, never created the kind of mass Zionist movement which existed in Poland. In 1921, there were only 8,685 shekel purchasers in the state; in 1938, 18,887 shekels were sold.[54] These figures demonstrate that a vote for the Jewish Party did not necessarily, or even usually, connote agreement with the Zionist program.

During the interwar years Czechoslovak Zionism showed many signs of weakness and a few signs of potential strength. The latter came from the east, where, as we have had occasion to note several times, the old Hungarian pattern of a split between Reform and Orthodox Judaism, rather than between religious and secular-national Jews, was not propitious for the rise of modern Jewish nationalism. But there is some indication that during the interwar years this pattern was beginning to change. Living in a new, modern state with compulsory secular education, many Orthodox youths came into greater contact with the modern world. The combination of Orthodox religious roots and secularization, in an environment heavy with nationalism and growing anti-Semitism, directed many youths here, as in Poland in an earlier period, toward Zionism. It is no accident that by the 1930s the pioneering movement in general and Ha-shomer ha-tsair in particular were concentrated in Slovakia and Subcarpathian Rus.[55] In these regions, therefore, the old anti-Zionist Orthodox tradition came to be challenged by a new pioneering, Palestine-oriented Zionism represented by the youth of the regions. In 1935, of the 1,500-odd pioneers (*halutsim*) in Czechoslovakia, over half came from Subcarpathian Rus.[56] But for the war, the growth of this new Zionism in the eastern provinces would surely have continued.

In the brief interwar period, however, the Czechoslovakian Jewries proved not only too acculturated or too Orthodox for Zionism to become a great factor, but also on the whole too secure. As many of its leading members had observed, the Bar Kochba type of Zionism in Bohemia was not an expression of a search for a new land in which to live, but the answer to a personal search for identity and roots. It was a reply not to *Judennot*, the physical needs of the Jews, but to a spiritual dilemma. This was typical of Zionism in the well-off communities of Central Europe, such as Germany, and its spiritual rather than "vulgar national" character set it off from Zionist movements in those lands of East Central Europe where the Jews felt much more strongly the need for a refuge in Palestine.[57] But while the Czechoslovak Zionist movement was somewhat similar to Masaryk's nationalist conceptions, just as some factions within Polish Zionism were close to Piłsudski's version of nationalism, the general well-being of the Jews in Czechoslovakia—the feeling of physical security, the lack of state-inspired anti-Semitism on the Polish model, the belief that there was a future here—meant that Zionism, at least in a sense of a Palestine-oriented political movement, would never win over too many adherents, and that most of its adherents would not seriously contemplate emigration to Palestine. In fact, there was precious little *aliyah* from Czechoslovakia during the interwar years. To be sure, the feeling of security began to erode in the middle and late 1930s, particularly in Slovakia. At that time, as we have seen, Zionism grew stronger, but these years were not characteristic of the period as a whole.

A twenty-year period is usually too short to produce profound cultural changes, but so far as the three Jewries of Czechoslovakia were concerned the interwar years signaled a sharp break with the past. The old non-Jewish ruling cultural orientations, German and Hungarian, gave way to Czech and Slovak, and, since most Jews growing up in the interwar years attended state schools, an important process of "czechization" and "slovakization" took place. The process naturally drove a wedge between the older generation, raised in Habsburg times and remaining by and large loyal to the old cultural (and sometimes political) orientations, and the youth. German remained the language of several major Jewish publications in the Republic, notably the Zionist organ *Selbstwehr*, and the most important journal of Jewish history in the Czech lands was published in Czech and German. But Czech and Slovak became the main languages of the new Jewish generation in the Czech lands and in Slovakia. (The language of the backward Rusyns, on the other hand, did not supplant Yiddish as the dominant language of Subcarpathian Rus Jewry.) It is noteworthy, however, that linguistic acculturation, no new phenomenon in the Czech lands and in Slovakia, was not necessarily accompanied by identification with either the Czech or the Slovak nationality. A comparison of the 1921 data (see above, table 3.4) and the 1930 data (see table 3.5) on the national identification of the Czechoslovak Jewries will bear out this point. In the Czech lands this nine-year period witnessed a slight rise in the percentage of Jews identifying themselves as Jews by nationality; here the old German orientation was declining, but its place was being taken not so much by a new Czechoslovak orientation as by a slowly growing identification with the Jewish nationality. The situation in Slovakia was somewhat different; here there was a significant desertion of the

TABLE 3.5
**National Identities of Czechoslovak Jews, 1930 (By Percentage)**

| Region | Nationality | | |
|---|---|---|---|
| | Jewish | Czechoslovak | German |
| Bohemia | 20.26 | 46.42 | 31.01 |
| Moravia-Silesia | 51.67 | 17.58 | 29.08 |
| Slovakia | 53.11 | 32.19 | 7.12 |

SOURCE: Franz Friedmann, *Einige Zahlen über die tschechoslovakischen Juden* (Prague, 1933), p. 25; Egbert Jahn, *Die Deutschen in der Slowakei in den Jahren, 1918–1919* (Munich and Vienna, 1971), p. 72; Bruno Blau, "Nationality among Czechoslovak Jewry," *Historica Judaica* 10 (1948):150–51.

old Hungarian orientation, thanks no doubt in part to pressure from the regime, and a substantial rise in the percentage of Jews identifying with the Czechoslovak nationality, while the number professing the Jewish nationality remained about the same. In Subcarpathian Rus, however, even more Jews than in 1921 proclaimed themselves adherents to the Jewish nationality.[58] For the entire country, the situation in 1930 was as follows: 57.20 percent of the Jewish population identified themselves as Jews by nationality (as opposed to 53.86 percent in 1921), 24.52 percent as Czechoslovaks, and 12.82 percent as Germans.[59] This does not mean that the majority of Czechoslovak Jews were Jewish nationalists, but it does mean that acculturation and identification with the dominant nationality did not necessarily go hand in hand. Thus in the Czech lands the high rate of intermarriage, which rose during the 1920s, coexisted with a modest rise in Jewish national identification during the same period. It may be argued that intermarriage is a more telling indication of which way the Jewish community was going than are responses to census forms. But the data on national identification point once again to the very different political-cultural situation which prevailed in Czechoslovakia and in Hungary.

In the prewar period Jews in the Czech lands were most likely to attend German-language state schools; and in Slovakia, Hungarian-language state schools. Indeed, these schools were the chief instruments of germanization and magyarization. In the interwar years Jewish children in these regions, as in Polish Galicia, continued the tradition of attending state schools, not private Jewish institutions, but now they flocked to schools in the Czech and Slovak languages. Even in Subcarpathian Rus, where the traditional Jewish religious school, or *kheyder*, had ruled supreme before the war, the state school became very important. According to government statistics there were, in the school year 1931–1932, 63,987 Jewish pupils and students in state schools (from kindergarten to university; the breakdown of the schools they attended, by language of instruction, is shown in table 3.6). Private Jewish schools were of importance only in Slovakia and in Subcarpathian Rus. In Slovakia there were, in the school year 1932–1933, 59 such schools, of which 35 were conducted in Slovak, 16 in Hungarian, and 5 in German. Particularly interesting is the situation in Subcarpathian Rus, where the Czech-language schools set up for children of Czech bureaucrats attracted many Jewish children whose parents did not care to send them to Ruthenian-language schools. Since there were relatively few Czechs living in this province, in many of these schools the majority of pupils were Jews.[60] Here, of course, was a repetition of the old and dangerous Jewish habit of sending children to the schools of the ruling nationality, a habit not appreciated by the Rusyns, just as it had not been appreciated by the

TABLE 3.6
**Jews in Czechoslovak State Schools, 1931–1932**

| Language | Number of Jewish Pupils* |
|----------|--------------------------|
| Czech and Slovak | 35,918 |
| German | 10,787 |
| Hungarian | 5,156 |
| Bilingual | 4,913 |
| Ruthenian | 3,885 |

SOURCE: Franz Friedmann, *Einige Zahlen über die tschechoslovakischen Juden* (Prague, 1933), pp. 17–19.

*Not included are Jewish pupils in rabbinical seminaries, in Hebrew-language schools, and in schools with English and French as languages of instruction.

Czechs in prewar Bohemia and Moravia. But Subcarpathian Rus was also the only region in Czechoslovakia where modern, Zionist-run Hebrew-language schools on the Polish Tarbut model were established. There were four such elementary schools there in 1932–1933, and there was also the famous Hebrew High School (*Gymnasium*) in Mukačevo. The high school was the center of Zionist life in the province; its director was a Russian Jew, Haim Kugel (1897–1966), who was also a leader of the Jewish Party and a delegate in the Czechoslovak parliament. Kugel's prominence in the 1930s marks the coming of age of the Enlightenment movement of the nationalist, East European type in this region. It is not surprising that the Hebrew High School was singled out for special abuse by the Hasidic leaders of the area, especially by the fanatic Mukačevo Rebe, who is said to have spat every time he passed its imposing building and who termed it a "house of abomination." Thomas Masaryk, on the other hand, viewed it with great favor, and made a generous private donation to it.[61] But just as the Hasidic majority here could not prevent Zionism from making inroads, so they could not prevent a small but active part of the Jewish population from supporting and sending their children to Zionist schools.

Zionist schools were unable to take root either in the Czech lands or in Slovakia, however. For, no matter to what extent they might have identified themselves as "Jewish by nationality," the Jews of these lands were too acculturated to consider the possibility of establishing modern Hebrew-language Zionist schools. This meant, in effect, that the Jewish National Council's demand for state-supported Jewish schools in a Jewish language made no impression among the Jewish population of Bohemia, Moravia, and Slovakia. We have seen the same pattern at work in Poland, where even the much less acculturated Galician Jews still preferred government schools in Polish to Tarbut schools in Hebrew. Only in

Subcarpathian Rus, where no "foreign" language had won the allegiance of the great majority of the Jews, and where Orthodoxy was at least to some extent breaking down under the impact of life in a modern state, were such schools possible. They were by no means as influential as the Tarbut school systems in Polish Lithuania, in Bessarabia, or in independent Lithuania, where Orthodox opposition was much weaker than in this extremely backward region, but their existence as a small pocket of modern Zionism in a hostile area is another sign that modern Jewish nationalism in Subcarpathian Rus possessed considerable potential.[62]

The data on educational trends clearly indicate that the cultural gap between the Czechs and Slovaks on the one hand and the Jews on the other was rapidly closing. So too were the cultural gaps among the Jewries of the Czech lands, Slovakia, and Subcarpathian Rus. Had the Republic endured another generation, the old German and Hungarian orientations would probably have completely disappeared. This process was particularly dramatic in Slovakia, where the Slovak culture had attracted very few Jews before the war.[63] (We shall see that the "slovakization" of the Jews did not, however, lessen anti-Semitism in this region.) The overrepresentation of Jews in high schools and universities, as apparent in Czechoslovakia as elsewhere in East Central Europe, and not impeded by any *numerus clausus*, naturally hastened the process. Thus, in the school year 1935–1936, 11.9 percent of all university students in the state were Jews, some five times higher than their proportion within the population.[64] And yet the Jewish penetration into high Czech and Slovak culture during the interwar years does not appear to have been very deep. There were a few fairly well-known Jewish Czech writers, such as the playwright František Langer, but the role of Jews in Polish and Hungarian culture in the interwar years was probably more impressive. Certainly there was no parallel in the interwar years to the brilliant German-Jewish cultural symbiosis of the late Habsburg period in Prague, which produced such luminaries as Kafka and Werfel. The brilliance of Prague German-Jewish culture was, after all, the result of a century of germanization in the Czech lands. The interwar Czechoslovak Republic was perhaps too short-lived to create a similar Czech or Slovak-Jewish culture.

### 5. The End of the Honeymoon: Anti-Semitism and the Collapse of Czechoslovakia

Jewish well-being in Czechoslovakia depended upon the political and economic stability of the state and its success in warding off irredentist challenges from Germany and Hungary. By the mid-1930s the state had succeeded in preserving its liberal, democratic political traditions, despite the economic depression, but the rise of Nazism and extreme Hungarian revisionism boded ill for the future. Internally the nationalities problem, Czechoslovakia's Achilles' heel, was becoming more acute. If in the early 1920s most of the Sudeten Germans had been willing to cooperate with the state, no matter how unhappy they were at the prospect of living under Czech rule, they were now coming more and more under the influence and control of Konrad Henlein's pro-Nazi party, which won a great electoral victory in 1935. The Magyar minority in Slovakia and Subcarpathian Rus was likewise strongly influenced by irredentist propaganda emanating from Horthy's Hungary. And many Slovaks, led by the Hlinka Slovak People's Party, were now in favor of breaking the Czech connection and founding either an autonomous Slovakia or their own state. The growth of German, Hungarian, Slovak, and also Rusyn nationalism in the 1930s was a bad omen for the Jewish minority. The anti-Czech and antistate sentiments of the minorities were inevitably accompanied by growing anti-Semitism, which was at any rate traditionally stronger among most of these nationalities than among the Czechs. And they very naturally provoked a national Czech reaction. The resulting hothouse environment was quite different from that of the 1920s, when the Czech-Jewish alliance had been forged.

For most Czechoslovak Jews the crisis of the 1930s was political, not economic. In this sense the situation here differed from that in most other East European countries, where economic decline was no less traumatic than the decline in personal security brought about by the rise of militant anti-Semitism. The Depression had a major impact, of course, but Czechoslovakia was richer than any other East European state and weathered the crisis more easily. The Jews of the Czech lands, and even of more backward Slovakia, held their own. It was only in Subcarpathian Rus that we may speak of a Jewish economic crisis, for this typically East European Jewish community shared the economic fate of similar communities in Poland, Romania, and the Baltic States. Here, as in Galicia, the kresy, Bessarabia, and Lithuania, new competition from a slowly emerging native professional and merchant class, as well as from peasant cooperatives, struck at the Jews' traditional economic strength, and the influx of Czech manufactured goods ruined many old-fashioned Jewish artisans. The general economic situation in the region improved during the 1920s, thanks to Czech efforts, but then came the Great Depression. But among the Jews the number of beggars and *luftmentshn* seems to have increased. Haim Kugel, leader of the Jewish Party in Subcarpathian Rus, described the desperate situation in the mid-1930s:

> Hundreds of Jewish workers, day laborers and wagoners, are without work. Hundreds of Jewish artisans, in the wake of the rise of industry, remain without bread. This situation has caused demoralization among

the youth. Thousands of youths wander about without work, without any skills, indifferent, without seeking meaning or content for their lives. In their life struggle for their physical existence they take steps with which we can never agree. Some fall under the unrestrained influence of the "wonder working" Rebe and of superstitious beliefs, and others fall victim to demagoguery because of their ignorance and lack of education.[65]

This description, excepting perhaps the Hasidic aspect so typical of Subcarpathian Rus, could be applied with equal accuracy to Jewish youth in Poland, which as we know was termed in the 1930s a "youth without a future." Such conditions naturally led to political extremism (Kugel's allusion to "demagoguery" presumably means Communism) and psychological despair. We should note that this aspect of the Jewish crisis in East Central Europe in the 1930s was part and parcel of the general economic crisis in most of the region, not necessarily the result of anti-Jewish policies. It was exacerbated, of course, by anti-Semitic economic policy in such countries as Poland and Romania, but it struck the Subcarpathian Jews of non–anti-Semitic Czechoslovakia (and the Jewish community of only moderately anti-Semitic Lithuania) no less harshly, while in highly anti-Semitic Hungary the Jewish economic situation remained fairly stable until the anti-Jewish laws of the late 1930s. The key to the crisis resided in the Jews' unhealthy economic situation in most of the more backward regions of East Central Europe. The East European-type communities in these regions were too vulnerable to rising local competition, and, even where there was no concerted anti-Semitic economic campaign, the general economic stagnation, made worse by the Depression, rendered impossible any breakthrough to Western-type economic status. As already pointed out, it was only in the Soviet Union that such a breakthrough occurred during the interwar years. But Soviet conditions were unique in East Europe.

Perhaps the most ominous internal political development in Czechoslovakia, from the Jewish point of view, was the rise of extreme anti-Czech nationalism in Slovakia. By the mid-1930s the deep-rooted anti-Semitic tradition in this region was receiving fresh impetus from the movement for Slovak independence, led by the most nationalistic of Slovak political forces. The combination of the lack of both a liberal and a left-wing political tradition, economic weakness, and national frustration made Slovakia a fertile area for the type of right-wing political movements which flourished in Romania and Hungary, and to a lesser extent in Poland, but not in the Czech lands. These movements were closely associated with the powerful Catholic church, which in Slovakia, as in Poland, looked upon the Jewish minority with great disfavor. The more extreme were openly fascist and received support from abroad, particularly from Nazi Germany.[66] The attitude of most Slovak nationalists toward the Jewish minority in the late 1930s is expressed well in a memorandum written by George Kennan in February, 1939, a few months after the Munich accord which created Slovak autonomy within the framework of the so-called Second Republic:

> The present Slovak autonomous regime grew out of the Hlinka movement, which had been subject to extensive and direct German influence for some time before the Munich Agreement. It is not surprising that it should have come to power with an out-and-out anti-Semitism as one of the principal planks in its platform. There is no point in reciting here the various statements of Slovak leaders with respect to the Jewish question. There have been many statements of this sort and their tenor has been all more or less the same: that the influence of the Jews in the political and economic life of Slovakia would have to be eliminated, and that the Slovak government would not shy at extreme measures in pursuing this purpose. . . . An important factor in the attitude of the Slovak authorities toward the Jews is the attitude of the Roman Catholic Church. Dr. Tiso [the prime minister of autonomous Slovakia] is himself a priest and the regime is strongly Catholic in character. Thus far, the Church has not seemed to be doing much to moderate the attitude of the government on the Jewish question. The Church's attitude was recently defined in detail by the Provincial of the Jesuit Order in Slovakia, Father Rudolph Mikus, who granted to the semi-official Bratislava newspaper, the *Slovak*, what was evidently a carefully prepared interview of this subject. . . . It will be seen that the Church, according to Father Mikus, favors the segregation of the Jews and the elimination of their influence in political and economic life in Slovakia.[67]

This analysis dates from a time when the more extreme Slovak nationalists were in the saddle, but, as Kennan remarks, this kind of thinking characterized Slovak national thought before Munich as well. And the Nazis, through their virulently anti-Semitic and anti-Czech propaganda broadcasts in Slovak, did their part to convince the Slovaks that their most dangerous enemy was the Jew.[68] In the Czech lands the situation was different, but even there the growing threats to the integrity of the Republic, both from abroad and from within, brought into the open anti-Semitic feelings which, as we know, were never lacking in Bohemia and Moravia. In July, 1938, a British diplomat remarked that "in Czechoslovakia . . . there is a deep-seated *popular* prejudice against them [the Jews] due largely to their success and 'encroachment' upon restricted fields of activity. Of this prejudice they are only too well aware, and it is a source of great anxiety to them."[69] This prejudice could only grow with the great political crisis of September, 1938.

The Munich agreement created a totally new situation in Czechoslovakia. As a direct result of the agreement, more than one-third of the territory of Bohemia and Moravia was ceded to Germany. In November, part of Slovakia, with close to one million inhabitants, along with part of Subcarpathian Rus, was "returned" to Hungary. In October, Poland took a share in this first dismemberment of the state by taking over the previously Czech part of Těšín (Teschen). Moreover, Slovakia received full autonomy, as did Subcarpathian Rus, now called Carpathian Ukraine. As a further concession to the Slovaks, the state was now called Czecho-Slovakia. This was a disaster for the Czechs, of course, and also for the Jews, whose fate was so closely tied to the integrity and prosperity of Czechoslovakia. The Jews of the Sudetenland, now annexed to the German Reich, were expelled by the Nazis and at first not admitted by the new Czech government. In October, 1938, they are described as "squatting in deplorable conditions in no man's land between Czech and German lines."[70] The Slovakian Jews "returned" to Hungary were not in such desperate straits, but they now found themselves in a virulently anti-Semitic state which had only recently begun to revoke Jewish emancipation and which was not grateful for the support some Jews had given there to the Magyar cause. As for the Jews who remained in the rump state of Czecho-Slovakia, they encountered unleashed anti-Semitism in autonomous Slovakia (and to a lesser extent in Carpathian Ukraine) and a new and hostile environment in the Czech lands. The situation was, of course, most dangerous in Slovakia, where (in the words of a British report of January, 1939) "the Slovaks were now at liberty to give free rein to the clerical and authoritarian ideals which appealed to a backward and fervently Catholic peasant people."[71] An authoritarian regime was established and the fascistlike Hlinka Guard was appointed to enforce the regime's will. The loss of some Slovak territory to Hungary in November fed the chauvinistic flames and stepped up the search for a scapegoat, while by no means relaxing Nazi Germany's growing hold. Already in late 1938, immediately following the proclamation of Slovak autonomy, anti-Semitic disturbances erupted in the country. In March, 1939, a sovereign Slovak state, which was in fact a Nazi protectorate, was established. One of its first steps, taken in April, 1939, was the promulgation of a "Jewish law" after the Hungarian model. This law defined as Jews all those who were Jewish by religion and had not converted to Christianity before 1918; as in Hungary, the Slovaks would not accept as Christians recent converts, whose motives were presumably suspect.[72] Persons of no religion with at least one Jewish parent were considered to be Jews, as were all persons who married Jews. Having thus defined its victims, the law went on to limit the number of Jewish lawyers to four percent of the total number, to exclude Jews altogether from the ranks of the notary publics, and to allow Jewish editors to work only for Jewish newspapers. It is interesting that this measure, which effectively brought to an end Jewish legal equality in Slovakia, struck only at the relatively small number of Jews in the legal profession and at editors. It indicates how much these Jewish professionals were hated by the new Slovak intelligentsia, which felt less threatened by Jewish shopkeepers and merchants than by Jewish lawyers. As for Jewish editors, they were regarded as symbols of the penetration of "alien" doctrines into Slovak culture.

This law was only the first step. As an American diplomat reported in May, 1939:

> . . . the purpose of the Slovak legislation may be said to have been to segregate out of the body of the population all those Jews who have not long since become Catholics, to stamp these people definitely as Jews, and to limit their participation in the free professions. This is, of course, only a portion of the anti-Semitic program of the Slovak leaders. The problems connected with the role of the Jews in the medical profession, with Jewish predominance in business and finance, and with Jewish ownership of land still remain for future legislative treatment.[73]

Indeed, after the outbreak of World War II such legislation was passed, and Jews (now defined according to much stricter criteria) were systematically ousted from the Slovak economy. In this regard the Slovaks followed in the footsteps of their otherwise hated Hungarian neighbors.[74] The great majority of Slovak Jews were eventually deported and put to death in Nazi concentration camps.

In what was left of the Czech lands the Jews fared somewhat better, but it was clear to them and to everyone else that the old liberal Czech world of Masaryk (who had died in 1937) and his partner Beneš (who resigned after Munich) was dead and buried. The new, post-Munich Czech regime was right wing and was obliged to seek accommodation with Germany. The popular mood, after the great loss of territory and betrayal by the Western powers, was ugly. Several Jewish leaders sadly reported that the old humanistic traditions had been replaced by an all too typical East European nationalistic and intolerant state.[75] Emigration, including *aliyah* to Palestine, increased. We have already seen that the Czechs would not admit Jewish refugees from the Sudetenland, and those who did eventually manage to enter encountered great difficulties in obtaining work permits. Writing in February, 1939, George Kennan remarked that the Czech government was under constant German pressure to do something about the "Jewish question," while the British and French, as well as most Czechs, opposed radical measures.[76] It was thanks, no doubt, to the lack of a Slovak-type anti-Semitic tradition in the Czech lands that no "Jewish law" was promulgated during the short-lived Second Republic, but new regulations on naturalization threatened many Jews with loss of Czech citizenship, and the civil service was purged of all Jewish employees. Jews were ousted also from all state-supported German institutions, such as the German university in Prague.[77] How much all this was the result of German pressure or how much the result of growing Czech anti-Semitism is impossible to determine. At any rate, in March, 1939, German troops put an end to the Second Republic, and the anti-Jewish measures and eventual annihilation of Czech Jewry were solely the responsibility of the Nazis. At the same time, Hungary took over the rest of Subcarpathian Rus, where anti-Semitic agitation had also been on the rise since that region had acquired autonomous status in November, 1938. Its Jews therefore came to share the tragic fate of Hungarian Jewry during the war years.

## 6. A Summing Up

Our brief survey of Jewish history in Czechoslovakia during the years 1918–1939 demonstrates that the uniquely benign condition of the Jews in this country was a function of the preservation both of Czech domination and of the Masaryk-Beneš tradition of Czech politics. The decline of Czech rule in Slovakia and Subcarpathian Rus inevitably brought a decline in the Jews' well-being. Nazi influence was certainly important in the unleashing of anti-Semitic attacks in these lands, but it was not crucial. For, in the typically East European environment of Slovakia and Subcarpathian Rus, the combination of extreme nationalism, authoritarianism, economic distress, and religious traditions and the identification of the Jews with economic domination, preponderance in the professions (particularly annoying to the new "native intelligentsia"), revolution, and the hated national oppressor led directly to such measures as the Slovak Jewish laws. The Germans encouraged such measures, but the Slovaks predominantly favored them as well. Only Prague could restrain such anti-Semitic manifestations, and only a Prague dominated by Masaryk's "nationalism with a human face."[78] The achievement of Slovak autonomy as a result of the Munich agreement and the establishment of a new type of Czech regime marked the beginning of the end of that Czech-Jewish alliance which was unparalleled in interwar East Central Europe and which had been lived up to by both sides until 1938.

From the standpoint of internal Jewish developments, most of the basic patterns of the prewar period continued to prevail. The Czech lands continued to be a good place for Jews, but not a very good place for Judaism in the sense of Jewish religious or cultural life. The remarkable success of the Jewish Party and the emergence of a secular, national Jewish leadership was, to be sure, a departure, but it was not accompanied by a dramatic upsurge of Zionist sentiment or the establishment of modern Jewish educational or religious institutions. Acculturation remained the hallmark of this Jewry, with Czech clearly becoming the main spoken language. This was the case despite a willingness on the part of many to identify as "Jews by nationality," such identification itself a function of the complex nationalities situation in the state. In the eastern provinces there were more striking changes. The hold of Orthodoxy remained strong, but a certain degree of secularization, speeded up by the compulsory school system, enabled modern Jewish nationalism to make an appearance, even in the Hasidic stronghold of Subcarpathian Rus. The Mukačevo Rebe remained a great force in Jewish life, but such new leaders as Haim Kugel also rose to prominence. Czech and Slovak culture made considerable inroads into Jewish life, most dramatically in Subcarpathian Rus, and this created an ever-growing link between the Western-type Jewry of the Czech lands and the very different Jewries of the eastern provinces. Had not war intervened, it might have been possible to speak before too long of a single Czechoslovakian Jewry. And in the two eastern sections, at least, this Jewry would have become progressively more secular-national and less Orthodox although, at least in Subcarpathian Rus, economically more vulnerable.

In 1943 the son of Thomas Masaryk, addressing a Jewish organization in England, remarked that "relations between the Jews and the Czechs were, in fact, excellent. We knew that when times were hard the Jewish minority would always stand by us. It never let us down."[79] This is a somewhat idealized but nonetheless basically accurate assessment, and Jan Masaryk, soon to be foreign minister of the postwar state, was right not to include the Slovaks in it. Most of the Jews of interwar Czechoslovakia would have agreed with him. It was neither their fault nor that of the Czechs that these relations did not endure. Those Jews lucky enough to survive the Holocaust in the Czech lands and Slovakia were not to witness a preservation of the Czech-Jewish alliance in Communist Czechoslovakia. In this sense, as in so many other ways, Communist Czechoslovakia was to have little in common with the Czechoslovakia of Masaryk.

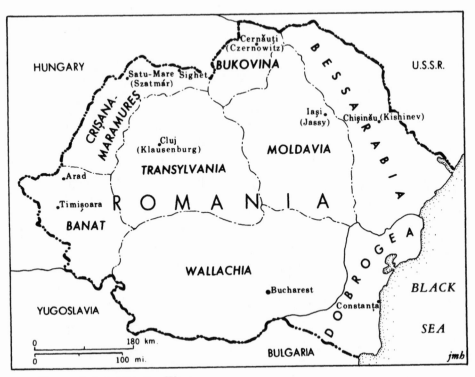

**Romania between the Wars**

# ROMANIA /4

Of all the countries surveyed in this book, Romania was the only one that existed as a fully sovereign state prior to World War I. There was, however, a great difference between prewar Romania and Romania of the interwar years. Known as the Old Kingdom, or the Regat, the prewar state comprised Moldavia, Wallachia, and part of Dobrogea. Because the population in these provinces was overwhelmingly Romanian, prewar Romania was very much a nation-state. All this changed after the war. In a series of diplomatic successes, which derived from Romania's having joined the victorious powers in 1918—successes which even the most optimistic Romanian nationalists could hardly have dreamed possible—neighboring lands having a substantial Romanian population were annexed to the Regat. These included formerly Russian Bessarabia, formerly Austrian Bukovina, formerly Bulgarian southern Dobrogea, and formerly Hungarian Transylvania (which consisted of three distinct regions: historical Transylvania, known in German as Siebenburgen, the Banat, and Crişana-Maramureş in the north). As a result of these unparalleled developments, Romania expanded tremendously in both population and territory. In this sense its experience was the very opposite of Hungary's, as Romania was transformed almost overnight from a small, insignificant country into the second largest state in East Central Europe. If Hungary, as a result of its humiliation, was a country devoted to irredentism, Romania was a country dedicated to the status quo. In this regard, Romania was similar to Czechoslovakia and to Poland, with whom it concluded defensive treaties against those rather numerous powers who coveted its territories.

The newly acquired territories also transformed Romania into a nationalities state on the Polish model. As in Poland, so in Romania only about two-thirds of the population was Romanian by nationality. Of the large number of national minorities in Romania the most important were the Hungarians, the Germans, the Russians, the Ukrainians, and the Jews. However, none of these nationalities was numerous enough to constitute the kind of challenge which the Ukrainians posed to the Polish state or, to choose another example, which the Germans or Slovaks posed to Czech rule in interwar Czechoslovakia. Nevertheless, the nationalities problem was a serious one for Romania, and here again the contrast with

Hungary is striking.[1] But in at least one sense interwar Hungary and interwar Romania were similar: they were both, from the outset, fiercely anti-Bolshevik and therefore counterrevolutionary. Hungary had the unpleasant experience of a short-lived Soviet regime, and Romania had annexed a province—Bessarabia—once tsarist and now coveted by the new Soviet regime. The Bessarabian issue, along with other obvious social and political differences, poisoned relations between the new Romania and the Soviet Union, and made anyone suspected of pro-Communist leanings into an enemy of Romanian nationalism. Indeed, one of the major themes of interwar Romanian anti-Semitism was the identification of the Jew as pro-Soviet and therefore as desiring the dismemberment of the state.

Like interwar Poland, interwar Romania faced the severe challenge of forging extremely diverse regions into a centralized nation-state. The Romanians of the Regat, who alone had enjoyed political power before the war, remained by and large the political masters of the new state, but they were looked down on by the Transylvanian Romanians, who regarded themselves as more Western (many were Uniate Christians, unlike the Orthodox Christians of the Regat). In different parts of the state different cultural orientations flourished—German in Bukovina, Hungarian in Transylvania, Russian in Bessarabia. If the Regat had achieved independence (and its own dynasty, of German origin) during the nineteenth century, in Transylvania the Romanians remained until World War I a powerless and oppressed people, inferior not only to the ruling Hungarians but to the local German minority as well. One thing which all the regions of the new state shared was economic backwardness, although in this aspect, too, important regional differences were apparent. Bessarabia was an extremely backward land, whereas Wallachia (in which the capital, Bucharest, was situated) and parts of Transylvania were considerably more advanced. The Romanians were a largely peasant people, and city life had been traditionally dominated by foreigners—Greeks, Germans, Hungarians, and Jews. Although by the late nineteenth century an important native intelligentsia had emerged, the Romanians, like most other East European peoples, had not developed much in the way of a commercial or industrial bourgeoisie. A large number of the great landowners of the country also were foreigners, although many were native Romanian "boyars" against whom the peasants of the Regat had staged a bloody jacquerie in 1907. Opposition to foreign domination of Romanian life, real or imagined, played a large role in the growth of Romanian nationalism, and since the Jews were almost invariably identified as foreigners, no matter how long they had lived in the country, Romanian nationalism was almost automatically anti-Semitic.

Interwar Romania, though officially a constitutional monarchy run on democratic principles, was not the ideal setting for the flourishing of Western-style liberalism. Politics in the Old Kingdom had been characterized by a great deal of corruption and by little sharing of power among the Romanian people, and these traditions were maintained after World War I. While party life was well developed and while opposition parties (with the exception of the Communists) were tolerated, elections were usually "arranged." As did most other countries of East Central Europe, Romania became increasingly less democratic and more right wing with the passing of time. By the 1930s the conservative, established right, best represented by King Carol, and the extreme right represented by the fascist Iron Guard and its various allies, were engaged in a great power struggle, one quite similar to that which characterized Hungarian political life in the 1930s. In both countries native fascism developed into a major force, and in both countries the moderate right-wing political establishment was obliged to oppose it in its struggle to maintain power. And, finally, in both countries the "Jewish question" occupied a strategic position of great importance in this struggle, while the fate of the Jews themselves hung in the balance.[2]

## 1. The Romanian Jewries

As were the Jews of Poland, Czechoslovakia, and Latvia, but unlike those of Lithuania and Hungary, the Jews of interwar Romania were divided into a number of very different communities. Indeed, the situation was probably more complex here than anywhere else in Eastern Europe.[3] The Jewish community of the Regat was in fact really two communities—that of Wallachia, relatively small and corresponding basically to the Western type, and that of Moldavia, much larger and much more Eastern. The Jewries of Bessarabia and Bukovina were both indisputably of the Eastern type, but in many ways they were quite different, the first having lived under Russian oppression, and the latter, which boasted a germanized elite in the capital city of Cernăuți (Czernowitz), having lived under tolerant Austrian rule. The situation in the former Hungarian regions was particularly complicated. In the northern region, known as Crişana-Maramureş, there resided an Eastern-type Jewry similar in many ways to that of Galicia, while in Transylvania proper and in the Banat there lived a Hungarian-type Jewry which in certain cities was as germanized as it was magyarized. In all, therefore, at least five distinct Jewries suddenly and quite unexpectedly found themselves living in the same state.

The Jews of the Regat, who had lived under Romanian sovereignty before World War I, were the only Jews in interwar Romania who had enjoyed (if that is the proper word) close contact with Romanian culture. In Wallachia, where the Jewish community was long established, relatively small, and concentrated in the capital, Bucharest, this contact had produced a considerable degree of acculturation (particularly in the case of the small but wealthy Sephardic community in the capital). In Moldavia, on the other hand, a much larger Jewish community, more recently arrived from the east, was much more prominent in urban life and more proletarian than Wallachian Jewry. As might be expected, in Moldavia the Jews still spoke Yiddish, many were under the influence of Hasidism, and in general they shared a number of characteristics with the Eastern-type community of nearby Galicia (whence, so all Romanian anti-Semites insisted, the Jews had "invaded" Romania in great numbers during the nineteenth century). But if Wallachian Jewry was in many ways a Western-type Jewry, and Moldavian Jewry an Eastern-type community, we must nonetheless use these terms with reservation. Reform Judaism of the German or Hungarian type never took root in Wallachia; nor, as we shall see, was the acculturation of Wallachian Jewry accompanied by the adoption of a Romanian national identity. In Moldavia, on the other hand, autonomous modern Jewish cultural and political life on the Galician, Polish, or Russian model was relatively weak. True, the modern Yiddish theater got its start in Jassy (Iaşi) in 1876, but this was largely the work of the Russian-born Avraham Goldfaden. In fact, Moldavia remained something of a Jewish backwater. There were no great centers of traditional Jewish learning here, and little in the way of a modern, national Jewish intelligentsia. Although the Haskalah movement was active, imported (like Hasidism) from Galicia, it failed to provide the impetus for the development of modern Hebrew or Yiddish culture and modern Jewish politics. In this sense Moldavian Jewry was something like the Jewry of Subcarpathian Rus, a "colony" of Galician Jewry cut off, thanks to political borders, from the great Jewish centers both in Galicia and in the Russian empire, and existing in a region not only economically backward, but culturally backward as well.[4]

So far as relations with the non-Jewish world were concerned, both Jewries of the Regat suffered from the same disabilities. Prewar Romania had a well-deserved reputation for being, along with Russia, the most anti-Semitic country in Europe. Despite pressure, at times quite intense, from the great powers of Europe, Romania had steadfastly refused to emancipate her Jewish subjects. As a result, by the eve of World War I only a tiny minority of Romanian Jews had acquired Romanian citizenship; the great majority were considered foreigners and therefore of inferior legal status.[5] It is instructive to compare this situation with that of Hungary. Unlike the Magyars, the Romanians had no need of Jewish services in ethnically mixed regions, since the Regat was a homogeneous,

Romanian nation-state. Also unlike the Magyars, the Romanian political elite was not prepared to leave the capitalist development of the country to "foreigners." The leading political force of the Regat, the Liberal Party, dominated by the Brătianu family, was devoted to the cause of industrializing Romania and of creating a native Romanian commercial and industrial class. The party was therefore anti-Semitic, although it was prepared, upon occasion, to cooperate with the Jewish bourgeoisie so long as the latter did not threaten its political power. Liberalism in prewar Hungary meant tolerating Jews and opposing anti-Semitism; in Romania its slogan was "through ourselves alone," "ourselves" meaning Christian Romanians, not Jews, Germans, Hungarians, or any other "foreigners." This slogan is reminiscent of the views of the Polish National Democrats, and, if the Brătianus were more moderate than Dmowski, they had little in common with the ideology of the old Hungarian gentry.[6] Moreover, also in contrast with Hungary, there existed in old Romania a tradition of violent popular anti-Semitism. In 1907 a great peasant revolt broke out, directed against both the Romanian landlords and their Jewish leasehold-ers (*arendaşi*). Concentrated in Moldavia, where most of the latifundia were located and where the role of Jewish *arendaşi* was especially con-spicuous, the revolt was marked by numerous anti-Jewish excesses.[7] In Romania, therefore, as in Poland, the Jews were hated by the peasants for being the symbols of wicked capitalist exploitation, and by the repre-sentatives of the "native" bourgeoisie for being obstacles to the forma-tion of a Romanian commercial class. This hatred of the Jews fit in well with the general hatred of foreigners so deeply embedded in Romanian consciousness. If in Hungary it was generally agreed in the prewar years that Jews might become good Hungarian patriots of the Mosaic faith, in Romania leading politicians and intellectuals, such as the great historian and nationalist Nicolae Iorga, insisted that the Jews were essentially foreign and that assimilation was impossible.[8] The dramatic expansion of the Romanian Jewish community as a result of the annexation of the new territories was to increase, rather than decrease, traditional Judophobia.

The history of the Jewish communities in these new territories was radically different from the history of Wallachian and Moldavian Jewry. In Bukovina, which during the nineteenth century was a crown land of the Habsburg empire, the Jews had been emancipated along with the rest of Austro-Hungarian Jewry and enjoyed complete equality. Indeed, in this multinational region, where no single nationality was able to achieve hegemony (as was not the case in Galicia), the Jews were even granted a certain degree of recognition as a separate but equal nationality. The high culture in the province was German, which was also the language of the university in Czernowitz. The Jews in the capital often knew this lan-guage, but the absence of a large German community precluded any kind of German assimilationist movement. Aside from a certain degree of German acculturation, Bukovinian Jewry was typically East European, although less steeped in traditional Jewish learning than the Jewries of Galicia and Lithuania. Outside the capital most Jews lived in small towns, spoke Yiddish, and retained Orthodox, and in many cases Hasidic, traditions. Indeed, Bukovina was the home of the famous Sadagura Hasidic dynasty, one of the best known in East Europe. Here, as in Moldavia, the influence of neighboring Galicia was strong. But even more important was the influence of the Austrian empire, much beloved by the *Kaisertreu* Jewish community and rightly seen as a guarantor of religious and national peace. So long as Habsburg rule was maintained, relations between Jews and non-Jews were as good as anywhere else in Eastern Europe, and probably better. If in Bohemia and Moravia the Jews were disliked for their German culture, this was much less the case in Bukovina, where the Jews were less germanized, where there were fewer Germans, and where the national movements of the other minorities— Romanians and Ukrainians—were weaker than that of the Czechs. And if the Jews were caught between Polish and Ukrainian nationalism in Galicia, the relative balance among the "weak" nationalities of Bukovina worked in their favor. All in all Bukovina was a reasonably good place for the Jews, despite its backwardness and poverty, and in the interwar period its now Romanian Jewish community looked back with longing to the good old days of Emperor Francis Joseph.[9]

In Bessarabia, on the other hand, the relatively large Jewish community had been under the oppressive fist of the tsarist regime, which was particularly harsh in this backward region. One of the most infamous of all modern pogroms had occurred in 1903 in its capital, Kishinev (Chişi-nău), which continued to be a center of anti-Semitic agitation during the interwar years. Bessarabian Jewry was typically East European—Yiddish speaking, Orthodox, lower middle class and proletarian, conspicuous both in the cities and in the small towns. Its modern intelligentsia was russified, not germanized as in Bukovina, and the great cultural center to which its enlightened inhabitants looked was Odessa, not Vienna. A part of the Russian Pale of Settlement, Bessarabia proved to be a fertile region for the development of modern Jewish culture and politics, more so than did the somewhat more acculturated and "Austrian" Jewry of Bukovina. Like Bukovina, Bessarabia was an ethnically mixed province, with significant Ukrainian, Russian, Romanian, and German groups. Unlike the Austrian regime, however, which saw in its germanized Jewish citizens important allies in the struggle to hold the multinational empire together, the anti-Semitic Russian state was hostile to the Jewish minority as it was hostile to the demands of the other national groups. Benighted tsarist rule and economic and social backwardness made this province a center of national and religious hatred which cannot be too strongly contrasted with the situation in Bukovina. At least at the beginning, the Jews of Bessarabia shed no tears upon being annexed to Romania, to which they appealed for protection against the pogroms then raging in the Ukraine.[10]

The same cannot be said of the Jews of Transylvania, who up until World War I lived in the Hungarian part of the Austro-Hungarian empire. As in Slovakia and other parts of the Hungarian realm, the Jews were regarded as useful allies in the heroic struggle for magyarization, and in Transylvania, as elsewhere, they were content to play the role of loyal Magyars. Having first undergone a process of germanization, influenced by the presence of a large and privileged German minority in the region, the Jews later underwent a process of magyarization. Many spoke both German and Hungarian. The Jews of historic Transylvania and the Banat were more urban and more middle class than those of the north, and often identified themselves as Magyars of the Mosaic faith. But Yiddish continued to be spoken, especially in historic Transylvania. As everywhere in Hungary a split had developed between Neologs and Orthodox, and there were important Neolog communities in Arad and Timişoara. On the whole, however, the reformers were historically weaker than in what was to become Trianon Hungary. In the north the Jewish community was much more like that of Subcarpathian Rus—very populous, very prominent in the few cities that existed in this backward area, mostly Yiddish speaking, and very strongly Hasidic (the most famous center of Hasidism being in Szatmár-Németi, or Satu-Mare, the home of the famous Satmar dynasty).[11]

Neither the Neolog, the Orthodox, nor the Hasidic communities of Transylvania were likely to provide fertile ground for the emergence of modern autonomous Jewish culture or politics. But, since Transylvania, like Bukovina and Bessarabia, was a multinational region and since traditional Judaism was so strong, Jewish acculturation and assimilation were much less pronounced than in Trianon Hungary. The transition from Hungarian to Romanian rule naturally lent impetus to Jewish separatism of the modern variety, since it dealt a severe blow to the magyarization process, and interwar Transylvania became something of a modern national Jewish center, at least in comparison with Trianon Hungary. As for Jewish-gentile relations, here as in Slovakia the Jews were perceived by the most numerous but oppressed nationality as the willing servants of the Magyars. Thus in Transylvania it was perfectly natural and almost inevitable for Romanian nationalists to be anti-Semitic, just as it was natural for Slovaks to be anti-Semites in Hungarian-dominated prewar Slovakia. The Romanian annexation of Transylvania therefore boded ill for the Jewish minority, which found itself suddenly ruled by a people whose culture and national aspirations had been severely repressed by Budapest.

## 2. The Jews of Romania: Demography, Economics, Group Identity

The number of Jews in the new, "great" Romania of the interwar period was an issue of interest not only to statisticians but also to politicians and polemicists concerned with the Jewish question. Certain anti-Semites asserted that there were as many as 1.5 million Jews in the country, the result of the "invasion" of Jews from Galicia and of the annexation of new territories abounding in Jewish subjects.[12] The official Romanian census of 1930, however, lists a grand total of 756,930 Jews (by religion), or 4.2 percent of the total population.[13] Assuming that this figure is more or less accurate (some Jewish sources maintained it was a bit too low), interwar Romania was the home of the second largest Jewish community in East Central Europe, but a community whose proportion within the total population was much lower than that of Polish Jewry and lower, too, than that of the Lithuanian, Latvian, and Hungarian Jewries. Moreover, the number of Jews remained stable during the 1930s, because of a low birth rate, and the percentage of Jews within the population declined.[14] The figures hardly bear out the alarming accusations of many Romanians that hoards of "Eastern" Jews were swarming over the country and stealing it from its rightful owners.

The distribution of Jews in the country was quite uneven (see table 4.1). In the areas which made up the old Regat, the demographic contrast between Wallachia and Moldavia is striking. In the latter province the pattern was not unlike the Polish or Galician model. The leading city, Iaşi, was over one-third Jewish, but the great majority of Moldavian Jews resided in the lesser towns and villages of this backward region. In more advanced Wallachia 76,480, the great majority of Wallachia's Jewish population, resided in the capital, Bucharest, but they constituted only 11.8 percent of the city's population. Such a large concentration of the Jewish population in one metropolitan area is reminiscent of the Hungarian, Bohemian, Moravian, and Livonian pattern, and is distinctly Western. There were few *shtetl* Jews in Wallachia, but many in less urban Moldavia. As for the two East European Jewries of Bessarabia and Bukovina, we should note in particular the very high percentage of Jews in Bukovina. In the cities of both provinces the Jewish percentage was also very pronounced: 36.05 in Chişinău, and 40.5 in Cernăuţi.[15] In both provinces significant numbers of Jews resided in small towns and villages; indeed, in Bessarabia nearly one-half the Jewish population resided in

## TABLE 4.1
### Jewish Population in Romania, 1930

| Region | Number | Percentage |
|---|---|---|
| Wallachia | | |
|   Muntenia | 94,216 | 2.3 |
|   Oltenia | 3,523 | 0.2 |
| Moldavia | 162,268 | 6.7 |
| Dobrogea | 4,031 | 0.5 |
| Bessarabia | 206,958 | 7.2 |
| Bukovina | 93,101 | 10.9 |
| Historic Transylvania | 81,503 | 2.5 |
| Banat | 14,043 | 1.5 |
| Crişana-Maramureş | 97,287 | 7.0 |

SOURCE: *Recensământul general al populaţiei româniei din 29 Decemvrie 1930*, 9 (Bucharest, 1938):441; ibid., 2 (Bucharest, 1938):xxv–xxvii.

small towns and villages.[16] In Transylvania the demographic situation was more complex. Northern Transylvania shows an Eastern pattern, including a very high percentage of Jews in the cities (23.1 in Satu-Mare, and 40.0 in Sighet) and a large number of Jews residing in small towns and villages. Historic Transylvania and the Banat show a more Western pattern; here the Jews were more urbanized, but the Jewish percentages in the cities were lower (13.4 in Cluj, 10.0 in Arad, and 10.0 in Timişoara). One should add, finally, that in certain regions of the state, in Dobrogea, for example, there were practically no Jews at all.

The socioeconomic situation of Romanian Jewry also differed sharply from one region to another. Let us consider, first of all, the situation for the entire country by comparing the activities of the economically active Jewish and non-Jewish populations (see table 4.2). As was usually the case in Eastern Europe, those non-Jews not employed in agriculture tended to be employed in industry, while the single largest Jewish group was concentrated in commerce. In the typically East European regions of Bessarabia and Bukovina the Jewish population, though on the whole very poor, played a dominant role in commerce, crafts, and the professions.[17] The Jewish role in the commercial and industrial life of Moldavia also was extremely important. In Wallachia there were a few famous Jewish banking families of great wealth, and a solid and influential Jewish bourgeoisie concentrated in Bucharest. But, since there were relatively few Jews here, their impact upon economic life in this province was less marked than in Moldavia. It cannot, at any rate, be compared to the Jews' impact on economic life in Hungary. In historic Transylvania and the Banat, too, the relatively middle-class Jewries were less conspicuous in

TABLE 4.2
**Jews and Non-Jews in the Romanian Economy,**
**1930 (By Percentage)**

|                                   | Jews | Non-Jews |
|-----------------------------------|------|----------|
| Agriculture                       | 4.1  | 73.7     |
| Industry and Crafts               | 32.8 | 11.3     |
| Commerce and Credit               | 48.3 | 4.2      |
| Transportation and Communication  | 2.4  | 2.3      |
| Army                              | 1.9  | 2.9      |
| Civil Service and Professions     | 2.7  | 3.1      |
| Other                             | 7.8  | 2.5      |

SOURCE: Leo Goldhamer, "Di yidn in rumenie," *Yidishe ekonomik* 2 (1938):149.

commercial and industrial life than they were in Bessarabia and Buko-vina, while in the north, in Crişana-Maramureş, the situation was akin to that in Moldavia, Bessarabia, and Bukovina.[18] In other words, the more backward the region the more impressive the Jewish role in the nonagrar-ian economic sector. We have already observed this pattern in the case of Poland, where the Jews constituted virtually the only bourgeoisie in the kresy but were somewhat less prominent in more advanced Congress Poland. As in Poland, so in Romania predominance in certain economic sectors did not imply wealth. On the contrary, the Jewish communities of Bessarabia and Bukovina were extremely poor, as was the Jewish com-munity in northern Transylvania. Such poverty, however, did not deter the Romanian anti-Semites from their diatribes against alleged Jewish control of the economy, just as it did not stop Dmowski and his allies from inveighing against the "Jewish character" of the economy in the kresy and in eastern Galicia.

Examination of the group identity of Romanian Jews reveals certain special characteristics, especially when compared to the existing data on Polish Jews. According to the Romanian census of 1930, which includes material on religious identity, nationality, and language, the great major-ity of Jews who proclaimed themselves to be Jews by religion also an-nounced that they were Jews by nationality; the data show 756,930 Jews by religion in the state, and 728,115 Jews by nationality. (Table 4.3 presents the absolute numbers of Jews according to each criterion.) The only two regions in which fairly significant numbers of Jews refrained from identifying themselves as Jews by nationality are Wallachia and Crişana-Maramureş. In Wallachia, where there was far more romaniza-tion than anywhere else, some eight thousand Jews by religion declared themselves to be Romanians by nationality. We may assume that in

TABLE 4.3
**Identities of Jews in Romania, 1930**

| Region | Jews by Religion | Jews by Nationality |
|--------|-----------------:|--------------------:|
| Wallachia | | |
| Muntenia | 94,216 | 86,545 |
| Oltenia | 3,523 | 3,305 |
| Moldavia | 162,268 | 158,421 |
| Dobrogea | 4,031 | 3,795 |
| Bessarabia | 206,958 | 204,858 |
| Bukovina | 93,101 | 92,492 |
| Transylvania | 81,503 | 78,626 |
| Banat | 14,043 | 11,248 |
| Crişana-Maramureş | 97,287 | 88,825 |

SOURCE: *Recensământul general al populaţiei româniei din 29 Decemvrie 1930*, 2 (Bucharest, 1938):xxiv–xxvii; ibid., 9 (Bucharest, 1938):409.

Crişana-Maramureş many Hasidic Jews were not happy with the idea that they should identify as Jews by nationality (implying that the Jews were a secular nation like all others) and therefore registered as belonging to some other nationality, either Romanian or Hungarian. In general, however, the number of Jews cleaving to Romanian or Hungarian national identity was surprisingly small. We may assume that the old Hungarian orientation was on the decline by 1930, and the fact that the regime was obviously not interested in having the Jews add their numerical weight to the Hungarian national minority may have also played a part in discouraging Jews from listing themselves as Magyars (or as Germans in Bukovina) and in encouraging them to register as Jews by nationality. More surprising is that so few Jews, even in the Regat, regarded themselves as Romanians of the Mosaic faith. There were proportionately many more Poles and Czechs of the Mosaic faith, not to mention, of course, Hungarians of the Mosaic faith. We can only speculate that the history of severe repression, and especially the refusal to grant citizenship to the Jews of the Regat, had the effect of retarding any assimilationist (though not necessarily acculturationist) tendencies. The addition of hundreds of thousands of "national Jews" from the new territories may also have had a nationalizing effect upon the Jews of Wallachia, as it did upon their political organization, the Union of Romanian Jews. Thus while the interwar period undoubtedly witnessed the romanization of Romanian Jews in the cultural sense, it clearly did not witness any strong tendency toward identification with the ruling nationality. This was the case in Poland, too, and we shall have the occasion to observe a similar phenomenon in the Baltic States of Latvia and Lithuania. Even in liberal and tolerant Czechoslovakia, acculturation was accompanied by an ever-growing readiness to identify with the Jewish nationality, although here, thanks to the enlightened policies of the Czechoslovak state, there was also a parallel trend toward identification with the "Czechoslovaks."

A glance at the linguistic situation of the Jews of Romania reveals a great difference between declaring oneself a Jew by nationality and declaring one's mother tongue a Jewish language.[19] As we can see from table 4.4, the Jews of Bessarabia and Bukovina were the least accultur-ated, whereas in Wallachia the great majority regarded Romanian as their mother tongue. In the three regions which made up greater Transyl-vania, the Jewish population of the Banat was the most acculturated, the great majority claiming Hungarian or German as their mother tongues. But significant numbers of Jews elsewhere in this former Hungarian possession were also to some degree linguistically acculturated, even in so strong a Hasidic region as northern Transylvania, where, apparently, those who did not list Yiddish listed Hungarian, although some of the Hasidic Jews may have listed Romanian out of loyalty to the regime. The Jews' continued adherence to the once dominant language in this region demonstrates how deeply Hungarian culture had penetrated even this highly religious, basically East European-type Jewry.

The 1930 data on national identification and linguistic affiliation allow us to conclude that the overwhelming majority of Romanian Jews felt very much apart from the ruling ethnic group; indeed, intermarriage and conversion were very unusual, in contrast with the situation in Hungary and in the Czech lands. But this strong national identification was not always filled with cultural content. Thus in the Regat the fact that most

TABLE 4.4
**Yiddish as the Language of Romanian Jews, 1930**

| Region | Number Declaring<br>Yiddish as Mother Tongue |
|---|---|
| Transylvania | 52,008 |
| Banat | 757 |
| Crişana-Maramureş | 58,510 |
| Wallachia | |
|     Muntenia | 19,842 |
|     Oltenia | 601 |
| Moldavia | 109,654 |
| Bessarabia | 201,278 |
| Bukovina | 74,288 |

SOURCE: *Recensământul general al populaţiei româniei din 29 Decemvrie 1930*, 2 (Bucha-rest, 1938):xxiv–xxvii; ibid., 9 (Bucharest, 1938):409.

Jews declared themselves Jewish by nationality did not mean that there existed in that region a Jewish national culture. As already pointed out, even in Moldavia there was little in the way of modern Yiddish culture; only in 1914 was an effort made, ultimately unsuccessful, to establish a Yiddish literary journal in Iaşi.[20] In Moldavia, we are informed, people spoke Yiddish but did not read it.[21] A Yiddish writer who visited the Moldavian town of Galaţi (Galatz) in 1918 remarked that there were many Jews residing there, "but, my God, are these really Jews? . . . no Jewish education, not a Yiddish word, only Jewish noses, that is all that is left."[22] Here is an important distinction between the Jewish community of the Regat and that of Poland, for in the latter case a sense of Jewish national identification was accompanied by a strong modern Jewish autonomous culture, whether in Yiddish or in Hebrew, and by the flourishing of modern Jewish politics. In Romania such phenomena were found only in Bessarabia, in Bukovina, and to a lesser extent in Transylvania.

### 3. The Jewish Question in Romania: Part One

In its dealings with its Jewish subjects, prewar Romania followed the Russian rather than the Hungarian (or Austrian) pattern.[23] And if interwar Hungary underwent a profound about-face in regard to its Jewish policy, interwar Romania carried on the anti-Semitic traditions of the old Regat. Although the Jewish community (or rather communities) of Romania changed out of all recognition as a result of the war, the attitude of the state was more one of continuity than of change.

During the nineteenth century international negotiations regarding the future of Romania had often taken into account the fate of the Jews residing in the Romanian lands. This tradition was maintained during the years 1918–1919, when the borders of the new, greatly enlarged Romania were hammered out in negotiations between Romanian leaders and the great powers. Thus in May, 1918, a treaty was signed between Romania and the Central Powers, then her allies, in which the annexation of Bessarabia to the Romanian state was confirmed. In this treaty Romania promised to grant citizenship to the Jewish inhabitants of the Regat (no such promise was made with regard to Bessarabia). In August, 1918, a new naturalization law, which granted citizenship to those Jews who had served in the army or who had been born in Romania of parents also born in Romania, was passed. Although it placed the burden of proof of eligibility for citizenship upon the Jews themselves, the law was nonetheless something of a departure because it granted citizenship to Jews en masse rather than on an individual basis. It was, however, interpreted by the authorities in such a way that the situation was not radically improved.

Nor was it welcomed by the leading organization of Romanian Jews, which demanded instead a law emancipating all Romanian Jews without exception.[24] The Jewish question was considered anew during the Paris peace conference of 1919, by which time Romania had changed sides and had allied herself with the victorious Western powers. Under the pressure of the Allies Romania agreed, in a treaty signed in December, 1919, to recognize as Romanian citizens "Jews inhabiting any Romanian territory who do not possess another nationality."[25] Like the Poles, the Romanians objected strenuously to the idea of safeguarding through a special treaty the rights of the national minorities, but after a spirited display of opposition on the part of the leader of the Liberal Party, Ion Brătianu, Romania signed an agreement quite similar to that accepted by the Poles. Thus the treaty of December, 1919, promised absolute equality to all citizens "without distinction as to race, language, or religion," and it went on to declare that there would be no discrimination in matters of employment. Moreover, it promised that "adequate facilities shall be given to Romanian nationals of non-Romanian speech for the use of their language, either orally or in writing before the courts." Finally, the state promised to provide primary education in the language of the national minority "in towns and districts in which a considerable proportion of Romanian nationals of other than Romanian speech are resident. . . ."[26] Minorities were also granted the right to maintain their own educational and charitable institutions at their own expense.

The treaty of 1919 in effect emancipated Romanian Jewry and was greeted with joy by Jewish organizations both in Romania and abroad. Their joy, however, was tempered by the realization that the Romanian political elite was not favorably disposed toward the Jews and had done its best to avoid making any promises with regard to national minority rights. Indeed, according to documents published by the Jewish Committee of Delegations to the Paris peace conference, Ion Brătianu had informed Woodrow Wilson in 1919 that the Jewish question in Romania had arisen as a result of the "immigration of masses of foreigners" during the nineteenth century and was analogous to the "yellow question" in the United States. The Jewish immigrants, Brătianu went on to inform the American president, "foreigners by their origin and by their language, directed by virtue of their education to certain professions to the exclusion of all others, too numerous to make a living in a poor country without compromising the interests of the other inhabitants . . . caused serious harm to the economic and social situation in Romania."[27] True, he admitted, things had changed since the nineteenth century; Romania had advanced economically, and the Jews had begun to assimilate. It was, therefore, possible to grant the Jews naturalization. But Jewish leaders could not take much comfort from the tenor of Brătianu's remarks, so similar to the kinds of statements being made by the perpetrators of the white terror in neighboring Hungary.

There was, however, nothing analogous to the white terror in the early years of Romanian independence. Indeed, Romania was largely spared the anti-Semitic violence which swept over most of the regions of Eastern Europe, from the Ukraine to Slovakia, in this period. Romania did not undergo the trauma of a Communist regime, as did Hungary; it did not have to wage wars with other nationalities in order to secure disputed territories, as was the case in Poland; and it was not invaded by Soviet troops. Moreover, Romania's status as the country which had profited the most from the war created a feeling of euphoria which was the very opposite of the national humiliation suffered by Hungary. These factors may have helped reduced the likelihood of anti-Jewish violence, just as Béla Kun's regime in Hungary and the struggles over Lwów and Vilna in Poland enhanced the prospects of anti-Jewish violence. It was also true that the Liberals, who dominated the political scene during most of the 1920s, were not interested in exacerbating Romanian-Jewish relations. And the coming to power of the National Peasant Party in 1928 did not signify any change in this regard. Thus during the 1920s Romania was ruled by moderate (if corrupt) politicians opposed to radical anti-Semitism. In this sense, at least, the situation was analogous to that which prevailed in Bethlen's post–white-terror Hungary. During these years there were even some friendly acts toward the Jews: large numbers of Jewish refugees were permitted to settle in Bessarabia after fleeing Soviet rule, and in certain cases the government actually encouraged national Jewish education.

If, however, Romanian Jewry was spared the traumas which Polish and Hungarian Jewry experienced in the immediate postwar years, its situation was far from ideal. Despite the emancipation of 1919, citizenship remained a problem. The 1923 constitution, while specifically recognizing the legal equality of the Jews, failed to solve the problem of the Jews in the new territories. Thus in Bukovina and Transylvania Jews were obliged to prove continuous residence since before the war; the many who were unable to do so were rendered stateless. In some cases bribes paved the way for Jews to gain citizenship, but such means were not always possible. An American delegation which visited Romania in 1928 found that

> there is a society in Cluj called "Actinea Romana" which was organized in 1922. It is made up principally of university professors, students, and army officers. It was frankly organized by anti-Semites to be used as a club over the heads of the Jews. For nearly five years this Society has had access to the lists of applicants for citizenship. Every individual who "opted" for Roumania had to go through certain formalities, and the

dossier of these individuals was handed over to this committee. Whenever a Jewish name was found, a protest was registered against it on some ground and in consequence very few Jews received the right of citizenship which the constitution guaranteed them.[28]

Along with citizenship problems, which continued into the late 1920s, Jews encountered discrimination in the civil service and in the army, as in most East European countries.[29] More serious, however, were the disquieting signs of violent anti-Jewish agitation in the 1920s, which was fostered by the propaganda of the radically anti-Semitic League of National Christian Defense. The leader of this party was Professor Alexandru Cuza of the University of Iaşi, who had a large following among university students. Indeed, the Romanian students were the main perpetrators of violent anti-Semitism in the 1920s, and some of the most dramatic anti-Jewish incidents occurred within university walls. In 1922, at the medical faculties of Cluj, Iaşi, and Bucharest, serious anti-Jewish violence was touched off by the demands of Christian students that Jews not be allowed to dissect non-Jewish cadavers.[30] Student disorders directed against Jews caused the government to close down the universities at the end of 1922, but the anti-Jewish agitation continued upon their reopening. In Iaşi the Christian students demanded the implementation of *numerus clausus*, a demand repeated ad nauseam throughout the interwar years, and upon occasion refused to allow their Jewish colleagues to enter the lecture rooms.[31] The University of Cernăuţi also was the scene of continual anti-Jewish agitation, and in 1926 a Jewish high school graduate seeking admission to the university was murdered by a Romanian student.[32]

Such incidents continued throughout the 1920s and rendered normal university life impossible, but the most dramatic outburst of violent anti-Semitism occurred not at a university but at a nationalist rally of Romanian students held in 1927 at Oradea Mare in Transylvania. These students, who hailed from the Regat, came to Transylvania in order to demonstrate the latter region's purely Romanian character (the city of Oradea Mare was inhabited chiefly by non-Romanians). Having assembled they began rioting in the streets, attacking both Hungarians and Jews (the latter, of course, being viewed as pro-Magyar). According to an account published in England, "The editorial and printing offices of two newspapers were demolished, and afterwards the crowd stormed a well-known Hungarian hotel, smashing everything they could lay hands on. The club where Hungarians met was also sacked. Two persons were killed and many were wounded during the riots."[33] At the same time, Jews were beaten, several synagogues in the town were vandalized, Torah scrolls were desecrated, and so forth. These activities spread to Cluj, the capital of Transylvania, and to other towns visited by the students on their way home to Bucharest and Iaşi.[34] The events made a powerful impression at home and abroad. The Central Jewish Organizations of Transylvania accused the students of having

> defiled the Sacred Law which not only constitutes the spiritual and moral treasure of our people, but has also served as the foundation of the Christian religion. Brandishing the handwritten Law, which we have cherished as a precious heirloom for centuries, they indulged in a wild war-dance uttering shouts of derision and whoops of mockery. They either burned or tore into pieces the Holy Law. They pillaged the sacred vessels of our temples, broke into peaceful Jewish homes and shops and sacked them, causing damages amounting to several millions. These scenes of barbarism, vandalism and devastation, are deeply engraven in our hearts, causing a wound never to be healed.[35]

The Jewish organizations went on to blame the authorities for failing to take a hard line against the students and their anti-Semitic professors. Their accusations were echoed by Jewish organizations elsewhere. The Joint Foreign Committee of the Board of Deputies of British Jews wrote to the Romanian foreign minister:

> Certain organizations have been permitted, in defiance of the law, to carry on a violent and anarchical agitation against the Jewish population and their religion, convulsing the country with riotous public meetings and flooding it with incendiary literature, in which the Jews are held up to hatred and contempt, and in which their expulsion from their native land, and even their wholesale massacre, are openly advocated under the patronage of high government officials.[36]

The government, in this case, did take steps to punish some of the students, but student-led anti-Jewish agitation continued unabated.

What is noteworthy about the riots in Transylvania, aside from their being led entirely by students under the influence of Cuza, was that they took place in an ethnically mixed region where the Jews were identified with the Magyar oppressors of Romanian freedom. In this sense they can be compared to the Polish pogroms in the ethnically mixed regions of Lithuania and eastern Galicia. A non-Jewish Romanian senator, commenting on the situation immediately after the riots, noted that "until the Great War we did not know what anti-Semitism [in Transylvania] was. Today it has become a national disgrace."[37] Here was a case of a minority, favored and protected by the old regime, paying a heavy price for its perfectly understandable Magyar patriotism.

Along with the identification of Jew with Magyar went the no less potent identification of the Jews with Bolshevism. The main venue for this charge was, naturally enough, Bessarabia, a former tsarist territory which became a focus of Soviet irredentism. In this backward and mis-ruled province unrest was habitually blamed on "Jewish Bolsheviks." In 1924 a Communist "revolt" led by people with Russian and Jewish names was uncovered in the little Bessarabian town of Tatar-Bunar.[38] Such incidents served to impress upon the population that the Bessarabian Jews monopolized the local Communist Party and favored Soviet annexation. And, of course, not only Bessarabian Jews were so accused.

Observers of the Romanian scene in the 1920s usually came to the conclusion that Romania was an extremely anti-Semitic country where deeply ingrained prewar anti-Jewish traditions were now augmented by resentment toward the annexation of large, nonassimilated Jewish communities and by a strong desire to even the score with pro-Hungarian, pro-German, and pro-Russian (or pro-Bolshevik) Jews. Of course, we should keep in mind that the students, the shock troops of the new anti-Semitic agitation and the perpetrators of anti-Jewish violence, did not as yet constitute a politically important force. Romanian politics was still monopolized by politicians of the old school. These politicians certainly did not like the Jews, and their attitude toward the Jews' tormentors was ambiguous; nonetheless, they were opposed to violent anti-Semitism and were not above making deals with various Jewish organizations. The various Liberal and Peasant governments did not initiate any anti-Jewish legislation during this period, in contrast with the Hungarian government, and undoubtedly the impact of anti-Semitism on the Jewish population during the 1920s was much less acute in Romania than in Poland. In the latter country more anti-Jewish violence occurred, and racial anti-Semitism within the ruling class was more prevalent. Romania was clearly not Czechoslovakia, but, so long as the radical right remained a negligible force, the Jewish situation did not appear to be particularly dangerous.

The most disturbing element in Romanian anti-Semitism of the 1920s was its impact among the students, who were, after all, the future elite of the country. It is true that universities all over East Central Europe were centers of anti-Semitism—we have only to recall Poland, with its "ghetto benches" introduced in the 1930s, and the demands for a *numerus clausus* in Hungary. In Romania, as elsewhere, young and impressionable students were attracted to the new militant, antipluralist nationalist movements, which combined xenophobia, anti-Communism, and anti-Semitism with an idealistic campaign directed against the compromise-prone, venal political and economic establishment. In Romania, more-over, perhaps more strikingly than in other backward East European countries, the rapid expansion of the university and high school systems was not accompanied by the state's ability to employ its graduates in remunerative positions. Economic insecurity turned many of the "new intellectuals" against their colleagues of "foreign" origin, whether Germans, Hungarians, or Jews. (The number of Jewish students far exceeded the Jewish percentage within the population.) And the nationalist doctrines, often imparted to them by their professors, supplied the ideological justification for this tendency.[39] To be sure, the professors were not always extremists. The greatest savant of interwar Romania, Nicolae Iorga, opposed violent anti-Semitism. In 1922 he warned the student extremists that "the Russians began with pogroms and ended up with dictatorship. There is a lesson here for the entire world."[40] But he also emphasized the Jews' foreign origins, their "invasion" of Romanian soil, and the need to build up a unitary, national Romanian state. Professor Cuza, however, openly preached extreme anti-Semitism at the University of Iaşi, as did Zelea Codreanu, father of the future leader of the Iron Guard, at a high school in Moldavia. Indeed, already in the 1920s those professors and teachers who dared speak out against anti-Jewish violence were occasionally "punished" by nationalist students.[41] In the 1930s the forces responsible for the sporadic violence which afflicted the universities and the numerous unpleasant incidents which Jewish and other minority students were obliged to put up with coalesced into a political movement of growing importance and of great danger to Romania's Jews.

## 4. Jewish Politics and Culture in Romania

The great theme of interwar Jewish politics in Romania was the struggle for hegemony between the Jewish community of the Regat and the new communities of Transylvania, Bessarabia, and Bukovina. Of course, as might be expected in a country where there were at least five, and perhaps as many as seven, distinct Jewries, the political scene was extremely complex. There were Jewish nationalists of every variety, as well as assimilationists of different types. There were Orthodox Zionists and Orthodox groups which were violently anti-Zionist. But most important was the basic distinction between the national Jewish politics of the annexed territories and the non-national Jewish politics of the Regat.

The leading political organization of Regat Jewry was the Union of Romanian Jews (Uniunea Evreilor Români, known as the UER), the interwar version of the prewar Organization of Native Born Jews founded in 1910. The Organization of Native Born Jews was chiefly a society of the Bucharest bourgeoisie and professional class which favored the romanization of Romanian Jewry and which fought for Jewish legal equality. In terms of its leadership and aims it was quite similar to the Society for the Promotion of Culture among Jews in Russia and to organizations elsewhere in Eastern and Central Europe which stood for

Jewish acculturation and enlightenment and at the same time waged the struggle for Jewish civic emancipation. The most noted leader of the Organization of Native Born Jews was the Bucharest lawyer Adolph Stern (1848–1931), a celebrated *shtadlen* of the prewar period.[42] During the interwar years the UER remained very much a Regat organization, failing, despite considerable effort, to put down roots in the annexed territories. Its most conspicuous leader was another Bucharest lawyer, Wilhelm Filderman (1882–1963, sometimes called the Louis Marshall of Romania), undoubtedly the most important Jewish figure in the Regat and probably the most prominent Jewish leader in interwar Romania.

The UER was castigated by its many Jewish enemies as an "assimilationist" organization, but, if that appellation could have been justly applied to its prewar ideology, it was inaccurate so far as the postwar period was concerned. True, the UER was non-Zionist and non-nationalist (but not, it should be emphasized, necessarily anti-Zionist or antinationalist). True, it continued to fight the good fight against anti-Semitism and for Jewish emancipation, not for Jewish national rights as demanded by the Zionists and other Jewish nationalists. Moreover, it strongly opposed the establishment of a Jewish party on the Czech model, preferring to ally itself with Romanian parties during elections. Nonetheless, some of its members were at the same time members of the Zionist movement (Stern himself drew close to the Bucharest Zionists toward the end of his life, and Filderman was a member of the Jewish Agency for Palestine), and some also contributed money to the Zionist organization. Indeed, several of its leaders came quite close to adopting a national Jewish position. Thus in 1927 Horia Carp, a UER delegate to the Romanian senate, declared that, while the Jews once regarded themselves as a purely religious minority, they now saw themselves as a special ethnic group ("nationalité ethnique"). At the same time he insisted that "we have no other political aspirations than those of the Romanian people" and that the Jews closely identified with Romanian history and with the Romanian culture and language. He also pointed out that the Romanians should logically prefer a separate Jewish consciousness to Jewish assimilation into the Hungarian or the Ukrainian nations, sounding rather like Yitshak Grünbaum or like the leaders of the Jewish Party in Czechoslovakia.[43] In 1927 the organization circulated a document calling upon the Jews to declare themselves "d'origine ethnique juive, de nationalité roumaine, de religion mosaïque."[44] It stood for political, but not for cultural, assimilation.

The quasi-national ideology of the UER, which suited well the not really national but very separatist nature of Regat Jewry, was also clearly influenced by the postwar situation in Romania. Both the addition of numerous Jewish communities of the East European type and the anti-

Semitic atmosphere in the Regat pushed the UER toward a more national, more "Jewish" platform. Carp himself noted in 1927 that the annexation of Bukovina, Bessarabia, and Transylvania had transformed Romanian Jewry from a religious to an ethnic minority.[45] All this illustrates the very great difference between the situation in Hungary, where the Jewish organizations were truly integrationist, and that in the Regat. To be sure, the UER continued to believe in *doikeyt*, in a Jewish future on Romanian soil (it did so even after World War II), and its members were all acculturated Jews, but it did not propagate the slogan "Romanians of the Mosaic faith."

While the Regat was the center of the basically nonpolitical, ideologically vague UER, the annexed territories boasted a large range of Jewish national parties and youth movements of the classic East European variety, along with Orthodox and antinational factions. The Bund, which in the prewar period was virtually nonexistent outside the Russian empire (except to a limited extent in Galicia), was active in interwar Bessarabia and to a lesser extent in Bukovina, but not in Transylvania. As the results of elections to the kehile in Chișinău demonstrate, the Bund was a powerful force in Jewish life there, and it also played an important role in the Yiddish school movement in Bessarabia.[46] Bukovina had a strong Folkist tradition—it was in Czernowitz (Cernăuți), after all, that a conference of Jewish cultural leaders and politicians, some of them of the Folkist persuasion, had proclaimed, in 1908, that Yiddish was "a national language of the Jewish people." One of Bukovinian Jewry's leading politicians, Benno Straucher, the head of the Jewish National People's Party, was an advocate of Folkist ideas.[47] Indeed, in prewar Bukovina the moderate Austrian political atmosphere and the Jews' position as a recognized national minority was conducive to the spread of the Folkist ideology, which was based on the idea of extraterritorial national autonomy but which, unlike the Bund and Poale Zion, was nonsocialist. In the new intolerant Romanian state the appeal of Folkism inevitably declined.

As for Orthodox Jewish politics, in Bessarabia Agudes yisroel dominated the scene. Its leader, Yehuda Leib Tsirelson (1860–1940), was the chief rabbi of the province and undoubtedly its most outstanding Jewish leader. The Agude in Bessarabia was relatively moderate, more so than in Poland and something like its sister organizations in the Baltic States. Thus Tsirelson was prepared to cooperate with the Zionists and went so far as to support the fund-raising efforts of the Zionist movement's National Fund (Keren Kayemet). The Agude's moderation was clearly the result of the personality of its leader, but it was also a consequence of the fact that in Bessarabia, as in Poland but not in Hungary, the Jewish community maintained its formal unity and did not split into two or three opposing factions.[48] In formerly Hungarian Transylvania the situation was quite different. Here the Agude was "Hungarian," not "Polish," meaning that it opposed all cooperation with secular Jewish organizations, while in the north the Hasidic rebes were famous for their fierce opposition to any form of modern Jewish politics and to modern Jewish schools, quite like the rebes of Subcarpathian Rus. Particularly vehement in this regard were the rebes of Satu-Mare, whose radical opposition to Zionism continues to this day.[49]

As elsewhere in Jewish communities of the East European type, Zionism was the single most powerful Jewish political movement in the new Romanian territories. Its strongest base was Bessarabia, where the old traditions of Russian Zionism were strengthened further by the influx of thousands of refugees from Soviet Russia. In tsarist times Kishinev (Chişinău) was a major Zionist center. The annexation of Bessarabia to Romania, which naturally put an end to the russifying tendencies of the local Jewish intelligentsia, gave an additional shot in the arm to Jewish nationalism. (As we know, virtually all Bessarabian Jews regarded themselves as Jews by nationality.) In this sense postwar Bessarabia may be compared to other parts of Eastern Europe where a cultural vacuum developed as the result of the change of regimes—Bohemia and Moravia, Slovakia, the Polish kresy, Bukovina, and Transylvania. No longer "Russians," certainly not Romanians, the Jews had to fall back upon their own resources. This turn of events, along with the fierce anti-Semitism in Bessarabia and, of course, their classically East European character, pointed them in the direction of Zionism.[50] The same may be said of Bukovina, where the transition from the golden age of Austrian tolerance and German culture to Romanian rule was particularly traumatic.[51]

The situation in Transylvania was more complex. Acculturation and even assimilation (into the Hungarian nationality) had gone much further here than in either Bessarabia or Bukovina, and in the north the Hasidic communities, untouched by modernization, were naturally unfriendly to modern Jewish nationalism. Nonetheless, the multinational character of this province and the rapid decline of both the Hungarian and the German cultural orientations during the interwar years did produce something of a national Jewish upsurge. Zionism may not have sprung here from the classical East European combination of a deeply rooted autonomous Jewish culture and the inroads of secularization and Haskalah-inspired modernization, but it did find much more fertile soil during the 1920s and 1930s than during the Hungarian era. A sign of the new times was the establishment in 1918 in Cluj of the National Jewish Union of Transylvania. The national Jewish Party was to receive considerable support in this part of Romania.[52]

Despite the evident power of the UER in the Regat, the Zionist movement became important in this region as well. In fact, its emergence in the Regat was not entirely a new development. Jews from prewar independent Romania had played a significant role in the early *aliyot* (waves of emigration to Palestine), and the Hibat Zion (Love of Zion) movement was well established in Romania by the late nineteenth century. Zichron Yaakov, the famous Jewish agricultural settlement founded in Palestine in 1882, was the work of Romanian immigrants.[53] The center of Zionist activity in the Regat was, of course, Moldavia, with its basically Galician-type Jewry; Wallachian Jewry, by and large the Jewish community of Bucharest, was much less involved. But during the interwar period the Zionist movement grew to significant proportions even in Wallachia, the result of the anti-Semitic environment and the influence of the "new Jewries" and their national-minded members, many of whom came to settle in the capital. We should recall in this context that even the non-Zionist UER, based in Wallachia, was not anti-Zionist and that the overwhelming majority of Regat Jews, despite the inroads of acculturation, regarded themselves as Jews by nationality. In Wallachia as in Transylvania, Jewish nationalism in the interwar period found more fertile soil than the nature of the local Jewish communities would lead one to expect.[54]

As in Poland, Zionism in Romania was highly fragmented. The activist youth-oriented and *aliyah*-oriented movements were strongest in the peripheral regions of the country, particularly in Bessarabia. In that province the Pioneer (He-haluts) flourished (many of its early members, here as in Poland, came from Soviet Russia), as did the Zionist youth movements. The numerical distribution of the pioneering youth movement Gordonia in the late 1920s demonstrates to what extent it was a movement of the new territories. In 1929, 75.3 percent of its members were from Bessarabia, 15 percent from Bukovina, and only 9.7 percent from the Regat (mostly from Moldavia, not Wallachia).[55] Ha-shomer ha-tsair in Romania originated in Bukovina, which was closely connected with the movement's birthplace, Galicia; it quickly spread to Bessarabia. The Pioneer began in Romania as a primarily Bessarabian phenomenon.[56] So far as the various pioneering Zionist movements were concerned, therefore, Bessarabia and to a lesser extent Bukovina functioned as the kresy did in Poland. As in Poland, in Romania too the Pioneer and the youth movements eventually penetrated the center, expanding from their base in the periphery (Ha-shomer, for example, reached the Regat in 1925).

Zionism in Bessarabia, unlike that in the Regat, was also characterized by a strong left-wing orientation. As might be expected in a province formerly part of the Russian empire, it was a center of the Zeire Zion (Youth of Zion) movement, which at a Zionist conference held in 1920 was represented by nearly fifty percent of the delegates.[57] There was,

however, no powerful Poale Zion tradition in Bessarabia in contrast with
the situation in the much more industrialized and Marxist-influenced
region of Congress Poland. In Bukovina, and certainly in Transylvania
and the Regat, the Zionist orientation was basically middle class. Perhaps
the most prominent Zionist leader in the Regat was the chief rabbi of
Romania, Yitshak Niemirover (1872–1939). Along with its rather "bale-
batish" (bourgeois) leadership, the Zionist movement in the Regat was
traditionally not interested in *Gegenwartsarbeit* (work in the diaspora)
and was hostile to Yiddish, much preferring a Hebraic orientation. This
was quite different from the situation in the new regions, at least in
Bessarabia and Bukovina, where Zionism meant not only building Palestine but also taking an active part in all aspects of local Jewish life.
Opposition to *Gegenwartsarbeit* and adherence to strict Hebraism was
typical of the Zionist movements in the more acculturated communities;
in this sense Wallachian Zionism was more akin to German Zionism than
to Polish Zionism.[58] Indeed, the aversion to *Gegenwartsarbeit* in the
Regat helps to explain why the Zionists and the UER were able to live
together in peace and harmony, and why members of the UER could also
be members of the Zionist movement. It was the refusal of Zionists in the
new territories to accept this division of labor, according to which the
Zionists would build Palestine while the UER would deal with Jewish
problems in Romania, which helped bring about the founding of the
Zionist-led Jewish Party.

In Romania, as in Poland, Czechoslovakia, and the Baltic States,
World War I and the dramatic changes wrought by the peace settlements
greatly strengthened national sentiment within the various Jewish communities. This was particularly the case, of course, in the new regions,
where the communities were not only more nationalist to begin with but
where the change of regimes also produced a vacuum which affirmation of
Jewish nationalism and support for Jewish national politics were able to
fill. As in most regions of East Central Europe (with the exception of
Hungary), Jewish national councils were established under the control of
nationalist Jewish elements. In Chişinău the Jewish kehile was transformed into a democratic institution in which the Zionists were the single
strongest faction. Led by the most prominent Zionist leader in Bessarabia, Bernstein-Cohen, the kehile worked out an intricate autonomy
scheme for Bessarabian Jewry which was later adopted at a conference of
kehiles held in 1921.[59] In Bukovina, too, the Jewish community of the
capital was taken over by Jewish nationalists. Even in Transylvania a
national council was formed. Only in the Regat, where there was no
transition from one national regime to another, did such an institution fail
to materialize.[60]

The Jewish national councils did their best to make their voices heard, on both Jewish and general, non-Jewish issues, but without success. In Bukovina, as in eastern Galicia, the National Council proclaimed its "neutrality" in the national conflict between the Romanians and the Ukrainians, a position which won it no support from either side. Like the Poles, the Romanians did not feel any need to court Jewish support, and thus in Romania the national Jewish politicians could not assume the role which they played, for a while at least, in Lithuania. The anti-Jewish attitude of Brătianu ruled out the support which Masaryk, in Czechoslovakia, lent to Jewish national institutions. It was in a hostile environment, therefore, akin to that in Poland, that Jewish political parties were obliged to struggle in order to ensure proper Jewish representation in the Romanian parliament. The argument over how best to achieve this goal dominated Jewish politics in Romania, as it did, throughout the 1920s at least, in Poland.

During the 1920s the prevailing strategy within the Jewish political camp was to seek alliances with Romanian parties. The UER, from which such behavior was certainly not unexpected, tended to ally itself with the Liberal Party, with which Filderman had close ties. But it also, upon occasion, lent its support to the National Peasant Party, and even allied itself for a time with Marshal Alexandru Averescu's People's Party.[61] As for the Jewish nationalists of the new regions, who might have been expected to denounce these tactics as dishonorable alliances with anti-Semites (in the style of Yitshak Grünbaum), they too made deals with Romanian groupings. Thus Meir Ebner (1872–1955), the outstanding leader of Zionism in Bukovina, was elected to parliament in 1926 as a result of an agreement with Averescu's victorious party, while his archrival, Benno Straucher, took a pro-Liberal line.[62] In the elections of 1927 the UER was allied with the Liberal Party, while the Jewish nationalists in Transylvania supported the National Peasant Party. There were a few efforts made at forming Jewish blocs, and even minority blocs on the Polish model, but they did not prove very successful.

Why did Jewish politics in Romania in the 1920s take the form of alliances with Romanian parties whereas in Poland Jewish parties formed their own national lists? One obvious answer is that there were many fewer Jews in Romania, and therefore independent Jewish lists were much less likely to succeed. Another is that most Romanian parties, with the obvious exception of the extreme anti-Semitic party led by Cuza, were quite willing to enter into agreements with the Jews, agreements which won them a certain amount of Jewish support. If the Polish National Democrats regarded a Jewish alliance as unthinkable, the Romanian Liberals were delighted to win the support of Filderman and his UER.

Moreover, there was no Jewish political force of any importance in Poland (with the possible exception of the Agude) which shared the UER's ideological distaste for truly independent Jewish politics. Finally, the deep historical divisions which separated the three annexed provinces of Bessarabia, Bukovina, and Transylvania made the formation of a common Jewish national bloc in those regions difficult, at least in the 1920s.

The policy of alliances in the 1920s, which succeeded in electing a fair number of Jewish representatives to the parliament, was based on the assumption that in return for Jewish support the ruling party would wage war against anti-Semitism. Thus in 1927, in an appeal to all Romanian Jews to vote for the Liberal Party, the UER justified its stand by declaring that "the Liberal Party has energetically disapproved of all agitation which tends to provoke discord among the citizens of the state and has made a firm promise to settle, through legal means, in full accord with the highest interests of the state, those problems which interest us. . . ." The well-informed journal of the French-based Alliance Israélite reported that in return for Jewish support the Liberals had pledged themselves to solve the citizenship problems and to grant equality to Jewish schools.[63] In 1928 the National Peasant Party, which the UER had formerly supported, came to power. Filderman now entered into negotiations with its leader, Iuliu Maniu, and angrily rejected suggestions that by so doing he was acting immorally. On the contrary, he replied, the Jewish interest resided in making alliances with whichever group was in the position to do the Jews the most good. "The Transylvanian Saxons," he observed, "have for a thousand years always supported the government in power." The Jews, after all, were a minority. And minorities cannot always make the rules of the game they play.[64]

But by the late 1920s the Jewish nationalists of the new territories were no longer willing to play this game. In 1928 four Zionist deputies—Theodor Fischer and Iosif Fischer from Transylvania, Meir Ebner from Bukovina, and Michael Landau from Bessarabia, all of whom had been elected in alliance with Romanian parties—formed a national Jewish club in parliament. It was immediately noted, with foreboding in certain Jewish circles, that this step was in direct imitation of the Jewish club in the Polish parliament.[65] The aim of the club, in the words of one of its founding members, was "the defense of collective [i.e., national] interests only," in contrast with the *shtadlones* and alliances with anti-Semites which characterized the approach of the non-nationalist Jewish leadership.[66] The nationalists now rejected the alliance policy of the UER as "immoral" and "disgusting" since "it transforms the Union into a loyal servant of great and dangerous forces which hate the Jewish population."[67] They also held high the banner of Jewish national rights in Romania, which no Romanian party supported and which obviously could not be achieved through the alliance system. In their official declaration in parliament the leaders of the club announced that they represented "the Jewish ethnic minority" in Romania, just as various political parties in the state represented other national minorities. While proclaiming its deep and "pure" Romanian patriotism and its loyalty to the state, the club announced its intention to struggle for the recognition "of all the rights of the Jewish ethnic minority" and demanded of the government "moral and financial aid for our national culture and language." It also announced its support for Maniu's National Peasant Party.[68]

The emergence of the Jewish national club (for all intents and purposes a national Jewish party), with a program similar to that of the General Zionists in Poland and of the Jewish Party in Czechoslovakia, was not greeted with unequivocal joy even in the Zionist camp. The Regat Zionist tradition of hostility toward *Gegenwartsarbeit* caused some of its leaders to regard the Jewish national club with suspicion. Niemirower, chief rabbi of Romania and a member of the Romanian senate, did not join the club. In the 1930s the General Zionist Federation in the Regat split; a radical group, allied with Grünbaum's faction in Poland and led by Stern-Kokhavi, favored *Gegenwartsarbeit* and, therefore, national Jewish politics in Romania, while the more conservative group, in a manner reminiscent of certain Galician General Zionists, continued to oppose it. On the whole, according to Landau, the Zionist leader from Bessarabia, the Regat Zionists were more inclined to support Filderman than they were the Jewish national party.[69] On the other hand, Rabbi Tsirelson of Agudes yisroel, a non-Zionist, supported the national party. Filderman himself, and his organization, naturally led the fight against the new national club. Filderman noted in 1929 that "the Romanian Jews must choose at this time between the enviable situation of their brothers in America, France, and England and the deplorable situation of their coreligionists in Poland." The Zionist politics of the national club, he added, were leading them in the latter direction.[70] The Polish experience, he believed, had demonstrated the bankruptcy of national Jewish politics, for the Polish Jews had certainly not benefited from the Zionists' preoccupation with *Gegenwartsarbeit* and had in fact suffered from the acrimonious debates and splits which this policy had caused.[71] The proper response to Romanian anti-Semitism, and the proper way to represent the legitimate Jewish interest, was to continue to seek alliances with progressive Romanian forces. This strategy was both more effective and had the advantage of proving to the Romanian people that the Jews sought "political assimilation," by which was meant "absolute, disinterested, and unconditional identification with all the interests of the state," while at the same time maintaining the Jews' separate religious and cultural identity.[72]

In 1931, for the first time, the Jewish nationalists (mostly Zionists) of the annexed territories, supported by Tsirelson of Agudes yisroel, ran a separate list in national elections. The Jewish Party of Romania, as it was called, did quite well. It received 64,175 votes, mostly from the new territories, and sent four deputies to parliament. A year later, in yet another round of national elections, the Jewish Party did even better, winning 67,582 votes and five mandates. In 1933, however, the party declined drastically, winning only 38,565 votes and failing to send even a single delegate to the parliament. It did not do much better in the elections of 1937.[73]

The emergence in 1931 of a Jewish national party as an electoral factor may be explained by some Jews' growing disillusionment with the tactic of alliances and with the increasingly close ties among Bukovina, Bessarabia, and Transylvania. The party's rapid demise is less easy to understand. One authority has attributed it to a planned campaign of terror against the party, whereas another is more inclined to believe that in the 1930s the Jews of Romania, taking fright at the ever-increasing extreme anti-Semitism, once again put their faith in alliances with large Romanian parties rather than in a necessarily small Jewish party whose influence in parliament was limited.[74] Whatever the case, the experience of 1931–1932 demonstrated that a base for national Jewish politics existed only in the new provinces. Even in Moldavia, with its Galician-style Jewish community, but with its lack of an autonomous Jewish political tradition, the Jewish Party performed poorly. The Regat, with about 35 percent of Romanian Jewry, provided only 13.36 percent of the vote for the Jewish Party in the elections of 1931–1932.[75]

As for those Jews who did not vote for the Jewish Party, they either followed the lead of the UER or voted for the socialists (the Communist Party being illegal). Both the socialist and the Communist parties included important Jewish figures; among the Communists, Anna Pauker, whose brother was a Yiddish writer, was to become famous as the foreign minister of Communist Romania. Indeed, one of the most prominent founding fathers of Romanian socialism was a Jew—Dobrogeanu-Gherea, whose real name was Katz—who, like so many prominent Romanian Jews, came from somewhere else (in his case from Russia). In Transylvania a small but important body of Jewish voters supported the Hungarian national list, despite the fact that the Hungarian cause was strongly marked by anti-Semitic tendencies. Their support was another touching example of Jewish loyalty to the old, pre-1918 political order and to Magyar nationalism.[76]

By the mid-1930s the traditional antagonism between the UER of the Regat and the nationalists of the new territories was beginning to wane. Under the impact of the rise of Romanian fascism the two organizations cooperated in the formation, in 1936, of the Central Council of Romanian Jews—an example, all too rare, of Jewish unity in the face of the growing anti-Semitic onslaught. By this time it had become clear that the main tasks of any Jewish organization were to defend the Jewish population against anti-Semitism and to organize Jewish emigration, not to press for the recognition of Jewish national rights in Romania. The leading figure in the Council was Filderman, whose long-established position on these issues now received at least partial vindication. He was to remain the leading spokesman of Romanian Jewry during the late 1930s and early 1940s.[77]

Jewish political leaders in Romania were never able to achieve even the temporary position of power and influence which the Polish and Lithuanian Jewish leaders enjoyed. We may assume that, as in Poland, the Jewish condition in Romania would have been even worse had the Jewish leaders not fought for equality and denounced anti-Semitism, but they were certainly unable to effect any fundamental change in the deteriorating Jewish condition. In the area of Jewish culture, of course, the prospects for success were brighter, and in this respect the nationalists were able to boast of considerable achievements. In Romania, as in Poland, Czechoslovakia, and the Baltic States, the struggle for national autonomy meant in fact the struggle for autonomous Jewish schools in Jewish languages. Bessarabia, for reasons of which we are already aware, was the perfect setting for such schools. By 1922 there were, in this relatively small province with only slightly more than 200,000 Jews, 75 Tarbut institutions, including 20 kindergartens, 40 elementary schools, and 15 high schools—more high schools than in all Poland, with its three million Jews. These institutions employed 450 teachers and educated some 10,000 pupils. In the same year there were as many as 52 Yiddish-language elementary schools.[78]

The early 1920s were the heroic years of modern, secular Jewish education in Bessarabia. The influx of Soviet refugees provided both teachers and pupils for these schools, and the Hebrew schools found an important ally in the person of Rabbi Tsirelson, whose pro-Zionist attitude we have already noted. The Romanian government, desiring to weaken Russian culture in Bessarabia, was at first quite amenable to the establishment of Hebrew and Yiddish schools. Thus many Yiddish schools were absorbed into the government public-school network. This policy did not last, however. As in Poland, pressure was brought to bear in order to increase the number of hours of instruction in the language of the land, and the state withdrew its financial support. Forced romanization virtually wiped out the Yiddish schools, just as it struck at Hungarian-language schools. But the Tarbut system, which was private from the beginning, continued to flourish. (It was fitting that in 1930 at a Tarbut conference an envious delegate from the Regat called Chişinău the "Romanian Jerusalem.") As late as 1935–1936 there were thirteen kindergartens, thirty-four elementary schools, and twelve high schools in the Tarbut system.[79] Its decline was partly due to the growing pauperization of the Jewish community, which was obliged to maintain these schools in the absence of state subsidies. Nonetheless, despite the decline, and despite the inevitable trend toward romanization among the new Jewish generation growing up in the interwar years, Bessarabia remained one of the three great bastions of secular Hebrew education in East Central Europe, sharing pride of place with the Polish kresy and independent Lithuania. It was no accident that when, in 1929, a Hebrew teachers' seminary was opened in Iaşi, capital of Moldavia, the great majority of its students hailed from Bessarabia.[80]

The optimal conditions for modern autonomous Jewish culture in Bessarabia were not duplicated in Bukovina. True, Bukovinian Jewry was of the Eastern type, but here, as in Galicia, it had been the custom in the prewar period to send Jewish children to state schools. Moreover, acculturation went deeper here than in the former tsarist province. In the early period of Romanian rule modern Hebrew and Yiddish schools were founded by Zionists and Bundists, but they were never very numerous and their impact upon Bukovinian Jewry was considerably less than was their impact in Bessarabia.[81]

In Transylvania, of course, the situation was even less propitious. The strong assimilationist trend, on the one hand, and the extreme Orthodoxy of the northern part of the province, on the other, militated against the emergence of a national secular culture, despite the dramatic rise of Jewish national politics in the region, and despite the government's desire that Jews open Hebrew or Yiddish schools rather than attend Hungarian ones.[82] There was no modern Yiddishist tradition here whatsoever, and although a few Tarbut-style schools were established, including a high school in Cluj, they did not last long. The traditional Orthodox yeshivas continued to flourish, as they had in prewar years.[83] That in Transylvania, as in Galicia, Bohemia-Moravia, and even in Congress Poland, the notable success of the Jewish Party was not accompanied by successes in the field of national education demonstrates once again that, while Jews may vote for Zionists, they do not necessarily want to send their children to Zionist (or Jewish nationalist) Hebrew or Yiddish schools. This held true for the Regat as well. The emergence of Zionism as a force in Jewish life there and the transformation of Bucharest into an important Zionist center in the 1930s did not lead to the triumph of Zionist schools. The first

Tarbut school was opened in Bucharest in as late as 1936.[84] The language of the Regat's Jewish press, including its Zionist press, was Romanian, just as in Transylvania it was in most cases Hungarian.[85]

Bessarabia was the center of the Yiddish press in Romania, and it was this province, along with Bukovina, which produced the most important secular Jewish cultural figures of the interwar period. These included Itsik Manger (1901–1969), one of the greatest Yiddish writers of the twentieth century, and the celebrated fabulist Eliezer Steinbarg (1880–1932). The former was born in Cernăuți, and the latter in a small town in Bessarabia. In the interwar period a number of Yiddish writers came to Bucharest from the newly annexed territories, in a manner reminiscent of the Litvak and Galician "invasion" of Warsaw, and brought to the Romanian capital the new Yiddish literature and the new Yiddish theater. Among them was Manger himself, the Galician-born Shloyme Bikel, and the Bessarabian poet Yankev Sternberg. Thus was maintained the tradition of foreign Jews bringing the "new word" to the Regat, a tradition which dates back to the Haskalah period and perhaps even to the period when Hasidism was imported from the Ukraine and Galicia. The interwar period, therefore, witnessed what one observer has termed the "flourishing" of Yiddish culture in Romania and its appearance, virtually ex nihilo, in the capital of Wallachia. It is extremely doubtful, however, that this new cultural growth would have truly taken root in the Regat, where, as we may recall, an earlier effort to establish a Yiddish journal in the much more Jewish town of Iași ended in failure. Certainly the prevailing cultural tendencies among the Jews of the Regat were not favorable to a long-term flourishing of Yiddish culture. The war years, of course, put an end to this new era of Yiddish culture in the Romanian heartland.[86]

We lack statistics on the extent of linguistic acculturation among Romania's Jewish communities during the interwar period, but it was certainly significant. To be sure, the Jewish masses in Bessarabia, Bukovina, northern Transylvania, and Moldavia continued to speak Yiddish, while the German and Hungarian orientations remained very much alive in Bukovina and Transylvania. But the new generation learned Romanian in school; in Bukovina, for example, the great majority of Jewish children attended government schools, and the same was true of Transylvania.[87] Acculturation did not necessarily imply the decline of Orthodoxy, at least not in its Transylvanian stronghold. And, as in Poland, acculturation went hand in hand not with assimilation, but with the nationalization of important segments within Romanian Jewry. During the interwar years Jews played an important role in certain areas of Romanian intellectual life, particularly in the press (everywhere a Jewish stronghold in Eastern Europe), and they produced a few well-known writers.[88] On the whole, however, they were less prominent in the host

culture than were the Jews of Galicia and Congress Poland, or the Jews of
Hungary. This is not surprising, since, in contrast with the situation in
Galicia, Congress Poland, and Hungary, the majority of Romanian Jews
encountered the dominant host culture only after World War I. Moreover, the majority of Regat Jewry lived in Moldavia, where Yiddish
remained the chief spoken, if not written, language. Finally, we should
recall that Romanian culture itself developed later. For all these reasons,
interwar Romanian Jewry did not create a high culture in the host
language. It is instructive to contrast the Romanian experience with that
of Bohemia and Moravia, where a relatively small Jewish community
exposed for a long period of time to German civilization dominated high
German culture in Prague.

### 5. The 1930s: The Triumph of Radical
### Anti-Semitism and Its Consequences

In Romania, as in Hungary, Poland, and the Baltic States, the 1930s
witnessed the rise of the radical right and the fateful political struggle
between it and the "moderate" right-wing establishment. Just as in
Poland, where the colonels faced a challenge from the extreme right wing
of the National Radical Camp and other groups, and as in Hungary,
where Horthy was challenged by the Arrow Cross, the same pattern
occurred in Romania. Here the moderates of the 1930s were represented
by the leaders of the historic parties and by King Carol, who returned to
the country in 1930 and played an increasingly large role in its political
life, while the radical right was most effectively represented by the
"legionary movement," also known as the Iron Guard, whose most
celebrated leader was Corneliu Codreanu. As in Hungary, relations
between the moderate right and the extreme right were ambivalent, since
both camps had much in common—hostility to Bolshevism, for example,
along with a strong belief in integral nationalism. Both also were anti-
Semitic, though here the difference being that Carol and the old-style
politicians were willing to tolerate the Jews while at the same time
promoting the romanization of the country whereas Codreanu and his
allies were racists who supported Nazi-like solutions to the Jewish question.

The political history of the second decade of interwar Romanian history may be quickly sketched. From 1930 to 1937 the country was run by
leaders of the historic parties—National Peasants and Liberals—while
King Carol wielded ever-growing power. In 1937 an extreme right-wing
government led by the poet Octavian Goga was installed—an event
reminiscent to some extent of the rise of the Gömbös regime in 1932 in

Hungary. But, whereas Gömbös held power for five years, Goga lasted only a few months, and the period 1938–1940 is generally referred to as the period of royal dictatorship, during which the king ruled supreme. External affairs, above all the loss of extensive territories to Soviet Russia, Hungary, and Bulgaria, cost Carol his throne in 1940. He was replaced by a fascist regime in which power was shared by the Iron Guard and Marshal Ion Antonescu. In 1941 Antonescu seized complete control by destroying the legionary movement.

The 1930s in Romania were dominated by the Great Depression, the rise of German influence, and the emergence of fascism as a powerful popular force. The latter two developments were to some extent a function of the first. It is true, of course, that Romanian fascism was a product of the 1920s, not of the 1930s. Its most famous leader, Corneliu Codreanu, a pupil of Cuza and Iorga, commenced his political career in 1919. During the 1920s he established a strong following among students and achieved considerable notoriety. Codreanu was from the outset fanatically anti-Bolshevik, and his creed included rejection of the corruption of the Romanian political system, devotion to the Orthodox church (which was extremely anti-Semitic), hatred of the city and of capitalism, and a belief in the great future of the Romanian peasantry. He was eventually to break with his more moderate teachers over their rejection of extraparliamentary methods and their refusal to lend support to the violent methods employed by his followers.

The Iron Guard was particularly strong in Moldavia (Codreanu having begun his political career as a leader of the nationalist students at the University of Iaşi), Bukovina, and Transylvania. It was predisposed against all the national minorities, but its anti-Semitism was particularly virulent. In his memoirs Codreanu insisted that between 2 million and 2.5 million Jews inhabited Romania, most of whom had invaded Romania during the nineteenth and twentieth centuries. These Jews had quickly taken over all commerce and industry and, in fact, totally dominated urban life in Moldavia. Moreover, they had also succeeded in enslaving millions of Romanian peasants. The extent to which the Jews had taken over Romania was best exemplified by the situation in Iaşi, where

> one can walk through streets and neighborhoods where there are no Romanians, where there is not a single Romanian house, where one cannot find a single Romanian shop. One may visit once great churches, which are today nothing but miserable ruins: the church of the leatherworkers, built by the Romanian leather workers guild, or the church of the harness makers, built by the harness makers guild. All in ruins. In Iaşi today there are no Romanian leather workers or harness makers.[89]

The struggle against the Jews, therefore, according to Codreanu, was a struggle of life or death for Romania, for there could be no thought of compromise. In an interview with an English journalist in 1938, Codreanu is reported as having said the following:

> The Jews, the Jews, they are our curse. They poison our state, our life, our people. The demoralise our nation. They destroy our youth. They are the archenemies. You talk of the Jewish problem; you are right. The Jews are our greatest problem, the most important, the most urgent, the most pressing problem for Romania. The Jews scheme and plot and plan to ruin our national life. We shall not allow this to happen. We, the Iron Guard, will stand in the way of such devilry. We shall destroy the Jews before they can destroy us. There are influences, important influences on the side of the Jews. We shall destroy them, too.[90]

Thus spoke the leader of a political movement which in the national elections of 1937 amassed nearly sixteen percent of the total vote and emerged as the third largest party in the state.

Codreanu, along with many other extreme right-wing Romanians, was much taken by the Nazi party, and was naturally pleased as Romania fell under increasing German influence following Hitler's rise to power. Germany came to play an ever-greater role in Romania's economic life, leading in turn to the rapid propagation of Nazi views in the country. It is true, of course, that Romanian nationalists had much to lose by linking up with Nazi Germany. In obvious contrast with Hungary, Romania's interest lay in preserving the international status quo, while Germany proved quite willing to preside over the dismemberment of its Romanian ally in order to cement its ties with Hungary and the Soviet Union. Nonetheless, Germany was by the late 1930s the great power in the region, aside from the hated Soviet Union, and even those Romanian leaders who feared the embrace of the Nazi state could find no other viable alternative. The failure of the moderate Romanian leadership to head off the growing power of the Iron Guard and the increasing Nazi influence paved the way for Romania's gradual transformation into a German satellite. This was, needless to say, a calamity for the Jewish population.

The early 1930s passed fairly quietly for the Jewish community of Romania, but a distinct rise in anti-Semitic agitation accompanied Hitler's rise to power. It was noted, for example, that the large German minority, undergoing a process of nazification, was now playing a notable role in the anti-Semitic movement.[91] In 1934 the Romanian government passed a "national work" law, which stipulated that eighty percent of the employees of economic enterprises must be "Romanians," as opposed to "foreigners." The law did not specifically denote Jews as foreigners, but was interpreted by Jewish leaders as an effort to oust the Jews from the economy in order to achieve what the National Peasant leader Vaida-Voevod called "the right proportion" of Romanians within the work force. In fact, in 1935 many Jews were thrown out of work as pressure was brought to bear on employers to reduce their "minority personnel."[92] All this took place while Romania was still being ruled by moderates, and, as in Hungary, the moderates did not hesitate to denounce the violent behavior of the extreme right. Thus in 1936 Gheorghe Tătărescu, leader of the liberal government from 1934 to 1936, declared:

> Between the government and the parties of the Right there was nothing in common; there was nothing but abysses, abysses of conception and abysses of method. The parties of the Right were characterized particularly by a nationalism expressed by aggressive means; the Government, however, could not forget that Romania was a State which, although national, included in its population 25 per cent of minority elements, towards which a policy of conciliation must be adopted by guaranteeing them the use of their language and their faith and free development within the framework of the laws.[93]

Such sentiments made Tătărescu something of a hero within the Jewish community, and it was generally believed that the king, too, shared his prime minister's contempt for the radical right. Carol, of course, did not love the Jews, although his celebrated mistress, Madame Lupescu, might have been of Jewish origin, and he had a millionaire friend of Jewish origin, Max Auşnit; but, like Horthy and other "moderate" Hungarians, he was willing to admit that there were good as well as wicked Jews. In January, 1938, Carol made the following remarks:

> The question of the Jews in Romania is the principal factor in the situation. It cannot be denied that there is a strong anti-Semitic feeling in the country. That is an old question in our history.
> The measure to be taken to deal with it is on the principle of revision of citizenship for those Jews who entered the country after the war.
> What happened was something in the nature of an invasion of Galician and Russian Jews who came in illegally. Their number has been exaggerated; some say as many as 800,000, but the maximum was about 250,000, who invaded the villages and are not a good element.
> Can people be regarded as good citizens who entered the country by fraud? Those Jews who lived in Romania before the war will remain untouched. But those who came after the war are without legal rights, except as refugees. About them we shall consider what to do.[94]

In a conversation with an English diplomat the king, echoing the "Zionist" views of contemporary Polish leaders, "expressed his hope that there would be no decrease in emigration to Palestine, which relieved the pressure of a most difficult problem. There was, he said, no doubt that a considerable number of Jewish immigrants obtained Romanian citizenship by fraud, and he was not sure that it might not be necessary to turn them out of the country."[95]

Such attitudes, while not very friendly, were obviously preferable to the views of Codreanu. Yet, as in Hungary and in Poland, the moderates in Romania found it expedient to placate the extremists by tightening the screws on the Jewish community. And, in Romania as elsewhere, this political game became more and more dangerous for the Jews. In 1937 the king actually went so far as to appoint a new government led by two of the most celebrated apostles of extreme anti-Semitism, the mentors of the Iron Guard, Octavian Goga and Alexandru Cuza. In interviews with foreigners the king let it be understood that his motives were not to raise the extreme right to power, but to reveal its inadequacies and to eliminate it. Thus in January, 1938, he proclaimed, "I must do everything I can to break extremism. There is a Beast abroad. We must smash and destroy the Beast. I may appear, at the moment, to be feeding the Beast, but in reality, the measures which I am taking are designed to stop the Beast and I shall destroy him."[96] The Iron Guard, he told an English diplomat, must be combatted, "and . . . the only way to do so was to adopt part of its program."[97]

This was small consolation for the Jews of Romania, who now found themselves, for the first time, ruled by a government whose Jewish policy differed little from that of the Nazis. Indeed, if we compare the proclaimed Jewish policy of the Goga-Cuza regime in Romania with that of the Gömbös regime in Hungary, there is no doubt that the Romanian facists were far more extreme. Their program called for the ousting of Jews from the economy and from the universities, the revocation of rights "improperly granted" to Jews, and the expulsion of all Jews who had entered the country after the signing of the peace treaty.[98] In its attitude toward national minorities, the new government distinguished between those which, from the very beginning, had identified themselves clearly with the dominant nationality and those which had proved themselves to be harmful to Romanian interests. Particularly harmful, according to a National Christian Party statement formulated prior to its rise to power, were "the Jews, who . . . owing to ancient extraterritorial impulses, to their too recent Romanian citizenship, and to their contact with the influences of the States to which they formerly belonged, form the dissolving element detrimental to the consolidation of the Romanian State. . . ." The government had the sacred duty, therefore, to protect its citizens against this danger.[99]

Once in power, the Goga-Cuza regime set about to realize its Jewish program—in contrast with the Gömbös regime, which quickly reached an understanding with the "Jewish enemy." Jewish newspapers and libraries were shut down, various professional organizations expelled their Jewish members, and efforts were made to apply the principle of *numerus clausus* to all sectors of the economy. In January, 1938, a law "concerning the revision of citizenship," according to which most Jews were obliged to prove that they were in fact Romanian citizens, was promulgated.[100] Fortunately for the Jewish community, the Goga-Cuza regime lasted a mere two months. Its fall was engineered by the king, who was supported by those elements in Romanian political life fearful of an Iron Guard takeover. Carol's task was made easier by the economic panic which swept over the country in the wake of Goga's rise to power and by the extremely negative foreign reaction to the government's Jewish policy. The new government, led by the Orthodox patriarch (also a convinced anti-Semite), inaugurated a new period in Romanian political history during which the king ruled supreme. In late 1938 Codreanu and several of his supporters were murdered, and a brutal, seemingly successful campaign was waged against the Iron Guard. Carol abolished the 1923 constitution, did away with the pluralistic party system, and assumed dictatorial power over a one-party corporate state.

Whatever its attitude toward the governing principles of Carol, Romanian Jewry breathed more easily after the demise of its most extreme enemies. The king's visit to London in 1938 in search of diplomatic support was also thought to be a sign of Romania's desire to extract itself from the Nazi embrace. In mid-1939 Armand Călinescu, a leading figure in the king's government, informed a foreign Jewish visitor that

> neither he nor his Government was anti-Semitic. Their suppression of the Iron Guard had rapidly altered the situation and, incidentally, had been of great benefit to the Jews. But they had to take certain elements in the life of the country into account. No Government could ignore them, and certain measures had to be taken "pour calmer l'opinion publique." But it had all been carried through deliberately in a spirit of moderation.[101]

By "certain measures" Călinescu was referring to the issue of Jewish citizenship. In this matter, at least, the policies of Goga-Cuza were continued. The king, regarded by the extreme right as a prisoner of the Jews (the proof being his moves against the Iron Guard, his "Jewish" mistress, and the presence among his friends of a Jewish millionaire), did not hesitate to prove to public opinion that he would take stern measures against the "bad Jews," although he continued to maintain, like Horthy, that not all Jews were bad. According to one account, by September, 1939, at least 270,070 Jews had been deprived of their citizenship.[102] Plans were made (but not carried out) to expel large numbers of "foreign Jews." Jews replaced by gentiles during the *numerus clausus* (or, as it was called in Romania, the *numerus vallachicus*) campaign, were not rehired. In the summer of 1940, after the loss of Bessarabia and northern Bukovina, in an atmosphere of growing desperation, the government passed a series of laws which resembled the Hungarian Jewish laws and which struck brutally at the Jewish interest. For the first time these laws defined the Jews also as a race, not only as a religion, thus affecting baptized Jews as well. On the other hand, the laws distinguished, in a manner now traditional in Romania, between different types of Jews. These who had been citizens before the war, and their descendants, were to some extent exempt from the new measures, and those Jews who had been resident in prewar Romania were also granted certain exemptions. The Jews of the new territories had no such good fortune. The laws, in the words of an authority, deprived "the great majority [of Romanian Jews], aside from a small privileged group . . . of their basic civil rights." Jews were prohibited from owning land in the villages, forbidden to publish newspapers, ousted from the army, and denied any role in public life. They were forbidden to deal in goods over which there were state monopolies, to marry gentiles, and to convert to Christianity. The property of the kehiles was nationalized, and many Jewish institutions were closed. A *numerus clausus* was established in the high schools. "A long list of similar instructions completed the legal, political, and social boycott of the Jews and paved the way for their economic ruin."[103] Just as Horthy and his moderate colleagues presided over the enactment of the Jewish laws in Hungary, so Carol, Călinescu, and other foes of extreme anti-Semitism presided over the demise of Jewish emancipation in Romania.

The years 1939 and 1940 were disastrous, not only for Romanian Jewry, but for Romania as well. In September, 1940, after the humiliating loss of Bessarabia, northern Bukovina, and northern Transylvania, the result of the implementation of certain provisions in the German-Soviet pact of 1939 and of Germany's pro-Hungarian policy, Carol abdicated. If his reign had been harmful to Jewish interests, the new Iron Guard government (allied with Marshal Antonescu) was far worse. Indeed, the establishment of the National Legionary State in September, 1940, in which the Iron Guard was the only legal party, may be regarded as the first chapter in the history of the Holocaust in Romania.

To what extent did the Jewish condition deteriorate during the decade of the 1930s? Quite apart from the growing anti-Semitic onslaught, the Jews' economic condition, along with that of the non-Jewish population, declined precipitously in the poorer regions where the impact of the Depression was particularly great. In 1929 the Jewish sociologist Yankev Leshchinski toured Bessarabia and found that the Jewish population in the little towns was undergoing a process of pauperization, the result of the loss of the Russian market and of general government neglect and misrule in the province. The Jewish bourgeoisie and professional class of the capital, however, was still doing well, and there is evidence that this was also the case in Bukovina, although in the latter province Jewish civil servants, employed by the old regime, were quickly replaced by Romanians.[104] As for the impact of state-inspired anti-Semitism, it seems that only in the late 1930s was the Jews' condition everywhere in the state seriously affected. Much depended upon local circumstances, since Romania had a poor record with regard to law enforcement, including the enforcement of anti-Jewish laws. In Arad there was little serious anti-Semitism until the crucial year 1940, while in Timişoara, another city in the Banat, the local polytechnicum was a hotbed of anti-Jewish agitation and an effort was made to ban the *shkhite* (ritual slaughter). In certain areas of Transylvania the nazified German population organized boycotts of Jewish stores, and in some towns in Bessarabia the German minority acted in the same manner.[105] In Bucharest, from 1937 on, Jews were ousted from merchant and professional associations, and Jewish merchants and industrialists were denied licenses. The same occurred in the towns of Moldavia.[106] Along with the economic damage, which is at any rate difficult to measure, the Jews suffered from frequent outbreaks of violence and from the inevitable despair which accompanied their loss of citizenship, the outlawing of their political organizations (the UER and the Jewish Party were dissolved in 1938), and their loss of legal protection. In 1939 the organ of the Alliance Israélite, a strong supporter of the UER and well informed as to the situation in Romania, came to the melancholy conclusion that the Jews had no alternative but to emigrate.[107]

Many Romanian Jews felt the same way. Filderman himself, the apostle of *doikeyt*, negotiated with government leaders in 1938 and agreed to support a plan whereby 50,000 Jews would leave the country each year.[108] From 1938 on, Romania became a center for illegal emigration to Palestine (known in Hebrew as *aliya bet*), an activity strongly supported by the government. But, of course, emigration could not solve the Jewish question in Romania. The general desire on the part of many Jews to leave Romania naturally had the effect of strengthening the Zionist movement, but (as in Poland) the ever-worsening condition of Romanian Jewry did not produce a united Zionist camp, while the difficulties in reaching Palestine eventually put a damper on Zionist enthusiasm. The pioneering youth movements grew in the 1930s, but after 1936 their graduates were barred by the British government from legally emigrating to the promised land. In 1939, the year of the last World Zionist Congress before World War II, 60,013 shekels were sold in Romania, more than ever before in Romania and second only to the number sold in Poland. *Aliyah*, on the other hand, which was never very impressive, declined in response to British policy in Palestine. In 1935, 3,616 Jews went to Palestine from

Romania; many fewer were able to do so during 1936–1939, despite the fact that the Romanian government, which outlawed the various youth movements in 1938, allowed the Pioneer to maintain its legal existence.[109] With the main Jewish organizations banned, only the Jewish kehiles remained to represent the community. During the war years it was Filderman, rather than the advocates of the new Jewish politics, who became the most important representative of the terrorized Jewish community.

### 6. The War Years and Some Final Thoughts

Although the period 1940–1944 lies beyond the proper scope of this book, the fact that Romania, like Hungary, preserved its independence justifies a quick survey of the events of these years. During the short-lived National Legionary State the Jewish condition deteriorated rapidly. In the last months of 1940 Jewish property was confiscated and Jewish shops were officially boycotted. An office of romanization was established in the ministry of labor. The Iron Guard celebrated its belated rise to power by organizing a bloody pogrom in Bucharest (in January, 1941). Soon after this event Marshal Antonescu, backed by the army, turned against the Guard and seized total power in the country. Antonescu was a loyal ally of Hitler, but he managed to preserve Romanian sovereignty just as Horthy was able to do in Hungary. And, like Horthy, Antonescu was also able to preserve some degree of freedom of action with regard to the Jewish question. His Jewish subjects were humiliated, deprived of all rights, ruined economically, and subjected to pogroms, but not all were destroyed during the war years. As Horthy sought to protect the "good Jews" of Budapest, so during Antonescu's regime the Jews of the Regat and southern Transylvania were to some extent protected. The Jews of Bessarabia and Bukovina, on the other hand, suffered disaster. Many were killed by German and Romanian troops during the reconquest of these regions from the Soviets, and those who survived were expelled to Transnistria, a part of the Soviet Ukraine conquered by Romania during the war. Here they were sent to concentration camps, where most died. The expulsion and murder of Bukovinian and Bessarabian Jewry was carried out with great enthusiasm by Antonescu and the Romanian authorities, who accused these Jewries of exhibiting pro-Soviet sympathies during the short-lived period of Bolshevik rule (1940–1941). But Antonescu did not agree to the mass murder of the Jews of the Regat and southern Transylvania, despite German pressure. The reasons for this policy resided not in his love for these Jews, but rather in his belief, the result of Stalingrad and other German reverses, that it would be wise not to burn his bridges with the Western Allies. Also involved was Romania's desire to maintain as much independence from Germany in internal affairs as possible. Thus in 1944, when Romania changed sides and joined the Allies after a coup against Antonescu engineered by the new king, the majority of Romanian Jews were still alive. According to one estimate, of 607,790 Jews under Romanian rule during the war (including the communities of Bessarabia and Northern Bukovina), 57 percent were saved—a higher percentage than anywhere else in the East Central European lands discussed in this book.[110]

Looking back on the Jews' experience in interwar Romania, the triumph of extreme anti-Semitism is hardly surprising. Here as elsewhere in the region, with the exception of Czechoslovakia, the general situation was conducive to the rise of the extreme right, and the Jews possessed no local allies to protect them from the rising danger. Indeed, the absence of a strong socialist movement and of an old-regime, Hungarian-type, pro-Jewish liberal tradition made the search for allies here more hopeless than even in Poland and Hungary. Nevertheless, that more Romanian Jews than Hungarian Jews, not to mention Polish Jews, were able to survive the war demonstrates that developments between the wars were by no means crucial with regard to the Jewish fate during the Holocaust. Whereas in Romania the extreme right Iron Guard was destroyed, finally, in 1941, in Hungary the Arrow Cross survived to take power in 1944 and to cooperate with the Nazis in the destruction of Hungarian Jewry. And while both Horthy and Antonescu were anxious to remain independent of the Germans, the latter was more successful. It is ironic that Romania, which refused to emancipate its Jewish subjects before World War I, pursued an anti-Semitic policy between the wars, and witnessed the development of the strongest native fascist movement in all Eastern Europe, turned out to be a safer place for Jews than did Hungary, Poland, Czechoslovakia, and the Baltic States. No less surprising is the fact that in the postwar Communist regime, for all its rabid Stalinism and Romanian nationalism, Jews have fared, and continue to fare, better than in most other Communist states of the region. If before World War I Romania and the tsarist empire were considered the most anti-Semitic countries in Europe, today the Soviet Union alone deserves that title.

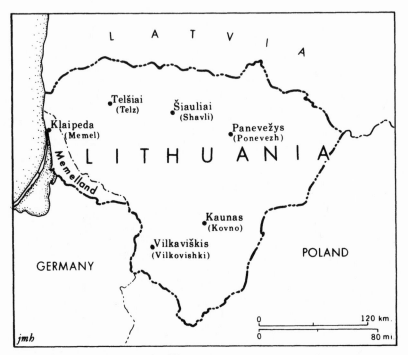

**Lithuania between the Wars**

# LITHUANIA / 5

Lithuania, like the other Baltic republics of Latvia and Estonia, attained political sovereignty after centuries of subjugation. Unlike Latvia and Estonia, however, Lithuania had once been, in the distant past, a great European power. But it had been incorporated into the medieval Polish-Lithuanian Commonwealth, and during the course of the centuries its ruling class had become polonized. Since an indigenous commercial class never developed in this land of great latifundia, the enserfed peasantry remained virtually the sole repository of the national culture. (The church was not, strictly speaking, a national institution, since it was heavily penetrated by Poles.) During the partitions of Poland in the late eighteenth century, almost all Lithuanian territory became part of Russia, and there it remained until the fall of the Romanovs. Throughout most of the nineteenth century it was subjected to russification measures, which were strongly resisted by the Polish gentry and by the Catholic church, some of whose priests eventually became leaders of a Lithuanian national movement directed against Warsaw, St. Petersburg, and the Russian Orthodox faith. Until the very end of the old regime, most of the landowning class was Polish; the peasantry, Lithuanian and, in some places, Belorussian; the urban, commercial population, Jewish (and to a lesser extent Polish); and the bureaucracy, Russian. The region was economically very backward, one of the least industrialized in European Russia. Only one city, Vilna (Vilnius), was of major importance, but this city, revered by Lithuanian nationalists as the historical capital of the nation, was in fact a Polish-Jewish town with few Lithuanian residents and with a rural hinterland inhabited mostly by Belorussian peasants.[1]

That this backward, multinational region should have attained political independence was quite unexpected. Lithuanian nationalists prior to World War I were content to demand some sort of national autonomy within the framework of a Russian federated republic. But here, as elsewhere in Eastern Europe, the dramatic events of the war and the immediate postwar period created a wholly new situation. During World War I Lithuania was occupied by Germany, which encouraged Lithuanian self-rule in the hope of establishing a satellite state in this strategic part of Europe. In 1917 a Lithuanian parliament, the Taryba, was established under German aegis in Vilna. After the German retreat the country was fought over by the resurgent Poles, who believed that all of Lithuania belonged by historical right to Poland, and by the Bolsheviks, who set up a short-lived Soviet republic there. After a bewildering sequence of events, during which Vilna changed hands some seven times, it turned out that neither the Poles nor the Soviets were strong enough to impose their will upon the Lithuanian people. The great powers, preferring an independent Lithuania to one totally dominated by either Poland or Soviet Russia, were glad to recognize the new state whose borders were not fixed until 1924. To the dismay of all Lithuanian nationalists, the new state did not include Vilna, which Poland had successfully seized in 1919. As compensation the new state gained from Germany the Memel region (Klaipeda in Lithuanian), which gave it an outlet to the Baltic. Despite their failure to incorporate Vilna into the new state, the Lithuanian nationalists had much to be proud of. Unlike the larger Ukrainian and Belorussian nations, Lithuania had achieved political independence and could now set about to right the wrongs of centuries of foreign rule.

It was, however, no easy task. The new state faced formidable internal and external problems. The economic situation, bad before the war, was now much worse. Unlike the Hungarians, Czechs, Poles, and Romanians, the Lithuanians had few trained people and no experience in self-government. Lithuanian national culture was still in its formative stages, and national consciousness was also not very well developed. In many ways everything had to be started from scratch. Lithuania was a more homogeneous country than most in East Central Europe (the only important minorities being the Jews and the Poles, with eighty percent of the population being ethnically Lithuanian), and it did not have the problem of different historical traditions, but it had more than its share of difficulties with its neighbors. The Soviet Union, while it recognized Lithuanian sovereignty, never forgot that this country had once been a Russian province, and Germany never renounced her claim to Memel. Meanwhile, the Lithuanian government in Kaunas (in Russian Kovno, the capital to which it had fled after Vilna had been seized by Poland) was obsessed with regaining the historic capital from Poland. The Vilna issue poisoned relations between Poland and the new Baltic state, and also lent to Lithuanian politics a particularly strident nationalistic tone lacking in Latvia and Estonia.[2] Lithuanian politics were pluralistic and multiparty at the beginning, but nationalism, hatred of the Soviet Union, and the prominence of the Catholic church, along with the political tradition inherited from tsarist Russia, led the country in a right-wing direction. From 1926 on, Lithuania, like Poland, was an authoritarian, right-wing state. This sort of regime, again as in Poland, did much to develop the national culture and national consciousness, but little to develop the backward economy. In this respect Lithuania remained in 1939 what it had been in 1919—an agrarian, peasant land with few cities and little industry.

## 1. The Historical Context

Lithuanian Jewry, unlike that of neighboring Latvia, was a historically homogeneous entity. Aside from the very small number of German-speaking Jews of the Memel region, annexed to the new state in 1924, the Jews of independent Lithuania shared a common history and culture. They all derived from the larger Lithuanian, or Lithuanian-Belorussian, Jewish community whose roots were in the Lithuanian part of the medieval Polish-Lithuanian Commonwealth. After the partitions of Poland they found themselves residing in the so-called North West region of the Russian empire and in the northeastern tip of Congress Poland. The political settlement after World War I partitioned this Jewry among four different states—the Soviet Union, Poland, Latvia, and Lithuania. The major urban centers of Lithuanian Jewry, Minsk and Vilna, were alloted to Soviet Russia and to Poland. Vilna was also Lithuanian Jewry's spiritual center, the home of a celebrated rabbinical, Haskalah, Zionist, and Bundist tradition. The Jewry of independent Lithuania was cut off from these centers, but the unique and celebrated Jewish tradition of the Lithuanian lands continued to shape its history during the interwar period.

We have already noted, in the chapter on Poland, the main characteristics of Lithuanian Jewry. It was, as we know, one of the least acculturated of all East European Jewries, since it resided in a buffer region between Russian and Polish culture and among peoples whose own national cultures held little attraction for members of other ethnic groups. Jewish Orthodoxy held sway here (there was, of course, no competing Jewish religious tendency) and Lithuania was famous for its great yeshivas and high religious culture, but Hasidism of the Polish and Galician (and, by extension, Hungarian-Romanian) variety was comparatively weak. Modernizing tendencies, encouraged by the tsarist regime, took root early here, and the Jewish Enlightenment (Haskalah) movement made deep inroads into the Jewish population. Vilna and other Lithuanian towns became great Haskalah centers, and, since the Haskalah in this part of the East European Jewish world possessed a strong nationalist, Hebraic cast, it was a precursor of the various modern Jewish national and cultural movements, all of which were very strong in Lithuania. The combination of little acculturation and a deeply rooted Orthodox Jewry undergoing a process of secularization encouraged by both the government and the Haskalah produced an environment in which modern Jewish nationalism flourished and competed with Orthodoxy for the allegiance of the youth.

Thus Lithuania became a center of Bundism, Folkism, and Zionism, as well as a bastion of modern Hebrew and Yiddish literature and journalism. In almost every way, its Jewry was the antithesis of the Jewries of Hungary, Bohemia, and Moravia. And Lithuanian Jews (Litvakn in Yiddish) maintained both their Orthodox and their secular nationalist traditions in the new states of the interwar period, with the obvious exception of the Soviet Union, where their autonomous Jewish politics and culture were ultimately crushed by the regime.[3]

Within the framework of the Russian empire prewar relations between Jews and Lithuanians do not appear to have been particularly bad. We may assume, of course, that the Lithuanian peasant as well as the Lithuanian priest shared the dislike of the Jews common everywhere in the Pale of Settlement, but on the whole the Jews in the Lithuanian-Belorussian lands probably had better relations with their non-Jewish neighbors than Jews did elsewhere in Russia. The Ukraine, along with Bessarabia, experienced the most infamous pogroms of the late nineteenth and early twentieth centuries, while Lithuania was relatively free of such disturbances. Congress Poland was the scene of much organized anti-Semitic activity, including the well-known boycott of Jewish shops organized in 1912, while nothing of the kind took place farther north. It is interesting to speculate just why this was the case. If we assume that growing Polish and Ukrainian nationalism had to do with intensity of anti-Jewish feelings in Poland and the Ukraine, it may well be that the retarded nature of Lithuanian national consciousness was responsible for the lack of such feelings in Lithuania. And if we assume that growing competition between the Jewish and the Polish bourgeoisies had a great deal to do with the emergence of the anti-Semitic National Democratic movement in Congress Poland, the lack of a Lithuanian commercial class in the prewar period may have had something to do with the failure of such a movement to emerge in Lithuania.[4] We have already noted that in the more backward regions of East Central Europe, in Subcarpathian Rus, for example, relations between Jews and non-Jews were often less tension-ridden than in rather more developed regions such as Slovakia or Poland. This fact demonstrates, if nothing else, that the strength or weakness of anti-Semitism is not related to the degree of acculturation or assimilation of the Jewry in question. At any rate, the Lithuanians did not bring to their new state anything comparable to the anti-Semitic baggage carried by the Poles or by the Romanians. And during the interwar years the Polish minority, identified with the hated regime which had seized Vilna from its rightful owners, was more feared and disliked than were the Jews. This situation helps explain the Jewish tendency in Vilna and elsewhere to prefer a Lithuanian to a Polish (or Soviet) "solution." It was one of the foundations on which the interesting although short-lived Lithuanian-Jewish alliance was based.

## 2. Lithuanian-Jewish Relations, 1918–1926: Hope and Disillusion

In most cases in Eastern Europe, when territories were transferred from one state to another, the opinions of the Jews were not consulted and their support was not solicited. Transylvanian Jews, for example, were not asked whether they preferred Romanian to Hungarian rule (they would have answered with a resounding no). The Lithuanian case, however, was different. The issue of whether or not Lithuania should be an independent state, and if so what her borders should be, was not resolved until 1920, although it had been actively debated since 1917. During these years the Jewish community did make its views known—or rather we should say that the various Jewish political factions made their views known. Moreover, their views were considered important, at least by the Lithuanian nationalists, who were extremely interested in obtaining Jewish support for their plans. The situation in Lithuania was in some ways comparable to that in eastern Galicia, whose fate also was not clear in the immediate postwar period and whose Jewish community was actively courted by one side in the dispute over control in that multinational region. But, whereas in eastern Galicia the official position of the Jewish leadership was one of neutrality in the face of conflicting Polish and Ukrainian claims, in Lithuania most Jewish leaders were openly pro-Lithuanian, welcoming the creation of a Lithuanian state (which they hoped would be large enough to include most Lithuanian Jews) and preferring it to the incorporation of their region into either Poland or Soviet Russia.

The Lithuanians had very good reasons to be interested in Jewish support. In the East European context Lithuanian nationalism was relatively weak, and its enemies very powerful. Lithuanian claims to statehood were by no means universally accepted, even by friendly Western powers. As already pointed out, the Lithuanian nation had no real ruling class—no gentry, no bourgeoisie, only a thin stratum of intellectuals. Given this position of weakness, the Lithuanians needed every bit of support they could muster, and the Jews appeared to be a logical and valuable source of such support. Unlike the other national minorities living on Lithuanian soil, the Jews obviously had no territorial claims of their own and could be expected to be much more friendly to the idea of Lithuanian sovereignty than the Poles, the Russians, or the Belorussians would be. The Jews' predominance in urban life and in Lithuanian commerce was such as to make their support very important, and it was also believed (not only by the Lithuanians, of course) that their influence on world public opinion and in world finance would be a factor in the postwar settlement. If Masaryk, representing a far more advanced nation, could consider Jewish support an important factor in the creation of Czechoslovakia, how much more so was this the case with Lithuanian nationalist leaders, who like the Czechs (but unlike the Ukrainians, who for similar reasons wanted the Jews in their camp both in eastern Galicia and in the Russian Ukraine) were not burdened by a strong anti-Semitic tradition. As for the cost of Jewish support, it was not considered excessive. The Lithuanian national movement would have little difficulty in proving itself less anti-Semitic than the Polish and less disruptive socially than Bolshevism. Moreover, the Jews' national demands for some sort of autonomy might be satisfactorily met, since the Lithuanians were not interested, at least not at first, in assimilating the Jews and since they were prepared, unlike the Poles, to consider the establishment of a "nationalities state" rather than a Polish-type nation-state. Like Masaryk, and like Ukrainian nationalists, they would be content if the Jews would put an end to "foreign" cultural and political orientations (whether Polish, Russian, or German) and develop their own Hebrew-Yiddish national culture.[5]

What seemed a good bargain from the Lithuanian side appeared no less attractive to many Jews. If the Ukrainians were not the most desirable of partners because of the fierce anti-Semitic tradition in the Ukraine (and the Jews needed no reminder of this tradition during 1918–1920), the Lithuanians, as we know, were a different case. If the Poles refused to consider Jewish national demands in eastern Galicia and Congress Poland, the Lithuanians promised them everything they desired. Moreover, Jewish nationalists welcomed the idea of an independent Lithuanian state because the Jews living in such a state would not be tempted to assimilate into the dominant culture, but would (so it was assumed) concentrate on developing their own national life. They would prefer to attend Hebrew or Yiddish schools rather than Lithuanian ones. This might not be the case in Poland, whose culture was obviously much more attractive and had already won over thousands of Jewish adherents. It made sense, therefore, for the Jews to support a Lithuanian state which would be by definition a multinational, federal state in which all the nationalities— Jews, Poles, Belorussians, and the majority Lithuanian people—would band together against the imperialist powers to create a kind of East European Switzerland. This position seemed all the more sensible in light of the fact that at least one great power, Germany, supported some sort of Lithuanian sovereignty, while the great powers were far from enthusiastic in support of Ukrainian claims in eastern Galicia. Much to the satisfaction of the Lithuanians, a Zionist conference held in Vilna in December, 1918, resolved to "greet the reconstruction of Lithuania as a free and democratic state based on full equality and national-personal autonomy for all its peoples." In the same month two leading General Zionists, Yaakov Vygodski (1855–1941) and Shimshon Rosenbaum (1860–1934), joined the Lithuanian government in Vilna, the former as minister without portfolio for Jewish affairs, the latter as vice-minister of foreign affairs.[6] Their decision to join the government was not given unanimous backing by the various Jewish political factions. The socialists, both Bundist and Poale Zion, were hostile toward "bourgeois" Lithuanian nationalism, all the more so since it was supported by imperialist Germany, and they were also naturally attracted to the great revolution taking place in Russia. Even within the General Zionist camp, voices warned against a commitment to Lithuanian nationalism, since it would surely alienate the Poles and endanger the Jews in the event of a Polish victory on the field of battle.[7] But the attractiveness of the Lithuanians as ideal partners in the creation of a new East European state in which all nationalities would be free to develop their culture as they saw fit outweighed these objections. For better or for worse, mainstream Jewish opinion opted for Lithuanian independence.

The fortunes of war and diplomacy created not the large Lithuania which Jewish (and Lithuanian) nationalists hoped for, but rather a small Lithuanian state located in a region from which many Jews had been expelled by the Russians in the early stages of World War I and which contained only a fraction of Lithuanian-Belorussian Jewry. Vilna, as we know, was captured by the Poles, and one of the first things they did in that city was to instigate a major pogrom (in April, 1919) to punish the Jews for their alleged pro-Lithuanian and pro-Bolshevik position. The Lithuanian government retreated to the provincial capital of Kaunas, taking along Rosenbaum but not Vygodski, who decided to stick it out with the rest of Vilna Jewry under Polish rule. We shall see that the reduced size of the new Lithuanian state had something to do with the ultimately unsatisfactory state of Lithuanian-Jewish relations. But in the meantime it appeared that the majority nationality was going to live up to its side of the bargain and grant its Jewish citizens not only full equality as individuals but also the status of a national minority with the right to its own state-supported national institutions. Since in Lithuania, as was not the case in Czechoslovakia, most Jews desired both to be recognized as members of a national minority and to make use of such national institutions, the stage was set for the implementation of one of the major Jewish political theories which had developed in the old Russian empire, namely, that of extraterritorial national autonomy.

In 1919, during the course of the Paris peace conference, Lithuanian leaders made their first official declarations with regard to the future status of the Jewish minority. According to their proclamation of August 5, 1919, Jews residing in the sovereign state of Lithuania would enjoy the following rights:[8]

1. Equality before the law for all "members of the Jewish nation."
2. Proportional representation for the Jews in legislative bodies, to be guaranteed by the establishment of a "Jewish national curia" or by some other means.
3. A special minister for Jewish affairs to represent the Jewish nation in the Lithuanian government.
4. The free use of Jewish languages in the courts and in government institutions.
5. The unlimited right to observe the Sabbath and other Jewish holidays.
6. Autonomy "in their internal affairs," including "religion, welfare, social help, education, and culture in general." The "organs of Jewish autonomy" would be the local Jewish communities (kehiles) and the union of these communities.
7. Free and obligatory education in Jewish schools, so long as such rights are granted to other primary schools as well.
8. Recognition of the organs of Jewish national autonomy as government organs whose acts are binding on all Jews and who are authorized to levy taxes.

This imposing program for extraterritorial autonomy which visionaries had only dreamed of during the prewar period was, of course, only a proclamation of intent, with no legal force, but it was signed by the future prime minister of Lithuania, Augustinas Voldemaras. The new state appeared to have every intention of making these declarations into law. The proclamation certainly excited the Jewish world, and many believed that a new era in Jewish-gentile relations had dawned in this small but significant corner of Eastern Europe. Lithuania would serve as a precedent of great importance for the principle of Jewish diaspora nationalism, a precedent that would be followed, eventually, by other states. If national autonomy had fallen victim to the Bolsheviks in the Russian Ukraine and to the Poles in eastern Galicia, it would triumph here.[9]

As the Lithuanian authorities were making their promises (which were also extended to the other national minorities of the new state, namely, the Poles and the Belorussians), the Jewish community, ravaged by war but full of hope now that Lithuanian sovereignty was being established, began to create its "national organs" and to choose its national leaders. Since Vygodski had remained in Vilna, a new candidate for the position of Jewish minister had to be found, and in the spring of 1919 Jewish representatives in the Kaunas city council selected Max Soloveitshik (1883–1957), a local Zionist leader, for the job.[10] Soloveitshik obviously did not have the political legitimacy which he would have derived from being chosen by a democratically elected all-Lithuanian Jewish conference, or from being chosen directly by the Jewish population. Like most other national Jewish leaders in the years 1918–1919, he had been chosen by other Jewish politicans, who themselves could hardly claim to be the democratically elected representatives of the Jewish people. Recognizing his position as temporary, Soloveitshik declared that his first task would be to establish a "network of democratically elected kehiles and at the same time to call for a conference of their representatives, which will decide all of the questions of Lithuanian Jewry including the issue of a minister for Jewish affairs."[11] In January, 1920, the first all-Lithuanian conference of kehiles met and elected the National Council (Natsional-rat in Yiddish; Vaad ha-arets in Hebrew) of thirty-four members. A month later the Lithuanian prime minister, Ernestas Galvanauskas, reiterated his country's commitment to national autonomy and further declared that "our country will be a model for all states made up of different nationalities."[12] The democratic kehile, he noted, would control "all the cultural and religious affairs of the Jewish population," while the all-Lithuanian organization of kehile representatives would have the authority to nominate the Jewish minister. In April, 1920, the government passed a law governing the authority and makeup of the kehile; it stipulated, among other things, that Jews could withdraw from the kehile's authority only via conversion or by proving that the documents stating that they were Jews were incorrect. The kehiles were granted very broad authority, ranging from education to the registry of Jewish births, deaths, and marriages.[13]

During 1920 Jewish enthusiasm over the Jewish policy of the Lithuanian government reached its apex. It appeared that the medieval Council of the Four Lands, which governed Jewish life in the old Polish-Lithuanian Commonwealth, was to be resurrected in a modern, secular form in the new state. In August the Jewish organization established to act as a watchdog over the implementation of Jewish national rights in Eastern Europe took time off from lambasting the Poles and the Romanians and congratulated Lithuania for "keeping her promises regarding the autonomy of minority nationalities."[14] When Vilna was briefly reunited with Lithuania, also in the summer, its Jewish leaders were ecstatic, comparing the enlightened attitude of the Lithuanians with the benighted policies of the Polish invaders. As Vygodski recalled in his memoirs, "Taking into account the experience we had with Kovno Lithuania [that is, with the independent Lithuanian state] and with Vilna

Lithuania [that is, with the Poles], it was entirely clear to us that Kovno Lithuania was a paradise in comparison with Vilna Lithuania."[15] The members of the Jewish National Council, especially Rosenbaum, were extremely active in promoting the Lithuanian cause, thus fulfilling their side of the bargain. When Vilna was returned, this time for good, to Polish sovereignty, the National Council issued the following statement:

> A new yoke, a hard regime of occupation is oppressing our brothers who have been cut off from us, and who together with the Lithuanians and Belorussians are now suffering under the yoke of foreign oppression.
>
> Although they are not with us, nonetheless the voice of Vilna Jewry has been heard, and we have heard the bold voice of people who desire to be free citizens in the free Lithuanian state.
>
> Through the artificial demarcation lines we send a brotherly greeting and call upon them to continue their stand as courageous fighters who embody the struggle for Jewish national self-rule.[16]

Further evidence of Lithuania's goodwill emerged in 1921, when the state formally agreed to allow Jewish deputies in the parliament to address that body in Yiddish if they so desired (their knowledge of Lithuanian, of course, was far from impressive). Moreover, street signs in Hebrew characters were permitted in the capital city of Kaunas.[17] All this was unimaginable in neighboring Poland, and although largely symbolic it did its part to convince many that Lithuania was truly a "paradise" for the Jewish population.

It was also in 1921, however, that doubts began to surface within the Jewish leadership regarding this widely held sentiment. In the debates on the nature of the Lithuanian constitution, held during 1921, the government put up considerable resistance to the idea of anchoring its promises to the Jewish minority in the basic laws of the new state. The constitution enacted in 1922 did not specifically mention the Jews (or any other national minority), and, while it did promise that the various nationalities would enjoy the right to run "their national and cultural affairs," it did not grant legal status either to the Jewish ministry or to the Jewish National Council. Nor was there any mention of the language rights of the Jews or of the "national curia" promised in 1919.[18] In deploring this situation, the second conference of kehiles, held in 1922, noted that "there are no complete guarantees for the development of national autonomy. The kehile conference believes that the constitution must stipulate that all the laws which deal with national minorities must be implemented by the Minister for the minorities."[19] Finding himself in an anomalous position, the Jewish minister, Soloveitshik, resigned his post in the fall of 1922 and left Lithuania. International Jewish organizations, once so full of praise for Lithuania, now became critical for the first time.

In 1923 the Lithuanian government appointed a new Jewish minister, Bernard Friedman, who served without the agreement of the national Jewish parties and was in fact boycotted by the organized Jewish community. Friedman's appointment had been preceded by an electoral law which the Jews perceived as being discriminatory in a way almost identical to that of the Polish law (which, we may recall, brought to life the minorities' bloc of 1922). Worse was yet to come. In 1924 the Ministry for Jewish Affairs was abolished, as was the Jewish National Council. In 1925 the kehile's central role in the scheme of Jewish national autonomy was dealt a devastating blow: a new law now specifically allowed more than one kehile to be established in a given locality, thus potentially robbing this institution of its authority within the local Jewish community. Moreover, all kehiles were now placed firmly under government control, as was the case in Poland. Finally, in 1926 the old kehiles, which had been elected democratically by the Jewish population during the early 1920s, were abolished altogether, and the new ones set up by the state were boycotted by the secular Jewish parties. In this sense, at least, the Jewish situation appeared now to be worse, not better, than in most other East European states. Little was left of the imposing edifice of national autonomy promised in 1919. Disillusion was widespread.[20]

How are we to explain this rapid and unexpected turn of events? In a remarkable interview given as early as the fall of 1921, Max Soloveitshik not only predicted with some accuracy what the future held in store for Lithuanian Jewry, but also presented an interesting if not entirely convincing analysis of why the glorious promises of 1919–1920 would probably not be kept. In his view the key was the failure of the Lithuanians to establish a large state which would be, by definition, a multinational one, including significant numbers of Jews, Poles, and Belorussians. Without the Vilna region, he pointed out, Lithuania was in fact a nation-state, not a state of nationalities, and such circumstances would provide little incentive, once the state got on its feet, to implement grandiose plans of extraterritorial national autonomy. On the contrary, Lithuanian nationalists, who were in reality no different from Polish or Romanian nationalists, would now have an excellent reason for opposing such plans, since they were no longer dictated by ethnic exigencies.[21] Whatever one may think of this argument, it was certainly true that, once the new state had been established within internationally recognized borders, the need for Jewish support, both internal and external, declined. At any rate, Jewish support had not succeeded in winning Vilna for Lithuania, so perhaps its value had been overrated. Moreover, it soon turned out that there were many fewer Jews in the new state than its leaders, and the leaders of Lithuanian Jewry, had previously believed. During the negotiations regarding Lithuania's future it had been assumed that the Jews made up about 13 percent of the country's population, but the loss of Vilna and the large number of Jews evacuated from the Kaunas region during the war substantially reduced their numbers. In 1920 the Lithuanian prime minister went on record as saying that 13 out of every 100 citizens of the state were Jews, but the census of 1923 revealed that Jews constituted only 7.26 percent of the total population.[22]

Not only was Jewish support and the Jewish weight within the country judged to be far less significant in 1921–1924 than in 1919–1920, but Lithuanian politics also took on a decidedly right-wing character in the early 1920s. This political tendency was obviously inimical to Jewish aspirations, as it was to the aspirations of other minorities. It stood for the creation of a unitary, authoritarian Lithuanian nation-state in which the slogan "Lithuania for the Lithuanians" was as natural as the slogans "Poland for the Poles" and "Romania for the Romanians."

Basically, the Lithuanian-Jewish alliance unraveled because it quickly became apparent from the Lithuanian side that it was a marriage of convenience only. The leaders of the Lithuanian state even in the first half of the 1920s were not Masaryk-type liberals, imbued with the spirit of tolerance; rather, they were more like the leaders of Hungary, and their policies toward the minorities in general, and toward the Jews in particular, were based upon the exigencies of the moment. When the Jews were perceived as useful allies, as in prewar Hungary and in the Lithuania of 1918–1920, they were wooed (and indeed won); when their usefulness came to an end, promises were forgotten and Jewish leaders' appeals for a return to the "good old days" fell on deaf ears. It is clear that in Lithuania, at any rate, national extraterritorial autonomy failed not because the Jews were uninterested (as was the case in the Czech lands), but rather because the Lithuanians lost interest. And such interest certainly did not reappear during the years 1926–1940, when the country was ruled by authoritarian, antidemocratic nationalists.

And yet, the fact is that the Jews of interwar Lithuania did enjoy a much greater degree of national autonomy than the Jews of Poland or Romania, even though there was no Jewish minister, no national curia, and no recognized Jewish national representative organization. The main institution of Jewish autonomy was the Jewish school, whether Hebrew or Yiddish. Thanks to the unique situation in the country, whose ruling language was quite unknown to the vast majority of its Jewish citizens, and thanks to the unique historical traditions of Lithuanian Jewry, Jewish schools flourished here as nowhere else in the East European diaspora. Moreover, as was not the case in Poland, these schools were given state subsidies; in this regard, at least, the Lithuanian government did not renege on its promises.[23] The moral of the story appears to be that national autonomy in the cultural sense (and this is certainly its most important aspect) can be achieved without Jewish ministers and Jewish parliaments, so long as the Jewry in question is interested in maintaining its own school system and so long as the state allows this school system to exist and grants it a certain amount of assistance. We shall see later how vital these schools were to Jewish life in interwar Lithuania.

### 3. Interwar Lithuanian Jewry: Demography, Economic Structure, Group Identity

According to official statistics dating from 1923, 157,527 Jews (by religion), constituting 7.26 percent of the total population, resided in Lithuania.[24] We have already seen that the absolute number was considerably lower than expected, a result of dislocations during the war and of the loss of the relatively large Jewish community in and around Vilna. But the Jewish percentage within the population was relatively high, exceeded in East Central Europe only in Poland. The percentage of Jews in the urban areas of the new state was also similar to that in Poland—31.9 in 1923. From a demographic point of view, Lithuanian Jewry was of the classic East European type, that is, very conspicuous in the few cities of this backward region, but also numerous in the many small towns (*shtetlekh*) which dotted the country. Over one-third of all Lithuanian Jews resided in nonurban areas—small towns and villages. By far the largest Jewish community was located in Kaunas, but this former provincial capital was not much of a metropolis and Jews numbered only 25,044 (in 1923).

During the interwar years the most striking demographic trend was the rapid "lithuanization" of the cities. In 1897 only 11.5 percent of the urban population of Kovno (Kaunas) Province, then under Russian rule, was Lithuanian, but already in the mid-1920s the city was more than 50 percent Lithuanian.[25] If Vilna, the great historic capital of Lithuania, remained during the interwar years a Polish-Jewish city with very few Lithuanians, Kaunas became a Lithuanian town, as did other, less known cities such as Panevėžys (Ponevezh) and Šiauliai (Shavli). Here was a striking success for the national policy of the Lithuanian state, made at the expense of Russians, Poles, and especially Jews. In the case of the Jews, the demographic losses suffered during the war were particularly heavy, and the birthrate of Jews was considerably lower than that of the urbanizing but largely peasant Lithuanians. Moreover, the rate of Jewish emigration was relatively high; during the years 1928–1936, 12,690 Jews left the country (many going to South Africa, which had already become an important center of Lithuanian Jewry in the "new world").[26] These factors created a Jewish demographic decline reminiscent less of the situation in neighboring Poland than of such Western-type Jewries as those in the Czech lands and in Hungary. By 1939 the absolute number of Jews had declined to about 150,000, and in the cities one could no longer speak of "Jewish domination."[27]

The economic profile of Lithuanian Jewry was of the classic East European type (see table 5.1). On the whole, Lithuanian Jewry, like that of Galicia, Poland, Bessarabia, Bukovina, and Subcarpathian Rus, was a lower-middle-class and proletarian community of small shopkeepers and artisans, with the usual thin but important stratum of wealthy businessmen, industrialists, and professionals. Since Lithuania was a much poorer country than Poland, with little industrial development, there was no equivalent here to the really wealthy Jewish factory owners and businessmen of Lodz or Warsaw. On the other hand, since the Lithuanian commercial class was much less developed than that of Poland, Jewish predominance in this branch of the economy was more striking. In 1923, of all those engaged in commerce fully 77.1 percent were Jews (a figure similar to that in the Lithuanian-Belorussian lands attached to Poland, but not to that in Congress Poland). In industry the situation was quite different: 21.1 percent were Jews, and 66 percent were Lithuanian.[28] This, too, is a familiar East European pattern—in the nonagricultural sector non-Jews gravitate toward industry, leaving commerce to Jews. Not showing up on the statistical table, but very important nonetheless, was the relatively large number of Jewish intellectuals active in the cultural life of the community, particularly the teachers, but also editors, journalists, writers, and the like. In Lithuania, in contrast with the situation in Poland, virtually no Jews played a role in the cultural life of the dominant nationality. Rather, the Jewish intellectuals staffed the Jewish cultural

TABLE 5.1
**Economic Profile of Jews in Lithuania, 1923**
**(Excluding Agriculture)**

| Profession | Percentage of Gainfully Employed Jews |
|---|---|
| Commerce | 31.90 |
| Industry* | 22.98 |
| Public Works | 5.30 |
| Communication and Transit | 2.98 |
| Other† | 36.84 |

Source: "The Jews of Lithuania, 1923," *American Jewish Yearbook* 32 (1930):281.
  *Meaning, by and large, "crafts."
  †Includes among other things, the large number of day laborers, beggars, and various types of Jewish *luftmentshn*.

institutions, which were the pride and joy of the small but vibrant community and which continued to flourish even after the collapse of Jewish national autonomy and the onset of the authoritarian regime in 1926.

It will come as no surprise that the overwhelming majority of members of this East European-type Jewry declared themselves to be Jewish by nationality. As late as 1937, after nearly a full generation of Lithuanian rule, 98 percent of all "Jews by religion" identified themselves as "Jews by nationality."[29] The old Russian orientation, which had attracted some Jews during the prewar period, had declined, but it had not been replaced by a new identification with the Lithuanian nationality. Jews growing up in the Lithuanian republic learned the language of the land, but rarely regarded themselves as Lithuanians by nationality. That they did not was doubtless the result both of the relative backwardness of Lithuanian culture and of the deep Jewish roots of Lithuanian Jewry, whose process of secularization was accompanied not by assimilation, but by the adoption of modern Jewish nationalism. The only Jews in the state who did not fit this pattern were the numerically insignificant German-speaking Jews of the Memel region, whose German acculturation was similar to that of the Courland Jews of independent Latvia. They were the only exception to the nonacculturated, Yiddish-speaking, Orthodox, and Jewish nationalist rule, and their presence did not alter the fact that the Jewry of independent Lithuania was not only one of the most homogeneous of all East European Jewries, but also undoubtedly the most "Jewish." Characteristically, virtually no marriages occurred between Jews and non-Jews. Poland, as we know, contained a significant number of highly acculturated Jews, and the same was true of Romania and Latvia, as also of Czechoslovakia and Hungary. In this regard Lithuania was unique.

### 4. Jewish Politics and Culture

Interwar Lithuania was, of course, an ideal place for autonomous Jewish politics. Not only were internal Jewish factors at work here, but also there was little Jewish participation in the politics of the dominant nationality. There were no Lithuanian equivalents to Rosa Luxemburg or Herman Diamand, famous Polish socialists of Jewish origin, although it is true that in Lithuania, as elsewhere, a notable percentage of Communists were of Jewish origin, indeed, according to one estimate, one-third of all Communist Party members by the end of the interwar period were Jews.[30] The lack of contact between mainstream Lithuanian politics and the Jewish population, more striking here than in Poland, meant that Jews would be more likely to lend their political support to specifically Jewish parties, which spoke their language and which best represented their interests in the wholly new environment of a sovereign Lithuanian state.

In this respect, the situation in Lithuania was similar to that in independent Latvia and in such regions as Bessarabia and Bukovina, whose Jewries also found themselves in a new cultural and political setting after the postwar settlement.[31]

On the whole, Jewish politics in Lithuania resembled Jewish politics in Poland and in other countries with East European-type Jewries. Politics were, however, less extreme than in Poland, in the sense that both the far left and the far right were weaker. As might be expected, Jewish politics in Lithuania closely followed the pattern of the Polish kresy and not that of Congress Poland. The Jewish left (Bund, Poale Zion) had a glorious tradition in old Russian Lithuania, but there were no great Jewish proletarian centers to rival Warsaw, Lodz, or Białystok, and Jewish Marxism as an organized, mass movement suffered as a result. In general, the small-town, homogeneous character of Lithuanian Jewry militated against political extremism of the Polish Jewish variety, although it should be noted that in Lithuania, as in Poland, Poale Zion was initially of the left-wing variety. Agudes yisroel, known here as "Ahdes" and supported by many prominent rabbis, was an important factor in Lithuanian Jewish life, but it tended to be, at least at first, less extreme and less anti-Zionist than its Polish counterpart. The Folkists were also strong. Within the Zionist movement the General Zionists were the most important faction at first, as in moderate Galicia. Later on, the moderate left—the Zionist Socialists—took the lead.[32]

This is not to say, however, that all was sweetness and light within the Jewish political community. All the classical sources of political divisiveness were present, and the challenge of creating Jewish political institutions within the framework of the projected national-autonomy scheme brought this divisiveness out into the open. Indeed, it was strong enough to lead at least one scholar to the conclusion that not only the Lithuanian government was responsible for the ultimate failure of autonomy.[33] Efforts to create a democratically elected Jewish leadership were something less than entirely successful, although they were certainly more successful than in Poland. The first attempt to convene an all-Lithuanian Jewish conference was made in January, 1920, when 141 representatives of 81 different kehiles met in Kaunas. The Marxist Jewish left boycotted the conference, which was dominated by middle-of-the-road and moderate-left-wing Zionists (61 delegates) and by members of Ahdes (54 delegates). The main bone of contention was the inevitable clash between Orthodoxy and secular nationalism, with the Ahdes representatives demanding that the kehile be defined as a religious institution and that Jewish schools sponsored by the institutions of Jewish autonomy bear a religious (which meant, of course, Orthodox) character.[34] As was not the case in Poland, however, secular nationalists and the Orthodox camp were able to establish a joint organization, the National Council, of which the president was a Zionist, and the vice-president a member of Ahdes. The National Council could not claim to be truly representative of all Lithuanian Jewry, however, since neither was it elected by direct vote nor did it include representatives of all factions within Lithuanian Jewry. It was also unsuccessful in its efforts to establish a unified Jewish school system. But it did manage to do something which the Polish Jews never succeeded in doing, namely, to establish a single Jewish list to run in the elections to the first Lithuanian parliament. The list consisted of two Zionists, two Folkists (the Folkist movement was quite strong here), and two Ahdes representatives.[35] In the Lithuanian parliament the Jewish delegation fought the good fight for national autonomy, while the National Council, aided by grants from the Joint Distribution Committee, did its best to improve the Jews' sorry economic condition and, on the political front, supported as strongly as it could the state's claims to the Vilna region.[36]

As time went on, and as the edifice of national autonomy began to crumble, internal Jewish political relations worsened, taking on more and more of a "Polish" rather than a "Galician" or a Polish kresy character. At the second conference of kehile representatives, held in 1922, the extreme left (representatives of Poale Zion-left and pro-Communist elements) appeared for the first time and bitterly contested such issues as the nature of the kehile and the orientation of the Jewish school. Moreover, the Zionists and leftists made no secret of their conviction that the members of Ahdes were not really interested in national autonomy, but rather in a much more narrowly defined and more traditional religious autonomy. A great debate was held on whether the word "religious" should be included in the formal definition of autonomy, and, when it was resolved that it should be, the Bund and the Poale Zion-left departed.[37] A sign of the times was the failure, in 1922, to establish a unified Jewish list during elections to parliament; instead, three separate lists, Zionist, Folkist, and Ahdes, competed for the Jewish vote. Things got even worse in 1923, when the government appointed its own candidate, the aforementioned Friedman, as minister for Jewish affairs. Friedman was bitterly denounced by the Zionists as an antinational "assimilationist" whose appointment had been made with the connivance of Ahdes. As in Poland and Czechoslovakia, in Lithuania the modern Jewish nationalists were certain that the Orthodox camp was cooperating with the regime in an unholy alliance directed against the new Jewish secular politics. "Cooperation" may be too strong a word, but it is certain that Ahdes refrained from participation in the struggle against Friedman, thus signaling its dislike of the Zionists' "oppositionist" tactics.[38]

In November, 1923, the first and only Jewish National Assembly, elected democratically by Lithuanian Jewry, convened in Kaunas. Ahdes boycotted the elections, however, and, while the extreme left did participate, it refused to be represented in the presidium. According to one observer, "the convention itself presented a picture of bickering over abstract party principles."[39] Nonetheless, as in 1920, a united Jewish list, including an Ahdes representative, was established for national elections and was included in an electoral bloc with representatives of the German, Polish, and Russian minorities in order to circumvent the Lithuanian electoral law. As in Poland, this tactic proved effective, and the national minorities' bloc elected fourteen delegates, half of whom represented the Jewish minority.[40] The parallel with Poland can be extended, for the Jewish representatives in parliament, from 1924 on the only elected Jewish leaders in the country, soon began to quarrel among themselves again, this time even more bitterly, over the question of the correct Jewish political line with regard to general political issues. The "democratic" Jewish representatives (Zionists and Folkists) strongly supported the moderate Lithuanian parties and denounced what they termed the "zoological nationalism" of the Lithuanian right. They also continued to accuse Ahdes of being indifferent to the political behavior of the gentiles and of being willing to ally itself with any political party so long as it did not threaten the rights and privileges of Jewish Orthodoxy. More specifically, the Zionists now argued that the Ahdes group had collaborated with the regime, behind the back of the Jewish Sejm faction, in drafting the new kehile legislation of 1925 so bitterly opposed by secular Jewish nationalists (Ahdes denied this charge).[41] As usual, Jewish political divisions between Orthodox and secular national forces played into the hands of the government. In the last free elections held in Lithuania, in 1926, the Zionists bitterly denounced Ahdes for its alleged collaboration with Lithuanian anti-Semites and antiautonomists, echoing the charges of secular Jewish nationalists in Poland and Czechoslovakia, while Ahdes accused the Zionists of a multitude of sins against Judaism. In its election platform the "Jewish Economic-Religious List" (sponsored by Ahdes) charged that the Zionists were attempting to dominate Lithuanian Jewry at the expense of Lithuanian Judaism. A proclamation of pro-Ahdes Lithuanian rabbis described the Zionist-Folkist list as being made up of "haters of religious Jewry, who wish to uproot our Torah and our religion."[42] If this were not enough, the moderate Zionist Socialists, who up to now had cooperated closely with the General Zionists, refused to run on the Zionist-Folkist ticket and joined with the Lithuanian Social Democrats. The Zionists and Folkists won the battle for Jewish votes, receiving three mandates to none for Ahdes and one for the Zionist Socialists. But the elections were closely followed by the right-wing coup, which put an end to Lithuanian democracy.

As in Poland, in Lithuania the establishment of an authoritarian regime, in 1926, rendered internal Jewish divisiveness much less important. However, the struggle among Zionists, Bundists, Folkists, and Ahdes for the allegiance of the Jewish population continued. Who won this contest? It is clear that, as in most East Central European countries, the Zionist movement was the most dynamic and most powerful single bloc. Zionists played the major role in the campaign for national autonomy, and it was from their ranks that the most notable leaders of Lithuanian Jewry during the 1920s emerged—Rosenbaum, Soloveitshik, Julius Brutzkus, and others. They also won the lion's share of Jewish seats in parliament. It was only to be expected that many sons and daughters of this intensely Jewish community should be attracted to the Zionist youth movements, which were very strong in Lithuania. True, the political environment was less hostile here than in Poland, but the economic prospects of the new generation of Lithuanian Jews were very bleak, while proportionally more Jews here than anywhere else were educated in modern Zionist schools in which whole classes adhered to such groups as Ha-shomer ha-tsair and Gordonia. In the early 1930s there were some 4,500 members of Ha-shomer ha-tsair in the country, a considerably higher number in proportion to the total Jewish population than in Poland.[43] Betar and Gordonia were also well represented, as was the Haluts (Pioneer) movement.[44] Lithuania was the cradle of the Mizrachi, and it remained an important center of religious Zionism during the interwar years. And in the 1930s Revisionism made converts here, as in Poland.[45] During the Jewish year 1932–1933, 29,500 shekels were sold in Lithuania, some 6,000 more than were sold in Czechoslovakia, where the Jewish community was over twice as large.[46] In 1934–1935, 47,038 shekels were sold, about nine times as many as in the much larger community in Hungary. Finally, during the years 1919–1941, over 9,000 Jews went from Lithuania to Palestine, again a considerably higher proportion than in Poland.[47]

All in all, it is safe to say that independent Lithuania possessed a higher percentage of Zionists than any other Jewish community in East Central Europe, a fact pointed out by the various Palestinian emissaries (shlihim) who visited Lithuania in the 1920s and 1930s. A local Haluts leader, on a fund-raising mission in the provinces, emphasized in his somewhat idealized description the strongly Zionist atmosphere of the Lithuanian towns:

> The small, poverty-stricken towns and the Jewish types there won me over, and the Lithuanian shtetl became a warm and comfortable home for me. Simplicity, poverty, wisdom and Jewish beauty were among the characteristics with which the Jews of the Lithuanian shtetlekh were blessed. Schools—entirely in Hebrew—brought Hebrew speech into the home, and the Yiddish language here was rich and spicy. Of course, here, too, there were wars between parents and children, and more than one

youth, in particular young girls, were forced to leave home in secret in order to join the *hakhshara* [vocational training] group. But generally speaking the Haluts was accepted and loved by the Jews of the *shtetlekh*, whose meagre livelihoods were shrinking all the time. The new Lithuanian intelligentsia was pushing the Jews out, and the Haluts, in its work and in its call to *aliyah*, provided something of a solution to the questions of the young generation. . . .

   Still fresh in my memory is my visit to the *shtetl* Yorburg. . . . The local Jews were angry over several incidents in which boys and girls had left their homes and families and joined the Haluts, and yet I was received with warmth as a representative of the organization. A good deal of money was collected, and the mother and daughter in whose house I slept treated me with special love. . . . Let me remember my visit in Taurage, which I reached by foot in order to save money. The boys and girls in the Haluts who were at home, who had not yet gone off to *hakhshara*, carried me around on their shoulders, and the house of the Sandler family, all of whose sons were in the Haluts, became a real home for me. . . . I see before me Poneveżys, almost a city, with a high school whose principal was Professor Kalvary, of blessed memory; my visit there was a great holiday. In his home one found a deeply rooted Jewish tradition combined with general culture, and this greatly influenced the young generation. Even the Orthodox Jews, led by their rabbi, who was a well-known fanatic and opponent of Zionism, not only did not interfere with the collection of funds but even contributed themselves, for the Haluts in their eyes was the historic continuation of the biblical soldier of God (*haluts*) who marches at the head of the army of Israel [see the passages in Joshua 6:7, 6:9, 6:13].[48]

The voices of Bundists, Folkists, and Agudes yisroel were certainly heard in the land, but none of these parties could compete with the Zionist appeal. A Jewry deeply rooted in traditional Jewish life but not dominated by Hasidism, the lack of a powerful indigenous left-wing movement, the triumph of modern Jewish national education, and the gradual but inexorable economic decline produced a pro-Zionist atmosphere duplicated in certain regions of other countries—Polish Lithuania, for example, and perhaps Bessarabia—but unparalleled so far as the Jewries of any other entire country were concerned. True, many young Jews were attracted to Lithuanian Communism (we have already noted the extraordinarily high percentage of the Jews in the Party and in its front organizations), but, while this fact is further evidence of the vital role played by Jews in East European Communist movements during the interwar period, we should remember that the actual number of Jews involved was not impressive—the entire Lithuanian Communist Party consisted of only about 2,000 members in 1940.[49] The vast majority of Lithuanian Jews had nothing to do with Communism, although the prominence of Jews within the Party, and especially in its upper echelons, became an important source of Lithuanian anti-Semitism.

As in its politics, so in its cultural life—Lithuanian Jewry clung to Jewish rather than to non-Jewish forms of expression. To be sure, the young generation learned Lithuanian in school, but, if there was at least the beginning of a process of "lithuanianization," modern autonomous Jewish culture maintained itself more successfully in Lithuania than anywhere else in Eastern Europe. Prewar Lithuanian Jewry, as we have noted, was renowned in the Jewish world for its learning and for its modern Jewish cultural achievements. Interwar Lithuania, however, cut off as it was from the Polish kresy and from the Soviet Union, the home of a poor, small, and isolated Jewish community, was not an important center of Jewish literature or theater. The major Jewish writers of the interwar years were attracted to the great Jewish communities of Poland, the Soviet Union, and, to a lesser extent, Romania.[50] Nonetheless, there was a certain amount of continuity with the glorious prewar tradition. Lithuania had been famous all over the Jewish world for its great yeshivas, and these institutions, located in such towns as Telšiai (Telz), Panevežys, and Slobodka (a suburb of Kaunas), continued to flourish during the interwar years. According to one source, the Telz yeshiva had over 500 pupils on the eve of World War II.[51] The Jewish community also established modern Jewish schools in Hebrew and Yiddish which attracted large numbers of students and were able to compete successfully with government schools—as was the case in the Polish kresy, but not in Galicia or in Congress Poland. The flourishing of these schools seemed to prove that it was possible to establish a modern Jewish school system teaching in Jewish languages in the twentieth-century diaspora, at least in the short run, even though graduates of the Tarbut system, at least, were not expected to live out their lives in Lithuania, but rather were encouraged to go on *aliyah* to Palestine. Jewish children were able to complete their entire educational careers, from nursery school to high school, in Hebrew or Yiddish, and the fact that so many did so made the autonomous Jewish school system in Lithuania a unique achievement.

We have already seen that efforts to establish a single, unified school system for Lithuanian Jewry were unsuccessful. Instead, three separate systems emerged—Tarbut (Hebrew Zionist, part of the larger Tarbut network which existed also in Poland, Romania, and elsewhere), Yavne (Orthodox schools sponsored by members of Ahdes and also by some members of Mizrachi), and Yiddish secular (supported by left-wing elements within the Jewish national camp such as Bundists and Poale Zion-left, along with the more moderate Folkists). The weakest of the three was the Yiddish school system, which suffered from the domination of left-wing elements whose views on the nature of Jewish education did not endear them to the vast majority of Lithuanian Jews. (We may recall that the Polish Tsisho schools suffered from a similar disability.) During the interwar period the number of Yiddish secular elementary schools ranged between 15 and 20, with between 1,300 and 1,700 pupils. There were also two Yiddish secular high schools, one in Ukmerge (Vilkomir) and the other in Kaunas.[52] More successful were the Yavne schools. In keeping with the relatively moderate political atmosphere in Lithuania, these schools were neither anti-Hebrew nor anti-Zionist; the language of instruction was often Hebrew, and secular subjects as well as Jewish religious subjects were taught. All in all, approximately one-third of all Jewish schools in the country were Yavne schools.[53] But it was the Tarbut system, here as in Bessarabia, which had the greatest appeal, thanks to its moderate secular Hebraic, Zionist orientation which best suited a nonacculturated Jewish community undergoing a process of modernization and beset by a severe economic crisis. During the school year 1930–1931 the Tarbut system included 18 kindergartens, 81 elementary schools, 11 high schools, and a total of 15,446 pupils and 542 teachers.[54] These impressive numbers are not that much lower than the number of Tarbut pupils in Poland. In fact, in 1931 there were fewer Tarbut high schools in giant Poland than in tiny Lithuania.[55]

The reasons for the remarkable success of the Tarbut system derive, as we have noted, both from the peculiar historical evolution of Lithuanian Jewry and from the fact that Lithuanian culture, as opposed to Polish culture, held little attraction for the Jewish population. Moreover, in contrast with the situation in Poland, in Lithuania Tarbut schools, as well as schools belonging to the other networks, received considerable government support. During the school year 1936–1937 nearly half the Tarbut budget derived from government aid, and nearly the entire budget for elementary education came from this source. In fact, the Jewish elementary schools were state schools, not private institutions, although this was not the case so far as kindergartens and high schools were concerned.[56] Thus, despite the formal failure of autonomy, the various Lithuanian governments never went back on the promises of 1918–1919 to subsidize Jewish national education, at least on the elementary level. In this regard, the Lithuanians appear to have been no less liberal than the Czechs, the difference being that in Lithuania the Jewish population was interested in national Jewish education, whereas in Czechoslovakia it was, on the whole, not.

Nevertheless, during the interwar years the state grew progressively less friendly toward Jewish education, cutting its subsidies (although not eliminating them) and increasing its demands for more subjects to be taught in Lithuanian. This was one reason for the impressive increase in the number of Jewish children who, by the 1930s, were studying in Lithuanian (and other "foreign-language") elementary schools. In the school year 1921–1922 only 954 Jewish children attended such schools; by 1935–1936 the number had increased to 3,483, constituting 20.4 percent of all Jewish elementary school pupils in that year (the rest studied in Yiddish- or Hebrew-language institutions).[57] Thus even in Lithuania, whose culture had been completely unknown to the Jews prior to the war, there was an obvious tendency on the part of more and more Jewish parents to register their children in schools of the dominant nationality, a pattern we have already noted in Romania, Czechoslovakia, and Poland. This was the result not only of government pressure but also of the Jewish parents' desire that their children receive a good education in the language of the land. That this was happening even in Lithuania, where conditions were ideal for the flourishing of autonomous Jewish national education, indicates that those Jewish educators and politicians who had never believed in the feasibility of Jewish national education in Jewish languages in the diaspora, at least not in the long run, may well have been right. True, until the very end of the interwar period, more Jewish children attended Jewish rather than non-Jewish schools in Lithuania, but how long would this situation have lasted? We may assume that had independent Lithuania existed for another twenty years a situation similar to that which prevailed in interwar Poland would have come to pass, with a minority of politically and culturally committed parents sending their offspring to Jewish national schools while most attended institutions of the majority culture. In this regard, Lithuania provides additional evidence that the ambitious programs of those who believed in extraterritorial autonomy for the Jewish nation in East Europe were built on sand. Nevertheless, the impact of the Tarbut, Yavne, and Yiddish schools on the young generation of Lithuanian Jews was enormous. Thousands of Jewish boys and girls received a good, modern education at the hands of dedicated teachers whose high standards were everywhere recognized. The schools played a great role in both the modernization and the nationalization of Lithuanian Jewry. It was in their classrooms that the "nests" of the various Zionist youth movements were located, and it was from there that the relatively numerous Lithuanian pioneers set out for Palestine. The Jewish school was the key factor in the formation of a modern national Lithuanian Jewish youth which had few parallels in the East European diaspora. Even if we can assume that this triumph of modern Jewish diaspora nationalism would probably not have endured forever, it does stand as the single most impressive achievement of the Jewish national movement in Eastern Europe.

### 5. The 1930s: Economic Decline and
### Lithuanian-Jewish Relations

As already noted, the tradition of anti-Semitism was weaker in the Lithuanian lands than in the Ukraine or in Poland, and it is true on the whole that Jewish-gentile relations in independent Lithuania were better than they were in independent Poland. Anti-Jewish feelings were certainly present, and Lithuania was by no means exempt from the wave of anti-Semitism which swept over nearly all of East Central Europe during the anarchical years 1918–1920. In 1919 the Lithuanian army perpetrated some minor pogroms as Jews were accused of opposing the formation of a Lithuanian state and of being either pro-Russian or pro-German (despite the strongly pro-Lithuanian stance of the official leadership of the Jewish community).[58] As the control of the state passed into the hands of right-wing elements, particularly after the coup of 1926, animosity directed against all national minorities increased, and, in the late 1930s in particular, anti-Semitic agitation became quite strong. But the "Jewish question" in Lithuania never was the subject of obsessive attention, as it was in Poland, Romania, and Hungary, and no Lithuanian government attempted to revoke Jewish emancipation. Moreover, Lithuania suffered little of the anti-Semitic violence endemic to Poland.

Nonetheless, during the interwar period the government did its utmost to further the economic interests of the majority nationality, and its efforts could only strike at the interests of the Jews. As in Poland, few Jews were hired in the state bureaucracy, and the state supported peasant cooperatives whose aim was to circumvent the Jewish middle man. Credit from state banks was denied to Jewish businessmen. Government monopolies over certain branches of trade were also used to promote Lithuanian commercial interests at the expense of the Jews. One of the results of this policy was the rise of a new Lithuanian commercial class, virtually unknown before the war, and the subsequent decline of Jewish commerce. The Jewish sociologist Yankev Leshchinski, who visited the country in 1936, had the following to say about this new phenomenon:

> During the '20s there were scarcely any Lithuanian-owned shops to be seen on the main streets of the average Lithuanian town. By 1936, however, during a tour of Shavli (Shaulyai), Panevezhis, Vilkaviskis, Kybartai and other towns, the writer was struck by the solid and secure appearance of the new Lithuanian business enterprises. The contrast between these vigorous, young proprietors and their worried, prematurely aged Jewish competitors, who had until recently monopolized the clothing trade, the wholesale business and others, symbolized the arrival of a new era.[59]

The decline of the Jewish commercial monopoly, which as in the Polish case may be attributed both to "artificial" (that is, state-inspired) causes and to the natural and inevitable process of Lithuanian urbanization and of the rise of a native bourgeoisie, was paralleled by a decline in other branches of the economy as well. In the crafts, where once Jewish artisans predominated, the government instituted new examinations and aided Lithuanian craft cooperatives; the percentage of Lithuanian craftsmen rose, and Leshchinsky writes that he discovered "a feeling of panic" among Jewish artisans in 1936.[60] The role of Jews in industry also declined, and, as almost everywhere else in East Central Europe, the percentage of Jews in higher education dropped. In 1922 Jewish students comprised 31.5 percent of the student body at the University of Kaunas, but in 1934 their percentage had declined to 15.9.[61] Thus was achieved the "lithuanianization" of the professions, which prior to World War I had been largely in the hands of non-Lithuanians. Not only did the Jewish community of Lithuania, in contrast with that of Soviet Russia, fail to make a dramatic breakthrough to middle-class status, but also its economic fortunes suffered a serious decline during the interwar years. In this respect its fate was similar to that of the other East European-type communities—those of Poland, Bessarabia, Bukovina, and Subcarpathian Rus. In these regions economic stagnation, the Great Depression of the 1930s, and official policies to strengthen the native nationality combined to reduce in a dramatic way the economic options of the Jews. Thus if Polish Jewish youth in the 1930s was described as a "youth without a future," Lithuanian Jewish youth may be similarly described, despite a much less strident anti-Semitic atmosphere in Kaunas than in Warsaw. In Lithuania, as elsewhere, observers remarked upon the economic collapse of the Jewish town, as in the following contemporary description of the *shtetl* Balbieriskis:

> During the past 3–4 years about 10 Jewish stores have closed down here and the rest, their shelves empty, are deserted for weeks at a stretch. . . . How does one really earn a living here? There are very few artisans, less than half of the number before the war. Certain trades that were once monopolized by Jews are now *Judenrein*. There is not a single Jewish blacksmith in town, not a house-painter, tinsmith or shoemaker (except for one cobbler). Their place had been taken in recent years by Lithuanians. . . . The few Jewish carpenters in town have been unemployed for years and have had to accept work as day-laborers in a factory. One Jewish carpenter, who was too proud to ask for a job in the gentile factory or whose health perhaps doesn't permit him, would long ago have forgotten how a plane or saw looks, if it were not for occasionally shaping a board for a coffin at some funeral.[62]

We have already noted similar descriptions of the dying Jewish *shtetl* in Poland and in Subcarpathian Rus. And although the grim situation doubtless did much to strengthen Zionism and encourage *aliyah*, emigration to Palestine (or to anywhere else, for that matter) could not solve the problem—nor could the many Jewish cooperative banking ventures, which flourished in the country, nor even the substantial aid received from American Jewry. It was not so much the failure of national autonomy which caused the Jewish crisis as it was the inexorable economic decline of the community, which must be seen in the context of the general economic crisis in East Central Europe in the 1930s. In Lithuania, as in Poland and parts of Romania and Czechoslovakia, the decline of the Jewish trader and artisan was matched by the sorry plight of the non-Jewish peasant and worker. The Jewish decline was obviously not the work of economic anti-Semitism alone, although the policies of the Lithuanian and Polish states certainly speeded it along. The same economic despair can be found in the *shtetlekh* of Subcarpathian Rus, which, after all, was part of a state which did not practice economic anti-Semitism. On the other hand, the more middle-class Jewries of Hungary and the Romanian Regat were better able to withstand the blatant anti-Semitic policies of their governments. The fact is that the economic crisis of the East European-type Jewries had deeper causes than state anti-Semitism. The example of Soviet Russia demonstrates that only major change and dynamic economic growth could alter the depressed character of the Jewish economy in the most backward areas of Eastern Europe. In the Soviet Union Jewish economic gains went along with the virtual extirpation of Jewish culture; in Lithuania autonomous Jewish culture remained, until the very end, stronger and more vigorous than in any other country in Europe, while the Jewish economic situation went from bad to worse. Independent Lithuania was certainly a good country so far as "Judaism" was concerned, but by the late 1930s it was becoming increasingly evident that it was not a very good country for Jews as individuals.

### 6. A Summing Up

In 1940 Lithuania was annexed to the Soviet Union. The coming of Communism, a calamity for Lithuanian nationalists, was welcomed by the left-wing elements within Lithuanian Jewry, whose importance within the small Lithuanian Communist Party has already been described. Having little support among the Lithuanian population, the new regime encouraged, at first, Jewish support, and a sizable number of Jewish leftists rose to positions of prominence in areas previously closed to them—the state apparatus, the army, the judiciary, and so forth.[63] The

Soviets therefore established a pattern which would be followed, after World War II, in the satellite states of Eastern Europe. The prominence of some Jews in the Communist regime, here as in Hungary in 1919, was a disaster for the entire Jewish community. It has been pointed out by several scholars that the Lithuanians' readiness to cooperate with Hitler in the extermination of Jews during the war, after the conquest of Lithuania by German arms, was greatly increased by their perception of the Jews as pro-Communist and therefore anti-Lithuanian.⁶⁴ Thus Lithuanian Jewry, whose leaders were such staunch adherents to an independent Lithuania in the interwar years, came to be identified during World War II as a partner of the hated Communist enemy which had destroyed the state altogether.

The history of interwar Lithuanian Jewry vividly demonstrates how the post–World War I settlement and the triumph of nationalism worked against the Jewish interest in Eastern Europe. Nowhere else were conditions, both internal and external, more ideally suited to the establishment of national autonomy, and yet this was not accomplished. Nowhere else, with the exception of Hungary and the Czech lands, was there less anti-Semitism in the prewar period, and yet the relatively weak anti-Semitic tradition did not prevent the state from waging a campaign to strengthen the Lithuanian sector at the expense of the Jews. Lithuania turned out to be not the great exception in Eastern Europe, as the leaders of Lithuanian Jewry had believed, but rather a state like all the others— nationalistic, bent on promoting the interests (as it saw them) of the dominant nationality. The hope that an alliance between the Jews and other "weak" nationalities in Eastern Europe (aside from the Lithuanians, other candidates for such an alliance were the Ukrainians and the Belorussians) would create the kind of environment in which Jews and Jewry would flourish was certainly not borne out by the Lithuanian experience. True, Lithuania was a considerably more pleasant place for the Jews than was Poland, but in the last analysis the differences were more of detail than of substance. The decision of the Jewish leadership to throw its weight behind the Lithuanian cause may have been unavoidable, given the circumstances prevailing in 1918–1919, but the poverty of the land and the nationalistic policies of its leaders dashed the hopes to convert Lithuania into an East European Switzerland. Even had Lithuania been constituted as a large state, including Vilna, it is doubtful whether the results would have been every different. In this regard, Soloveitshik's remarks of 1921 were probably mistaken. In all other respects, however, his warning that the Lithuanian leadership was not much different from that of most other newly awakened nationalities of Eastern Europe, implying that the Jewish fate in Lithuania would not differ very much from that of other East European Jewries, was very much to the point.

**Latvia and Estonia between the Wars**

# LATVIA AND ESTONIA / 6

In many ways independent Latvia was quite similar to its neighbor, Lithuania. Latvia's history, too, was marked by centuries of subjugation by foreigners and, also like Lithuania, it had been ruled by tsarist Russia during the nineteenth century. Moreover, in Latvia as in Lithuania there was no native aristocracy or middle class, the bearers of the national heritage being the Latvian-speaking peasantry (the great majority of the population) and the small intelligentsia. But there were also some very significant differences between the two neighboring countries. For one thing, there had never been an independent Latvian state, so that the interwar entity was a completely new phenomenon. More important were certain cultural and economic differences. Latvia, like Estonia but unlike Lithuania, was a predominantly Lutheran country, the result of many centuries of German domination. Ever since the Middle Ages the Germans, while never very numerous, had constituted the ruling class in this land, the result being that the high culture became German and the main religion Protestant, in sharp contrast with polonized and Roman Catholic Lithuania. (Only in the southeastern part of interwar Latvia was Catholicism predominant.) German domination was maintained during most of the nineteenth century, but at the same time Russian culture began to penetrate the region, so that by the eve of World War I there were two competing high cultures, German and Russian, along with the Latvian culture of the peasantry. The coexistence of two cultural orientations, one representing the politically dominant Russians and the other the socially and economically dominant Germans, was in some ways reminiscent of the situation in the prewar Lithuanian lands, where Polish and Russian competed for supremacy. The Germans, however, unlike the Poles, were a privileged minority in Russia, and their strength in the Baltic region was much greater than that of the Lithuanian Polish minority. This naturally had an important bearing on the Jewish population, whose own cultural situation was remarkably complex.

Latvia, although a mostly peasant, agrarian land, was nonetheless a more developed country than Lithuania. Latvia's cities had for centuries been active participants in the lively economic life of the Baltic, and Riga, by the end of the nineteenth century, was one of the leading commercial and industrial centers of the Russian empire. This meant that there was a larger working class here than in Lithuania, and consequently a relatively strong socialist tradition. Indeed, the Bolsheviks enjoyed considerable support in Latvia during 1917, and during the interwar years the Social Democratic Party remained a force to reckon with.

Despite these differences, the history of interwar Latvia does not deviate very much from that of the two other Baltic republics. Having repulsed Soviet efforts to annex this former tsarist territory, and having endured several years of chaos and occupation, the new state was officially antirevolutionary and strongly nationalist (although there was no irredentist problem to speak of). Constitutional democracy and political pluralism lasted longer here than in Lithuania, but in 1934 Latvia joined the ranks of the other authoritarian, though not totalitarian, states of East Central Europe. The ultimate fate of independent Latvia was identical to that of her Baltic neighbors. Latvia too was "reunited" with the Soviet Union in 1940, and it too has never regained political sovereignty.[1]

## 1. The Jewries of Latvia: The Historical Context

In sharp contrast with Lithuania, Latvia contained not one but three distinct Jewries—Courland Jewry, the Jewry of Latgalia, and the Jewish community of Livonia (of which Riga Jewry was by far the most important component).[2] Latgalia, in the southeastern part of the country, was the home of a Jewish community more or less identical to that of the Lithuanian-Belorussian Jewish communities of independent Lithuania and of the Polish kresy. Before World War I Latgalia was administratively part of the North West region of the Russian empire. Its population was largely Roman Catholic, the high cultures were Polish and Russian (the latter much stronger than the former), and the economic situation was one of extreme backwardness. The great majority of the Jews were Yiddish-speaking and Orthodox, while the intelligentsia spoke Russian. The Jews played a predominant role in urban life (in the leading city of the region, Daugavpils, known as Dvinsk before the war, 44 percent of the population in 1897 were Jewish), in commerce, and in industry. Modern Jewish national politics flourished here, as it did in other regions of Lithuania. Had there been a Jewish logic to the reconstruction of Eastern Europe after World War I, Daugavpils would have been in the same country as Vilna, Minsk, and Kaunas.

Quite different was the situation in Courland, which, prior to its annexation by Russia in 1795, had been a semi-independent duchy linked to Poland. Courland's never having been part of the Pale of Settlement retarded the growth of a Jewish community. It was a more urban region than rural Latgalia, and its cities, the largest of which were Libau (Lie-paja) and Mitau (Jelgava), were dominated by Germans. The relatively small and basically middle-class Jewish communities which did emerge here were closer to the German Jewish than to the Lithuanian Jewish model, although many observers have remarked that they represented something of a synthesis between these two contrasting types.[3] Under German influence, but more backward than Germany and somewhat isolated from the great centers of both Jewish and non-Jewish learning, Courland was not a region to produce either highly "Jewish" Jews or highly assimilated ones. Both German and Yiddish were spoken here. While Orthodoxy maintained itself, Hasidism was not strong, although some Hasidic Jews from the Pale did settle here during the nineteenth century.

Livonia, too, had been in tsarist times outside the Pale, but this did not prevent the establishment in Riga of an important Jewish community made up chiefly of Jews from Courland and from the Pale itself, mainly from Lithuania-Belorussia. The Jewish community of Riga had long been one of the most modern in the empire (a distinction it shared with the more important community of Odessa). It was in Riga that one of the first modern Jewish schools in Russia was established, in 1840, and it was from here that the rabbi of the German synagogue, Max Lilienthal, set out to spread the message of Enlightenment to the benighted Pale of Settle-ment. Acculturation was quite marked here, both in its German and its Russian form, as was embourgeoisement, but, as in the case of Courland Jewry, it would be incorrect to speak of Riga Jewry as an assimilated community. On the contrary, here as elsewhere the existence of compet-ing cultural orientations acted as a brake on assimilation, as did the fact that both the Riga and Courland Jewries were constantly receiving rein-forcements from the intensely Jewish Pale of Settlement. Moreover, neither in Livonia nor in Courland was the German or Russian popula-tion numerous enough to facilitate Jewish integration. Riga Jewry may have been similar to German and Hungarian Jewry in its social and economic structure, but its members, were not inclined to describe them-selves as Germans or Russians of the Mosaic faith.[4]

It may be said, therefore, that even if two of the three components of Latvian Jewry shared several characteristics of Western-type Jewish com-munities, they were much more Jewish by culture and by identity than were the Jewries of Hungary or even of the Czech lands. In both Courland and Riga the Jewish communities were fairly new and far from being great centers of Jewish learning, in sharp contrast with the Jewish communities of Lithuania; nonetheless, they were not on the road to losing their Jewish identity. And even the rather modest process of acculturation which they had undergone during the course of the nineteenth century was halted, at least temporarily, by the emergence of an independent Latvian state and the consequent decline of both German and Russian influence.

## 2. Latvian Jews: Demography, Economic Life, National Identity

According to official statistics from the year 1925, Latvian Jews numbered 95,675, or 5.2 percent of the total population.[5] These figures represent a considerable decline from prewar times, the reason being that here, as in Lithuania, large numbers of Jews had been expelled during the war and had failed to return. Of all Latvian Jews, 41 percent resided in Riga, a phenomenon typical of such Western-type Jewries as the communities of the Czech lands and Hungary. An additional one-third lived in Latgalia, and the remainder in Courland. The great majority of Latvian Jews resided in cities, another Western characteristic. Of all Latvian Jews, 86.5 percent lived in the thirty-eight largest cities in the country, the three largest Jewish communities being those of Riga (39,296), Liepaja (9,825), and Daugavpils (12,647). Jewish *shtetlekh* were common in the backward region of Latgalia, but were less prevalent in more advanced Courland and Livonia. As is also to be expected, the percentage of Jews in the cities of Latgalia was very high, as it was everywhere in Jewish Lithuania-Belorussia. Of the population of Daugavpils, 40.8 percent was Jewish, as was 41.5 percent in Rezekne (Rezhitsa) and 40.6 percent in Ludza (Lutsin). In Courland the percentages are significantly lower (19 percent in Liepaja, 7.7 percent in Jelgava), whereas in Riga 13.45 percent of the population was Jewish.[6] Here is an illustration of the very different demographic patterns of a typically East European Jewry, on the one hand, and of an intermediary type on the other. As was the case almost everywhere else in East Central Europe, the Jews suffered demographic decline during the interwar years. By 1935 the absolute number of Jews in Latvia had sunk to 93,479, and their percentage within the total population to 4.8.[7]

As for the economic profile of Latvian Jewry, 48 percent of the gainfully employed were active in commerce, 27 percent in industry, 7 percent in "intellectual work," and 2.75 percent in communications and transit.[8] The Jewish role in the nonagricultural sector was not so great in Latvia as in Lithuania, at least not in Courland and Livonia. But Jews were prominent enough in the economic life of the country, particularly in the capital, to recall on a less dramatic scale the situation in Hungary, which, like Latvia, was a relatively backward, agrarian state but which nonetheless could boast of at least one highly developed economic center where a very high percentage of the Jewish community lived. Thus in Riga over one-fourth of all commercial and industrial enterprises were in Jewish hands, as were a number of banks, and Jews were conspicuous in the professions.[9] An important Jewish artisan proletariat of the typical East European variety existed in Latgalia, but characteristically enough a Jewish industrial proletariat in Riga failed to emerge. In Latvia, as elsewhere in Eastern Europe, the larger the industrial enterprise, the smaller the number of Jewish workers.[10]

As for the question of the national identity (or identities) of the Jews residing in independent Latvia, the situation was in a way quite similar to that which prevailed in neighboring Lithuania. As in the other Baltic republic to the south, virtually all Jews declared themselves to be Jewish by nationality. Indeed, in some regions of Latvia the census of 1930 yielded more Jews by nationality than by religion, a most unusual circumstance. In Daugavpils, for example, 11,585 Jews declared themselves to be Jews by religion and 11,636 registered as Jews by nationality, despite the fact that a considerable degree of acculturation had taken place in Latvia, as was not the case in Lithuania.[11] Here is proof that the acculturation process had not been accompanied by the adoption of a German or a Russian national identity by the Jews of Livonia or Courland. As the case of the Jewries of the Romanian Regat and the Czech lands demonstrates, acculturation does not automatically mean the loss of Jewish national identity. It is clear, too, that the rise of an independent Latvia was an important factor in the nationalization of the Jews living within its borders, both because it dealt German and Russian culture a serious blow and because the regime certainly preferred its Jewish citizens to identify as Jews rather than as either one of the previously dominant nationalities. Thus the pattern was quite similar to that in the Czech lands, in Slovakia, and in Transylvania. As in Romania, hardly any intermarriage took place between Jews and gentiles—further evidence that Latvian Jewry was quite different from the Western-type Jewries of Hungary and the Czech lands.[12]

If virtually all Latvian Jews regarded themselves as Jews by nationality, there was less unanimity with regard to their linguistic loyalties. The data pertaining to "language of common usage" (*Umgangssprache*) among the Jewish population in 1925 (see table 6.1) give us some indication of the degree of acculturation among Latvian Jews, although we must remember that many Jews from Courland and Riga who listed Yiddish as their language also spoke Russian or German, or both. Despite this acculturation, the impact of external events upon the Jewish communities of Livonia and Courland was such as to make them, in terms of cultural and national orientations, much more similar to Latgalian Jewry than had been the case prior to the establishment of an independent Latvian state. So it was that the rather Western-type Jewries of the former two prov-

## TABLE 6.1
### Languages of Latvian Jews, 1925

| Language | Number of Jews (by Nationality) |
|---|---|
| Yiddish | 78,143 |
| German | 8,692 |
| Russian | 4,550 |
| Latvian | 527 |

SOURCE: Paul Michaelis, "Die jüdische Bevölkerung in den Baltischen Randstaaten, unter Berücksichtigung ihrer Umgangssprache," *Zeitschrift für Demographie und Statistik der Juden* 3, no. 4–6 (1926):121.

inces made up, together with the typically Eastern-type Jewry of the Southeast, a Jewish community which, in the interwar period, was among the most national and separatist in Eastern Europe.

### 3. Jews and Latvians: The Question of Autonomy

In Latvia, as in Lithuania, the new masters of the country were not heirs to an especially strong anti-Semitic tradition. Their attitude was certainly not the result of a particularly liberal, tolerant political tradition, as was the case in the Czech lands, but may have resulted from the fact that the young Latvian national movement was directed chiefly against the Germans and the Russians, while the small Jewish community in Courland and Livonia was not regarded as constituting a serious threat to the national aims of the Latvian people. There were relatively few anti-Semitic incidents in prewar, tsarist times, and in the early years of independence the Latvians had good reasons for not alienating the Jewish population. As a weak state, like Lithuania, Latvia sorely needed international recognition; as a state with small but potentially troublesome German and Russian minorities, it naturally preferred the Jews to develop their own national identity rather than to identify with either of these groups. Thus the stage was set, not only for granting the Jews legal emancipation, but also for granting them some form of national autonomy. Autonomy was also desired by most of the Jews of the new state, some of whom demonstrated their enthusiasm for Latvia by volunteering for the army of liberation.[13] To be sure, the dramatic Lithuanian-Jewish alliance found no exact parallel in the Latvian lands. Latvia had nothing comparable to the Vilna issue, which weighed so heavily in Lithuanian thinking and was so important in the forging of the Lithuanian-Jewish partnership. And if the Lithuanians believed that there were nearly twice as many Jews in the country than there actually were, the rulers of Latvia made no such mistake. There was little talk in Latvia of Jewish ministers or Jewish representative organizations, and as a result the Jewish world, enamored of Lithuania, tended to ignore events to the north. But in the long run the results in the two Baltic republics were more or less the same.

Latvia never signed the Minorities' Treaty forced upon an unwilling Poland, but it did take steps early on to ensure the support of the Jewish population. Jews were given equitable representation in the National Council formed in 1918, and the government established in 1919 included a Jewish member. Also in 1919 a special law established a Jewish section in the ministry of education, whose purpose was to direct a network of Jewish schools which would enjoy state subsidies. Plans to establish a more comprehensive law governing Jewish autonomy came to nothing, and the failure of the government to go beyond cultural autonomy was roundly criticized in some Jewish quarters. But at least there was no parallel here to the trauma of Lithuanian Jewry during 1922–1926, when its glorious autonomous institutions were dismantled. So far as schools were concerned, the Latvian government kept its promises, as did the government of Lithuania. Indeed, the experience of the Jews in the Baltic republics indicates that subsidizing Jewish schools in Jewish languages was as far as any state might be reasonably expected to go in satisfying the demands of Jewish autonomists. It was not what Dubnov and his Folkists had hoped for; rather, it was more along the lines of the more modest Bundist proposals. But it did make possible, in the unique environment of Latvia and Lithuania, the national education of a new Jewish generation.[14]

### 4. Jewish Politics and Culture in Latvia

The Jewish political scene in independent Latvia was not essentially different from that in the other former tsarist Jewish regions—Poland, Bessarabia, and independent Lithuania. If we compare the situation in Latvia with that in Lithuania, however, a few differences do emerge. The Jewish left, particularly in the form of the Bund, was stronger in Latvia than in Lithuania. In the prewar era this Jewish socialist party was important both in Latgalia and in Riga, and it did not go into eclipse during the interwar years. A Bundist (Noyakh Meyzel, who hailed from Daugavpils) was elected to the Latvian parliament. The Bund also succeeded in allying itself very closely with the powerful Latvian Social Democratic Party, for a time the strongest party in the state. In this respect, as in its electoral triumphs, the Bund was more successful here than it was in its great center, Poland.[15]

The Folkists were also quite active in Latvia, where they participated in the establishment of an impressive Yiddish school system. More important, however, was Agudes yisroel, which lacked the great Hasidic base available to it in Poland but which was blessed both with government backing (particularly after the right-wing coup of the nationalist leader Kārlis Ulmanis in 1934) and with several outstanding leaders. Of these, the most important was Mordecai Dubin (1889–1956), one of the best examples in all Eastern Europe of the classical *shtadlen* type. Dubin was a member of the National Council in 1918, an extremely active delegate to parliament, and after 1934 the most important Jewish politician in the country.[16] An additional Jewish political force was the National Democratic Party, backed by the wealthy, "non-national" stratum. Professor Paul Mintz, a member of this group, was the Jewish representative (serving as state comptroller) in the Latvian government of 1919. This small group of acculturated, middle-class Jews, inconceivable in Lithuania, was in its ideology and social makeup not unlike the much larger Union of Romanian Jews (UER) of the Romanian Regat.

The strength of non-Zionist forces in Latvia demonstrates that Zionism did not dominate the Jewish political stage to the same extent that it did in Lithuania. It was, nonetheless, an important force. The Zionist Socialists (Zeire Zion-Ts. s.) were able to elect a delegate to most of the Latvian parliaments prior to 1934. The Mizrachi was also quite active. This religious Zionist party produced a particularly distinguished leader in Rabbi Max (Mordecai) Nurok (1879–1962), who hailed from Courland and who had received there both a sound Jewish and a general education, thus personifying that synthesis which the Mizrachi preached.[17] From a Zionist perspective, however, Latvia is best known as the cradle of the Revisionist movement and of Betar, its youth movement. Vladimir (Zev) Jabotinsky, the Russian-born founder of the Revisionist movement, made a series of highly successful tours of Latvia, beginning in 1923, and Betar was established in that year by a group of Jewish high school students in Riga. From Riga it spread to Poland, where it reached its greatest heights in the 1930s. Just why Latvia played so important a role in the history of Revisionism is not clear, although it had something to do with the success of Jabotinsky's Russian oratory in this one formerly Russian area of the "free world" where the Jewish population had undergone a significant process of russification.[18] But Betar had no monopoly on the Zionist youth. Ha-shomer ha-tsair, known here as Netsah, flourished too, and the other groups were also present.[19]

Interwar Latvia was obviously an ideal setting for Jewish national politics, including Zionism, though perhaps not quite so ideal as Lithuania. During the 1920s considerably fewer shekels were sold here than in the fortress of Zionism to the south, but by the 1930s Latvia began to catch up.[20] During the years 1919–1941, 4,547 Jews went from Latvia to Palestine, about one-half the number who went from Lithuania but proportionately about the same as the number of Jews who went on *aliyah* from Poland.[21]

The internal political quarrels within the Latvian Jewish community were not essentially different from those in other former Russian possessions. In the minds of its politicians, at least, there was a clear distinction between the "progressive" Jewish forces (the Bund and the Zionist Socialists) and the "right-wingers" (the Agude representatives), with Nurok of the Mizrachi usually siding with the former. One of the most divisive Jewish issues was the problem of Hebrew versus Yiddish, inevitable in a country where Jewish autonomy meant modern Jewish schools and where such schools were among the most important institutions of the community. Aside from the language issue, the Jewish delegates in parliament argued chiefly over which Latvian faction to support. In this regard, two interesting aspects of Jewish political life in Latvia should be mentioned. First, the Jews were usually successful in electing five percent of the total number of delegates, thus matching their percentage within the population; this feat was not paralleled anywhere else in Eastern Europe. Second, there were close ties between the Jewish representatives and the German minority, reminiscent of the situation in Poland in the 1920s. Indeed, one of the leaders of the German community, Paul Schiemann, was an enthusiastic exponent of the "nationalities state" idea and a firm ally of the Jews. In Latvia, however, as elsewhere, the nazification of the German minority in the 1930s put an end to this alliance.[22]

Perhaps the most interesting clash between contending Jewish forces in Latvia was between the two Orthodox leaders, Nurok and Dubin. Dubin, the great *shtadlen*, was despised by nationalist Jewish exponents of the "new politics," but was extremely popular among the Jewish population, which found his interventions with the authorities to be of considerable value. He was, like all Agude leaders, a political conservative, and he cultivated good relations with the regime and with the nationalist (as opposed to socialist) Latvian parties. Thus, in 1928, he issued a stinging attack on the readiness of some Jews to ally themselves with the socialists, whereupon Nurok replied as follows:

> We talk different languages. I cannot sit at the same table with people [Latvian right-wing politicians] who trample on our national honor and our human self-respect, who fling mud at all that is precious and holy to us, who make proclamations of hatred against the Jews from this platform and even make use of the Bible for the purpose.
>
> If all this seems to you to be just a bargaining matter, then let each of you trade as much as you like. But I, for my part, am not interested in bargaining. To fight back—that is my intention. That is the difference

between me and you. The question is one of attitudes, plans, regime, and not in any way a question of trading. . . .

As before, I shall continue to fight for our rights from the place where I stand. I am imbued with ideals, and therefore I cannot change my place. That, Mr. Dubin, is the whole of the difference.

On this side [pointing to the left] are freedom, democracy, human qualities, understanding and a program, a clear policy, outlook and future. While there [pointing to the right] are misanthropy, Jew-hatred . . . suppression of freedom, open and black anti-Semitism. The past and the future of my people, the existence of Latvia, the inner voice of my heart and my conscience—all these mark out for me the way which I have chosen. Absolute equality for minorities and a free Governmental system can come about only as a result of proceeding with democracy, step by step.[23]

This resounding speech would certainly have won the full approval of Yitshak Grünbaum, who also believed in linking the Jewish minority with "progressive" forces. But in Latvia, as in Poland, the parties of the left were no match for those of the right, and in 1934 the dictatorship of Ulmanis put an end to them altogether. The Jewish parties, with the exception of the Agude, were also outlawed, and their leaders were imprisoned. (The Zionists were allowed to continue their *aliyah* activities, but not to play a role in Latvian politics.) Now Dubin and his colleagues acquired something of a monopoly over Jewish affairs; the all-important Jewish section in the ministry of education was handed over to them, and the only Jewish newspaper permitted was edited by an Agude member.[24] If the Polish Agude's proposed alliance with the right-wing regime failed dramatically after the death of Piłsudski, Dubin had greater success in the more moderate, less anti-Semitic climate of dictatorial Latvia. And while Nurok, the Zionist Socialists, and the Bundists regarded his political behavior as "dishonorable," it nonetheless enabled him to continue his useful interventions on behalf of the Jewish community until the very end of the interwar period.

We have had occasion to remark that the most important area of autonomous Jewish activity in Latvia was education. In this case, too, while the general situation resembled that in Lithuania, there were certain interesting differences. As in Lithuania, the overwhelming majority of Jewish children attended Jewish-run schools. In 1928–1929, of 12,022 Jewish children in elementary school, 10,325 attended Jewish schools. The breakdown by language of instruction in these Jewish schools is of particular interest (see table 6.2). On the secondary level, a higher proportion of Jewish pupils attended non-Jewish schools, but a majority nonetheless studied in Jewish institutions. Of these, 18 percent studied in Hebrew, 24 percent in Yiddish, 41 percent in Russian, and 17 percent in German.[25]

TABLE 6.2
**Jewish Schools in Latvia, 1928–1929**

| Language of Instruction | Number of Students | Percentage of Students |
|---|---|---|
| Hebrew | 3,204 | 31 |
| Yiddish | 4,978 | 48 |
| German | 1,438 | 14 |
| Russian | 705 | 7 |

SOURCE: Z. Michaeli, "Jewish Cultural Autonomy and the Jewish School Systems," in *The Jews in Latvia* (Tel Aviv, 1971), p. 209.

Nowhere else in the East European diaspora was the language situation in Jewish schools so complex as it was in Latvia. In Liepaja, for example, there were in 1925 two Jewish elementary schools and one Jewish high school. In one of the elementary schools the language of instruction was Yiddish; in the other, German, except for the first two grades, which were taught in Hebrew. The language of the high school was German.[26] Moreover, the language situation in Jewish schools was extremely fluid. German-language schools sometimes were transformed into Yiddish-language schools, or the opposite. There were no Jewish schools in which Latvian was the language of instruction, but this language was of course taught in all the Jewish schools and made the situation even more complicated. In all this linguistic babble the successes of the Yiddish schools stand out. If in Lithuania the Tarbut schools dominated, in Latvia the institutions of the Central Jewish School Organization and other Yiddish-language schools ruled the roost. The strength of the Bund and the Folkists was important in this regard, as was the fact that the law governing minority schools in the country prescribed that these schools be operated in the "language of the family." This might mean Yiddish, Russian, or German, but could hardly be construed to mean Hebrew.[27] The Yiddishists were also faster on their feet and organized more quickly than did the Hebraists. Under the short-lived Communist regime in 1919 they succeeded in opening several schools, and this act, too, was to their advantage later on. More important, neither in Courland nor in Livonia was there much of a modern Hebrew tradition, in contrast with the situation in Jewish Lithuania-Belorussia. Thus, when the German and Russian cultural orientations declined with the emergence of an independent Latvian state, the most natural step was to go over to Yiddish, which was spoken by most Jews in these semi-acculturated regions. Even the local Zionists here were not much interested in Tarbut-style schools, as was the case in another area where the Jewish political leadership was highly acculturated—Galicia.[28] Moreover, because the Yiddish schools in

Latvia were not very politicized—much less so than those in Poland—
they were more acceptable to the Jewish population.[29]

During the course of the interwar period the number of Jewish pupils in
Latvian-language schools tended to increase, at the expense not so much
of Yiddish and Hebrew but of German and Russian. In 1922–1923 a mere
3.1 percent of all Jewish elementary school students were enrolled in
Latvian-language schools; by 1935–1936 the percentage had increased to
12.6.[30] Even more impressive is the fact that by the mid-1930s nearly
one-third of all Jewish high school students attended Latvian-language
institutions. In Latvia as in Lithuania, a process of acculturation into the
language of the land was gaining strength, proceeding, as Leshchinski
writes, "quite slowly but organically."[31] It is safe to venture that, had
independent Latvia endured for another generation, the Hebrew and
Yiddish schools also would have declined.

The interwar years produced an unprecedented flourishing of autonomous Jewish culture in Latvia which was in the main the result of the
dramatic changes in the external environment. It was the reaction of a
somewhat acculturated Jewry (at least in Courland and Livonia) which,
finding itself in a wholly new cultural setting where the language of the
majority held little attraction while the formerly leading languages were
also discredited, fell back willy-nilly upon its own resources. It may well
be that this flourishing of Jewish culture was, in contrast with that in
Lithuania and Poland, somewhat artificial, not deeply rooted in the
Jewish past in this small corner of Eastern Europe. Autonomous Jewish
culture in Latvia meant above all Jewish national schools, not a thriving
Yiddish or Hebrew literature. Nonetheless, those Jews fortunate enough
to grow up in independent Latvia and to attend Jewish schools there
retained both a knowledge of things Jewish and a Jewish national identity
which quite often were maintained even in the very different and much
more hostile environment of Soviet Russia.

## 5. The End of the Road in Latvia

The right-wing takeover in 1934 and the consequent decline of Latvian
democracy was not accompanied by anti-Jewish violence. Ulmanis and
his allies, like the antidemocratic right in Lithuania but in marked contrast with the extreme right in Hungary, Romania, and Poland, were not
obsessed with the "Jewish question." That they were not led some Jewish
observers to believe that life under the new regime might not be substantially different from what it had been before.[32] In this belief they were
at least to some extent mistaken. The new government, while not instigat-
ing pogroms or revoking Jewish emancipation, stepped up efforts to
"nationalize" the economy, with predictably harmful consequences for

the Jews and the other minorities.[33] The number of Jewish students at the University of Riga declined sharply.[34] If the more or less middle-class Jewish communities of Courland and Livonia withstood the anti-Jewish onslaught with greater success than their counterparts did in most other East European countries, the Jewish youth, as in Lithuania, Poland, and every other country with the exception of pre-Munich Czechoslovakia, faced dim prospects. Thus it is not surprising that many Jews welcomed the arrival of Soviet troops in Latvia in 1940. During the short-lived Soviet regime Jewish organizations were finally outlawed altogether, completing the work begun by Ulmanis in 1934. But, as in Lithuania, Jews were absorbed into the bureaucracy and the army, something quite unknown in the years of Latvian sovereignty. Many also joined the Communist Party and the Komsomol, in the hope that the new regime would be more friendly and less discriminatory than the old.[35] As in Lithuania, the entire Jewish community paid a price for the pro-Communist enthusiasm of some of its members when the Nazis invaded the country and, with the help of Latvian collaborators, destroyed the Jewish population.

In retrospect, interwar Latvia must be seen as a relatively benign environment, both for Latvian Jewry in the collective sense and for Latvian Jews as individuals. Cultural autonomy prevailed, and the nationalization of Latvia, while boding ill for all the minorities, was not carried out in a particularly brutal way. This does not mean, however, that Latvia was like Czechoslovakia (or at least the Czech lands), in that it was an exception to the general rule that the new, nationalistic states of East Central Europe were inimical to the Jewish interest. Had Latvia continued to exist as a sovereign state for another generation, we may speculate not only that Jewish cultural life would have suffered as a natural result of acculturation into the dominant language, but also that the Jewish role in the economy and in the free professions, and indeed in all aspects of Latvian life, would have been more and more curtailed. Latvia was surely a more pleasant country for Jews to live in than was Poland, Hungary, or Romania, but the same forces which worked against the Jews with such devastating effect in those countries were far from absent in this smaller and more peaceful state.

### 6. A Note on Estonian Jewry

Estonia, the smallest of all East European countries, also contained the smallest of all East European Jewish communities. So small was it, and so far removed, spiritually at least, from the great Jewish centers of the Russian Pale of Settlement, that it has received virtually no scholarly attention. The Jews of Estonia, however, who numbered 4,566 in 1922

(0.4 percent of the total population), constituted something of a unique community. In tsarist times Estonia, like Courland, was outside the Pale. Most Jews who settled there during the nineteenth century were veterans of the tsarist army, who were allowed to live outside the Pale after having survived their long-term service. Included among them were some of the so-called Cantonists, Jews recruited at an early age and in a particularly brutal way during the regime of Nicholas I. During the course of the century some nonmilitary Jews filtered in from Courland and from the Pale, but there was no large center here of the sort which developed in Riga and no tradition of Jewish learning. Estonian Jewry was, by the eve of World War I, a fairly homogeneous community and a mostly urbanized one; well over 50 percent lived in the two largest cities, Tartu (Dorpat) and Tallin (Reval). Its economic profile was very similar to that of Latvian Jewry.[36]

The masters of the independent state of Estonia, like the ruling classes of the other two Baltic republics, were not particularly anti-Semitic and were also inclined to bestow autonomy upon the national minorities. Their readiness to do so in Estonia may have been influenced by the fact that the minorities made up a smaller percentage of the population than in any other East European state, with the exception of Hungary. Whatever the reason, the tiny Jewish community of Estonia enjoyed full cultural autonomy guaranteed by the laws of the land. Indeed, in regard to their institutions, their situation more closely approximated that so devotedly hoped for by Dubnov and other ideologues of extraterritorial autonomy than it did anywhere else in the diaspora. A national register ("kataster"), on which all Jews were listed, was established. A "cultural council," consisting of twenty-seven members, was elected by the Jewish community and ran its cultural affairs. As in Latvia and Lithuania, Jewish schools were subsidized by the state. The political shift to the right in the 1930s did not shake the foundations of this autonomy, which was fully maintained until the Russian takeover in 1940.[37]

In essence the history of Estonian Jewry in the interwar years closely followed the Courland-Riga pattern. In Estonia, too, a modernizing and somewhat acculturated Jewish community, living in a backwater of Jewish life, underwent something of a nationalist revival thanks to the radically new political circumstances of the interwar period. And here, too, native nationalism, while bent on establishing a homogeneous nation-state, was not obsessed with the Jewish question, thus allowing the Jews to live in relative tranquility. The end came, in Estonia as in Latvia, with the Nazi conquest of 1941.

# CONCLUDING REMARKS

The foregoing pages have been chiefly concerned with two major themes: Jewish-gentile relations, on the one hand, and Jewish efforts to find political and cultural solutions to the "Jewish question" on the other. As for the first, it is apparent that relations between the Jews and their gentile neighbors developed in a rather paradoxical fashion. During the interwar period in East Central Europe Jews became, at least outwardly, more and more similar to non-Jews. Old-style Orthodoxy by no means disappeared, but the young generation was exposed to a greater extent than ever before to the non-Jewish world.

We have seen how Jews everywhere were learning the language of the country in which they lived and were attending state schools in greater numbers than ever before. Languages utterly unknown to the prewar generation, such as Lithuanian and Latvian, were by the 1930s spoken by large numbers of Jews. Polish Jews were undergoing a marked process of polonization, and the Jews of Bohemia, Moravia, and Slovakia were abandoning German and Yiddish in favor of Czech or Slovak. The process of acculturation, however, did not contribute to the improvement of Jewish-gentile relations, thus giving the lie to the old accusation that the cultural separateness of East European Jewry was largely responsible for anti-Semitism. In fact, it is clear that the degree of Jewish acculturation had little or nothing to do with the strength or weakness of anti-Jewish prejudices. Such prejudices were particularly strong in Hungary, whose Jewish community was the most acculturated in East Central Europe, and they were relatively weak in Lithuania, where the Jewish community was the most unacculturated.

Nor can it be asserted that the Jews' peculiar economic role was responsible for the dramatic rise of violent anti-Semitism during the interwar years. Jewish "domination" of the Hungarian economy is often cited as a cause of the anti-Semitic hysteria of interwar Hungary, but the Jewish role in the Hungarian economy was certainly no less striking in the late nineteenth century, and yet in those years Hungarian anti-Semitism was a much less powerful force. This book has documented the catastrophic economic decline of the Eastern-type Jewish communities, the result of rising competition from non-Jews, general economic misery, and anti-Jewish government policy. Everywhere in Eastern Europe Jewish economic influence declined during the interwar years while at the same time anti-Semitic pressures increased. In Poland in the 1930s the economic structure of the Jewish community was actually becoming more similar to that of the Poles, a result of the tendency to abandon trade in favor of industry. But, of course, those were precisely the years when violent anti-Semitism reappeared on the scene. Finally, the well-known belief that anti-Semitism is a function of the number of Jews in a given country is disproved by the East European experience. After all, the percentage of Jews in Lithuania was higher than the percentage of Jews in Hungary.

In a general way, then, we must conclude that what the Jews did in interwar East Central Europe had little impact on attitudes and policies toward them. The case of Czechoslovakia demonstrates that Jewish-gentile relations were basically a function of the political situation in each country. In Masaryk's state, where liberalism and democracy were preserved until 1938, anti-Semitism was minimal. It existed, of course, as it existed and exists everywhere in the Christian and Moslem world, but it never became a major political issue. Elsewhere, the decline of liberalism and democracy and the rise of the radical right combined to create a situation in which the "moderate" right struck at the Jews in order to appease the extreme right which by the mid-1930s was so powerful a force in Hungary, Poland, and Romania. The collapse of democracy in East Central Europe signaled, among other things, the end of Jewish emancipation. It is true, of course, that the demise of liberalism did not automatically mean the rise of extreme anti-Semitism. Fascism in the Baltic States was less anti-Jewish than in Romania and Hungary, while Yugoslavia and Bulgaria, both of which followed the familiar East Central European political pattern during the interwar years, did not become centers of anti-Semitic agitation. Obviously, local historical and cultural factors must be taken into account in determining the development and impact of anti-Semitism. But it can be said with certainty that in those lands which boasted of a long and deeply rooted anti-Semitic tradition, such as Poland and Romania, the demise of democracy and liberalism and the triumph of right-wing integral nationalism unleashed anti-Jewish passions and served to destroy whatever hopes had existed for peaceful coexistence between Jew and gentile. Even in Czechoslovakia, after all, the collapse of the first republic and the birth of its short-lived but authoritarian successor led to a serious deterioration in Jewish-Christian relations.

If the Jews had little influence over the ways in which their neighbors and their rulers behaved toward them, the historical experience of the interwar years shows that the various efforts the Jews made to "solve" the

Jewish question also foundered because the Jewish minority was not in a position to determine its own fate. Jewish national autonomy in the East European diaspora failed not only because many Jews did not always support it but also because the states of the region refused to fund Jewish national institutions. Zionism possessed a multitude of supporters in East Europe, especially in Poland, Romania, and the Baltic States, but the number of Jews able to leave East Europe for the promised land was severely limited by English immigration laws. It is true that *aliyah* from Eastern Europe during the interwar years greatly strengthened the Jewish community in Palestine, but it also was the case that Zionism was unable to solve the dilemma of the East European Jewish communities. Whereas Zionism's prognosis with regard to the future of the Jews in Europe was proved all too accurate, its impact on the fate of the various Jewish communities was all too limited. In this sense, the Bund's critique of Zionism as a utopian movement of doubtful relevance to the condition of East European Jewry was justified. But the Bund's faith in the coming revolution and in the solidarity of Jewish and non-Jewish workers proved to be no less utopian. In the last analysis, the Jews could neither emigrate from Eastern Europe in significant numbers nor find reliable allies among the Christian population. These two basic facts doomed all Jewish political solutions—from that of the Zionists to that of Agudes yisroel—to failure.

The Jewish historical experience in Poland, Hungary, Czechoslovakia, Romania, and the Baltic States during the years 1919–1939 may be viewed in two ways. These years witnessed a growing animosity toward the Jews which greatly facilitated the eventual implementation of Hitler's "final solution." They also constituted the last chapter in the history of the unique Jewish civilization of Eastern Europe. To be sure, small Jewish communities remained in these countries after the terrible years of destruction during World War II, and Soviet Russian Jewry, less affected by the Holocaust than were the Jewries west of the Soviet Union, still numbers close to two million people. But autonomous Jewish culture and politics—the yeshivas, the Tarbut and Tsisho schools, the Yiddish and Hebrew press and literature, the great Jewish political parties—no longer exist. The unique combination of a nonacculturated but modernizing Jewry, rooted in the traditional Jewish world but open to outside influences, which characterized the Jewish community of interwar Poland and which was responsible for the flourishing of Jewish culture and politics in that country, and in neighboring lands, will not be seen again in Eastern Europe. Nor can it be found in this form in the great East European Jewish diasporas of North America, the British Commonwealth, South America, and South Africa. Today, of course, autonomous

Jewish culture and politics are concentrated in Israel. The Zionist movement may have failed in its efforts to save interwar East European Jewry,
but it has succeeded in establishing a state which in some ways preserves
and carries on the historical traditions of East European Jewry.

# *Notes*

## Introduction

1. The best survey of this region is Joseph Rothschild, *East Central Europe between the Two World Wars* (Seattle and London, 1974), which includes Poland, Romania, Czechoslovakia, Hungary, Bulgaria, Yugoslavia, Albania, and the Baltic States. Antony Polonsky, *The Little Dictators: The History of Eastern Europe since 1918* (London and Boston, 1975) includes Austria but omits the Baltic States and Albania. Alan Palmer, *The Lands Between: A History of East-Central Europe since the Congress of Vienna* (London, 1970), includes Greece, omits Austria, and has little material on the Baltic States. Alan Palmer and C. A. Macartney, *Independent Eastern Europe* (London and New York, 1962), has the broadest conception of all, going so far as to include Turkey and Finland. On the other hand, the old classic, Hugh Seton-Watson, *Eastern Europe between the Wars, 1918–1941*, 1st ed. (Cambridge, 1945), emphasizes only Poland, Czechoslovakia, Hungary, Romania, Yugoslavia, and Bulgaria.

2. A strong case could be made for including Austria, which was also, of course, a successor state of the Habsburg empire. But I would argue that the cultural, economic, and social characteristics of the Austrian Jewish community, so similar to those of German Jewry, make it much more a Central than an East Central European Jewry.

## 1. Poland

1. The best guides in English to pre-World War I Polish history are Piotr S. Wandycz, *The Lands of Partitioned Poland, 1795–1918* (Seattle and London, 1974); Robert F. Leslie et al., eds., *The History of Poland since 1863* (Cambridge, Eng., 1980). A new and important study of German Poland is William W. Hagen, *Germans, Poles, and Jews: The Nationality Conflict in the Prussian East, 1772–1914* (Chicago and London, 1980).

2. For data and a discussion of the difficulties of ethnic statistics, see Rothschild, *East Central Europe*, pp. 34–36.

3. The best English-language studies of interwar Polish politics are Antony Polonsky, *Politics in Independent Poland* (London, 1972); Hans Roos, *A History of Modern Poland* (London, 1966); Edward Wynot, *Polish Politics in Transition* (Athens, Ga., 1974). The best short treatment is Rothschild, *East Central Europe*, pp. 27–72.

4. See Ezra Mendelsohn, "From Assimilation to Zionism in Lvov: The Case of Alfred Nossig," *The Slavonic and East European Review* 49, no. 117 (October 1971): 521–34; idem, "Jewish Assimilation in Lvov: The Case of Wilhelm Feldman," *Slavic Review* 28, no. 4, (December 1969): 577–90.

5. Prewar Congress Poland included the historically Lithuanian province of Suwalki, the northern part of which was annexed to the independent state of

Lithuania after World War I. The central provinces of interwar Poland include Białystok Province, the eastern part of which was not part of prewar Congress Poland.

6. On Jewish history in Congress Poland, see Artur Eisenbach, *Kwestia równouprawnienia Żydów w Królestwie Polskim* (Warsaw, 1972); Yankev Shatski, *Geshikhte fun yidn in varshe*, 3 (New York, 1953): 27–94; Refael Mahler, *Hahasidut ve-ha-haskala* (Merhavya, 1961), pp. 209–86. The subject of Jewish-Polish assimilation is treated in Mendelsohn, "A Note on Jewish Assimilation in the Polish lands," in *Jewish Assimilation in Modern Times*, ed. Bela Vago (Boulder, 1981), pp. 141–50.

7. Moshe Mishkinsky, "Regional Factors in the Formation of the Jewish Labor Movement in Czarist Russia," *Yivo Annual of Jewish Social Science* 14 (1969): 27–52.

8. *The Letters and Papers of Chaim Weizmann*, 2, A (London, 1971): 276–77.

9. Eisenbach, *Kwestia równouprawnienia*, pp. 456–544.

10. On Jewish demography in Poland, see Mahler, *Yehude polin ben shte milhamot ha-olam* (Tel Aviv, 1968), pp. 18–36; Szyja Bronsztejn, *Ludność żydowska w Polsce w okresie międzywojennym* (Warsaw, 1963). See also Bronsztejn, "The Jewish Population of Poland in 1931," *Jewish Journal of Sociology* 6, no. 1 (July 1964):3–29. The 1921 census did not include parts of the provinces of Vilna and Silesia.

11. S. Fogelson, "Przyrost naturalny ludności żydowskiej w Polsce, *Sprawy narodowościowe* 11, nos. 4–5 (1937):405–19.

12. For figures on Jewish emigration 1921–1931, see Bronsztejn, *Ludność żydowska*, p. 97. During this period 292,832 Jews emigrated; of these, 184,500 left during 1921–1925. See also Aryeh Tartakower, "Jewish Emigration from Poland in the Post-War Years," *Jewish Social Service Quarterly* 16, no. 3 (March 1940): 273–79.

13. On the remarkable changes in Soviet Jewish demography, see Mordecai Altshuler, *Ha-kibuts ha-yehudi be-vrit ha-moatsot bi-yamenu* (Jerusalem, 1980), pp. 11–20.

14. Mahler, *Yehude polin*, p. 76. For a thorough analysis of the Jews' economic situation, see ibid., pp. 37–195.

15. Janusz Żarnowski, *Społeczeństwo drugiej rzeczypospolitej* (Warsaw, 1973), p. 391.

16. For a discussion of this question, see Mendelsohn, *Class Struggle in the Pale* (Cambridge, Eng., 1970), pp. 19–23.

17. Mahler, *Yehude polin*, p. 133.

18. See Żarnowski, *Społeczeństwo*, pp. 263–78.

19. S. M. Ulam, *Adventures of a Mathematician* (New York, 1976), p. 24.

20. As quoted in Celia Heller, *On the Edge of Destruction: Jews of Poland between the Two World Wars* (New York, 1977), p. 192.

21. On the "assimilated" community, see Heller, *On the Edge of Destruction*, pp. 183–210.

22. See Jonathan Frankel, *Prophecy and Politics: Socialism, Nationalism, and the Russian Jews, 1864–1918* (Cambridge, 1981); Oscar Janowsky, *The Jews and Minority Rights (1898-1919)* (New York, 1966), pp. 49–85.

23. Shlomo Netser, *Maavak yehude polin al zekhuiyotehem ha-ezrahiyot ve-ha-leumiyot (1918–1922)* (Tel Aviv, 1980), pp. 146–67; Moshe Landau, *Hayehudim ke-miut leumi be-shnoteha ha-rishonot shel polin ha-atsmait* (Ph.D. diss., Hebrew University, 1972). See also Mendelsohn, *Zionism in Poland: The Formative Years, 1915–1926* (New Haven and London, 1981), pp. 106–07; Pawel Kor-

zec, *Juifs en Pologne, La question juive pendant l'entre-deux-guerres* (Paris, 1980), pp. 69–95.

24. The text is in Janowsky, *The Jews*, pp. 360–65.

25. For the quotation see Mendelsohn, *Zionism in Poland*, p. 107. See also Netser, *Maavak yehude polin*, p. 162.

26. The Polish text is quoted in Aleksander Hafftka, "Ustawodawstwo Polski odrodzonej w stosunku do. żyd. mniejszości narodowej," in *Żydzi w Polsce odrodzonej*, ed. Ignacy Schipper et al., 2 (Warsaw, 1933):236–38.

27. See the following Polish studies: Andrzej Chojnowski, *Koncepcje polityki narodowościowej rządów polskich w latach 1921–1939* (Wrocław, etc., 1979); Jerzy Tomaszewski, "Konsekwencja wielonarodowościowej struktury ludności Polski 1918–1939 dla procesów integracyjnych społeczeństwa," in *Drogi integracji społeczeństwa w Polsce XIX-XX w.*, ed. Henryk Zielinski (Wrocław, etc., 1976), pp. 109–38. See also Alexander Groth, "Dmowski, Piłsudski, and Ethnic Conflict in Pre-1939 Poland," *Canadian Slavic Studies* 3 (1969):69–91; Joel Cang, "The Opposition Parties in Poland and Their Attitude towards the Jews and the Jewish Question," *Jewish Social Studies* 1, no. 2 (1939):241–56.

28. A good example of this position is Leon Wasilewski, *Die Judenfrage in Kongress-Polen* (Vienna, 1915). For the typical views of a leading Polish socialist (of Jewish origin), see Henryk Piasecki, "Herman Diamand w okresie II Rzeczypospolitej, (Maj 1926–Luty 1931)," *Biuletyn Żydowskiego Instuytutu Historycznego w Polsce* 1, no. 113 (January-March 1980):44–45.

29. See, for example, Roman Dmowski, "Żydzi wobec wojny," in idem, *Polityka Polska i odbudowanie państwa* (Warsaw, 1926), pp. 301–08. See also Andrzej Micewski, *Roman Dmowski* (Warsaw, 1971), pp. 351–55. Dmowski's views on Zionism were definitely not echoed by Polish leaders in the late 1930s, who did all they could to open Palestine to mass Jewish emigration (see below, pp. 71–72, 79–80); see also Alvin M. Fountain, *Roman Dmowski: Party, Tactics, Ideology 1895–1907* (New York, 1980).

30. Wincenty Witos, *Moje wspomnienia*, 2 (Paris, 1964):184–45, 307–08, 391–92.

31. As quoted in Groth, "Dmowski, Piłsudski, and Ethnic Conflict," pp. 73–74, from Dmowski, *Myśli nowoczesnego Polaka*, 7th ed. (London, 1953), p. 91.

32. On the status of Jewish schools, see Yitshak Grünbaum, "Ha-yehudim u-vate ha-sefer be-folaniya," in idem, *Milhamot yehude polin* (Jerusalem, Tel Aviv, 1941), pp. 172–91; Khaim Shloyme Kazdan, *Di geshikhte fun yidishn shulvezn in umophengikn poyln* (Mexico City, 1947); Nathan Eck, "The Educational Institutions of Polish Jewry (1921–1934)," *Jewish Social Studies* 9, no. 1 (January 1947):3–32.

33. Grünbaum, ed., *Di yidishe kehile* (Warsaw, 1920); William Glicksman, *A Kehillah in Poland during the Inter-War Years* (Philadelphia, 1969). For a survey of the legal situation of Polish Jewry, see Leon Brandes, "Der rekhtlekher matsev fun yidn in poyln tsvishn beyde velt milkhomes," *Yivo bleter* 42 (1962): 147–86.

34. Quoted in Mendelsohn, *Zionism in Poland*, p. 89. See also Max Blokzyl, *Poland, Galicia, and the Persecutions of the Jews at Lemberg* (n.p., 1919).

35. Mendelsohn, *Zionism in Poland*, pp. 88–91; and the survey by Korzec, "Antisemitism in Poland as an Intellectual, Social, and Political Movement," in *Studies on Polish Jewry [Shtudies vegn yidn in poyln] 1919–1939*, ed. Joshua Fishman (New York, 1974), pp. 12–58. See also the important new study by Frank Golczewski, *Polnisch-Jüdische Beziehungen 1881–1922* (Wiesbaden, 1981), pp. 181–245.

36. Quoted in Mendelsohn, *Zionism in Poland*, p. 90.

37. Ibid., pp. 41–42; Golczewski, *Polnisch-Jüdische Beziehungen*, pp. 121–80.

38. Mahler, *Yehude polin*, pp. 159–60.

39. Ibid., p. 170.

40. Ibid., p. 172.

41. On economic anti-Semitism, see the survey by Yeshaye Trunk, "Der ekonomisher antisemitizm in poyln tsvishn di tsvey velt-milkhomes," in *Studies*, ed. Fishman, pp. 3–98.

42. This term was used by Yitshak Grünbaum at a Zionist conference in 1925; see Mendelsohn, "Polish Zionism between Two Wars," *Dispersion and Unity* 17-18 (1973):82, quoting from *Haynt* 55 (5 March 1925).

43. By far the best analysis of the genesis of modern East European Jewish politics is Frankel, *Prophecy and Politics*.

44. Mendelsohn, *Zionism in Poland*, pp. 44–87.

45. For a pioneering study of Agudes yisroel in Poland and its struggle against Jewish modernization, see Gershon Bacon, *Agudath Israel in Poland, 1916–39: An Orthodox Jewish Response to the Challenge of Modernity* (Ph.D. diss., Columbia University, 1979; Ann Arbor: University Microfilms, 1981).

46. Mendelsohn, *Zionism in Poland*, pp. 91–96; see also Netser, *Maavak yehude polin*, pp. 47–72.

47. This lack of unity is emphasized by Emanuel Meltser, *Yahadut polin ba-maavak ha-medini al kiuma be-shnot 1935–1939* (Ph.D. diss., Tel Aviv University, 1975), pp. 314–28.

48. For the results, see Hafftka, "Życie parlementarne żydów w Polsce odrodzonej," in *Żydzi w Polsce odrodzonej*, ed. Schipper, 2:289. Elections were not held in eastern Galicia and in regions in the east ultimately attached to Poland.

49. The Jewish left did do better, however, in municipal elections. Moreover, the Bund split in 1919 over whether or not to take part in the elections. The split was quickly overcome and the party gained strength rapidly. See Bernard Johnpoll, *The Politics of Futility* (Ithaca, 1967), pp. 82–142.

50. Mendelsohn, *Zionism in Poland*, pp. 96–101; Ruvn Fan, *Geshikhte fun der yidisher national oytonomie inm period fun der mayrev-ukrainisher republik* (Lwów, 1935).

51. Mendelsohn, *Zionism in Poland*, pp. 101–04; see also below.

52. See Mendelsohn, "The Dilemma of Jewish Politics in Poland: Four Responses," in *Jews and Non-Jews in Eastern Europe* (New York, 1974), ed. Bela Vago and George Mosse, pp. 203–20; Joseph Rothschild, "Ethnic Peripheries Versus Ethnic Cores: Jewish Political Strategies in Interwar Poland," *Political Science Quarterly* 96, no. 4 (Winter 1981–82):591–605.

53. On the Polish Bund, see Johnpoll, *The Politics of Futility*; Y. Sh. Herts et al., eds., *Di geshikhte fun bund*, vol. 4 (New York, 1972).

54. Mendelsohn, *Zionism in Poland*, pp. 213–22; Netser, *Maavak yehude polin*, pp. 282–314; Landau, *Ha-yehudim ke-miut*, pp. 84–123; Korzec, *Juifs en Pologne*, pp. 122–34.

55. Yitshak Schwarzbart, *Tsvishn beyde velt-milkhomes* (Buenos Aires, 1958), p. 223.

56. Quoted in Mendelsohn, *Zionism in Poland*, p. 217, from a letter to S. Rothfeld dated 30 December 1927, Central Zionist Archives, L9/269.

57. Landau, "Mekoma shel ha-'ugoda' (mi-shnat 1925) be-masekhet ha-yahasim ha-hadadiim ha-polaniim-yehudiim," *Tsiyon* 47 (1972):66–110; Korzec, *Juifs en Pologne*, pp. 152–60; Korzec, "Heskem memshelet V. Grabski im ha-netsigut ha-yehudit," *Gal-ed* 1 (1973):175–201 (also available in German: "Das Abkommen zwischen der Regierung Grabski und der Jüdischen Parlaments-

vertretung," *Jahrbücher für Geschichte Osteuropas* 20, no. 3 [September 1972]:331–66); Mendelsohn, "Reflections on the 'Ugoda,' " in *Sefer Refael Maler* (Merhavya, 1974), pp. 87–102.

58. Quoted in Mendelsohn, *Zionism in Poland*, p. 220, from an article by Yehoshua Thon in *Haynt* 53 (3 March 1925).

59. Mendelsohn, "The Politics of Agudas yisroel in Inter-War Poland," *Soviet Jewish Affairs* 2, no. 2 (1972): 47–60; Bacon, *Agudath Israel*, pp. 347–455.

60. Vilner arkhiv, Chorno seminar, *Yivo Archives*.

61. Mendelsohn, *Zionism in Poland*, pp. 108, 184–85, 218.

62. Ibid., pp. 180–81.

63. Ibid., pp. 261–69.

64. Ibid., pp. 178–79.

65. For a survey of the Jewish youth movements, see Moyshe Kligsberg, "Di yidishe yugnt-bavegung in poyln tsvishn beyde velt-milkhomes," in *Studies*, ed. Fishman, pp. 137–228. The best study of a particular movement is Elkana Margalit, *'Ha-shomer ha-tsair'—me-edat neurim le-marksizm mahapkhani, (1913–1936)* (Tel Aviv, 1971).

66. On the "fourth *aliyah*," see Mendelsohn, *Zionism in Poland*, pp. 253–99. Somewhat lower figures on the Polish *aliyah* are given in David Gurevich and Aharon Gerts, *Ha-aliya, ha-yishuv ve-ha-tnua ha-tivit shel ha-ukhlusiya be-erets yisrael* (Jerusalem, 1944), p. 61; according to this source the number was 30,832.

67. See Mark Kiel, "The Ideology of the Folks-Partey," *Soviet Jewish Affairs* 5, no. 2 (1975):75–89.

68. For material on Jews in the Communist Party, see Ester Rozental-Shneiderman, "Ha-yehudim ba-tnua ha-komunistit be-folin," *Molad* 3, no. 13 (January–February 1970):81–96; *Unter der fon fun k.p.p., zamlbukh* (Warsaw, 1959), which includes a list of Yiddish-language Communist periodicals which appeared in the interwar years; Sh. Zakhariash, *Di komunistishe bavegung tsvishn der yidisher arbetndiker bafelkerung in poyln* (Warsaw, 1954); P. Mints, *Di geshikhte fun a falsher iluzie (zikhroynes)* (Buenos Aires, 1954).

69. Sh. Z. Kahana, "Ha-moreshet ha-masoratit shel yehude polin," *Sefer ha-shana/yorbukh* 2 (1967): 34–70; Yitshak Levin, "Yeshivat hokhme lublin," ibid., pp. 381–88; Shmuel Mirski, ed., *Mosdot tora be-iropa be-vinyanam u-ve-horbanam* (New York, 1956), pp. 1–413, 561–603.

70. See Nakhmen Mayzel, *Gevn amol a lebn* (Buenos Aires, 1953), pp. 17–18.

71. For bibliographies of the Yiddish press, see Yisroel Shayn, *Bibliografie fun oysgabes aroysgegebn durkh di arbeter parteyen in poyln in di yorn 1918–1939* (Warsaw, 1963); idem, "Bibliografie fun yidishe periodike in poyln," in *Studies*, ed. Fishman, pp. 422–83. For studies of the Jewish press, see *Fun noentn over*, vol. 2 (New York, 1956), which deals with the Jewish press in Warsaw; Khaim Finkelshtein, *Haynt, a tsaytung bay yidn, 1908–1939* (Tel Aviv, 1978). See also David Flinker et al., eds., *Itonut yehudit she-hayta* (Tel Aviv, 1973), and Marian Fuks, *Prasa żydowska w Warszawie 1823–1939* (Warsaw, 1979).

72. See Mikhol Vaykhert, *Zikhroynes, Varshe*, vol. 2 (Tel Aviv, 1961), for a memoir on the Yiddish theater in Poland. See also Yitskhok Turkov-Grudberg, "Dos yidishe teater in poyln tsvishn beyde velt-milkhomes," *Sefer ha-shana/yorbukh* 2 (1967):325–58.

73. Dov Sadan, *Sifrut yidish be-folin ben shte milhamot ha-olam* (Jerusalem, 1964); Y. Y. Trunk, *Di yidishe proze in poyln in der tkufe tsvishn beyde velt-milkhomes* (Buenos Aires, 1949); Mayzel, *Gevn amol a lebn*.

74. Philip Friedman, "Polish Jewish Historiography between the Two Wars, (1918–1939)," *Jewish Social Studies* 11, no. 4 (1949):373–408.

75. Kazdan, *Di geshikhte fun yidishn shulvezn*, pp. 19–407; Mendelsohn,

*Zionism in Poland*, pp. 198–205; Nathan Eck, "The Educational Institutions"; Miriam Eisenstein, *Jewish Schools in Poland* (New York, 1950).

76. Mendelsohn, *Zionism in Poland*, p. 205; Kazdan, *Di geshikhte fun yidishn shulvezn*, p. 549. For somewhat lower figures, see Stanisław Mauersberg, *Szkolnictwo powszechne dla mniejszości narodowych w Polsce w latach 1918–1939* (Wrocław, etc., 1968), p. 167.

77. The word "renaissance" is used by Trunk, *Di yidishe proze*, p. 17.

78. On the Tarbut schools, see Eck, "The Educational Institutions"; Mendelsohn, *Zionism in Poland*, pp. 188–96; Grünbaum, "Ha-yehudim u-vate ha-sefer be-folin"; Menahem Gelerter, *Ha-gimnaziya ha-ivrit 'tarbut' be-rovno* (Jerusalem, 1973).

79. The figures for 1921 are from Mendelsohn, *Zionism in Poland*, p. 205. See also Kazdan, *Di geshikhte fun yidishn shulvezn*, p. 549; Mauersberg, *Szkolnictwo*, p. 169.

80. On these schools, see Haim Ormian, "Bet ha-sefer ha-ivri ha-tsiburi be-folin ben shte milhamot ha-olam," *Gal-ed* 4-5 (1978):231–63; Kazdan, *Di geshikhte fun yidishn shulvezn*, pp. 536–46.

81. For statistics on the number of Jews in religious schools and for a discussion of the Orthodox schools for Jews, see Kazdan, *Di geshikhte fun yidishn shulvezn*, pp. 479–501, 549.

82. Kazdan, *Di geshikhte fun yidishn shulvezn*, pp. 550–51.

83. A. Druyanov, *Tsiyonut be-folaniya* (Tel Aviv, 1933), pp. 11-12.

84. For general remarks, see Aleksander Hertz, *Żydzi w kulturze polskiej* (Paris, 1961).

85. Moshe Landau, "Hafikhat mei 1926—tsipiyot be-yahadut polin le-tmura medinit ve-tahalikh hitbadutan," *Gal-ed* 2 (1975):237–86; Korzec, *Juifs en Pologne*, pp. 165–238.

86. Chojnowski, *Koncepcje polityki*, pp. 69–83.

87. Meltser, *Yahadut polin*, p. 13. See also Roman Wapiński, *Narodowa Demokracja 1893–1939* (Wrocław, etc., 1980), pp. 299–329.

88. Polonsky, *Politics*, p. 370.

89. Micewski, *Z geografii politycznej II rzeczypospolitej. Szkice* (Warsaw, 1964), p. 21.

90. Yosef Teeni, *Aliyat Hitler la-shilton ve-hashpaata shel ha-antishemiyut al matsavam shel yehude polin ba-shanim 1933–1939* (Ph.D. diss., Hebrew University, 1980), p. 61. See also Meltser, "Yahse polin-germaniya ba-shanim 1935–1938 ve-hashpaatam al baayat ha-yehudim be-folin," *Yad va-shem, kovets mehkarim* 12 (1977):145–70.

91. See the remarks of Hugh Seton-Watson, "Fascism, Right and Left," in *International Fascism, 1920–1945*, ed. Walter Laqueur and George Mosse (New York, 1966), pp. 183–97.

92. For a good analysis of the situation, see Wynot, " 'A Necessary Cruelty': The Emergence of Official Anti-Semitism in Poland," *American Historical Review* 76, no. 4 (October 1971):1035–58. See also Korzec, *Juifs en Pologne*, pp. 239–74.

93. As quoted in Polonsky, *Politics*, p. 424.

94. As quoted in Trunk, "Der ekonomisher antisemitizm," p. 65. See also Meltser, *Yahadut polin*, pp. 45–46.

95. Meltser, *Yahadut polin*, pp. 127–54; Leni Yahil, "Madagascar: Phantom of a Solution for the Jewish Question," in *Jews and Non-Jews in East Central Europe*, ed. Vago and Mosse, pp. 315–34; Meltser, "Ha-diplomatiya ha-polanit u-vaayat ha-hagira ha-yehudit ba-shanim 1935–1939," *Gal-ed* 1 (1973): 211–49.

96. Meltser, *Yahadut polin*, pp. 137–49.

97. Teeni, *Aliyat Hitler*, pp. 11–12.

98. As quoted in Joel Cang, "The Opposition Parties in Poland," p. 249.

99. Meltser, *Yahadut polin*, p. 12.

100. Ibid., pp. 85–98.

101. Ibid., pp. 99–105; Korzec, "Antisemitism in Poland," pp. 94–98.

102. Trunk, "Der ekonomisher antisemitizm," p. 52. On the boycott, see ibid., pp. 48–60; Meltser, *Yahadut polin*, pp. 42–50, 190–205.

103. Trunk, "Der ekonomisher antisemitizm," p. 54; Yankev Leshchinski, "Ha-praot be-folin," *Dapim le-heker ha-shoa ve-ha-mered* 2 (February 1952):37–92; Leshchinski, *Erev khurbm* (Buenos Aires, 1951).

104. Meltser, *Yahadut polin*, p. 204.

105. Sh. Berkovich, "Ankete vegn der peysekh untershtitsungsaktsie in yor 1934," *Dos virtshaftlekhe lebn* 4-5 (1934):6. See also Leshchinski, "Di poyperizirung fun di yidishe masn in poyln," *Yivo bleter* 6, no. 2 (March-April 1934):201–28.

106. On the work of the Joint Distribution Committee in Poland in the 1930s, see Yehuda Bauer, *My Brother's Keeper: A History of the American Jewish Joint Distribution Committee 1929–1939* (Philadelphia, 1974), pp. 190–209.

107. Leshchinski, *Erev khurbm*, pp. 142–49.

108. Quoted in Maks Vaynraykh, *Der veg tsu unzer yugnt* (Vilna, 1935), p. 210.

109. The quotation and the figures are from Joseph Shechtman, *Fighter and Prophet*, 2 (New York and London, 1961): 345. On the rapid growth of the movement, see Yaakov Shavit, *Me-rov le-medina. Ha-tnua ha-revizionistit: ha-tokhnit ha-hityashvutit ve-ha-raayon ha-hevrati* (Tel Aviv, 1968), pp. 69–73; Shechtman, *Fighter and Prophet*, p. 147, 191.

110. Shavit, *Me-rov le-medina*, p. 73. In general, see H. Ben-Yeruham, ed., *Sefer betar, korot u-mekorot*, vol. 1, (Jerusalem–Tel Aviv, 1969).

111. Levi Arye Sarid, *He-haluts u-tnuot ha-noar be-folin, 1917–1939* (Tel Aviv, 1979), p. 467; Leyb Shpeyzman, *Khalutsim in poyln*, 1, (New York, 1959): 652; Yisrael Otiker, *Tnuat he-haluts be-folin, 1932–1935* (Tel Aviv, 1972), pp. 30–35.

112. Yisroel Openhaym, "Prokim tsu der geshikhte fun der kholutsisher hokhshore in tsvishnmilkhomedikn poyln," in *Studies*, ed. Fishman, p. 291.

113. Meltser, *Yahadut polin*, pp. 106–14, 258–71; Johnpoll, *The Politics of Futility*, pp. 220–24.

114. Collection of Jewish autobiographies, *Yivo Archives*, no. 3501.

115. Quoted from a Yivo autobiography in Heller, *On the Edge of Destruction*, p. 246.

116. *Yivo Archives*, no. 3507.

117. Ibid., no. 3545.

118. Ibid., no. 3565.

119. Ibid., no. 3571.

120. Meltser, *Yahadut polin*, pp. 35–42, 244–58.

121. Meltser, *Yahadut polin*, pp. 127–54; Shechtman, *Fighter and Prophet*, pp. 338–47.

122. Meltser, *Yahadut polin*, pp. 106–14, 206–17. See also Leonard Rowe, "Politics under Stress: The Jewish Response in Poland," *Bennington Review*, no. 4 (1968); idem, "Jewish Self-Defense: A Response to Violence," in *Studies*, ed. Fishman, pp. 105–49.

## 2. Hungary

1. For a remarkable study of interwar Hungary, see C. A. Macartney, *October Fifteenth: A History of Modern Hungary 1929–1945*, 2 vols. (Edinborough, 1956–1957). For an attractive survey, see also Paul Ignotus, *Hungary* (New York, 1972). On the Hungarian right, see M. Lackó, *Arrow-Cross Men, National Socialists, 1935–1944* (Budapest, 1969); Nicholas M. Nagy-Talevera, *The Green Shirts and Others: A History of Fascism in Hungary and Rumania* (Stanford, 1970).

2. Istvan Deak, *The Lawful Revolution: Louis Kossuth and the Hungarians, 1848–1849* (New York, 1979), especially pp. 115–16, 314–15.

3. See Robert Kann, "Hungarian Jewry During Austria-Hungary's Constitutional Period (1867–1918)," *Jewish Social Studies* 7 no. 4 (October 1945):357–86.

4. William McCagg, "Hungary's 'Feudalized' Bourgeoisie," *Journal of Modern History* 44 no. 1 (March 1972):65–78; H. Seton-Watson, "Two Contrasting Policies towards Jews: Russia and Hungary," in *Jews and Non-Jews in Eastern Europe*, ed. Vago and Mosse, pp. 99–112; McCagg, *Jewish Nobles and Geniuses in Modern Hungary* (New York, 1972); Iván Berend and György Ránki, *Economic Development in East Central Europe in the Nineteenth and Twentieth Centuries* (New York and London, 1974), pp. 123–65; Andrew Janos, "The Decline of Oligarchy: Bureaucratic and Mass Politics in the Age of Dualism (1867–1918)," in *Revolution in Perspective: Essays on the Hungarian Soviet Republic of 1919*, ed. Andrew Janos and William Slottman (Los Angeles and London, 1971), pp. 1–60.

5. See the brillant essay of Yaakov Katz, "Yihuda shel yahadut hungariya," in *Hanhagat yehude hungariya be-mivhan ha-shoa* (Jerusalem, 1976), pp. 13-24 (also available in English as "The Uniqueness of Hungarian Jewry," *Forum* (1977): 45–53.

6. Scotus Viator [Robert Seton-Watson], *Racial Problems in Hungary* (London, 1908), p. 188.

7. Netanel Katzburg, "Toldot yehude hungariya mi-reshit ha-hityashvut ad shnot milhemet ha-olam ha-shniya," in *Pinkas ha-kehilot, Hungariya* (Jerusalem, 1975), pp. 24–28.

8. See the important material on the various Jewish communities of Hungary in *Pinkas-ha-kehilot. Hungariya.* See also Moshe Eliyahu Gonda, *Mea shana le-yehude debretsen* (Tel Aviv, 1970); Aharon First, "Budapesht," *Arim ve-imahot be-yisrael* (Jerusalem, 1948), 2:109–86.

9. Ignotus, *Hungary*, p. 93.

10. Oscar [Oszkár] Jászi, *The Dissolution of the Habsburg Monarchy* (Chicago, 1961), p. 174 (for further remarks on this interesting figure, see below, p. 111); Seton-Watson, *Racial Problems*, p. 206.

11. Katz, "Yihuda," pp. 20–21. See also Macartney's observation that "the Jews always remained something of outsiders," in his *October Fifteenth*, 2: 21; conversion did not do much to alter this situation.

12. Macartney, *The Habsburg Empire 1790–1918* (New York, 1969), p. 710.

13. McCagg, *Jewish Nobles*, pp. 17, 31. See also Istvan Veghazi, "The Role of Jewry in the Economic Life of Hungary," in *Hungarian-Jewish Studies*, ed. R. L. Braham (New York, 1969), 2:35–84; the statistical material in McCagg, "Hungary's 'Feudalized' Bourgeoisie"; the remarks of Jászi, *The Dissolution of the Habsburg Monarchy*, p. 173; the detailed study by Victor Karady and István Kemény, "Les juifs dans la structure des classes en Hongrie: essai sur les an-

técéndents historiques des crises d'antisémitisme du XXe siècle," *Actes de la recherche en sciences sociales* 22 (June 1978):25–59.

14. McCagg, "Hungary's 'Feudalized' Bourgeoisie." On the alliance of the Jewish financial and commercial elite and the Magyar ruling class, see Berend and Ránki, *Economic Development*, p. 164; Janos, "The Decline of Oligarchy," pp. 34–37.

15. McCagg, *Jewish Nobles*; Katzburg, "Toldot yehude hungariya," pp. 61–63.

16. McCagg, "Jews in Revolutions: The Hungarian Experience," *Journal of Social History* (Fall 1972):78–105; Shlomo Yitshaki, "Ha-yehudim be-mahapechot hungariya, 1918–1919," *Moreshet* 11 (November 1969):113–34; Ignotus, *Hungary*, pp. 117–18; Rudolph Tökés, *Béla Kun and the Hungarian Soviet Republic* (New York, 1967), p. 1.

17. Alexander Scheiber, ed., *Ignaz Goldziher, Tagebuch* (Leiden, 1978), p. 34.

18. Ignatus, *Hungary*, pp. 97–98.

19. Katsburg, *Antishemiyut be-hungariya 1867–1914* (Tel Aviv, 1969). See also McCagg's review of Judit Kubinszky's book on Hungarian anti-Semitism in *The American Historical Review* 83, no. 1 (1978): 215–16; and Katz, *From Prejudice to Destruction: Antisemitism, 1700–1933*, (Cambridge, Mass., 1980), pp. 230–44.

20. Quoted in Livia Rotkirchen, "Hitpathut ha-antishemiyut u-redifot ha-yehudim be-hungariya ba-shanim 1920–1945," in *Shana le-en kets*, ed. Moshe Zandberg (Jerusalem, 1966), p. vii. See also the comments in George Barany, "Magyar Jew or Jewish Magyar? Reflections on the Question of Assimilation," in *Jews and Non-Jews in Eastern Europe*, ed. Vago and Mosse, pp. 51–98.

21. The history of Hungarian Jewry in the interwar period is the subject of two recent and important books: Braham, *The Politics of Genocide: The Holocaust in Hungary*, 1 (New York, 1981); Katzburg, *Hungary and the Jews, 1920–1943* (Ramat-Gan, 1981).

22. On Jewish support for Károlyi, see Peter Pastor, *Hungary between Wilson and Lenin: The Hungarian Revolution of 1918–1919 and the Big Three* (New York, 1976), pp. 39, 45; Jászi, *Magyarens Schuld, Ungarns Sühne, Revolution and Gegenrevolution in Ungarn* (Munich, 1923), pp. 24–27; McCagg, "Jews in Revolutions"; Rothschild, *East Central Europe Between the Two World Wars*, p. 139. Károlyi is described as a Jewish stooge in the violently anti-Semitic book by Cécile Tormay, *An Outlaw's Diary: Revolution* (London, 1923), especially p. 70.

23. Yitshaki, "Ha-yehudim be-mahapekhot hungariya." See also McCagg, "Jews in Revolutions," and Deak, "Budapest and the Hungarian Revolutions of 1918–1919," *Slavic and East European Review* 46, no. 106 (January 1968):129–40.

24. Quoted in Janos, "The Agrarian Opposition at the National Congress of Councils," in *Revolution in Perspective*, ed. Janos and Slottman, p. 97.

25. Jászi, *Magyarens Schuld*, p. 129. For valuable material on Jews and the left in Hungary, see also McCagg, *Jewish Nobles*.

26. Tormay, *An Outlaw's Diary: The Commune* (Hereford, 1923), p. 5.

27. Jerome and Jean Tharaud, *When Israel Is King* (New York, 1924), p. 190.

28. Deak, "Budapest and the Hungarian Revolutions of 1918–1919," pp. 131–32; Ignotus, *Hungary*, p. 151. For details on the pogroms see Katzburg, "Redifot ha-yehudim be-hungariya 1919–1922," *Universitat bar-ilan, sefer shana* 3 (1965): 225–51; idem, *Hungary and the Jews*, pp. 32–59. See also "La terreur blanche en Hongrie et les juifs," *Bulletin du comité des délégations juives auprès de la conférence de la paix* 14 (12 May 1920): 3–5; ibid. 15 (6 July 1920): 6–11; the testimony of one of Horthy's aides in 1919, in Anton Lehar, *Erinnerungen*.

*Gegenrevolution und Restaurationsversuche in Ungarn 1918–1921* (Munich, 1973), pp. 112–27. There appear to be no statistics on the number of Jews killed; the reference to fifty cities is in Katzburg, *Hungary and the Jews*, p. 41.

29. See, for example, Nicholas Horthy, *Memoirs* (London, 1956), pp. 98–109. Horthy does write in his memoirs that he opposed the pogroms, but he also writes that he did not regret the white terror, which was necessary in order to rid the country of Bolshevism.

30. Stephen Béla Vardy, *Modern Hungarian Historiography* (New York and Guildford, 1976), 62–69. See also Asher Cohen, "The Attitude of the Intelligentsia in Hungary toward Jewish Assimilation between the Two World Wars," in *Jewish Assimilation in Modern Times*, ed. Vago, pp. 57–74.

31. For material on Jewish demography see B. D., "Di yidn in ungarn," *Yidishe ekonomik* 1 (1937):184–88; "The Jews of Hungary: Census of 1920," *American Jewish Year Book* 29 (1927–28):265–68. The latter source gives as the total number of Jews in Hungary in 1920 473,310.

32. "The Jews of Hungary, Census of 1920," p. 265. An excellent map of the locations of the various Jewish communities is found in *Pinkas ha-kehilot, Hungariya*.

33. David Shmuel Levinger, ed., *Shivim shana, hoveret ha-yovel le-vet ha-midrash le-rabanim be-vudapest ba-shana ha-shivim le-hivasdo* (Budapest, 1974); A. N. Ts. Rot, "Bet ha-midrash le-rabanim be-hungariya," in *Mosdot tora be-iropa be-vinyanam u-ve-horbanam*, ed. Sh. Mirski (New York, 1956), pp. 635–54. For the figure on the percentage of Neologs, see Katzburg, "Toldot yehude hungariya," pp. 74–75.

34. Tsvi Yaakov Avraham, "Al ha-yeshivot be-hungariya ha-nirheva," in *Mosdot tora be-iropa*, ed. Mirsky, p. 438.

35. On the existence of large numbers of poor Jews, see Braham, *The Politics of Genocide*, 1: 78–80.

36. "Di yidn in ungarn," *Yidishe ekonomik* 1 (1937):271. These figures do not include doctors and lawyers employed in various government offices, where the percentage of Jews was much lower. For statistics on Jews in the civil service see ibid., p. 269. By 1930 only 4.3 percent of all civil servants were Jews; in 1920 the figure was 7.4 percent.

37. Ibid., pp. 280, 282. These statistics are admittedly not completely accurate, since the religious affiliation of the owners was not always listed.

38. Macartney, *October Fifteenth*, 1: 19.

39. M. Norin, "Gemishte khasenes bay yidn in budapesht," *Yidishe ekonomik* 3 (1939):254. For figures for all of Hungary from 1913 to 1932, see "20 yor gemishte khasenes bay yidn in ungarn," ibid., p. 271.

40. "The Jews of Hungary, Census of 1920," p. 281. In 1920 the figure was 1,925; in 1921, 827; in 1922, 277.

41. Horthy, *Memoirs*, p. 98.

42. Paul Teleki, *The Evolution of Hungary and Its Place in European History*, reprint ed. (Gulf Breeze, 1975), pp. 141–42.

43. Quoted in L. Tilkovszky, *Pál Teleki (1879–1941): A Biographical Sketch* (Budapest, 1974), pp. 28–29.

44. Introduction to Nicholas [Miklós] Kállay, *Hungarian Premier* (Westport, 1970), p. xv. For details on Jewish-gentry cooperation, see Bernard Klein, "Hungarian Politics and the Jewish Question in the Inter-War Period," *Jewish Social Studies* 28, no. 2 (April 1966): 79–98.

45. *The Jewish Minority in Hungary. The Hungarian Law No. XXV of the Year 1920 ["Numerus Clausus"] Before the Council of the League of Nations, Dec. 10 &*

*12, 1925*, Report of the Joint Foreign Committee of the Board of Deputies of British Jews (London, 1926), p. 5.

46. Ibid., p. 48. For details see Karady and Kemény, "Antisémitisme universitaire et concurrence de classe: la loi du *numerus clausus* en Hongrie entre les deux guerres," *Actes de la recherche en sciences sociales* 34 (September 1980): 67–96; Katzburg, *Hungary and the Jews*, pp. 60–79. See also Thomas Spira, "Hungary's Numerus Clausus, the Jewish Minority, and the League of Nations," *Ungarn-Jahrbuch* 4 (1972): 115–28.

47. *Paix et Droit* 6 (June 1923).

48. *The Jewish Minority in Hungary*, p. 34.

49. For statistics on the period 1918–1922, see "The Jews of Hungary: Census of 1920," *American Jewish Yearbook* 29 (1927–28): 275. In 1932 14.3% of all students were Jews, but in the late 1930s there was a rapid decline. See Klein, "Hungarian Politics," p. 84.

50. Katzburg, "Ha-maavak be-hever ha-leumim neged hok ha-'numerus klausus' be-hungariya," *Universitat bar-ilan, sefer ha-shana* 4-5 (1967):270–88; idem, *Hungary and the Jews*, pp. 73–79. Katzburg believes that foreign intervention, along with Hungary's desire to receive a foreign loan, led the government to remove the law from the statute book.

51. Jászi, *Magyarens Schuld*, pp. 193–97.

52. Quoted in Livia E. Biton, "Zionism in Hungary: the First Twenty-Five Years," *Herzl Institute Year Book* 7 (1971):285. On Hungarian Zionism, see also Braham, "Legitimism, Zionism, and the Jewish Catastrophe in Hungary," *Herzl Institute Year Book* 6 (1964–65):239–52; Y. Tsvi Zahavi, *Me-Ha-Hatam Sofer ve-ad Hertsel. Toldot ha-tsiyonut be-hungariya* (Jerusalem, 1965).

53. On the number of shekels, see the report on Hungary in *Report of the Executives of the Zionist Organization and of the Jewish Agency for Palestine* (Jerusalem, 1939), p. 76.

54. See "Briefe aus Ungarn," *Allgemeine Zeitung des Judentums* (28 November 1919):545–46.

55. "Di Zukunft des ungarischen Judentums," ibid. (2 January 1920):6–7. The name of the organization was the Landeshilfskommission der ungarischen Juden.

56. *The Confidential Papers of Admiral Horthy* (Budapest, 1965), p. 7. On Vázsonyi, see also Katzburg, "Redifot"; idem, "The Jewish Question in Hungary during the Inter-War Period: Jewish Attitudes," in *Jews and Non-Jews in Eastern Europe*, ed. Vago and Mosse, pp. 114–15.

57. Katzburg, *Hungary and the Jews*, p. 242. The discussion took place in 1923.

58. Katzburg, "The Jewish Question," p. 114.

59. *The Jewish Minority in Hungary*, p. 46. For details, see Katzburg, "The Jewish Question"; idem, "Ha-maavak"; idem, *Hungary and the Jews*, pp. 60–79.

60. Katzburg, "The Jewish Question."

61. See above, p. 49.

62. Quoted in McCagg, *Jewish Nobles and Geniuses*, p. 106.

63. Jászi, *The Dissolution of the Habsburg Empire*, p. 174. On this interesting figure, see Lee Congdon, "History and Politics in Hungary: The Rehabilitation of Oscar Jaszi," *East European Quarterly* 9 (1975–76): 315–29; McCagg, *Jewish Nobles and Geniuses*, pp. 102–05.

64. *Ignaz Goldziher, Tagebuch*, p. 159.

65. On education, see Aron Moskovits, *Jewish Education in Hungary (1848-1948)* (New York, 1964), pp. 215–93. In the school year 1929–1930 there were 157 private Jewish elementary schools in Hungary, but the language of instruction was, of course, Hungarian. There were also a few private Jewish high schools.

Moskovits concludes that during the interwar years Hungarian Jewry was headed toward "the gradual abandonment of its schools" (p. 293). For a survey of the Jewish role in Hungarian culture, see Erzsebet Bella, "The Jews of Hungary: A Cultural Overview," in *Hungarian-Jewish Studies*, ed. Braham, 2: 85–136.

66. Ingomar Senz, *Die nationale Bewegung der ungarlandische Deutschen vor dem ersten Weltkrieg* (Munich, 1977); Thomas Spira, *German-Hungarian Relations and the Swabian Problem from Károlyi to Gömbös, 1919–1936* (New York, 1977); G. C. Paikert, *The Danube Swabians* (The Hague, 1967).

67. *The National Program of the Hungarian Gömbös Government* (Budapest, 1932), paragraph no. 83.

68. See the documents in Elek Karsai, ed., "The Meeting of Gömbös and Hitler in 1933," *The New Hungarian Quarterly* 3 (1962):170–96; from the German perspective, Gömbös' visit broke the "official isolation of national socialism" (p. 196).

69. Macartney, *October Fifteenth*, 1: 117.

70. Quoted in Klein, "Hungarian Politics," p. 83.

71. Lackó, *Arrow-Cross Men*, p. 10; J. Eros, "Hungary," in *European Fascism*, ed. S. J. Woolf (New York, 1969), pp. 126–28. See also Nagy-Talavera, *The Green Shirts*, pp. 83–90.

72. This term is used by Nagy-Talavera, *The Green Shirts*, p. 90.

73. On the Jewish question and foreign policy, see Macartney, "Hungarian Foreign Policy during the Inter-War Period, with Special Reference to the Jewish Question," in *Jews and Non-Jews in Eastern Europe*, ed. Vago and Mosse, pp. 125–36.

74. Laszlo Ottlik, "The Hungarian Jewish Law," *The Hungarian Quarterly* 4 (1938–39): 399. See also Johann Weidlin, *Der ungarische Antisemitismus in Dokumenten* (Schorndorf, 1962), p. 51; Katzburg, *Hungary and the Jews*, pp. 94–113; Braham, *The Politics of Genocide*, 1: 122–27.

75. Ottlik, "The Hungarian Jewish Law," pp. 401–02.

76. "Declaration of Protest of Hungarian Jews against the Introduction of the Occupational Restriction Law of May, 1938," *Contemporary Jewish Record* 1, no. 2 (1938–39):26.

77. Ibid., pp. 27–28. Those named are great Hungarian patriots of past centuries.

78. Katzburg, *Hungary and the Jews*, p. 98. See also the correspondence between Halifax and Norman in Vago, *The Shadow of the Swastika* (London, 1975), p. 313.

79. See the remarks of Dr. Rassay quoted in Weidlin, *Der ungarische Antisemitismus*, p. 66. For the debate in general, see ibid., pp. 53–94; Katzburg, *Hungary and the Jews*, pp. 94–113.

80. Weidlin, p. 76.

81. Katzburg, "Paul Teleki and the Jewish Question in Hungary," *Soviet Jewish Affairs* 2 (November 1971):106–07.

82. Weidlin, *Der ungarische Antisemitismus*, pp. 31–32; Braham, *The Politics of Genocide*, 1: 123–25.

83. Katzburg, "Paul Teleki," p. 109.

84. This is also the position of Macartney, *October Fifteenth*; see, for example, his discussion of the first Jewish law (1: 218–19).

85. Israel Cohen, "The Jews in Hungary," *The Contemporary Review*, (November 1939):10. See also Weidlin, *Der ungarische Antisemitismus*, pp. 95–137; Katzburg, *Hungary and the Jews*, pp. 114–57; Braham, *The Politics of Genocide*, 1: 147–56.

86. "Memorandum of Count István Bethlen and some other politicians," *Admiral Horthy's Confidential Papers*, pp. 114–15.

87. Ibid., pp. 117–18.

88. Ibid., p. 112; Horthy, *Memoirs*, p. 175.

89. See the account in Macartney, *October Fifteenth*, 1: 327–28. It appears that Horthy used Imrédy's "Jewish descent" as a means to get rid of a man whose radical right policies he disliked.

90. Ibid., pp. 350–51.

91. See, for example, "Memorandum des Deutschen Aussenministeriums an die Ungarische Regierung," 1943, which accuses the government even at that late date of doing nothing to reduce Jewish influence; Lajos Kerekes, ed., *Allianz Hitler-Horthy-Mussolini* (Budapest, 1966), p. 347.

92. Cohen, "The Jews in Hungary." For the situation in the small towns, see the invaluable material in *Pinkas ha-kehilot, Hungariya*.

93. Braham, *The Hungarian Labor Service System 1939–1945* (New York, 1977), pp. 5-13.

94. Katzburg, "Hanhagat ha-kehilot," in *Hanhagat yehude hungariya be-mivhan ha-shoa*, pp. 81–84.

95. Quoted in Braham, *The Politics of Genocide*, 1: 96. Stern was also the president of the National Bureau of the Jews in Hungary.

96. During the years 1928–1935, 2,609 Jews emigrated; see Sh. Friedman, "Yidishe emigratsie fun ungarn," *Yidishe ekonomik* 3 (1939):89–94.

97. Rotkirchen, "Korot tkufat ha-shoa," *Pinkas ha-kehilot, Hungariya*, p. 104.

98. Vago, "Tmurot be-hanhagat yehude hungariya bi-yeme milhemet ha-olam ha-shniya," *Hanhagat yehude hungariya be-mivhan ha-shoa*, pp. 61–76; Yosef Shefer, "Hanhagat ha-mahteret ha-halutsit be-hungariya, ibid., pp. 135–49; Rot, "Bet ha-midrash le-rabanim," p. 649.

99. Kerekes, *Allianz* p. 385.

100. For details on the definition of "Jew" in the first three Hungarian laws, see Raul Hilberg, *The Destruction of the European Jews* (Chicago, 1961), p. 513. On anti-Jewish legislation during the war years, see Katzburg, *Hungary and the Jews*, pp. 158–211; Braham, *The Politics of Genocide*, 1: 192–382.

101. See "Notes prepared by Andor Szentmiklósy," 1943, in *Admiral Horthy's Confidential Papers*, pp. 241–43.

102. Kállay, *Hungarian Premier*, pp. 75–76.

103. For details, see Braham, *The Hungarian Labor Service System*.

104. Braham, *The Destruction of Hungarian Jewry: A Documentary Account* (New York, 1963), 1:xi–xxxi.

105. Ibid., 2: 971. For details, see Braham, *The Politics of Genocide*, vol. 2.

106. Weidlin, *Der ungarische Antisemitismus*, p. 76.

## 3. Czechoslovakia

1. In the use of the terms "Rusyn" and "Subcarpathian Rus," I follow Paul R. Magocsi, *The Shaping of a National Identity: Subcarpathian Rus, 1848-1948* (Cambridge and London, 1978). The peasant people which made up the majority in this province are referred to sometimes as Ruthenian, sometimes as Ukrainian. The language they spoke shall be referred to here as Ruthenian.

2. For general information on the minority nationalities, see ibid.; Owen Verne Johnson, *Sociocultural and National Development in Slovakia, 1918-1938:*

*Education and Its Impact* (Ph.D. diss., University of Michigan, 1978); Peter Brock, *The Slovak National Awakening: An Essay in the Intellectual History of East Central Europe* (Toronto, 1976); Elizabeth Wiskemann, *Czechs and Germans*, 2d ed. (New York, etc., 1967). On interwar Czechoslovakia in general, see Victor Mamatey and Radomír Luža, eds., *A History of the Czechoslovak Republic 1918–1948* (Princeton, 1973).

3. Ruth Kestenburg-Gladstein, "The Jews between Czechs and Germans in the Historic Lands," *The Jews of Czechoslovakia*, 1 (New York and Philadelphia, 1968): 21–71; Guido Kisch, "Linguistic Conditions among Czechoslovak Jewry," *Historia Judaica* 8, no. 1 (April 1946):19–32; Max Brod, *Haye meriva* (Jerusalem, 1967), p. 109; Hans Tramer, "Prague: City of Three Peoples," *Leo Baeck Institute Yearbook* 9 (1964): 305–39.

4. Yitshak Zev Kahana, *Nikolsburg, Arim ve-imahot be-yisrael* (Jerusalem, 1950), 4:210–313; Sh. H. Bergman, "Petah davar," *Yahadut chekhoslovakiya, Gesher* 2-3 (1959–1960):7–10; idem, "Prag," ibid., pp. 83–91; Kestenberg-Gladstein, "The Jews between Czechs and Germans."

5. "Zikhronot mi-tkufat ha-hitbolelut," in *Prag vi-yerushalayim. Sefer zikaron le-Yan Herman*, ed. Feliks Weltsh (Jerusalem, 1954), p. 52.

6. See his introduction to Jiři Langer, *Nine Gates to the Hasidic Mysteries* (New York, 1976), p. viii.

7. *Letter to His Father* (New York, 1966), pp. 69–81.

8. Langer, *Nine Gates*, p. ix.

9. Ibid., p. xi.

10. Brod, *Haye meriva*, p. 128. See also Hans Kohn, "Before 1918 in the Historic Lands," in *The Jews of Czechoslovakia*, 1: 12–20; Kestenberg-Gladstein, "The Jews between Czechs and Germans"; Zigmund Katsnelson, "Be-maavak ha-leumim," in *Prag vi-yerushalayim*, ed. Weltsh, pp. 57–63. See also the new study (which I was unable to consult) Gary Cohen, *The Politics of Ethnic Survival: Germans in Prague, 1861-1914* (Princeton, 1981).

11. Quoted in Kisch, *In Search of Freedom: A History of American Jews from Czechoslovakia* (London, 1949), pp. 36–37.

12. For a reappraisal of the Jewish-Czech movement, see Hillel Kieval, *Nationalism and the Jews of Prague: The Transformation of Jewish Culture in Central Europe, 1880-1918* (Ph.D. diss., Harvard University, 1981). For an analysis of the linguistic situation, see Michael Riff, "Czech Antisemitism and the Jewish Response before 1914," *Wiener Library Bulletin* 29,no. 39/40 (1976): 17–18. See also Oskar Donath, "Jüdisches in der neuen tschechischen Literatur," *Jahrbuch der Gesellschaft für Geschichte der Juden in der Cechoslovakischen Republik* 3 (1931): 1–144; Vlastimila Hamackova, "Débuts du mouvement assimilateur Tchéco-Juif," *Judaica Bohemiae* 14, no. 1 (1978): 15–23. As is so often the case in ethnically mixed regions, the Jews in Bohemia and Moravia were more bilingual than either the Germans or the Czechs, and some played an important role in bringing Czech culture to the attention of German Prague. See Tramer, "Prague"; Brod, *Haye meriva*, 228–48; Eve Bock, "The German-Jewish Writers of Prague: Interpreters of Czech Literature," *Leo Baeck Institute Yearbook* 23 (1978): 239–46. See also Wilma Iggers, "The Flexible National Identities of Bohemian Jewry," *East Central Europe* 7, no. 1 (1980): 39–48.

13. Kohn, *Living in a World Revolution* (New York, 1964), pp. 28–29. Brod, *Haye meriva*, pp. 41–42; Haim Yahil, *Dvarim al ha-tsiyonut ha-chekhoslovakit* (Jerusalem, 1967).

14. Phillip Frank, *Einstein: His Life and Times* (New York, 1947), pp. 83–85; Roman Szporluk, *The Political Thought of Thomas Masaryk* (New York, 1981), pp. 34–35.

15. N. M. Gelber, "Kavim le-kidmat toldoteha shel ha-tsiyonut be-vohemiya u-moraviya," in *Prag vi-yerushalayim*, ed. Weltsh, pp. 48–49.

16. See the essays in *Prag vi-yerushalayim*, ed. Weltsh; Yehoshua Borman, "Ha-'zerem ha-pragai' ba-tnua ha-tsiyonit ha-olamit," *Yahadut chekhoslovakiya*, pp. 243–50; Stuart Borman, *The Prague Student Zionist Movement, 1896-1914* (Ph.D. diss., University of Chicago, 1972), in which he also discusses several other student Zionist movements in the capital of Bohemia.

17. Donath, "Jews in Masaryk's Life," in *Thomas G. Masaryk and the Jews: A Collection of Essays*, ed. Ernest Rychnovsky, trans. Benjamin Epstein (New York, 1941), p. 130.

18. See, for example, Bruce M. Garner, *The Young Czech Party 1874-1901 and the Emergence of a Multi-Party System* (New Haven and London, 1978), pp. 141, 302–03. For a rather different view, which emphasizes the strength of Czech anti-Semitism, see the excellent article by Christoph Stölz, "Zur Geschichte der böhmischen Juden in der Epoche des modernen Nationalismus," *Bohemia. Jahrbuch des Collegium Carolinum* 14 (1973): 179–221; ibid., 15 (1974): 129–57; idem, *Kafkas böses Böhmen. Zur Sozialgeschichte eines Prager Juden* (Munich, 1975). See also Michael Riff, "Czech Antisemitism and the Jewish Response before 1914," *Wiener Library Bulletin* 29 (1976): 8–20.

19. Frantisek Červinka, "The Hilsner Affair," *Leo Baeck Institute Yearbook* 13 (1968):142–57; Ernest Rychnovsky, "The Struggle against the Ritual Murder Superstition," in *Thomas G. Masaryk and the Jews*, trans. Epstein, pp. 148–234.

20. Hugo Stránský, "The Religious Life in Slovakia and Subcarpathian Ruthenia," in *The Jews of Czechoslovakia*, 2 (New York and Philadelphia, 1971): 347–92; Livia Rothkirchen, "Slovakia: I, 1848-1918," ibid., 1: 72–84.

21. Ladislav Grosman, "Harhek me-erets avot," *Yahadut chekhoslovakiya*, pp. 104–24; Eran Laor, *Vergangen und Ausgeloscht. Erinnerungen an das slowakisch-ungarische Judentum* (Stuttgart, 1972), pp. 83–131; Shmuel Ha-kohen Veingarten, *Toldot yehude bratislava (presburg), Arim ve-imahot*, 7 (Jerusalem, 1960).

22. Oskar K. Rabinowicz, "Czechoslovak Zionism: Analecta to a History," *The Jews in Czechoslovakia*, 2: 24–25.

23. Veingarten, "Le-korot ha-yehudim be-karpatorus," in *Karpatorus, Entsiklopediya shel galuiyot*, ed. Yehuda Erez, 7 (Jerusalem and Tel Aviv, 1959): 17–88. See also Herman Dicker, *Piety and Perseverance: Jews from the Carpathian Mountains* (New York, 1981).

24. Data are based on Franz Friedmann, *Einige Zahlen über die tschechoslovakischen Juden* (Prague, 1933); Bruno Blau, "Yidn in der tshekhoslovakay," *Yidishe ekonomik* 3 (1939):27–54.

25. Friedmann, *Einige Zahlen*, pp. 9–14; Blau, "Bafelkerung-bavegung bay yidn in tshekhoslovakay," *Yidishe ekonomik* 3 (1939):172–94. Because very few Jews emigrated from Czechoslovakia during the interwar years, emigration was not an important factor in the demographic decline. See "Yidn in der emigratsie fun tshekhoslovakay," *Yidishe ekonomik* 3 (1939):96-97.

26. Herman, "The Development of Bohemian and Moravian Jewry," p. 201.

27. Aryeh Sole, "Subcarpathian Ruthenia: 1918-1938," in *The Jews of Czechoslovakia*, 1: 129.

28. Johnson, *Sociocultural and National Development in Slovakia*, p. 385; Rothkirchen, "Slovakia," pp. 76–77; Juraj Kramer, *Slovenské autonomistické hnutie v rokoch 1918-1929* (Bratislava, 1962), p. 116. Jews were also important in Slovakia as landowners and estate managers, as they were in ethnic Hungary.

29. Herman, "The Development of Bohemian and Moravian Jewry," p. 202; Friedmann, *Einige Zahlen*, p. 15; Blau, "Bafelkerung-bavegung," p. 177.

30. In 1934 only 19 Jews converted to Catholicism in Prague, although an additional 123 officially quit the Jewish community without converting to any other religion. See Blau, "Bafelkerung-bavegung," p. 192. In 1938, at the height of prewar anti-Semitism, 389 Prague Jews officially quit the Jewish community.

31. Thomas Masaryk, *The Making of a State: Memoirs and Observations 1914-1918* (New York, 1969), p. 222.

32. Quoted in Felix Weltsch, "Masaryk and Zionism," in *Thomas G. Masaryk and the Jews*, trans. Epstein, p. 86. See also the articles by Brod and Bergmann in ibid.

33. Josef Penizek, "Masaryk and the Jewish Czechs," in ibid., pp. 115–24; Jindrich Kohn, "Masaryk's School of Thought and its Relation to Judaism," in ibid., pp. 25–47. Szporluk, *The Political Thought of Thomas Masaryk*, pp. 120–21, emphasizes Masaryk's reluctance to accept Jews as Czechs, but this reluctance did not imply that he regarded them as less than equal citizens of the state.

34. *The Making of a State*, p. 389. See also the remarks of Masaryk's colleague Eduard Beneš, *My War Memoirs* (Boston and New York, 1971), pp. 493–94.

35. Quoted from a report of the meeting published in Aharon Moshe Rabinowicz, "The Jewish Minority," in *The Jews of Czechoslovakia*, 1: 175.

36. See the documents in ibid., pp. 232–42. See also "La Tchéco-Slovaquie reconnaît la nationalité juive," *Bulletin du comité des délégations juives auprès de la conférence de la paix* 13 (30 March 1920):8; ibid., pp. 9–10. The recognition of the Jews as a separate nationality was based on a later interpretation of the constitution, which did not specifically mention the Jews. The fact that the "Jewish articles" of the Polish Minorities' Treaty were not incorporated into the Czechoslovak treaty caused considerable anger in Zionist circles. See Aharon Moshe Rabinowicz, "The Jewish Minority," pp. 230–32.

37. From a report quoted in Aharon Moshe Rabinowicz, "The Jewish Minority," p. 222.

38. Veingarten, *Toldot yehude bratislava*, pp. 129–32; Egbert Jahn, *Die Deutschtum in der Slowakei in den Jahren 1918-1929* (Munich and Vienna, 1971), p. 36; Rothkirchen, "Slovakia: II, 1918-1938," in *The Jews of Czechoslovakia*, 1: 85–87.

39. Quoted in Aharon Moshe Rabinowicz, "The Jewish Minority," pp. 226–27.

40. Joseph A. Mikus, *Slovakia. A Political History: 1918–1950* (Marquette, 1963), p. 96.

41. J. W. Brügel, "Jews in Political Life," in *The Jews of Czechoslovakia*, 2: 243–52.

42. Quoted in Brügel, *Czechoslovakia before Munich* (Cambridge, 1973), p. 104.

43. Aharon Moshe Rabinowicz, "The Jewish Minority," p. 218. See also idem, "The Jewish Party," *The Jews of Czechoslovakia*, 2: 253–346.

44. See the memorandum from the Jewish National Council to the Czechoslovak government, October, 1918, in Aharon Moshe Rabinowicz, "The Jewish Minority," p. 219.

45. Ibid.

46. On this organization, see Aharon Moshe Rabinowicz, "The Jewish Party," pp. 253–346.

47. Ibid. See also Bela Vago, "The Attitude toward the Jews as a Criterion of the Left-Right Concept," in *Jews and Non-Jews in Eastern Europe*, ed. Vago and Mosse, pp. 42–43. In 1920 Subcarpathian Rus did not participate in the elections.

48. Gertrude Hirschler, "The History of Agudath Israel in Slovakia (1918-

1939)," *The Jews of Czechoslovakia*, 2: 155–72; Aharon Moshe Rabinowicz, "The Jewish Party," pp. 271–72; Vago, "The Attitude toward the Jews," p. 42; Veingarten, *Toldot yehude bratislava*, p. 146.

49. The proclamation is published in A. Sole, "Ben shte milhamot ha-olam," in *Karpatorus*, ed. Erez, p. 207. An English version is in Sole, "Subcarpathian Ruthenia," pp. 148–49.

50. Sole, "Ben shte milhomot olam," pp. 163–69; Yehuda Shpigel, "Ungvar," *Arim ve-imahot be-yisrael*, 4 (Jerusalem, 1950): 47–48. Rabinowicz, "The Jewish Party," p. 269. Shimon Ha-kohen Veingarten, "Munkatsh," in *Arim ve-imahot be-yisrael*, 1 (Jerusalem, 1946): 368–69.

51. Sole, "Ben shte milhamot olam," p. 178.

52. See Yeshayahu Jelinek, "The Communist Party of Slovakia and the Jews: Ten Years (1938-48)," *East Central Europe 5*, pt. 2 (1978):186–202; the author notes that "a respectable part of the young Jewish intellectuals in Slovakia" became Communists (p. 187). According to Brügel, "Quite a few of Czechoslovakia's leading Communists were of Jewish origin . . ." ("Jews in Political Life," p. 251).

53. Aharon Moshe Rabinowicz, "The Jewish Party," pp. 294–96.

54. Figures in Oscar K. Rabinowicz, "Czechoslovak Zionism," p. 55. For estimates on the strength of the movement, see also Yahil, "Al ha-tsiyonut ha-chekhoslovakit," *Yahadut chekhoslovakiya*, p. 132.

55. Oscar K. Rabinowicz, "Czechoslovak Zionism," p. 87 (on Ha-shomer ha-tsair); Sole, "Ben shte milhamot ha-olam," in *Karpatorus*, ed. Erez, p. 209 (on the Pioneer). The pioneering movement, however, originated in the Czech lands. See Haim Kafri, "Nitsanim rishonim shel tnuat he-haluts be-chekhoslovakiya," *Measaf* 10 (1978): 108–11; Fini Brada, "Emigration to Palestine," *The Jews of Czechoslovakia*, 2: 589–98.

56. Sole, "Modern Hebrew Education in Subcarpathian Ruthenia," *The Jews of Czechoslovakia*, 2: 431.

57. See, for example, Kohn, *Living in a World Revolution*; Kohn later became disappointed that "Zionist nationalism went the way of most Central and Eastern European nationalisms" (p. 53). See also the articles in *Prag vi-yerushalayim*; Yahil, *Dvarim al ha-tsiyonut ha-chekhoslovakit*; Oscar K. Rabinowicz, "Czechoslovak Zionism." On the similarities between Masaryk's views and those of the Czech Zionists, see Brod, "A Conversation with Prof. Masaryk," in *Thomas G. Masaryk and the Jews*, trans. Epstein, pp. 279–83.

58. Aharon Moshe Rabinowicz, "The Jewish Party," p. 285. Now 93% claimed to be Jews by nationality.

59. Blau, "Nationality among Czechoslovak Jewry," p. 150.

60. Friedmann, *Einige Zahlen*, pp. 17–19; Yehuda Erez, "Be-ene shaliah eretsyisraeli," in *Karpatorus*, ed. Erez, pp. 245–46.

61. Details in Sole, "Modern Hebrew Education in Subcarpathian Ruthenia," and idem, "Ben shte milhamot ha-olam"; the quotation is from the latter article (p. 185).

62. For an appreciation of the schools, see Erez, "Be-ene shaliah."

63. There are interesting data on this in Johnson, *Sociocultural and National Development in Slovakia*, pp. 132–40, 242–51, 288–322.

64. B. D., "Yidishe studentn in tshekhoslovakay," *Yidishe ekonomik* 2 (1938): 79–85.

65. The speech is published in Sole, "Ben shte milhamot ha-olam," p. 208, and in part in English in idem, "Subcarpathian Ruthenia," p. 132. On the Jews' economic decline, see also Erez, "Be-ene shaliah," pp. 236–42.

66. Jelinek, "The Slovak Right: Conservative or Radical? A Reappraisal," *East Central Europe* 4, pt. 1 (1977): 20–34; Jörg Hoensch, "The Slovak Republic, 1939-1945," in *A History of the Czechoslovak Republic, 1918-1945*, ed. Mamatey and Luža, pp. 271–95.

67. George F. Kennan, *From Prague after Munich: Diplomatic Papers, 1938-1940* (Princeton, 1968), pp. 50–51.

68. Henry Delfiner, *The Vienna Broadcasts to Slovakia, 1938-1939: A Case Study in Subversion* (New York and London, 1974), especially pp. 71–83.

69. Notes of R. H. Hadow in Vago, *The Shadow of the Swastika*, p. 324.

70. Telegram to the British Foreign Office, in ibid., pp. 335–36. On these refugees, see also Kurt R. Grossmann, "Refugees to and from Czechoslovakia," *The Jews of Czechoslovakia*, 2: 571–74.

71. Report of B. C. Newton to Lord Halifax in Vago, *The Shadow of the Swastika*, p. 370.

72. For the text, see Linnell's report to the U.S. Department of State in Kennan, *From Prague after Munich*, pp. 151–56.

73. Ibid., p. 150.

74. Bernhard Adolf, *Die Wirtschaft der Slowakei* (Prague, 1941), pp. 161–69, on economic measures. See also Yan Shteiner, " 'Hasine ha-nasi' shel dr Tiso," *Shvut* 3 (1975): 64-69. Details on the fate of Slovak Jewry are available in Hilberg, *The Destruction of the European Jews*, pp. 458–73.

75. Brod, *Haye meriva*, p. 251; David Merts, "Ha-'haavara' ha-chekhit—hatsala be-shaat tsara," in *Prag vi-yerushalayim*, ed. Weltsh, pp. 160–76.

76. *From Prague after Munich*, pp. 42–50.

77. Ibid.

78. The phrase is from Szporluk, *The Political Thought of Thomas Masaryk*, p. 147.

79. Jan Masaryk, *Minorities and the Democratic State* (London, 1943), p. 13.

## 4. Romania

1. For statistics, see Rothschild, *East Central Europe*, p. 284.

2. On the interwar period in general, see ibid., pp. 281–322; Henry Roberts, *Romania: Political Problems of an Agrarian State* (New Haven, 1951). On Romanian fascism, see Eugen Weber, "The Men of the Archangel," in *International Fascism, 1920–1945*, ed. Laqueur and Mosse, pp. 101–27; idem, "Romania," in *The European Right: A Historical Profile*, ed. Hans Rogger and Eugen Weber (Berkeley and Los Angeles, 1966), pp. 501–74. Another important study is Andrew Janos, "Modernization and Decay in Historical Perspective: The Case of Romania," in *Social Change in Romania, 1860-1940*, ed. Kenneth Jowitt (Berkeley and Los Angeles, 1978), pp. 72–116.

3. For the best general survey of Jewish history in interwar Romania, see Bela Vago, *Jews and Anti-Semitism in Interwar Romania, 1919-1940: Prologue to the Holocaust*, forthcoming.

4. For general studies of Regat Jewry, see Carol Iancu, *Les juifs en Roumanie 1866-1919. De l'exclusion à l'émancipation* (Provence, 1978); T. Lavi, "Toldot yehude ha-regat," in *Pinkas ha-kehilot, Romaniya*, 1 (Jerusalem, 1969): 19–224; the very interesting work of Yitshak Berkovich, *Pirke romaniya* (Tel Aviv, 1975). On Hasidism in Moldavia, see Yitshak Alfasi, *Ha-hasidut be-romaniya* (Tel Aviv, 1973), pp. 20–29.

5. Joshua Starr, "Jewish Citizenship in Rumania (1878-1940)." *Jewish Social Studies* 3 no. 1 (January 1941): 57–80.

6. Maurice Pearton, *Oil and the Rumanian State* (Oxford, 1971), p. 13; Janos, "Modernization and Decay," pp. 91–92.

7. Philip Gabriel Eidelberg, *The Great Rumanian Peasant Revolt of 1907* (Leiden, 1974), pp. 37–39.

8. William O. Oldson, *The Historical and Nationalistic Thought of Nicolae Iorga* (Boulder, 1973), p. 47. For more details on the attitude of this great savant and prominent politician toward the Jews, see Ana Kolombo, "Yorga ve-ha-yehudim," *Toladot* 6 (January-March 1972): 11–13.

9. Hugo Gold, ed., *Geschichte der Juden in der Bukowina*, vol. 1 (Tel Aviv, 1958); *Pinkas ha-kehilot, Romaniya*, 2 (Jerusalem, 1980): 419–32; Manfred Reifer, *Dr. Mayer Ebner. Ein jüdisches Leben*, (Tel Aviv, n.d.); Tsvi Yavets, "Chernovits ha-yehudit lifne ha-shoa," *Shvut* 2 (1973): 17–76; Alfasi, *Ha-hasidut*, pp. 30–34. On the especially favorable position of the Jews here see Robert Kann, *The Multinational Empire*, 1 (New York, 1970); 329–32.

10. See the collection of articles in *Yahadut besarabiya* (Jerusalem-Tel Aviv, 1971), especially Eliyahu Feldman, "Toldot ha-yehudim be-vesarabiya ad sof ha-mea ha-19," pp. 6–246. See also L. Kupershtein and Y. Korn, eds., *Pirke besarabiya*, vol. 1 (Tel Aviv, 1952); David Vinitski, *Besarabiya ha-yehudit be-maarakhoteha*, vols. 1-2 (Jerusalem-Tel Aviv, 1973). For the influence of Hasidism, see Alfasi, *Ha-hasidut*, pp. 35–40.

11. Vago, "Toldot yahadut transilvaniya ha-dromit," *Pinkas ha-kehilot, Romaniya*. 1: 261–71; idem, "Yahadut transilvaniya ha-tsfonit," ibid., 2: 3–56; Alfasi, *Ha-hasidut*, pp. 52–61, 102–06.

12. Leo Goldhamer, "Di yidn in rumenie," *Yidishe ekonomik* 2 (1938): 144; Wilhelm Filderman, *Adevărul asupra problemei Evreești din România in lumina textelor religioase și a statisticei* (Bucharest, 1925), pp. xi–xii. See also Vago, *Jews and Anti-Semitism*, pp. 22–53.

13. *Recensământul general al populației româniei din 29 Decemvrie 1930*, 2 (Bucharest, 1938): xxiv. The census data are also available in Charles Upson Clark, *Racial Aspects of Romania's Case* (n.p., 1941).

14. Vago, *Jews and Anti-Semitism*, pp. 39–45.

15. Details on the Jews' demographic situation in Bessarabia are available in Vinitski, *Besarabiya ha-yehudit*, 2: 391–410. See also *Pinkas ha-kehilot, Romaniya*, 2: 451–520, 323–416.

16. Goldhamer, "Di yidn," 146.

17. On Bessarabia, see Leshchinski, "Ha-yehudim be-vesarabiya ba-meot ha-19 ve-ha-20," *Yahadut besarabiya*, pp. 677–746; according to him, one-half of all the doctors in the capital of the province were Jews, and over 90 percent of the dentists (p. 727). An eyewitness account of Bessarabia in 1919 notes that trade in Bessarabia was monopolized by Jews; see Em. de Martonne, *What I Have Seen in Bessarabia* (Paris, 1919), pp. 38–39. See also Irina Livezeanu, "The Impact of Urbanization on Ethnic Processes in the Moldavian Soviet Republic" (unpublished paper, University of Michigan, 1979) p. 7. On Bukovina, see Hermann Sternberg, "Zur Geschichte der Juden in Czernowitz," *Geschichte der Juden in der Bukowina*, ed. Gold, 2 (Tel Aviv, 1962): 35–36.

18. Details on the Jews' economic structure in the Regat and in southern Transylvania are found in the article on Jewish communities in *Pinkas ha-kehilot, Romaniya*, 1: 3–256, 272–345. See also Vago, *Jews and Anti-Semitism*, pp. 62–63. On northern Transylvania, see *Pinkas ha-kehilot, Romaniya*, 2: 1–56, 59–275.

19. The data on language are taken from *Recensământul general*.

20. Dov Sadan, "Ben unikum le-kuriyoz," *Toladot* (1976): 1–4.

21. Yankev Botoshanski, *Mame yidish* (Buenos Aires, 1949), pp. 135–36.

22. Botoshanski in the literary journal *Likht* 1 (1918): 19.

23. For a comparison of the two patterns see Hugh Seton-Watson, "Two Contrasting Policies towards the Jews: Russia and Hungary," in *Jews and Non-Jews in Eastern Europe*, ed. Vago and Mosse, pp. 99–112.

24. N. M. Gelber, "The Problem of the Rumanian Jews at the Bucharest Peace Conference, 1918," *Jewish Social Studies* 12, no. 3 (July 1950): 223–46. See also Iancu, *Les juifs*, pp. 271–72.

25. Iancu, *Les juifs*, p. 274. The text is also published in Zsombor de Szász, *The Minorities in Romanian Transylvania* (London, 1927), p. 407.

26. Szász, *The Minorities*, p. 407; Iancu, *Les juifs*, pp. 274–75. See also the comments in Sherman David Spector, *Rumania at the Paris Peace Conference* (New York, 1962), pp. 217–19. The clauses in the Polish Minorities' Treaty specifically relating to the Jews were not included in the Romanian treaty.

27. "L'Histoire selon M. Bratiano: Documents," in *Bulletin du comité des délégations juives auprès de la conférence de la paix* 11 (19 February 1920): 12.

28. *Roumania Ten Years After* (Boston, 1929), p. 42. See also Starr, "Jewish Citizenship," pp. 66–67.

29. See *Paix et Droit* (10 December 1928) for a description of how Jews were discriminated against in these areas. On the ousting of Jews from the civil service in Bukovina, see Leshchinski, "Ha-yehudim be-vesarabiya," p. 726.

30. *Paix et Droit* (10 December 1922).

31. Ibid. (2 February 1923).

32. On this affair, see Manfred Reifer, *Dr. Mayer Ebner*, pp. 128–35; Gold, ed., *Geschichte der Juden in der Bukowina*, 2: 174–76. See also *Paix et Droit* (9 November 1926 and 10 December 1926).

33. *The Jewish Minority in Roumania: Further Correspondence with the Roumanian Government respecting the Grievances of the Jews* (London, 1928), p. 3.

34. Details in *Paix et Droit* (10 December 1927). See also the materials published by the Counseil pour les droits des minorités juives (Comité des délégations juives), *La situation de la minorité juive en Roumanie* (Paris, 1928).

35. "Appeal to the Rumanian People by the Central Jewish Organizations of Transylvania . . . ," *La situation de la minorité juive*, pp. 40–41.

36. *The Jewish Minority in Roumania*, p. 9.

37. "Declaration du senateur non-juif Romulus Boila . . . ," *La situation de la minorité juive en Roumanie*, p. 28.

38. Charles Upson Clark, *Bessarabia, Russia and Roumania on the Black Sea* (New York, 1927), pp. 239–64. Georges Tatarescu, *Bessarabie et Moscou* (Bucharest, 1926). On the anti-Semitic overtones of a trial of suspected Communists in Bucharest in 1922, see *Paix et Droit* (2 February 1922). See also Stephen Fischer-Galati, "Fascism, Communism, and the Jewish Question in Romania," in *Jews and Non-Jews in Eastern Europe*, ed. Vago and Mosse, pp. 157–76.

39. Janos, "Modernization and Decay in Historical Perspective," pp. 107–09.

40. *Paix et Droit* (2 February 1923). According to the same journal, in 1927 thirty-six professors at the University of Iaşi issued a proclamation deploring anti-Semitism (ibid. [5 May 1927]).

41. See the examples given by Livezeanu, "Sowing the Wind: Romanian Student Antisemitism in the 1920s" (unpublished paper, University of Michigan, 1980), p. 41.

42. Lavi, "Toldot yehude ha-regat"; Berkovich, *Pirke romaniya*, pp. 60–67; Shleyme Bikel, *Rumenie, geshikhte, literatur-kritik, zikhroynes* (Buenos Aires,

1961), pp. 21–24. Jean Ancel, *Yahadut romaniya ben 23.8. 1944 le-ven 30.2 1947* (Ph.D. diss., Hebrew University, 1979), pp. 52–6, 177–80.

43. *Paix et Droit* (9 November 1927).
44. *Ibid.* (5 May 1927).
45. *Ibid.* (9 November 1927).
46. Vinitski, *Besarabiya ha-yehudit*, 2: 413. On the Bund in Bukovina, see J. Kissman "Zur Geschichte der jüdischen Arbeiterbewegung 'Bund' in der Bukowina," *Geschichte der Juden in der Bukowina*, ed. Gold, 1: 129–40; Bikel, *Rumenie*, pp. 61–70.
47. On the Czernowitz conference, see Emanuel S. Goldsmith, *Architects of Yiddishism at the Beginning of the Twentieth Century* (Cranbury, N.J., 1976), pp. 183–222. On Straucher, see Reifer, *Mayer Ebner*, pp. 92–96; Chaim Erlich, "Zur Charakteristik der Zionistischen Bewegung in der Bukowina zwischen beiden Weltkriegen," in *Geschichte der Juden in der Bukowina*, ed. Gold, 2: 134–36.
48. Mordecai Slipoi, "Agudat yisrael be-vesarabiya," *Yahadut besarabiya*, pp. 869–80. On Tsirelson, see also Michael Landau, *Ishim u-zmanim* (Ramat-Gan, 1975), pp. 73–79.
49. There are a few remarks on this subject in Alfasi, *Ha-hasidut*. On the anti-Zionist campaign waged by the Rabbi of Tăşnad, a town in northern Transylvania not far from Satu-Mare, see Avraham Fuks, *Tăşnad* (Jerusalem, 1973), pp. 47–48.
50. See in general Vinitski, *Besarabiya ha-yehudit*, vol. 1; Yisrael Klauzner, "Ha-tnua ha-tsiyonit be-vesarabiya," *Yahadut besarabiya*, pp. 497–526; Landau, *Maavak hayei* (Ramat-Gan, 1970), pp. 45–50; *Sefer Bernshtein-Cohen* (Tel Aviv, 1946).
51. Erlich, "Zur Charakteristik," pp. 133–34; Reifer, *Dr. Mayer Ebner*, pp. 78–85.
52. Vago, "Toldot yehude transylvaniya ha-dromit," *Pinkas ha-kehilot, Romaniya*, 1: 261–71; idem, "Yahadut transilvaniya ha-tsfonit," ibid., 2: 7–9.
53. Lavi. "Toldot yehude ha-regat," pp. 58–61.
54. Berkovich, *Pirke romaniya*, pp. 124–39; Landau, *Maavak hayei*, pp. 19–50; Aryeh [Leon] Mizrahi, *Im dori u-maavakav* (Tel Aviv, 1970); Landau, "Ha-tnua ha-leumit ha-yehudit be-romaniya ba-mea ha-esrim," *Gesher* 1 (1957): 77–94; ibid. 2 (1957): 78–91; ibid. 3 (1957): 101–13.
55. Meir Zayit, ed., *Sipura shel tnua. Gordoniya—Makabi ha-tsair be-romaniya* (Tel Aviv, 1978), pp. 70–71.
56. On the Shomer, see David Goren, *Paamayim al safsal ha-neeshamim* (Tel Aviv, 1980); Shunya Dorfman, "Toldot ha-shomer ha-tsair be-romaniya," *Sefer ha-shomer ha-tsair*, 1 (Tel Aviv, 1956): 376–81. On the Pioneer, see Vinitski, *Besarabiya ha-yehudit*, 1: 175–286; Landau, *Ishim u-zmanim*, pp. 65–68.
57. Landau, *Ishim u-zmanim*, pp. 69–72; Jaakow Polesink-Padani, "Die Geschichte des 'Haschomer Hazair' in der Bukowina," in *Geschichte der Juden in der Bukowina*, ed. Gold, 1: 145–52; Landau, *Maavak hayei*, pp. 45–50; Vinitski, *Besarabiya ha-yehudit*, 1: 38 (on the conference).
58. See the comments by the Regat Zionist leader Aryeh (Leon) Mizrahi, *Im dori u-maavakav*, pp. 33–35, 47–56. Mizrahi was very critical of the anti-*Gegenwartsarbeit* tradition and championed a more Polish version of Zionism.
59. Details in Vinitski, *Besarabiya ha-yehudit*, 2: 413–15.
60. On Bukovina, see Reifer, "Geschichte der Juden in der Bukowina (1919-1944)," in *Geschichte der Juden in der Bukowina*, Gold, ed., 2: 1–4.
61. Vago, "The Jewish Vote in Romania between the Two World Wars," *Jewish Journal of Sociology* 14, no. 2 (1972): 232–33. The question of whom to

cooperate with sometimes created splits within this organization. Thus Filderman's preference for the Liberals was disliked by Adolf Stern; see Bikel, *Rumenie*, pp. 21–29.

62. Reifer, *Dr. Mayer Ebner*, p. 125; Vago, "The Jewish Vote in Romania," p. 235.

63. *Paix et Droit* (6 June 1927); ibid. (7 September 1927).

64. Ibid. (10 December 1928).

65. Ibid. (3 March 1929). On the formation of the bloc, see Landau, *Maavak hayei*, pp. 50–53.

66. Landau, *Maavak hayei*, p. 53.

67. Mizrahi, *Im dori u-maavakav*, pp. 96–97 (from an article written in 1927).

68. Text in Vinitski, *Besarabiya ha-yehudit*, 2: 633–35.

69. Landau, "Ha-tnua ha-leumit ha-yehudit be-romaniya," *Gesher* 2 (1957): 79–85. For the views of the radicals see the articles in Mizrahi, *Im dori u-maavakav*.

70. *Paix et Droit* (4 April 1929).

71. Vago, "The Jewish Vote in Romania," p. 237.

72. *Paix et Droit* (10 December 1934). The quotation is from Filderman.

73. Figures in Vago, "The Jewish Vote in Romania," pp. 237–41, and in Vinitski, *Besarabiya ha-yehudit*, 2: 479–81.

74. Vago, "The Jewish Vote in Romania," pp. 239–41; Vinitski, *Besarabiya ha-yehudit*, 2: 485–87.

75. Vinitski, *Besarabiya ha-yehudit*, 2: 481.

76. Vago, "The Jewish Vote in Romania." On Jews in the Communist Party, see the remarks in Ancel, *Yahadut romaniya*, pp. 197–204, 243; Ancel writes that "the Communist Party between the wars was based mainly on Jewish activists" (p. 243). See also Stephen Fischer-Galati, "The Radical Left and Assimilation: The Case of Romania," in *Jewish Assimilation in Modern Times*, ed. Bela Vago (Boulder, 1981), pp. 89–103, where the author generally plays down the importance of Jews in the Communist Party, stating that ". . . in fact, neither the number nor the influence of the Jewish members in the Communist party itself or in its top echelons overrode that of other nationalities, although it is fair to say that the intellectual wing of the party was dominated by Jews" (p. 91).

77. His role in the late 1930s and 1940s is reviewed in Ancel, *Yahadut romaniya*, pp. 170–80.

78. The figures are from Vinitski, *Besarabiya ha-yehudit*, 2: 515–16.

79. Ibid., pp. 565, 606. On the Yiddish schools, see the article in the *Algemayne entsiklopedie* (New York, 1943), 3: 405–06.

80. Menachem Brayer, "Toldot ha-hinukh ha-ivri be-romaniya," in *Ha-hinukh ve-ha-tarbut ha-ivrit be-iropa ben shte milhamot ha-olam*, ed. Tsvi Sharfstein (New York, 1957), p. 231.

81. Brayer, "Ha-hinukh ha-ivri be-vukovina," in *Ha-hinukh ve-ha-tarbut*, ed Sharfshtein pp. 248–72.

82. For evidence on the latter point, see *The Grievances of the Hungarian Minority in Roumania* 1 (1919-1922), (n.p., 1922), p. 23. We read here that "Josip Moldovan the Arad School Superintendent informed the Jewish Community that the Jewish schools at Arad would not be allowed to use Hungarian as the language of tuition, as according to the regulations in force they must adopt either the Yiddish-Hebrew language [*sic*] as the language of the Jewish minority, or else the Roumanian language and the further use of the Hungarian language would be prohibited."

83. Shlomo Yitshaki, *Bate sefer yehudiim be-transilvaniya ben shte milhamot*

*ha-olam* (Jerusalem, 1970). Brayer, "Ha-yeshivot be-romaniya," in *Mosdot tora be-iropa be-vinyanam u-ve-horbanam*, ed. Mirski, pp. 517-60.

84. Berkovich, *Pirke romaniya*, pp. 140–53; Brayer, "Toldot ha-hinukh ha-ivri be-romaniya."

85. Meir Zayit, "Ha-itonut ha-yehudit be-romaniya," in *Itonut yehudit she-hayta*, ed Yehuda Gothelf et al. (Tel Aviv, 1973), pp. 457–72.

86. See the introduction by Avraham Feler to the Hebrew version of Bikel's book *Rumenie, Yahadut romaniya* (Tel Aviv, 1978), p. ix. On the Yiddish cultural scene, see Bikel, *Rumenie*; Botoshanski, *Mame yidish*.

87. Yitshaki, *Bate sefer yehudiim*, p. 146; Brayer, "Ha-hinukh ha-ivri be-vukovina," *passim*.

88. See the anthology *Shorashim ve-saar*, ed. by K. A. Bartini, A. B. Yafe, and Dora Litman-Litani (Tel Aviv, 1972).

89. Corneliu Zelea Codreanu, *Eiserne Garde* (Berlin, 1939), p. 71. On the strength of the movement in different regions of the country, see Weber, "The Men of the Archangel," pp. 110–14.

90. A. L. Easterman, *King Carol, Hitler, and Lupescu* (London, 1942), pp. 229–30.

91. *Paix et Droit* (5 May 1933).

92. Ibid. (1 January 1936). For the reaction of the UER, see ibid. (2 February 1935); for Vaida-Voevod's remarks see, ibid. (5 May 1935). Vaida-Voevod, who left the National Peasant Party in 1934 and subsequently established the right-wing Romanian Front, was well known for his advocacy of a *"numerus vallachicus,"* which aimed at increasing Romanian participation in the economy at the expense of the Jews.

93. Quoted in a communication from R. Hoare to A. Eden, 23 April 1936, in Vago, *The Shadow of the Swastika*, pp. 176–77.

94. Easterman, *King Carol*, pp. 260–61.

95. Vago, *The Shadow of the Swastika*, p. 224 (from a communication from Hoare to Eden, 19 May 1937).

96. Easterman, *King Carol*, p. 95. See also, for a similar interpretation, Hector Bolitho, *Roumania under King Carol* (New York, 1940), p. 43.

97. Hoare to Eden, 19 January 1938, in Vago, *The Shadow of the Swastika*, p. 268.

98. *Paix et Droit* (7 September 1935) summarizes the Goga-Cuza program as of 1935, the year when these two leaders joined forces in establishing the National Christian Party.

99. Quoted in *Politics and Political Parties in Roumania* (London, 1936), p. 176, from the 1935 platform of the National Christian Party.

100. *Paix et Droit* 1 (January 1938); ibid. 2 (February 1938); Vago, "Ha-mediniyut ha-yehudit shel ha-diktatura ha-malkhutit be-romaniya (1938-1940)," *Tsiyon* 29 (1964): 133–37; Starr, "Jewish Citizenship in Rumania," pp. 72–73; *Pinkas ha-kehilot, Romaniya*, 1, table on anti-Semitic decrees, pp. 168–69.

101. Hoare to Halifax, 15 June 1938, in Vago, *The Shadow of the Swastika*, p. 412.

102. Starr, "Jewish Citizenship in Rumania," p. 76. See also Hilberg, *The Destruction of the European Jews* p. 488.

103. The quotations are from Vago, "Ha-mediniyut ha-yehudit," pp. 149, 150. For details, see Hilberg, *The Destruction of the European Jews*, pp. 488–89; the table in *Pinkas ha-kehilot, Romaniya*, 1: 168–69; Fischer-Galati, "Fascism, Communism, and the Jewish Question," pp. 168–70.

104. Leshchinski, "Ha-yehudim be-vesarabiya ba-meot ha-19 ve-ha-20," pp.

707–32. On Bukovina, see Reifer, "Geschichte der Juden," in *Geschichte der Juden in der Bukowina*, ed. Gold, 2: 8–9; the article by Steinberg on Czernowitz in the same volume, pp. 39, 42–43. For details on the Jewish economic crisis in a small town in Bessarabia, see K. A. Bartini, *Pinkas britshiva* (Tel Aviv, 1970). On Jewish cooperative ventures as a means to struggle against pauperization, see Moshe Ussoskin, *Maavak le-kiyum* (Jerusalem, 1975).

105. Details on these and other towns in Transylvania in *Pinkas ha-kehilot, Romaniya*, 1: 272–345. On Bessarabia, see Lavi, "Yehude besarabiya tahat ha-shilton ha-romani ben shte milhamot ha-olam (1918-1940)," in *Yahadut besarabiya*, pp. 337–41.

106. *Pinkas ha-kehilot, Romaniya*, 1: 60 (on Bucharest); ibid., *passim* (on Moldavia). See also Israel Cohen, *The Jews in Rumania* (London, 1938).

107. *Paix et Droit* (2 February 1939).

108. See Efraim Ofir, "Al aliya bet mi-romaniya ve-darka (1938-1941)," *Yalkut Moreshet* 31 (April 1981):39–74.

109. *Encyclopedia of Zionism and Israel*, 2: 959; *Ha-kongres ha-tsiyoni ha-21, din ve-heshbon stenografi* (Jerusalem, 1939).

110. The figures are from the article on Romania in *Encyclopedia Judaica*, 14: 404. On this period, see Hilberg, *The Destruction*, pp. 488–509; Ancel, *Yahadut romaniya*; Vago, "The Ambiguity of Collaborationism: The Center of the Jews in Romania (1942-1944)," in *Patterns of Jewish Leadership in Nazi Europe, 1933-1945*, ed. Yisrael Gutman and Cynthia Heft (Jerusalem, 1979) pp. 287–309.

## 5. Lithuania

1. For general information on Lithuania, see Alfred Erich Senn, *The Emergence of Modern Lithuania* (New York, 1959); idem, *The Great Powers: Lithuania and the Vilna Question, 1920-1928* (Leiden, 1966); idem, *Basanavicius: The Patriarch of the Lithuanian National Renaissance* (Newtonville, 1980); Manfred Hellmann, *Grundzüge der Geschichte Litauens und des litauischen Volkes* (Darmstadt, 1966).

2. Rothschild, *East Central Europe*, p. 377.

3. See the material on the Lithuanian Jews of the Polish kresy, above, pp. 21–22, and the general article by Yaakov Robinson, "Yahadut lita ha-atsmait ba-aspaklariya ha-historit ve-ha-hashvaatit," *Yahadut lita*, 2 (Tel Aviv, 1972): 26–28.

4. See, however, the remarks in Azriel Shohat, "The Beginnings of Anti-Semitism in Independent Lithuania," *Yad Washem Studies* 2 (1958): 7–9.

5. For details, see Mendelsohn, *Zionism in Poland*, pp. 101–04. See also Leib Garfunkel, "Maavakam shel yehude lita al zekhuiyot leumiyot," *Yahadut lita*, 2: 35–72.

6. Mendelsohn, *Zionism in Poland*, p. 102. The quotation is from "Die erste Landeskonferenz der Zionisten Litauens," in the Central Zionist Archives, Jerusalem, Z3/135, pp. 1–2.

7. Mendelsohn, *Zionism in Poland*, pp. 102–03.

8. "La Lithuanie accorde aux juifs l'autonomie nationale," *Bulletin du comité des délégations juives auprès de la conférence de la paix* 6 (18 September 1919).

9. For an example of enthusiasm in Jewish national circles, see "La Lithuanie veut tenir ses engagements relatifs à l'autonomie des minorités nationales," *Bulletin du comité* 16 (18 August 1920).

10. Details in *Tsirkular-briv No. 1* (20 June 1919) issued by the *Biuro fun minister far idishe ongelegenhaytn in Kaunas*.

11. Ibid.

12. "Le président du conseil lithuanien sur l'autonomie en Lithuanie," *Bulletin du comité* 12 (16 March 1920).

13. Garfunkel, "Maavakam shel yehude lita," p. 43. The law is also summarized in Samuel Gringauz, "Jewish National Autonomy in Lithuania (1918-1925)," *Jewish Social Studies* 14, no. 3 (July 1952): 235.

14. See above, n. 9.

15. *In Shturm* (Vilna, 1926), p. 200, quoted in Mendelsohn, *Zionism in Poland*, p. 104.

16. "Rezolutsie vegn vilne," in *Der yidisher natsional rat in lite. Barikht vegen zayn tetikeyt 1920-1922* (Kaunas, 1922), pp. 7–8. On Jewish efforts on behalf of Lithuania, and especially for the important role of Rosenbaum, see Garfunkel, "Maavakam shel yehude lita."

17. See "Déclaration de M. Soloweitchik," *Bulletin du comité* 21 (3 September 1921). The Jewish Minister also noted that "several non-Jewish parliamentarians understand this language [Yiddish]."

18. For details, see Garfunkel, "Maavakam shel yehude lita"; Gringauz, "Jewish National Autonomy." On the constitution of 1922 and the minorities, see *Bulletin du comité* 23 (13 August 1922): 1.

19. "La deuxième conférence des communautés juives de Lithuanie," *Bulletin du comité* 23 (13 August 1922).

20. See the remarks of Leo Motzkin, a leading Zionist and champion of Jewish national autonomy, in ibid., pp. 9–11, and of the American Jewish Congress, also in ibid., p. 12. On the resignation of Soloveitshik, see Garfunkel, "Maavakam shel yehude lita," p. 62; Gringauz, "Jewish National Autonomy," pp. 237–38. For details on the steps taken in 1923, see "La violation des droits des juifs en Lithuanie," *Bulletin du comité* 25 (15 May 1923). On the new kehile law see Mark Friedman, "The Kehillah in Lithuania 1919-1926: A Study Based on Panevezys and Ukmerge (Vilkomir)," *Soviet Jewish Affairs* 6, no. 2 (1976): 101–02. For general remarks on the demise of autonomy, see Garfunkel, "Me-igra rama le-bira amikta," *Yahadut lita*, 2: 28–34. See also *Barikht fun der yidisher seymfraktsie fun II litvishn seym (1923-1926)* (Kaunas, 1926).

21. *Bulletin du comité* 21 (3 September 1921): 3–4.

22. "Le président du conseil lithuanien sur l'autonomie en Lithuanie," ibid. 12 (16 March 1920).

23. See below, pp. 232–34. Another important Jewish institution which flourished throughout the interwar period was the co-operative bank; see Gringauz, "Jewish National Autonomy."

24. L. Hersh, "Tsu der demografie fun der yidisher bafelkerung in kovner lite erev der tsvayter velt-milkhome," *Yivo bleter* 34, (1950): 274–76. See also "The Jews of Lithuania, 1923," *American Jewish Yearbook* 32 (1930):276–80; Leshchinski, "Ha-kalkala ve-ha-demografiya shel yahadut lita (1919-1939)," *Yahadut lita*, 2: 91–100.

25. Leshchinski, "Ha-kalkala."

26. "Yidishe emigratsie fun lite," *Yidishe ekonomik* 2 (1938):86–87.

27. Hersh, "Tsu der demografie," p. 276.

28. Leshchinski, "Ha-kalkala." For slightly different figures, see Mintsen, "Handl un industrie bay yidn in lite," *Bleter far yidishe demografie, statistik, un ekonomik* 5 (1925):110–15. See also M. Lindner, "Yidishe mlokhe in lite," *Yidishe ekonomik* 3 (1939):1–8.

29. Hersh, "Tsu der demografie," p. 274.

30. Dov Levin, "The Jews in the Soviet Lithuanian Establishment, 1940–41," *Soviet Jewish Affairs* 10, no. 2 (May 1980): 24. Of course, there were not many Communists in Lithuania; see below p. 232.

31. See the remarks of Garfunkel, "Ha-yehudim ba-seimim ha-litaiim," *Yahadut lita*, 2: 73.

32. See the collection of articles "Miflagot u-tnuot" on the various political parties in *Yahadut lita*, 2: 189–246.

33. Gringauz, "Jewish National Autonomy," pp. 243–46.

34. Garfunkel, "Maavakam shel yehude lita," pp. 43–45. See also the material in *Der yidisher natsional rat in lite*.

35. Garfunkel, "Ha-yehudim ba-seimim."

36. *Ibid.* See also *Der yidisher natsional rat in lite*.

37. Details in Garfunkel, "Maavakam shel yehude lita," pp. 52–55.

38. See the accusations of the Zionists in *Barikht fun der yidisher seym-fraktsie fun II litvishn seym (1923-1926)* (Kaunas, 1926), pp. 12–13. For details, see also Levin, " 'Ahdes' be-tsel pilug—'ha-reshima ha-kalkalit-datit ha-yehudit' la-seim ha-shlishi be-lita ha-demokratit (1926)," in *Mikhael* 6 (1980):69–73 (Hebrew section).

39. Gringauz, "Jewish National Autonomy," p. 239. For details see Garfunkel, "Maavakam shel yehude lita," pp. 64–66.

40. *Barikht fun der yidisher saym-fraktsie*, 14–28.

41. Ibid., p. 35 (for the quotation) and pp. 31–53. See also Levin, "Ahdes be-tsel pilug."

42. Levin, "Ahdes be-tsel pilug," pp. 95, 97–98.

43. Yaakov Amit, " 'Ha-shomer ha-tsair,' " *Yahadut lita*, 2: 203–06.

44. Pesah Rudnik, "'Gordoniya'," ibid., pp. 211–14; Mordechai Kats, "Ha-tnua ha-reviziyonistit be-lita," ibid., p. 222; Mordechai Elyashiv, "Tnuat 'he-haluts' be-lita", ibid., pp. 236–39.

45. David Reznik, "Ha-'mizrahi' u-tnuat 'tora va-avoda' be-lita," ibid., pp. 215–17; Kats, "Ha-tnua ha-reviziyonistit," pp. 218–25.

46. Figures in *Ha-Kongres ha-tsiyoni ha-19, . . . din ve-heshbon stinografi* (Jerusalem, 1935), pp. xvii–xviii.

47. For details, see the article "Zionism in Lithuania" in *Encyclopedia of Zionism and Israel*, (New York, 1971), 2:726–67.

48. David Cohen, "Im ha-halutsim be-lita," *Yahadut lita*, 2: 241.

49. Levin, "The Jews in the Soviet Lithuanian Establishment," p. 24.

50. For material on Jewish literary life see the articles in *Lite*, ed. Mendl Sudarski et al., 1 (New York, 1951): 1015–1118.

51. Elyohu Meyer Blokh, "Di telzer yeshive," in *Lite*, ed. Sudarski et al., 1:629. See in general ibid., pp. 483–690; Gedaliya Alon, "Yeshivot lita," in *Kehilot yisrael she-nehravu* (Tel Aviv, 1944), pp. 91–99; M. Gifter, "yeshivat telz," in *Mosdot tora be-iropa*, ed. Mirski, pp. 133–68.

52. Yudel Mark, "Bet ha-sefer ha-idi be-lita ha-atsmait," *Yahadut lita*, 2: 166–96. Also Elyohu Shulman, "Di yidishe veltlekhe shuln in lite," in *Lite*, ed. H. Laykovich, 2 (Tel Aviv, 1965): 323–50.

53. Yitshak-Refael Ha-levi Etsion, "Ha-zerem ha-hinukhi 'yavne' be-lita," *Yahadut Lita*, 2: 160–65.

54. Dov Lipets, "Ha-hinukh ha-ivri ve-ha-tnua ha-ivrit be-lita ha-atsmait," ibid., pp. 113–29; the figures are from p. 119. There is a great deal of material on these Hebrew schools; see the articles in ibid., pp. 132–59.

55. See above, p. 66 for the relevant Polish figures.

56. Lipets, "Ha-hinuch ha-ivri," pp. 115–17.

57. Ibid., p. 117. See also "Yidishe kinder in di folkshuln fun lite," *Yidishe ekonomik* 2 (1938):285.

58. Shohat, "The Beginnings of Anti-Semitism," pp. 7–48.

59. "The Economic Struggle of the Jews in Independent Lithuania," *Jewish Social Studies* 8, no. 4 (1946):276.

60. Ibid., p. 281. See also Lindner, "Yidishe mlokhe in lite."

61. Leshchinski, "The Economic Struggle," p. 285.

62. Ibid., pp. 292–93.

63. Levin, "The Jews in the Soviet Lithuanian Establishment," pp. 27–37.

64. Levin, "Be-khaf ha-kele," *Yahadut lita*, 2: 349–52; Shohat, "Jews, Lithuanians, and Russians, 1939-1941," in *Jews and Non-Jews in Eastern Europe*, ed. Vago and Mosse, pp. 301–14.

## 6. Latvia and Estonia

1. On interwar Latvia, see Rothschild, *East Central Europe*, pp. 367–81; Alfred Bilmanis, *A History of Latvia* (Princeton, 1951).

2. For general surveys of the Jewries which together constituted the Jewish community of Latvia, see Mendel Bobe, "Four Hundred Years of the Jews in Latvia," in *The Jews in Latvia* (Tel Aviv, 1971), pp. 21–77; Bobe, *Yidn in letland* (Tel Aviv, 1972), pp. 9–122; Avraham Itay and Mordecai Nayshtat, *Koroteha shel tnua, netsah be-latviya* (Tel Aviv, 1972), pp. 17–32.

3. Abraham Godin, "Jewish Traditional and Religious Life in the Latvian Communities," in *The Jews in Latvia*, pp. 217–21; Shaul Lipshitz, "The Jewish Communities in Kurland," in ibid., pp. 276–84; Aryeh Tartakover, Yitshak Refael, Mendel Bobe, eds., *Zekher Mordechai. Mukdash le-hayav u-faalo shel ha-rav Mordechai Nurok zikhrono levrakha* (Jerusalem, 1967), pp. 56–57.

4. Bobe, "Riga," in *The Jews in Latvia*, pp. 243–61.

5. "The Jews of Latvia: Census of 1925," *American Jewish Yearbook* 32 (1930):266–67. For additional statistical material, see M. Shats-Anin, *Di yidn in letland* (Riga, 1924): Bobe, "Yahadut latviya be-misparim," in *Yahadut latviya, sefer zikaron*, ed. B. Eliyav, A. Kremer, and M. Bobe (Tel Aviv, 1953), pp. 18–29.

6. The figures for Courland and Latgalia are from Anin, *Di yidn in letland*, p. 16, and refer to the year 1920; the figures on Riga refer to the year 1925.

7. Bobe, "Yehude latviya be-misparim," p. 21. On the low natural increase of Latvian Jewry (in 1934 it was zero), see ibid., p. 25. For emigration figures, see ibid., p. 27.

8. "The Jews of Latvia: Census of 1925," pp. 269–70.

9. Anin, *Di yidn in letland*, p. 63. See also B. Sieff, "Jews in the Economic Life of Latvia," in *The Jews in Latvia*, pp. 230–42.

10. Anin, *Di yidn in letland*, p. 70.

11. *Annuaire statistique de la Lettonie pour l'année 1930* (Riga, 1931). In Riga 42,328 Jews declared themselves Jews by nationality, while only 41,586 declared themselves Jews by religion. We may assume that some of the Jews by nationality who did not register as Jews by religion were Bundists or members of Poale Zion.

12. Bobe, "Yehude latviya be-misparim," p. 26.

13. Bobe, *Yidn in letland*, pp. 125–26.

14. M. Laserson, "The Jews and the Latvian Parliament," in *The Jews in Latvia*, pp. 94–185; Z. Michaeli, "Jewish Cultural Autonomy and the Jewish

School Systems," in ibid., pp. 186–216; Bobe, *Yidn in letland*, pp. 131–33. For a Jewish critique of Latvian policy, see "La politique anti-juive de la Lettonie," *Bulletin du comité des délégations juives auprès de la conférence de la paix* 22 (9 January 1922): 1–3.

15. Y. Levin-Shatskes, "Noah Meizel—shaliah ha-tsibur shel ha-'bund' be-latviya," in *Yahadut latviya* ed. Eliyav, Kremer, and Bode, pp. 62–73.

16. See the description of him in Bobe, *Yidn in letland*, pp. 147–48.

17. See the book devoted to him, *Zekher Mordechai*.

18. H. Ben-Yeruham, *Sefer betar* (Jerusalem and Tel Aviv, 1969), pp. 30–54; Schechtman and Benari, *History of the Revisionist Movement*, 1: 21–25.

19. On Ha-shomer ha-tsair, see the excellent book by Itay and Nayshtat, *Koroteha shel tnua*.

20. During the Jewish year 1926–1927 only 4,250 shekels were sold, but by 1932–1933 this figure had increased dramatically to 22,246. The figures are in *Protokoll der Verhandlungen des XV Zionisten-Kongresses* (London, 1927), p. xviii, and in *Protokoll der Verhandlungen des XVIII Zionisten-Kongresses . . .* (Vienna, 1933), p. 18.

21. See the article on Latvia in *Encyclopedia of Zionism and Israel*, 2: 705–06.

22. On Schiemann's views, see Michael Garleff, "Paul Schiemanns Min-derheitentheorie als Beitrag zur Lösung der Nationalitätenfrage, *Zeitschrift für Ostforschuung* 25 (1976): 632–60.

23. Quoted in Laserson, "The Jews and the Latvian Parliament," pp. 161–62.

24. Bobe, *Yidn in letland*, pp. 186–88. See also Itay and Nayshtat, *Koroteha shel tnua*, pp. 166–76.

25. Michaeli, "Jewish Cultural Autonomy and the Jewish School Systems," p. 11.

26. See the report on this town in *Yidishe shul bavegung in letland* (Riga, 1926), p. 49.

27. *Yidishe shul bavegung*, p. 60; Mendel Mark, "A kurtser iberblik iber der yidisher shul in letland," *Yivo bleter* 44 (1973): 233.

28. Michaelis, "Jewish Cultural Autonomy and the Jewish School System," p. 195; this was the case, so the author claims, in Riga.

29. Mark, "A kurtser iberblik," p. 236; *Yidishe shul bavegung*, pp. 41–43.

30. Leshchinski, "Dos yidishe kultur-lebn in letland," *Yidishe ekonomik* 1 (1937):31.

31. Ibid., p. 32.

32. See, for example, the description of the Jewish reaction in Levin-Shatskes, "Noah Meizel," p. 164. See also Itay and Nayshtat, *Koroteha shel tnua*, p. 171.

33. Bobe, *Yidn in letland*, 186–88; Dov Levin, "Yehude latviya ben histeigut le-ven histaglut la-mishtar ha-sovieti," *Behinot* 5 (1974): 73–74; Levin-Shatskes, "Noah Meizel," p. 164.

34. Leshchinski, "Dos yidishe kultur-lebn," p. 50. In 1920–1921, 15.7% of all students at the University of Riga were Jews; by 1935–1936 the percentage had dropped to 7.1.

35. Levin, "Yehude latviya."

36. For general surveys, see E. Amitan-Wilensky, "Estonian Jewry," in *The Jews of Latvia*, pp. 336–47; Emanuel Nodel, "Life and Death of Estonian Jewry," in *Baltic History*, ed. A. Ziedonis, W. Winter, and M. Valgemae (Cleveland, 1973), pp. 227–36.

37. For a description of Jewish autonomy in Estonia, see Max Laserson, "The Jewish Minorities in the Baltic Countries," *Jewish Social Studies* 3, no. 3 (July 1941):276–77.

# Bibliographical Essay

Serious research on the Jews of East Central Europe between the wars is still in its early stages, and although a fair amount has been written on this subject in Hebrew and in Yiddish, as well as in German and in the local East European languages, scholarly books and articles in English are few and far between. I have listed the major English-language publications in my bibliography, *Yehude mizrah-merkaz iropa ben shte milhamot ha-olam, bibliografiya nivheret* [*The Jews of East Central Europe between the Two World Wars: A Selected Bibliography*], published by the Zalman Shazar Center (Jerusalem, 1978). Aside from my own book there is only one other general survey of Jewish history in the lands between Germany and the Soviet Union—a collection of essays by different hands in Hebrew, edited by Yaakov Tsur, *Ha-tfutsot: mizrah iropa* [*The Diaspora: Eastern Europe*] (Jerusalem, 1975). Two other important collections of essays devoted to various aspects of Jewish history in this region are Bela Vago and George Mosse, eds., *Jews and Non-Jews in Eastern Europe, 1918-1945* (New York, 1974), which includes a survey of the period by Shmuel Ettinger; and Bela Vago, ed., *Jewish Assimilation in Modern Times* (Boulder, 1981). Also worthy of mention is Bela Vago's book *The Shadow of the Swastika: The Rise of Fascism and Anti-Semitism in the Danube Basin, 1936-1939* (London, 1975), which contains a good deal of primary material on the anti-Jewish movement in the region. A much older monograph with material on anti-Semitism in East Central Europe is Oscar Janowsky, *People at Bay: The Jewish Problem in East Central Europe* (London, 1938). A valuable work on the question of Jewish minority rights in the region is Jacob Robinson, Oscar Karbach, and Max Laserson, *Were the Minorities' Treaties a Failure?* (New York, 1943).

There are a few articles dealing with the general subject of Jewish history in East Central Europe, among them my study "Jewish Leadership between the Two World Wars," in *Patterns of Jewish Leadership in Nazi Europe, 1933-1945*, ed. Yisrael Gutman and Cynthia Haft (Jerusalem, 1979), pp. 1–12, and Bela Vago, "The Attitude Towards the Jews as a Criterion of the Left-Right Concept," in *Jews and Non-Jews in Eastern Europe*, ed. Vago and Mosse, pp. 21–50. Articles comparing the Jewish fate in several of the countries of the region are uncommon, but the reader may be referred to the recently published research of Antony Polonsky and Michael Riff on the Jewish question in Poland and Czechoslovakia in Volker Berghahn and Martin Kitchen, eds., *Germany in the Age of Total War: Essays in Honor of Francis Carsten* (London, 1981). Another interesting comparative study is Hugh Seton-Watson, "Two Contrasting Policies Towards the Jews: Russia and Hungary," in *Jews and Non-Jews in Eastern Europe*, ed. Vago and Mosse, pp. 99–112.

It is natural that interwar Polish Jewry, over three million strong, has attracted more scholarly attention than any of the other Jewish communities of East Central Europe. Even so, the situation is far from satisfactory. There is only one general scholarly study in English—Celia Heller, *On the Edge of Destruction:*

*Jews of Poland between the Two World Wars* (New York, 1977). This book is certainly preferable to the earlier study by Harry Rabinowicz, *The Legacy of Polish Jewry* (New York, 1965), but it suffers from being based largely on secondary materials which are not always accurate guides to the subject. Another general study, emphasizing anti-Semitism, is the French-language book by Pawel Korzec, *Juifs en Pologne. La question juive pendant l'entre-deux-guerres* (Paris, 1980). There are two book length studies of Jewish politics in Poland—my own, *Zionism in Poland, 1915-1926: The Formative Years* (New Haven and London, 1981), and Bernard Johnpoll, *The Politics of Futility: The General Jewish Workers Bund of Poland 1917-1943* (Ithaca, 1967). A useful collection of articles on interwar Polish Jewry, some of which are in English and others in Yiddish, is Joshua Fishman, ed., *Studies on Polish Jewry, 1919-1939* (New York, 1974). Other book-length studies in English deserving of mention are Simon Segal's discussion of anti-Semitism in *The New Poland and the Jews* (New York, 1938); William Glickson, *A Kehillah in Poland During the Inter-War Years* (Philadelphia, 1969); William Glickson, *In the Mirror of Literature* (New York, 1966), which is a discussion of the Jews in Polish literature, and Miriam Eisenstein, *Jewish Schools in Poland* (New York, 1950). There is also the biography by Israel Biderman, *Mayer Balaban: Historian of Polish Jewry* (New York, 1976).

The number of scholarly articles on Jewish life in interwar Poland is also not impressive. For statistics on Jewish demography, the reader can consult Szyja Bronsztejn, "The Jewish Population of Poland in 1931," *Jewish Journal of Sociology* 6, no. 1 (July 1964):3–29, and Jacob Lestchinsky [Leshchinski], "The Jews in the Cities of the Republic of Poland," *Yivo Annual of Jewish Social Science* 1 (1946):156–77. Material on the Jews' economic situation is found in the following studies: Jacob Lestchinsky, "Economic Aspects of Jewish Community Organization in Independent Poland," *Jewish Social Studies* 9, no. 4 (October 1947): 319–38; Jacob Lestchinsky, "The Industrial and Social Structure of the Jewish Population of Interbellum Poland," *Yivo Annual of Jewish Social Science* 11 (1956/57):243–269; Raphael [Refael] Mahler, "Jews in Public Service and the Liberal Professions in Poland, 1918-1939," *Jewish Social Studies* 6, no. 4 (October 1944):291–350.

The subject of anti-Semitism is better represented. Particularly important are the following articles: Edward Wynot, " 'A Necessary Cruelty': The Emergence of Official Antisemitism in Poland, 1936–39," *American Historical Review* 76, no. 4 (October 1971):1035–58; Pawel Korzec, "Antisemitism in Poland as an Intellectual, Social and Political Movement," in *Studies on Polish Jewry*, ed. Fishman, pp. 12–104; Joel Cang, "The Opposition Parties in Poland and Their Attitude Towards the Jews and the Jewish Question," *Jewish Social Studies* 1, no. 2 (April 1939): 241–56; Leni Yahil, "Madagascar: Phantom of a Solution for the Jewish Question," in *Jews and Non-Jews in Eastern Europe*, ed. Vago and Mosse, pp. 315–34; Pawel Korzec, "The Steiger Affair," *Soviet Jewish Affairs* 3, no. 2 (1973): 38–57; Jacob Lestchinsky, "The Anti-Jewish Program: Tsarist Russia, the Third Reich, and Independent Poland," *Jewish Social Studies* 3, no. 2 (April 1941): 141–58. A new and very important book-length study in German is Frank Golczewski, *Polnisch-Jüdische Beziehungen 1881-1922* (Wiesbaden, 1981).

So far as Jewish politics in Poland are concerned, the reader may be referred to my articles, "The Dilemma of Jewish Politics in Poland: Four Responses," in *Jews and Non-Jews in Eastern Europe*, ed. Vago and Mosse, pp. 203–20; "The Politics of Agudas Yisroel in Inter-War Poland," *Soviet Jewish Affairs* 2, no. 2 (1972):47–60; "Reflections on the 'Ugoda,' " in *Sefer Refael Mahler* (Merhaviya, 1974), pp. 87–102; and "Polish Zionism between Two Wars," *Dispersion and*

*Unity* 17-18 (1973):81–87. A very useful study of the Folkist Party is Mark Kiel, "The Ideology of the Folks-Partey," *Soviet Jewish Affairs* 5, no. 2 (1975):75–89. An interesting general study is Leonard Rowe, "Politics under Stress: The Jewish Response in Poland," *Bennington* Review 4 (Spring, 1968). An important contribution to the literature is the work by Gershon Bacon, *Agudath Israel in Poland, 1916-39: An Orthodox Jewish Response to the Challenge of Modernity* (Ph.D. diss., Columbia University, 1979); this is the first full-length study of an important but much neglected political force in interbellum Poland.

The following articles on various aspects of Polish Jewish cultural life can be recommended: Phillip Friedman, "Polish Jewish Historiography between the Two World Wars (1919–1939)," *Jewish Social Studies* 11, no. 4 (October 1949):373–408; and Nathan Eck, "The Educational Institutions of Polish Jewry (1921-1934)," *Jewish Social Studies* 9, no. 1 (January 1947):3–32. The Jewish reaction to growing anti-Semitism in the 1930s is the subject of Leonard Rowe, "Jewish Self-Defense: A Response to Violence," in *Studies on Polish Jewry*, ed. Fishman, pp. 105–49. Finally, no one interested in interwar Polish Jewry should overlook the valuable collection of photographs edited by Lucjan Dobroszycki and Barbara Kirshenblatt-Gimblett, *Image before My Eyes: A Photographic History of Jewish Life in Poland, 1864-1939* (New York, 1977).

The literature in English on Hungarian Jewry has been greatly enriched by the recent appearance of two books on the subject. Randolph Braham has published a major study, *The Politics of Genocide: The Holocaust in Hungary*, 2 vols. (New York, 1981); despite the title, the first volume deals extensively with the interwar years. Less extensive, but also of importance, is Nathaniel Katzburg, *Hungary and the Jews, 1920-1943* (Ramat-Gan, 1981), which concentrates on the various Hungarian governments' attitude toward the "Jewish question." The reader should also consult the essays by different hands edited by Randolph Braham, *Hungarian-Jewish Studies*, 2 vols. (New York, 1966, 1969), and the very interesting monograph by William McCagg, *Jewish Nobles and Geniuses in Modern Hungary* (Boulder, 1972). The latter book, unlike the new studies of Braham and Katzburg, emphasizes the internal development of Hungarian Jewry both before World War I and during the interwar years. Another book-length study of certain aspects of Jewish cultural life is A. Moskovits, *Jewish Education in Hungary, 1848-1948* (Philadelphia, 1964).

For shorter general studies of Jewish history in interwar Hungary, the following articles may be recommended: Randolph Braham, "Hungarian Jewry: An Historical Retrospect," *Journal of Central European Affairs* 20, no. 1 (1960):3–23; Randolph Braham, " 'Legitimism,' Zionism, and the Jewish Catastrophe in Hungary," *Herzl Institute Yearbook* 6 (1964–65):239–52; and Nathaniel Katzburg, "Hungarian Jewry in Modern Times: Political and Social Aspects," in *Hungarian-Jewish Studies*, ed. Braham, 1: 137–70. Demographic data is furnished by Erno Laszlo, "Hungary's Jewry: A Demographic Overview, 1918-1945," in *Hungarian-Jewish Studies*, ed. Braham, 2: 137–82. The following articles deal with economic issues: William McCagg, "Hungary's 'Feudalized' Bourgeoisie," *Journal of Modern History* 44, no. 1 (March 1972): 65–78; and Istvan Veghazi, "The Role of Jewry in the Economic Life of Hungary," in *Hungarian-Jewish Studies*, ed. Braham, 2: 35–84. The role of Jews in Hungarian radicalism is the subject of an important study by William McCagg, "Jews in Revolutions: The Hungarian Experience," *Journal of Social History* (Fall 1972):78–105. The problem of Jewish-Hungarian assimilation is analyzed in George Barany, "Magyar Jew or Jewish Magyar?" in *Jews and Non-Jews in Eastern Europe*, ed. Vago and Mosse, pp. 51–98, and in two articles which appear in *Jewish Assimilation in Modern Times*, ed. Vago; Asher Cohen, "The Attitude of the Intelligentsia in Hungary towards Jewish Assimilation between the Two World Wars," pp. 57–74; and George Schöpflin, "Jewish Assimilation in Hungary: A Moot Point," pp. 75–88. The Zionist movement is discussed in Livia Bitton, "Zionism in Hungary: The First Twenty-Five Years," *Herzl Institute Yearbook* 6 (1964–65): 239–52.

There are a number of articles on various aspects of the "Jewish question" in Hungary. Along with several studies (by Braham, Katzburg, and C. A. Macartney) on this subject in Vago and Mosse, eds., *Jews and Non-Jews in Eastern Europe*, the following may be recommended: Bernard Klein, "Hungarian Politics and the Jewish Question in the Inter-War Period," *Jewish Social Studies* 28, no. 2 (April 1966): 79–98; Janos Kovacs, "Neo-Antisemitism in Hungary," *Jewish Social Studies* 8, no. 3 (July 1957): 147–60; and Bela Vago, "Germany and the Jewish Policy of the Kallay Government," in *Hungarian-Jewish Studies*, ed. Braham, 2: 183–210. For those who read French, two important articles by Victor Karady and István Kemény must be mentioned: "Les juifs dans la structure des classes en Hongrie: Essai sur les antécédents historiques des crises d'antisemitisme du XXe siècle," *Actes de la recherche en sciences sociales* 22 (June 1978): 25–59; and "Antisémitisme universitaire et concurrence de classe. La loi du *numerus clausus* en Hongrie entre les deux guerres," *Actes de la recherche en sciences sociales* 34 (September 1980): 67–96. A useful contribution to the literature on the Jewish question in the 1920s is Thomas Spira, "Hungary's Numerus Clausus, the Jewish Minority, and the League of Nations," *Ungarn-Jahrbuch* 4 (1972): 115–28.

Pre–World War I Jewish life in the Czech lands has attracted considerable interest, due in large measure to the figure of Franz Kafka and his Prague circle. But the interwar period has been generally neglected; there is no satisfactory treatment of Jewish history in interwar Czechoslovakia in any language. There does exist, however, a very important collection of essays, *The Jews of Czechoslovakia*, 2 vols. (Philadelphia, 1968, 1971). Also of great value is the collection of articles edited by Ernest Rychnovsky, *Thomas Masaryk and the Jews* (New York, 1941). Jewish demography in the Czech lands is covered by Jan Herman, "The Development of Bohemian and Moravian Jewry, 1918-1938," in *Papers in Jewish Demography*, ed. U. O. Schmelz, P. Glikson, and S. Della Pergola (Jerusalem, 1969), pp. 191–206. Jewish economic life is the subject of Joseph Pick, "The Economy," in *The Jews of Czechoslovakia*, 1: 359–438. The Jewish question in the Czechoslovak Republic is dealt with by Aharon Moshe Rabinowicz, "The Jewish Minority," in *The Jews of Czechoslovakia*, 1: 155–266. Jewish politics is the subject of two important articles: Aharon Moshe Rabinowicz, "The Jewish Party," in *The Jews of Czechoslovakia*, 2: 253–346; and Oskar K. Rabinowicz, "Czechoslovak Zionism: Analecta to a History," in *The Jews of Czechoslovakia*, 2: 19–136. The two-volume *Jews of Czechoslovakia* also includes articles on Jewish religious and cultural life in the Republic, including the Jews' contribution to German and Czech literature (by Harry Zohn and Egor Hostovsky), and Jewish education (by Aryeh Sole). For other articles of interest, the reader may be referred to Hans Tramer, "Prague: City of Three Peoples," *Leo Baeck Institute Yearbook* 9 (1964):305–39; Bruno Blau, "Nationality among Czechoslovak Jewry," *Historica Judaica* 10 (1948):147–54; and Wilma Iggers, "The Flexible National Identities of Bohemian Jewry," *East Central Europe* 7, no. 1 (1980): 39–48. The latter article deals primarily with the pre–World War I period, as does the study by Michael Riff, "Czech Antisemitism and the Jewish Response before 1914," *Wiener Library Bulletin* 29, no. 39/40 (1976): 8–20.

If interwar Czechoslovak Jewry has been generally ignored by scholars writing in English, the situation with regard to Romania is even worse. There is no general study of interwar Romanian Jewry, although this will no longer be the case when Bela Vago's pioneering two-volume work (the first volume of which is entitled *Jews and Anti-Semitism in Inter-War Romania, 1919-1940: Prologue to the Holocaust*) is published. There are two short contemporary accounts of the Jewish condition in Romania in the 1920s and 1930s—Salo Baron, *The Jews in Rumania* (New York, 1930), and Israel Cohen, *The Jews in Rumania* (London, 1938). The "Jewish question" in Romania is the subject of the following articles: Stephen Fischer-Galati, "Fascism, Communism, and the Jewish Question in Romania," in *Jews and Non-Jews in Eastern Europe*, ed. Vago and Mosse, pp. 157–75; Fischer-Galati, "The Radical Left and Assimilation: The Case of Romania," in *Jewish Assimilation in Modern Times*, ed. Vago, pp. 89–104; N. M. Gelber, "The Problem of the Rumanian Jews at the Bucharest Peace Conference," *Jewish Social Studies* 12, no. 1 (April 1950):223–46; and Joshua Starr, "Jewish Citizenship in Rumania (1878-1940)," *Jewish Social Studies* 3, no. 1 (January 1941):57–80. There is nothing on Jewish politics, but there is an interesting contribution by Bela Vago on Jewish voting behavior, "The Jewish Vote in Romania between the Two Wars," *Jewish Journal of Sociology* 14, no. 2 (December 1972):229–44.

Studies in English on the Jews of the Baltic region are also rare. Relations between Jews and Lithuanians have been described by Azriel Shochat in two articles: "Jews, Lithuanians, and Russians, 1939-1941," in *Jews and Non-Jews in Eastern Europe*, ed. Vago and Mosse, pp. 301–14, and "The Beginnings of Anti-Semitism in Independent Lithuania," *Yad Vashem Studies on the European Jewish Catastrophe and Resistance* 2, (1958):7–48. Dov Levin has also written on this subject, and the reader may be referred to two of his articles: "The Jews in the Soviet Lithuanian Establishment, 1940-1941," *Soviet Jewish Affairs* 10, no. 2 (1980):21–38, and "The Jews and the Election Campaigns in Lithuania," *Soviet Jewish Affairs* 10, no. 1 (1980):39–51. The subject of Jewish autonomy is well treated in S. Gringauz, "Jewish National Autonomy in Lithuania (1918–1925)," *Jewish Social Studies* 14, no. 3 (July 1952):225–46. Jewish internal organization is analyzed by Mark Friedman, "The Kehillah in Lithuania, 1919-1926: A Study Based on Panevezys and Ukmerge (Vilkomir)," *Soviet Jewish Affairs* 6, no. 2 (1976):83–103. On Jewish economic life there is an important article by Jacob Lestchinsky, "The Economic Struggle of the Jews in Independent Lithuania," *Jewish Social Studies* 8, no. 4 (October 1946):267–96.

As for Latvia, articles on all aspects of Jewish life may be found in *The Jews in Latvia* (Tel Aviv, 1971), which also contains a brief discussion of Jewish life in Estonia and which may be augmented by Emanuel Nodel, "Life and Death of Estonian Jewry," in *Baltic History*, ed. A. Ziedonis, W. Winter, and M. Valgemae (Cleveland, 1973), pp. 227–36. A general article on the Jewries of all three Baltic lands is Max Laserson, "The Jewish Minorities in the Baltic Countries," *Jewish Social Studies* 3, no. 3 (July 1941):273–84.

Since the completion of the manuscript of the hardcover edition of this book a number of important studies relevant to its subject have appeared. Few, however, are written in English. Of these I should mention the diary of the writer Emil Dorian, *The Quality of Witness. A Romanian Diary 1937-1944*, ed. Marguerite Dorian (Philadelphia, 1982), which sheds considerable light on the immediate pre-war period in Romania as well as on the war years. There is also the controversial but undoubtedly important study by Joseph Marcus, *Social and Political*

*History of the Jews in Poland 1919-1939* (Berlin, New York, Amsterdam 1983). The first issue of a new periodical devoted to Jewish Polish studies, *Polin,* appeared in 1986, as did a collection of essays based on a conference held in Oxford in 1984 on Jewish history in Poland, *The Jews in Poland,* ed. Chimen Abramsky, Maciej Jachimczyk, and Antony Polonsky (Oxford, 1986). Both these volumes include material on the inter-war period. The publication of the papers presented at a conference on Polish Jewry held at Brandeis University in 1986, which dealt exclusively with the inter-war years, is promised in the not too distant future. The journal *Studies in Contemporary Jewry* has published the following articles of interest: Ezra Mendelsohn, "Recent Work on the Jews in Inter-war East Central Europe: A Survey," I, (1984): 316-337; Victor Karady, "Jewish Enrollment Patterns in Classical Secondary Education in Old Regime and Inter-war Hungary," *ibid.,* 225-252; Gershon C. Bacon, "The Politics of Tradition: Agudat Israel in Polish Politics, 1916-1939," II, (1986): 144-163. Finally, let me mention the forthcoming publication in Jerusalem (in 1987) of a volume honoring the memory of Paul Glikson, which also contains material relevant to the inter-war period.

# Index

Acculturation
  and assimilation, 2
  in Czech lands, 133–135
  of Hungarian Jews, 87–91
  in Latvia, 243–244
  in Romania, 192, 201–202
Agrarian Party, Czech, 155
Agudes yisroel
  in Czechoslovakia, 155
  in Latvia, 248
  in Lithuania, 228–232
  in Poland, 44–50, 55–56, 61–63, 66, 77–
    82
  in Romania, 191–192
Ahdes, 228–232
*Aliyah*, 59, 60, 77, 167, 193
*Aliyot*, 193
Alliance Israélite, 109, 196, 209
Anti-Semitism
  in Czechoslovakia, 136–139, 148–152,
    164–169
  in East Central Europe, 255–258
  in Galicia, 19
  in Hungary, 93–98, 104, 113
  in Lithuania, 217, 236–238
  in Poland, 36–43, 68–83
  in Romania, 172–177, 183–189, 202–210
  in Slovakia, 141
Antonescu, Ion, 203, 208, 210–211
*Arendaşi*, 175
Arrow Cross Party, 115, 123, 126, 129, 211
Asch, Sholem, 63
Ashkenazi Jews, 3
Askenazy, Szymon, 42, 68
Assimilation
  and acculturation, 2
  of Hungarian Jews, 87–91
  in Poland, 39
  *see also* Acculturation
Auşnit, Max, 205
Austrian Social Democratic Party, 33
Autonomy for Jews. *See* National auton-
    omy for Jews
Averescu, Alexandru, 195

Bałaban, Majer, 64
Balfour Declaration, 33, 49, 60, 147

Banat, 171, 173, 177–182; *see also*
    Romania
Bar Kochba, 138
Bartel, Kazimierz, 69
Begin, Menachem, 77
Belorussians, 14, 20–21, 52, 213, 217–219
Beneš, Eduard, 149, 167
Bergmann, Hugo, 138
Bernstein-Cohen, 194
Bessarabia, 171–173, 176–182, 187–193,
    199–201, 208; *see also* Romania
Betar, 59, 77, 248
Bethlen, István, 97, 98, 103–105, 112, 114,
    120–121, 125
Beys yankev schools, 66
Bikel, Shloyme, 201
Birthrate
  of Czechoslovakian Jewry, 144
  in West European vs. East European
    community, 6–7
Bohemia, 132–139; *see also* Czechoslo-
    vakia
Bolshevism, in Romania, 187–188, 210
Boycott of Jewish business, 73–74
Brătianu, Jon, 184, 195
Brătianu family, 175
Bratislava, 140
Braude high schools, 66
Brod, Max, 134–137, 153
Brutzkus, Julius, 231
Bucharest, 174–179, 189, 200–201
Budapest, 92, 99–101, 108, 126
Bukovina, 171–182, 185, 189–195, 200; *see
    also* Romania
Bund
  in Latvia, 247, 251
  in Poland, 22, 34, 46–53, 56, 61, 72, 77–
    80
  in Romania, 191

Călinescu, Armand, 207
Camp of National Unity, 70
Cantonists, 254
Carol, king of Romania, 173, 202–208
Carp, Horia, 190, 191
Carpathian Ukraine. *See* Subcarpathian
    Rus

293

Catholic Church
anti-Semitism in Hungary, 118–119
anti-Semitism in Poland, 71
in Lithuania, 213–214
and Slovak nationalism, 164–166
Central Council of Romanian Jews, 199
Central Region of Poland. See Congress Poland
Cernăuţi, 173
Chorin, Aron, 90
Christian Democratic Party in Poland, 16
Cities, Jewish population in
Czechoslovakia, 135, 143
Lithuania, 225–226
Poland, 23–25
Romania, 179
Civil service, exclusion of Jews from Polish, 42–43
Cluj, 186
Codreanu, Corneliu, 202–206
Codreanu, Zelea, 189
Commerce, Jewish role in Polish, 25–28
Communist Party
in Latvia, 253
in Lithuania, 227, 229, 232, 238–239
in Poland, 15, 51, 53, 62, 78
in Romania, 188, 198
Congress Poland: history of, 12–13; pogroms and anti-Semitism in, 40–41; Jewish politics in, 50–51, 55; see also Poland
Conversions
in Czechoslovakia, 145
in Hungary, 123
Council of the Four Lands, 221
Courland, 242–244, 253, 254
Crişana-Maramureş, 171, 173, 180, 181; see also Romania
Culture, Jewish
in Czechoslovakia, 152–162
in East Central Europe, 255–258
in Latvia, 252
in Lithuania, 233–235
in Poland, 63–68
in Romania, 199–202
Cuza, Alexandru, 186–187, 195, 206–207
Czech lands, 131–139, 142–146; see also Czechoslovakia
Czechoslovakia, 131–169: overview of, 131–132; history of, 132–142; three separate Jewries of, 132–133; biculture in Czech lands, urbanization, departure from Judaism, 134–139; Slovakian Jewry, 139–141; Subcarpathian Rus, 141–142; demographic profile of Jewry of, 142–146; Jews' relation with state, 146–152; national identities,

146–148, 159–160; Czech-Jewish alliance, 148–150; popular anti-Semitism, 150–152; Jewish politics and culture, 152–162; nationalism, 152–154; Jewish Party, 154–157; Zionism, 157–158; education, 160–162; anti-Semitism and collapse of state, 162–168; Nazism, 162–163; Slovak nationalism, 164–166; dismemberment of, 166; Jewish "law," 166–167; summary, 168–169

Danzig, 13–14
Darányi, Kálmán, 116, 125
Daugavpils, 242, 245
Deák, Ferenc, 89
Demography of Jews
in Czechoslovakia, 142–146
in Hungary, 99–102
in Latvia, 244
in Lithuania, 225–226
in Poland, 23–25
in Romania, 173–179
Depression
in Czechoslovakia, 163–164
in Romania, 208–209
Diamand, Herman, 227
Distanzliebe, 136
Dmowski, Roman, 16, 21, 38, 41, 70, 104
Dobrogea, 171; see also Romania
Dobrogeanu-Gherea, 198
Doikeyt, 44, 45, 191
Drod, 59
Druyanov, A., 67
Dubin, Mordecai, 248–250
Dubnov, 247, 254

East Central Europe: interwar years summarized, 1–8; politicization of Jewry in, 2; definition of, 3; diversity of, 3–4; shared characteristics in, 4–5; two basic types of Jewish communities in, 6–8; Jewish-gentile relations in, 255–258; Jewish culture in, 255–258
Eastern Region of Poland. See Kresy
East European type of Jewish community, 6–8
Ebner, Meir, 195, 196
Economic conditions
of Czechoslovakian Jewry, 145
diversity within East Central Europe, 3–4
of East Central European Jewry, summarized, 255–256
in Hungary, 92–93, 100–101
in Latvia, 244–245
of Lithuanian Jews, 226, 236–238

in Poland, 14–15, 25–29, 73–76
in Romania, 172, 179–180
Education
  in Czechoslovakia, 160–162
  in Latvia, 250–252
  see also Schools
Eichmann, Adolph, 126
Einstein, Albert, 137
Elijah of Vilna, 22
Emigration
  aliyah, 59, 60, 77, 167, 193
  from Czechoslovakia, 158–159, 167
  from Hungary, 123
  from Lithuania, 225
  from Poland, 25, 39, 60, 71–80
  as Polish solution to Jewish problem, 39
  from Romania, 208–209
Endek. See National Democratic Party of
  Poland
"Enlightenment." See Haskalah
Eötvös, József, 89, 93
Estonia, 253–254
Ethnic diversity, 3
Extraterritorial autonomy. See National
  autonomy

Fascism
  in Hungary, 113
  native movements, 5
  in Romania, 203–204
  see also Nazism
Fischer, Iosif, 196
Fischer, Theodor, 196
Folkism and Folkspartey
  in Latvia, 248, 251
  in Lithuania, 228–232
  in Poland, 46–51, 62
  in Romania, 191
Francis Joseph, Austrian emperor, 176
Frayheyt, 59
Freud, Sigmund, 135
Friedman, Bernard, 223, 229

Galicia: history of, 13; Jewry of, 18–19, 24;
  pogroms in, 40; Jewish politics in, 51,
  54–55; see also Poland
Galileo Circle, 96
Galvanauskas, Ernestas, 221
Gegenwartsarbeit, 57–58, 153, 194, 197
General Zionism
  in Lithuania, 219, 228
  in Poland, 46, 50–59, 65, 76–78
  in Regat, 197
German culture, conflict with Czech culture, 133–137, 152–153
Goebbels, Josef, 70

Goga, Octavian, 202–203, 206–207
Goldfaden, Avraham, 174
Goldziher, Ignaz, 93, 100, 111
Gömbös, Gyula, 97, 102–103, 113–115,
  121, 202–203
Gordon, A.D., 59
Gordonia, 59, 193, 231
Grabski, Władysław, 56
Great Depression. See Depression
Group identity. See National identities of
  Jews
Grünbaum, Yitshak, 53–58, 190, 195, 197,
  250

Haluts, 231–232
Habsburg rule of Poland, 12
Ha-shomer ha-tsair
  in Czechoslovakia, 158
  in Latvia, 248
  in Lithuania, 231
  in Poland, 32, 59, 79
  in Romania, 193
Hasidism
  in Congress Poland, 20, 61
  in Galicia, 18
  in Poland, 61
  in Romania, 176–177
  in Slovakia, 155
  in Subcarpathian Rus, 141–142
Haskalah movement
  in Czechoslovakia, 133–134
  in Lithuania, 215
  in Poland, 19–22
  in Romania, 174
Havlíček-Borovský, Karel, 136, 138, 148
Hebrew
  culture in Poland, 65
  as mother tongue of Jews, 30–32
  vs. Yiddish, as political issue, 46
Hebrew High School, in Mukačevo, 161
Henlein, Konrad, 163
Herzl, Theodore, 91, 94, 107
Hibat Zion, 193
Hisner, Leopold, 139, 147
Hirsch, Samson Rafael, 134
Hitahdut, 59
Hitler, Adolph
  and Antonescu, 210
  and Horthy, 124
  influence on Hungary, 113, 114
  and Poland, 70
  see also Nazism
Hlinka Guard, 166
Hlinka Slovak People's Party, 163
Hlond, August, 7
Horthy, Miklos, 97–98, 103–110, 119–127,
  210

Hungary, 85–128; national obsession with Trianon treaty revision, 85–87; history of, 87–94; magyarization of Jews, 87–91; religious split, 90–91; social ostracism of Jews, 91–93; role of Jews in economy and culture, 91–94; Jews' special role after World War I, 94–99; Béla Kun regime, 95–97; anti-Semitism wave, 97–98; demography of Jews, 99–100; characteristics of Jewry, 101–102; "Jewish question" under Horthy and Bethlen, 102–107; *numerus clausus*, 105–107; Jewish politics, 107–112; nondemocratic Jewish leadership, 109–112; Gömbös regime, 113–115; pressure to solve Jewish question, first "Jewish laws," 115–124; World War II, 124–126; relationship of Magyars and Jews reviewed, 126–128

Iaşi, 178, 186, 200
Identity, national. *See* National identities of Jews
Ignotus, Paul, 91
Imrédy, Béla, 119–122, 125
Industry, Jews in Polish, 26–28
Intermarriage
  in Czechoslovakia, 145–146, 160
  in East-European vs. West-European type communities, 6–7
Iorga, Nicolae, 175, 187
Iron Guard, 202–203, 208–211

Jabotinsky, Vladimir, 71, 76–80, 248
Jászi, Oszkár, 91, 96, 111, 112
Jewish Board of Deputies, 109
Jewish Economic Party of Slovakia, 155
"Jewish law" in Slovakia, 166–167
Jewish National Council of Prague, 153
Jewish National People's Party of Romania, 191
Jewish Party of Czechoslovakia, 154–157
Jewish Party of Romania, 192–194, 198, 209
Jewish Scientific Institute, 64
Jewish Workers' Union. *See* Bund
Judaism
  in Czech lands, 134–139
  in Czechoslovakia, 140
  Hasidism, 18–20, 61, 141–142, 155, 176–177
  in Hungary, 90–95, 100, 107
  influence on political parties, 4, 44–46
  in Lithuania, 22, 215
  misnagdic, 32
  Neology, 90–108, 140, 177
  in Poland, 44–45, 62, 90

pluralism in East Central Europe, 3
Reform, 90
  in Romania, 176–177
  in Slovakia, 140
Status Quo, 90, 140
  in Subcarpathian Rus, 155–156
  *see also* Orthodox Judaism

Kafka, Franz, 134–135, 137
*Kaisertreu*, 176
Kállay, Miklós, 125
Kalwaria, Góra, 20
Kapper, Siegfried, 136, 148
Károlyi, Mihály, 85, 95
Kaunas, 219, 225
Kautsky, Karl, 38
Kehiles
  in Lithuania, 221–222, 228–230
  in Poland, 34–35, 39
Kennan, George, 165, 167
*Keren Kayement*, 191
Khoyrev schools, 66
Kingdom of Poland, 12–13
Kishinev, 176, 192
*Klal yisroel*, 50, 53
Kleinbaum, Moshe, 70
Kohn, Hans, 137, 138
Kohn, Samuel, 107
Komsomol, 253
Kossuth, Lajos, 88
Kresy: history of, 13; Jewry of, 21–23; demographics of, 24; *see also* Poland
Kugel, Haim, 161, 163
*Kultusgemeinde*, 153, 157
Kun, Béla, 85, 95–97, 103–108, 150

Landau, Michael, 196, 197
Langer, František, 134–135, 162
Language
  Czech vs. German in Czech lands, 136–137
  of Czechoslovakian Jews, 159
  Hebrew as mother tongue, 30–32
  Hebrew vs. Yiddish as political issue, 46
  of Hungarian Jews, 100
  of Latvian Jews, 245–246, 251
  of Polish Jews, 30–31, 65
  of Romanian Jews, 182–183
Latgalia, 242
Latvia, 241–253: history of, 241–244; three distinct Jewries of, 242–244; demography of Jews, 244–245; national identity and languages, 245–246; autonomy issue, 246–247; Jewish politics, 247–252; education, 250–252; culture, 252; Nazi destruction of, 252–253
League of Israel. *See* Agudes yisroel

League of Nations, and anti-Semitism in Hungary, 105, 109–110
Lenin, N., 38
Leshchinski, Yankev, 74, 208, 236, 252
Liberal Party of Romania, 175, 184–188, 195–196, 202
Lilienthal, Max, 243
Linder, Menakhem, 74
Literature, Yiddish renaissance in Poland, 63–65
Lithuania, 213–239: Jewry of, 20–22; pogroms in, 40; Polish Jews' attitude toward, 52; overview of, 213–214; history of, 215–217; Lithuanian-Jewish relations and Jewish extraterritorial autonomy, 217–225; Jewish National Council, 221–223; demography, 225–226; Jewish politics, 227–233; Jewish culture, 233–235; school system, 233–235; decline in economy and Jewish-Lithuanian relations, 236–238; annexation by Soviets, 238–239
Litvaks, 20–21, 63, 216
Livonia, 242–243, 253
Lodz, 20
Löw, Leopold, 90
*Luftmentshn*, 145, 163
Lukács, George, 111
Lupescu, Magda, 205
Luxemburg, Rosa, 227
Lwów, 40, 41, 52
Lwów Polytechnicum, 73

Macartney, C.A., 92, 101, 104, 122
Magyarization
  in Czechoslovakia, 131–132
  in Romania, 177, 187
  in Slovakia, 140–141
Magyars, 85–90, 105
"Magyars of the Mosaic persuasion," 87, 91–92, 105, 128
Mahler, Gustav, 135
Makabäa, 138
Manger, Itsik, 201
Maniu, Iuliu, 196, 197
Margulies, Emil, 157
Marriage with gentiles. *See* Intermarriage
Marx, Karl, 38
Marxism, 45, 96; *see also* Communist Party
Masaryk, Jan, 169
Masaryk, Thomas, 131, 137–139, 147–148, 161, 167–169, 218
Maskilim, 19; *see also* Haskalah movement
Memel, 214
"Men of Szeged," 97, 113
Meyzel, Noyakh, 247
Mikus, Rudolph, 165

Minorities' Treaty, 35, 36, 39, 149–150, 247
Minority nationalities
  as Czech problem, 131, 148, 163
  in East Central Europe, 5
  in Poland, 14, 53–54
  *see also* National identity of Jews; Nationalism
Mintz, Paul, 248
Misnagdic Judaism, 32
Mizrachi
  in Latvia, 248
  in Lithuania, 231–233
  in Poland, 22, 46, 50, 62–66
Moldavia, 171–175, 178–179, 183, 193; *see also* Romania
Molnár, Ferenc, 89, 112, 123
Moravia, 132–139; *see also* Czech lands; Czechoslovakia
Mother tongues. *See* Language
Mukačevo Rebe, 155, 161
Munich agreement, 165–166

National autonomy for Jews
  in Czechoslovakia, 133–138, 152–157
  as failure in East Central Europe, 257
  in Latvia, 246–247
  in Lithuania, 219–224
  in Poland, 32–39
  secular ideology of, 32–35
  *see also* Nationalism
National Council of Lithuania, 221–223, 229
National Councils of Romania, 194–195
National Democratic Party of Poland (Endek), 15–17, 21, 38–39, 69–73, 104
National identities of Jews
  in Czechoslovakia, 133–138, 146–147, 152–160
  in Latvia, 245
  in Lithuania, 227
  in Poland, 29–32
  in Romania, 180–182
Nationalism
  and anti-Semitism, 41–42
  in Czech lands, 133–138
  in Czechoslovakia, 152–157
  in East Central Europe, 5
  and Jewish politics, 33–35
  in Poland, 29–32
  in Romania, 194–198
  in Slovakia, 164–166
  *see also* National autonomy for Jews
National Jewish Union of Transylvania, 192
National Labor Party of Poland, 16
National Legionary State of Romania, 208, 210
National Party of Poland, 70

National Peasant Party of Romania, 185, 188, 195–197, 202
National Radical Camp (ONR), 70
Nazism, influence on
  Hungarians, 113–119, 126
  Poland, 69–70
  Romania, 204
  Slovakia, 165–166
Neolog Judaism, 90, 95, 100–101, 107–108, 140, 177
Netsah, 248
Newspapers, Yiddish, 63
New Zionist Organization, 77
Niemirover, Yitshak, 194
Nordau, Max, 91, 107
*Numerus clausus*
  in Hungary, 105–110, 119–120, 125
  in Romania, 186–187, 207–208
*Numerus vallachicus*, 208
Nurok, Max, 248–250

ONR (National Radical Camp), 70
Oradea Mare, 186
Organization of Native Born Jews, 189–190
Orthodox Judaism
  in Czechoslovakia, 140
  in Hungary, 90, 100, 107
  in Lithuania, 22, 215
  in Poland, 44–45, 62, 90
  in Romania, 177
OZON (Camp of National Unity), 70

Pale of Settlement, 21, 25, 176, 218, 243, 254
Palestine
  role in Polish-Jewish politics, 58–60
  *see also* Emigration; *Aliyah*
Pauker, Anna, 198
Peasant Party of Poland, 72
Peasant Party of Romania, 185, 188, 195–197, 202
People's Party of Romania, 195
Perets, Y.L., 63, 65
Piast party, 16
Piłsudski, Józef, 16–17, 39, 55, 69–70
Pioneer youth movement
  in Czechoslovakia, 158
  in Lithuania, 231–232
  in Poland, 47, 57–59, 77–79
  in Romania, 193, 210
Poale Zion
  in Lithuania, 229–230
  in Poland, 46–53, 59, 66, 155
Pogroms
  in Hungary, 97
  in Poland, 40, 73–74
  in Romania, 176

Poland, 11–83: history of, 11–17; German-held lands, 11–12; Habsburg-held lands, 12; Russian-held lands, 12–13; national minorities problem, 14; economic deficiencies, 14–15; political parties, 15–16; Jewries of interwar period, 17–23; Galicia, 18–19; Congress Poland, 19–21; Kresy, 21–23; demographic structure, 23–25; economic structure, 25–29; national character of Jewries, 29–32; Jewish demands for autonomy, 32–35; Jewish question in new Poland, 32–43; polonization, 37; exclusion of Jews from bureaucracy, 42–43; Jewish politics in the 1920s, 43–63; prewar Russian influence, 43–46; Zionism vs. "hereness," 44; secular vs. religious forces, 44–45; social ideologies, 45–46; issue of Yiddish vs. Hebrew, 46–47; divisiveness, 47–48; political activism of youth, 48; triumph of "new" Jewish parties, 48–49; lack of unified Jewish leadership, 50–51; alliance with other minorities, 53–54; failure of Jewish political strategies, 56; Zionism, 57–61; Jewish cultural life, 63–68; reemergence of violent anti-Semitism, 68–81; economic boycott of Jews, 73–76; growth of Bund, 77–78; emigration to Palestine, 79–80; summary, 81–83; claims on Lithuania, 213–214
"Poles of the Mosaic faith," 19, 20, 29, 51
Polish-Lithuanian Commonwealth, 213
Polish Socialist Party (PPS), 15–16, 38, 45–46, 56, 62, 72
Polish-Soviet War, 40–41
Political parties, Jewish
  in Czechoslovakia, 152–162
  effectiveness of, 255–258
  in Latvia, 247–251
  in Lithuania, 227–233
  in Poland, 43–63
  in Romania, 189–199
Polonization, 20, 37, 67, 213
Pomorze, 13, 18
Population. *See* Demography of Jews
Poznań, 13, 18
PPS. *See* Polish Socialist Party
Prague, 134–139
Press, Yiddish
  in Poland, 63
  in Romania, 201
Pressburg, 140, 150
Professions, Polish Jews in, 27
Proletariat, Polish, 27
Prussia, and Poland, 12

Rappaport, Shlomo Yehuda, 134
Rebe of Bełz, 61
Rebe of Ger, 20, 61
Rebe of Mukačevo, 155, 161
Reform Judaism, in Hungary, 90
Regat, 171–175, 181–183, 190–198; *see also* Romania
Reich, Leon, 54
Religion. *See* Judaism
Revisionism, 47, 76–77, 80, 231, 248
Riga, 242–245
Romania, 171–211: historical background on, 171–173; differing Jewries of differing regions, 173–178; Jewish demography, 178–183; Jewish economics, 179–180; Jewish identity, 180–182; language, 182–183; state dealings with Jews, 183–189; citizenship for Jews, 185–186; anti-Semitism, 186–189; Jewish politics, 189–199; UER, 189–191; Zionism, 192–194; nationalism and Jewish Party, 194–198; schools, 199–200; culture, 199–202; acculturation, 201–202; triumph of anti-Semitism, 202–210; moderate right under King Carol vs. radical right under Iron Guard, 202–207; end of Jewish emancipation, 206–208; emigration to Palestine, 208–209; war years, 210–211; overview of, 211
Rosenbaum, Shimshon, 219, 222, 231
*Rozvoj*, 136
Russia
  rule of Poland, 12–13, 44–46
  *see also* Soviet Union
Rusyns. *See* Subcarpathian Rus

Sadagura dynasty, 176
Salanter, Israel, 22
Sanacja, 69, 72
Satmar dynasty, 177
Satu-Mare, 192
Schipper, Ignacy, 64
Schools, Jewish
  in Czechoslovakia, 160–161
  in Latvia, 247, 250–252
  in Lithuania, 233–235
  in Poland, 34, 39, 64–68
  in Romania, 199–200
Schwarzbart, Ignacy, 54
Sejm, 15–16, 51, 57–58, 73
*Selbstwehr*, 159
Sephardic Jews, 3
Seton-Watson, Robert, 89, 91
Shapira, Haim Eliezer, 155, 161
Shenirer, Sarah, 66
Shir, 134

*Shkhite*, 55, 73, 209
Shtadlones, 56, 110–111
*Shtetl*, 6–7, 22, 237–238
*Shtetlekh*, 24
Shul-kult schools, 66
Silesia, 13, 18
Singer, Isaac Bashevis, 63
Singer, I.J., 63
Sławoj-Składkowski, 71
Słonimski, Antoni, 68
Slovakia: history as part of Hungary, 115–116, 131–132; Jewry in, 139–141; demography of Jews in, 142–146; Hasidism in, 155; education in, 162; extreme anti-Czech nationalism, 164–166; *see also* Czechoslovakia
Social Democratic Party
  in Czechoslovakia, 157
  in Latvia, 242, 247
Socialist Party of Poland. *See* Polish Socialist Party
Sofer, Moses, 140
Sokolow, Nahum, 149
Soloveitshik, Max, 221–223, 231, 239
Soviet Union: environment for Jews, 6; claims on Lithuania, 214, 238–239; Latvian rule, 253; Jewry of, 257
Šrobár, Vavro, 150–151
"Status Quo" Judaism, 90, 140
Steinbarg, Eliezer, 201
Stern, Adolph, 190
Stern, Samu, 123
Sternberg, Yankev, 201
Stern-Kokhavi, 197
Straucher, Benno, 191, 195
Subcarpathian Rus: history as part of Hungary, 115–116, 119, 131–132; Jewry of, 141–146, 160; Jewish politics and religion, 155–156; schools, 160–162; economic crisis, 163–164; *see also* Czechoslovakia
Sudetenland, 132, 166
Swabian Germans, 113, 118
Szabasówki schools, 67
Szálasim, Ferenc, 115, 126
Széchenyi, István, 89
Szekfü, Gyula, 98
*Szlachta*, 11, 15

*Takhles*, 65
Tarbut school system, 65–68, 200–201, 233–235
Taryba, 213
Tătăresco, Gheorghe, 205
Teleki, Pál, 97, 103, 104, 118–122, 125
Temporary Jewish National Council of Poland, 50–51

"Territorialists," 44
Tiso, Dr., 165
Transylvania, 177–180, 185–195, 200; see also Romania
Trianon Treaty, 86–87, 100, 105
Trotsky, Leon, 97
Trunk, Y.Y., 63
Tsirelson, Yehuda Leib, 191, 197–199
Tsisho school system, 64–68
Tuwim, Julian, 68

Ugoda of 1925, 54–56
Ukrainians
in Galicia, 19
history of, 13–14
nationalism of, 51–52
Ulam, S.M., 29
Ulmanis, Kārlis, 248, 250, 252
Union of Hungarian Jews, 116
Union of Romanian Jews (UER), 181, 189–192, 195–196, 209
Universities
anti-Semitism of Romanian, 186–189
Polish, 73
Urbanization, 135–136; see also Cities

Vaida-Voevod, 205
Vámbéry, Arminius, 89
Varshavsky, Oizer, 63
Vaynraykh, Maks, 76
Vázsonyi, Vilmos, 105, 108, 109, 127
Vilna: as Haskalah center, 22; Polish capture of, 52–53; Lithuanian claims to, 213–225
Vohryzek, Viktor, 137
Voldemaras, Augustinas, 220
Volynia, 22
Vygodski, Yaakov, 219–221

Wallachia, 171–174, 178–181, 193–194; see also Romania
Warsaw, 20–21
Weissenberg, I.M., 63
Weizmann, Chaim, 21, 76, 150
Werfel, Franz, 135
West European type of Jewish community, 6–8
West Ukrainian Republic, 52
Wielopolski, Aleksander, 21

Wilson, Woodrow, 184
Windischgraetz, Lajos, 108
Witos, Wincenty, 38
Workers' Union. See Bund
Workers of Zion. See Poale Zion
World Zionist Organization, 57, 60, 77, 150, 209
Wyzwolenie (Emancipation) party, 15–16

Yavne schools, 66, 233–235
Yeshivas
Lithuanian, 233
Polish, 63
Yiddish
culture in Poland, 63–68
culture in Romania, 201
vs. Hebrew, as Polish political issue, 46
as language of Poles, 30–32
as language of Romanians, 182–183
schools in Latvia, 251–252
schools in Lithuania, 233–235
Yivo, 64
Young Czech Party, 138
The Young Pioneer, 59; see also Pioneer movement
Youth movements
in Czechoslovakia, 158
in Lithuania, 231–232
in Poland, 43, 47–48, 59–60, 77–79
in Romania, 191, 209–210
Youth of Zion. See Zeire Zion

Zeire Zion, 46, 193
Zionism
in Galicia, 19, 80
in Hungary, 91, 107–108
languages of, 30–32
in Latvia, 248–249
in Lithuania, 22, 219, 228–232
in Poland, 29–30, 34–35, 46–51, 56–59, 65–66, 76–80
in Regat, 197
in Romania, 190–194, 209
weaknesses of, 60–63
Zionist Federation of Bohemia, 153
Zionist Organization of Congress Poland, 59
Zionist Socialists, 228–230, 248